MESOPOTAMIA
VOLUME 10

PAUL D. SANSONE, O.F.M.

MESOPOTAMIA
Copenhagen Studies in Assyriology

Vol. 1: *Bendt Alster*, Dumuzi's Dream, 1972
Vol. 2: *Bendt Alster*, The Instructions of Suruppak, 1974
Vol. 3: *Bendt Alster*, Studies in Sumerian Proverbs, 1975
Vol. 4: *Mogens Trolle Larsen*, The Old Assyrian City-State and its Colonies, 1976
Vol. 5: *Harriet Crawford*, The Architecture of Iraq in the Third Millennium B.C., 1977
Vol. 6: *Flemming Johansen*, Statues of Gudea. Ancient and Modern. With a chapter by Bendt Alster, 1978
Vol. 7: *Mogens Trolle Larsen* (ed.), Power and Propaganda. A Symposium on Ancient Empires, 1979
Vol. 8: *Bendt Alster* (ed.), Death in Mesopotamia. XXVI[e] Rencontre assyriologique internationale, 1980
Vol. 9: *Benjamin R. Foster*, Administration and Use of Institutional Land in Sargonic Sumer, 1982

MESOPOTAMIA

Copenhagen Studies in Assyriology

VOLUME 10

THE SUMERIAN LANGUAGE

AN INTRODUCTION TO ITS HISTORY AND GRAMMATICAL STRUCTURE

BY

MARIE-LOUISE THOMSEN

AKADEMISK FORLAG

Copenhagen 1984

The Sumerian Language

Mesopotamia

Copenhagen Studies in Assyriology

Volume 10

Copyright © 1984 by Marie-Louise Thomsen and Academic Press Copenhagen

2. edition 1987

Reprinted 1991

Illustration on the cover is from the Old Babylonian grammatical text published in Arno Poebel, *Historical and Grammatical Texts. (University of Pennsylvania, The Museum, Publication of the Babylonian Section,*V.) Philadelphia 1914. Nr. 152 col. 5,7-10.

Printed in Denmark

by B. Stougaard Jensen,

Copenhagen 1991

ISBN 87-500-2516-3

Publication of this book was made possible by grants from the University of Copenhagen, The Danish Research Council for the Humanities, and Knud Højgaards Fond.

TABLE OF CONTENTS

The Verb

ACKNOWLEDGMENTS

It gives me great pleasure to express my gratitude to the following of my colleagues and teachers: to Professor Jørgen Læssøe for his encouragement and interest in my work; to Lektor Aage Westenholz who read the manuscript of this book and made many valuable suggestions and corrections for which I am very grateful; to Lektor Mogens Trolle Larsen for his painstaking care in editing this volume and help in technical and practical matters. I wish also to thank Professor R. Borger for reading the manuscript and for his useful corrections especially as regards the transliterations.

Special thanks go to the University of Copenhagen, to Statens Humanistiske Forskningsråd, and to Knud Højgaards Fond for generously providing the means for the publication.

The manuscript was completed at the end of 1982. Literature and texts published since then could, as a rule, not be incorporated.

PREFACE

As it will be demonstrated in the introduction below (p. 15ff.) the study of the Sumerian language is not easy: the meaning of many words and grammatical elements is far from evident, the writing is defective and we are not able to analyse the grammar very well. In the history of Sumerology many studies about Sumerian grammar have been published, but as I.M. Diakonoff puts it: 'there are as many Sumerian languages as there are Sumerologists' (1976 p. 99). At least there are many different theories concerning particular grammatical problems.

It is of course not possible here to give an account of all these studies and much less to estimate the various theories. I shall therefore only mention the most important grammatical works which form the basis of our grammatical understanding of Sumerian today. The studies mentioned below are those most often used and referred to by the Sumerologists when translating and editing a text, even if they do not agree with them. For other studies I refer to the Bibliography.

The first systematic description of the Sumerian language, to which we still owe much today, is Arno Poebel's *Grundzüge der sumerischen Grammatik*, published in 1923. Poebel based his grammatical study on a variety of Sumerian texts: pre-Sargonic royal inscriptions as well as Neo-Assyrian bilinguals. In this book as well as in several articles (see Bibliography) he defined many grammatical categories: tenses, cases, the verbal morpheme /ed/ etc. The weakness of Poebel's grammar, however, is perhaps due to the fact that he based his work on texts from different periods which cover a long space of time without paying enough attention to the different stages of the language and the consequences of the contact with the Akkadian language and of the death of the language. However, although it is partly obsolete, Poebel's work stands in many respects as the traditional grammatical study of Sumerian.

Another important work is Adam Falkenstein's *Grammatik der Spra-che Gudeas von Lagas̆*, I-II, published 1949-1950, as well as many articles on grammatical problems (see Bibliography). Falkenstein follows to some extent the basic work of Poebel, but the fact that he limited himself to a single group of texts, namely the Gudea inscriptions which linguistically seem to be the most reliable textual material, meant that he could revise the grammar of Poebel on various points. In a more general way Falkenstein presented his grammatical theories in *Das Sumerische* (1959) which is an extremely short but practical outline of the Sumerian language.

The main objections against Falkenstein's description of Sumerian is that he did not sufficiently realize the specific character and structure of the language, but introduced categories from Indo-European languages into the Sumerian grammar, which fact resulted in some obscure interpretations and reconstructions of 'original' forms. However, Falkenstein's grammar as well as that of Poebel represents the traditional, and probably the most widespread, view on Sumerian grammar among scholars today.

A grammar dealing with the royal inscriptions of the Isin and Larsa dynasties is I. Kärki, *Die Sprache der sumerischen Königsinschriften der frühaltbabylonischen Zeit* (1967). This study is almost identical with Falkenstein's grammar of the Gudea language, as regards both terminology, composition as well as the treatment of grammatical categories.

The Old Sumerian inscriptions from the first dynasty of Lagas̆ were treated by E. Sollberger, *Système verbal* (1952), where a grammatical view is presented which in many respects differs widely from that of both Poebel and Falkenstein. However, because of the defective writing of the texts under consideration the alternative interpretations cannot easily be confirmed.

Beside these grammars studies on individual grammatical problems, especially the verb, have been published, for instance R.R. Jestin, *Le verbe sumérien*, in three volumes (1943-1954).

Thorkild Jacobsen contributed to the study of the Sumerian verb with his important articles 'Introduction to the Chicago Grammatical Texts' (1956) and 'About the Sumerian Verb' (1965). There he presented an original view of the verbal system which goes far beyond the studies of Poebel and Falkenstein, and which gives many interesting and detailed suggestions as to the meaning and analysis of the verbal morphemes.

Several other Sumerologists, especially in the last 10-15 years, have contributed to the understanding of Sumerian grammar with studies on various grammatical problems. For instance, a new theory of the occurrence of case elements in the prefixe chain was published by Gene B. Gragg (see §§ 425-426), and several studies of the verbal categories *hamṭu* and *marû* have been written by M. Yoshikawa and D.O. Edzard (see §§ 231-241 and Bibliography). However, the most important discovery of the last years is perhaps the realization that Sumerian belongs to the so-called ergative languages. This fact implies a new basis of the study of the Sumerian language which in the future probably will improve our understanding of Sumerian in many respects.

It is not my intention here to give a totally new and different representation of the Sumerian language. I rather think it useful to present a general description of Sumerian, as coherent as possible. Therefore, textual material from various periods has been included, and, consequently, the present grammar will also to some extent show the changes and development of the language by comparing certain forms and phrases. In my opinion, the Sumerian texts represent first of all the literary language and in the most important period, from the beginning of Ur III to the end of the Old Babylonian period, it has no connexion with a spoken language, since Sumerian probably died out in the last centuries of the 3rd mill. B.C. 'Development' means therefore not the development of the spoken vernacular, but rather the changes of the written language. Partly for this reason the grammar often seems contradictory and we shall probably never understand the Sumerian language completely.

Instead of developing elaborate systems according to which for instance every verbal form shall be explained, or instead of citing all instances of a certain form or morpheme I have tried to describe how the language functions by citing whole sentences and passages in order to illustrate the context in which this or that form can be used. In many cases I follow the basic work of the Sumerologists mentioned above, in other cases I have tried to improve or modify earlier theories; but also when I do not agree with them I have referred to various theories in order to present a varied picture of the Sumerian language and to point out other possibilities which may some day turn out to be right after all.

INTRODUCTION

History of the Sumerian Language

The peculiar situation of the Sumerian language and the special problems connected with it are not so much due to the status of Sumerian as a dead language, but mainly to the fact that it was probably no longer spoken already in that period from which by far the most Sumerian texts date.

The Sumerian text material forming the basis of the present grammar is a part, but the most important part, of the Sumerian sources from Mesopotamia, namely including the Old Sumerian inscriptions from Lagaš from ca. 2500 B.C. on and ending with the literary texts written during the Old Babylonian period, i.e. until ca. 1600 B.C. These ca. 900 years are the period when Sumerian gradually changed from a spoken language to a literary language only. We can say for certain that it was still spoken at the beginning of this period and that without doubt it was dead at the end of the OB period, but the advancing steps of the process cannot be followed in details.

It must of course have some consequences for the study of a language whether it should be regarded as a spoken everyday language or whether it is used exclusively as a literary language written during generations by people having another language as their mother tongue. In the following I shall therefore try to outline the history of the Sumerian language.

The heartland of the Sumerians is assumed to be the southern part of Mesopotamia called Sumer, the boundary being somewhere north of Nippur; in the later part of the Early Dynastic period maybe not very far from that city.[1] We do not know when the Sumerians had their

---

1. Cf. D.O. Edzard, 1965 p. 63: 'Wir können in der Periode frühdynastisch II mit einer weitgehend semitischen Besiedlung Nordbabyloniens und des Dijāla-Gebietes rechnen und damit einen Gegensatz 'semitischer Norden — sumerischer Süden' annehmen.'

first contacts with the Akkadians, but they are probably of a very early date, ca. 3000.[2] There seems to be indications for a long period of close contact between Sumerians and Akkadians, at least in the boundary districts, although we cannot follow this in written sources before ED III (ca. 2600 B.C.). As a result of this situation Akkadian as well as Sumerian underwent some changes such as the adoption of loanwords. The Sumerian influence may already rather early have caused the Akkadian word order: Subject − Object − Verb, which is unusual for a Semitic language.[3] Most clearly the early contact is shown in the archaic texts from Fara and Abū Ṣalābīkh (i.e. ED III ca. 2600 B.C.). In these texts there is a considerable amount of Akkadian personal names, and the scribes have Akkadian names as well. Although an Akkadian name of course does not necessarily mean that the person is an Akkadian, the names must be taken as evidence for the presence of Akkadian speakers in Sumer.[4] In the Abū Ṣalābīkh texts the Akkadian loanword u 'and' is the earliest certain evidence of an Akkadian loanword in Sumerian context.[5] It thus seems probable that there was a rather large number of bilingual persons at that time (ED III) in the northern part of Sumer to which Abū Ṣalābīkh belonged. In view of what happens later on, we can perhaps say that in ED III the Sumerian speaking population was reduced compared with the preceding period. The Akkadian language thus spread from the North where bilingual regions were established, whereas the population in the southern part probably was still mostly Sumerian-speaking.

During the reign of the Akkadian dynasty of Sargon the official language was primarily Akkadian, royal inscriptions and year dates were,

---

2. A. Falkenstein, 1960 p. 302, dates the earliest contacts to 'Frühdynastisch II'.
3. Cf. W. von Soden, 1952, p. 183 § 130b, and, for general remarks on the Sumerian influence on the Akkadian language, 1965 p. 105. For the adoption of Sumerian loanwords, see Lieberman, 1977. The Sumerian influence on the Akkadian language before the Sargonic period cannot be proven because of the very limited number of sources for the Akkadian language (cf. Gelb, 1961 p. 1-6). For the Akkadian influence on Sumerian, see A. Falkenstein, 'Kontakte zwischen Sumerern und Akkadern auf sprachlichem Gebiet.' *Genava* 8 (1960) p. 301-314.
4. Cf. R.D. Biggs, 1967: 'Semitic Names in the Fara Period.' *OrNS* 36 p. 55-66; and 1974, p.27. See also n. 6 below.
5. Cf. Biggs, 1974 p. 32.

however, mostly bilingual. Both languages are also used in religious texts like incantations. In other contexts, however, Sumerian is found only in Sumer proper. It thus seems probable that Sumerian as an everyday language in this period began seriously to vanish and that at least a-part of the Sumerian population has become bilingual, since Akkadian sources now also are found in Sumer.[6]

Nevertheless, after the Sargonic period, especially during the 3rd dynasty of Ur, the use of Sumerian increased in official documents. Royal inscriptions, juridical and administrative documents and letters are almost entirely written in Sumerian, whereas Akkadian texts are extremely rare.[7] Neo-Sumerian literary texts are scarce (the Gudea cylinders are an outstanding exception), but a part of the Sumerian literature attested in OB is assumed to have been composed during this period.[8] This so-called Sumerian 'renaissance', however, affected most probably the written language only, and the trends from the Sargonic period continue in the direction that a still greater part of the Sumerian population becomes bilingual and finally gives up the Sumerian language. In Ur III the use of Sumerian as a spoken language seems thus to have been very limited.

In the following OB period Sumerian must be regarded as a dead language, even if still used as an official and literary language. By far the most literary texts of this period are thus Sumerian, and so are the royal inscriptions until the 1st dynasty of Babylon (see Textual Material).

In the OB period the Sumerian tradition was continued in the 'school', the Eduba, where the literary texts were copied and studied. Sumerian was here spoken by the scholars and the more advanced students, who learned it, however, as a foreign language.[9] Before Sumerian thus finally became the language of a limited number of 'scientists', there was perhaps a period when a part of the population in Sumer was able to understand, at least in part, the Sumerian hymns, royal proclaims. etc. by recognizing some Sumerian words and expressions, although they did not speak Sumerian themselves.

---

6. For the distribution of Sumerian and Akkadian sources, see Gelb, 1960 p. 268. A catalogue of the Akkadian texts until OB times is given by Gelb 1961 p. 1-19.
7. Cf. Gelb, 1961 p. 16-19.
8. See W.W. Hallo, 1976 p. 198f.
9. See Å.W. Sjöberg, 1976 p. 161f. and cf. also below: Writing and Language Reconstruction, p. 20-26.

The history of the Sumerian language as outlined here is based chiefly on the important study of I.J. Gelb: 'Sumerians and Akkadians in their Ethno-Linguistic Relationship' (1960), and most recently the article of J.S. Cooper: 'Sumerian and Akkadian in Sumer and Akkad' (1973). Both argued for a comparatively early date of the extinction of Sumerian as a spoken language and concluded that Sumerian speakers were very few during Ur III.[10] However, the question is disputed, other Sumerologists are thus inclined to the opinion that Sumerian was still a living language in NS but died out somewhere during the Old Babylonian period.[11] The process of language death of course involves many cultural and social factors and there can hardly be given any general rules for the individual stages of its progress or of its duration. In our case historical and archaeological sources give only little direct information about the contact and relation of Sumerians and Akkadians, and the date of the language death must be deduced from such secondary circumstances as the spreading of Sumerian and Akkadian personal names,[12] the occurrences of Sumerian inscriptions versus Akkadian, and the increasing number of Akkadian loanwords in Sumerian texts.[13] All these indications are, however, rather uncertain and may allow for different interpretations.

However, an early date of the language death would agree best

---

10. Cf. Gelb, 1960 p. 270: 'While the Sumerian renaissance [i.e. Ur III] affected the use of the written language the country as a whole continued in the direction of total Akkadization and elimination of Sumerian elements. This can be clearly established by the growing number of Akkadian personal and geographical names in the South of the country, of Akkadian loanwords in Sumerian, and by the fact that the last three rulers of the Ur III dynasty bore Akkadian names, in contrast to the first two rulers, whose names are Sumerian'. Cooper, 1973 p. 241: 'Sumerian as a spoken language was in all probability dead or nearly so in Ur III.'

11. See F.R. Kraus, 1970 p. 86ff. for an outline of the various viewpoints. Cf. also Lieberman, 1977 p. 21 n. 50: 'In all likelihood Sumerian continued to be graced with native speakers down into the Old Babylonian period, through the Isin-Larsa period, although certainly the numbers of native speakers and the areas in which they lived gradually diminished and had already been significantly decreased before the Ur III period.'

12. For the problematic relation between the language of the name and the 'nationality' of its bearer, see W. Heimpel, 'Sumerische und akkadische Personennamen in Sumer und Akkad'. AfO 25, 1974-77, 171-174; and F.R. Kraus, 1970 p. 83-86. For a list of Sumerian names in the Sargonic period, see B.R. Foster, 1982.

13. Cf. Gelb, 1960 and n. 10 above.

with the available lingustic data. In fact the language of the non-canonical texts like documents and letter-orders, which presumably would be close to the spoken language, are very much influenced by Akkadian,[14] thus indicating that the Neo-Sumerian scribes did not have Sumerian as their mother tongue.

The process of the extinction of the Sumerian spoken language may, however, be more complicated as briefly outlined here. The conclusions drawn on the basis of the linguistic material are thus expected to concern only a part of the population, namely those who wrote the texts. Theoretically it is quite possible, if not very likely in my opinion, that there were more or less isolated Sumerian-speaking pockets in the South as late as in the Old Babylonian period. Their language, however, had obviously no influence on written Sumerian, since they lived without linguistic contact to the literary strata of the society.[15] Such possible smaller groups of Sumerian speakers are therefore of very limited importance to our grammatical study.

If the history of the Sumerian people and language as described here is correct, we must conclude, I think, that the last period where Sumerian was still a living language, spoken by the majority of the population, lies before the NS period. The NS and OB texts of various genres, both economic and literary, reflect the high status of Sumerian as the language of literature and of official and religious life, but not as the everyday language which was now almost exclusively Akkadian.

Bibliography

See also the bibliography to 'Writing and Language Reconstruction'.

R.D. Biggs, 1967. 'Semitic Names in the Fara Period'. *OrNS* 36: 55-66.

J.S. Cooper, 1973. 'Sumerian and Akkadian in Sumer and Akkad'. *OrNS* 42: 239-246.

---

14. This can for instance be seen in the use of the verbal prefixes /mu-/ and /ba-/ in the NS period which differs from the distribution of /mu-/ and /ba-/ in the Gudea and OB literary texts, cf. §§ 342-343.

15. So for instance Lieberman, 1977 p. 20 n. 50: 'It is not certain when Sumerian ceased to be spoken; most likely it died out in Northern Babylonia before there were no longer any native speakers in Sumer. Pockets or families of native speakers may have persisted long after the linguistic milieu had changed to Akkadian.'

D.O. Edzard, 1960. 'Sumerer und Semiten in der frühen Geschichte Mesopotamiens.' *Genava* 8: 241-258.

A. Falkenstein, 1960. 'Kontakte zwischen Sumerern und Akkadern auf sprachlichem Gebiet.' *Genava* 8: 301-314.

B.R. Foster, 1982. 'Ethnicity and Onomastics in Sargonic Mesopotamia.' *OrNS* 51: 297-354.

I.J. Gelb, 1960. 'Sumerians and Akkadians in their Ethno-Linguistic Relationship'. *Genava* 8: 258-271.

I.J. Gelb, 1961. *Old Akkadian Writing and Grammar.* Second Edition, Revised and Enlarged. (*Materials for the Assyrian Dictionary* 2) Chicago.

W. Heimpel, 1974-77. 'Sumerische und akkadische Personennamen in Sumer und Akkad'. *AfO* 25: 171-174.

F.R. Kraus, 1970. *Sumerer und Akkader. Ein Problem der altmesopotamischen Geschichte.* (*Mededelingen der Koninklijke Nederlandse Akademie van Wetenschappen. Afd. Letterkunde.* Nieuwe Reeks — Deel 33 — No. 8) Amsterdam-London.

Writing and Language Reconstruction

The Sumerian writing never attempted to render the language phonetically correct, exactly as it was spoken. The very first stages of writing as attested in Uruk and Ǧemdet Naṣr (about 3000 B.C.) were pictographic or ideographic in nature, thus rendering only the most important words like the catchwords of an account or a literary text. This principle was never totally abandoned in the Sumerian writing, although more and more grammatical elements and phonetic complements were gradually added. The original catchword principle is also apparent in the fact that for instance in the inscriptions from Lagaš the signs were not written in that order in which they had to be read until ca. 2470 (the reign of Eanatum). Note, however, that Akkadian names were always written in the right order, although the order of signs of the Sumerian context was free.

The ideographic writing system without phonetic signs for grammatical elements means that the identification of the language behind the written records is not immediately evident. On the basis of homonymous signs it is, however, made certain that the language of the Uruk and Ǧemdet Naṣr texts is Sumerian. The picture of a reed, Sumerian: gi = 'reed', is thus used for the verb gi = 'to return'. The texts must therefore be considered Sumerian, since it is not very likely that exactly the words for 'reed' and 'return' would be homonymous in any other language besides Sumerian.

See A.A. Vaiman, 1974 'Über die protosumerische Schrift', *Acta Antiqua* 22 p. 15f. A. Falkenstein, 1936 p. 37ff., argued for the Sumerian language in the Ǧemdet Naṣr texts in the same way based on the signs: EN LÍL TI, which he interpreted as a personal name: 'Enlil erhalte am Leben!'. TI which is the picture of an arrow is thus used for the homonyms 'arrow' and 'life' both = ti. The correct reading of the sign group is, however, É.EN.TI as stated by A.A. Vaiman, 1974 p. 15.

The development of the Sumerian writing and its function primarily as an aid to memory has been described by I.M. Diakonoff, 1976 'Ancient Writing and Ancient Written Language' (*AS* 20 p. 99-121): (The Sumerian writing system) 'even when using a maximum of phonetic values created for its signs according to the rebus principle, still remained in its essence a mnemonic system in which an exact rendering of the pronunciation was not aimed at. Thus when we try to find out the morphophonological structure of the Sumerian language, we must constantly bear in mind that we are not dealing with a language directly but are reconstructing it from a very imperfect mnemonic writing system which had not been basically aimed at the rendering of morphophonemics' (p. 112). Cf. also M. Civil, 1973b 'The Sumerian Writing System: Some Problems', *OrNS* 42: 21-34.

The typical differences between the old and the young scribal tradition can be illustrated by the following passage of 'Instructions of Šuruppak to his son Ziudsudra' of which both a version from Abū Ṣalābīkh (ca. 2600) and an Old Babylonian version exist:

(1) [ǧeš]tug$_2$ inim zu kalam til-la Šuruppak dumu na [n]a-mu-ri
(2) ud-ba (...) Šuruppak ǧeštug$_2$ tuku inim galam inim zu-a ka· lam-ma ti-la-àm, Šuruppak^{ki}-e dumu-ni-ra na na-mu-un-ri-ri '(On that day Šuruppak), the wise one, the one knowing (elaborate) words, who lives in Sumer, Šuruppak gave instructions to (his) son.'
(1) = Abū Ṣalābīkh version = *OIP* 99, 256 I 4-6, see Alster, 1974 p. 11; (2) = OB version 5-6, see Alster, 1974 p. 34; in parenthesis the additions of the OB version.

The addition of pronominal elements in verbal forms can be illustrated by the following examples:

(3) ensi$_2$-da Lagaš^{ki}-e hé.ǧál-la šu mu-da-peš-e (Gudea, cyl. B XIX 14-15)
(4) ^{D}En.líl-da kalam-e hé.ǧál-la šu mu-un-da-an-peš-e (Enki and the World Order 329, text H)

(3): 'with the ensi (the city) Lagaš expands in abundance';
(4): 'with Enlil the land (or: the people = uĝ-e) expands in
abundance'.

Other comparisons of texts from different periods can be found in:
M. Civil et R.D. Biggs, 1966 'Notes sur des textes sumériens archaïques', *RA* 60 p. 12; and I.M. Diakonoff, 1976 p. 104-108.

For the orthographic style called UD.GAL.NUN which occurs in
the Early Dynastic texts from Fara and Abū Ṣalābīkh and which apparently is based on a simple substitution of signs, see: R.D. Biggs,
1974 p. 32; W.G. Lambert, 1976 and 1981; J. Krecher, 1978b; B. Alster, 1982.

Bearing in mind the special character of the Sumerian writing as demonstrated above: an aid to memory rather than a phonetic transcrip-
tion of the spoken language, we must state that strictly speaking the
only thing we can do on this basis is to try to describe how some
grammatical relations are expressed *in the writing*. Since we cannot
take the texts at their face value a detailed grammatical description
of the language as presumably spoken would be a rather uncertain
task of reconstructing. As stated by M. Civil one of the pitfalls facing
the Sumerologist is the assumption that 'what is not written in the
texts is not in the utterance' (1973b p. 21), and other pitfalls are er-
roneous reconstructions of grammatical elements, where they perhaps never were present.

Nevertheless it is not only tempting but also necessary, I think, at
least to try to draw some conclusions about the spoken language behind the written records. The case of Sumerian is, however, a special
one, since we have two stages of linguistic tradition which have to be
treated differently: 1. the 'mnemonic' rendering of the spoken language, and 2. the literary tradition of the dead language. The turning-
point is, as described elsewhere, probably somewhere in the last centuries of the 3rd millennium.

1. Before the language death the writing was mainly an aid to memory rendering the most important words and morphemes in an ideographic manner, omitting many things which were not thought absolutely necessary for the understanding of the text. The omissions
were not solely a choice of the individual scribe, but follow some
scribal rules and conventions.

2. After the extinction of spoken Sumerian the writing was still

'mnemonic' in character, since the Sumerian literary tradition was not only scribal, but also oral, and the texts were thus still a supplement to oral representation.

Cf. M. Civil, 1976a p. 130: 'The OB Nippur scribe learned to associate sounds and meanings with the signs he was being trained to write from the teacher's oral instruction, and certainly not from consulting a tablet.'

Cf. also I.M. Diakonoff, 1976 p. 108f.: 'A scribe who was sure he would not be misunderstood could allow himself to leave out an ending here and an ending there, even as late as Ur III and probably later. (...) The better trained the scribe and the more routine the text, the less need there was to express in writing everything that existed in the language.'

However, as Sumerian became a foreign language to the scribes the need for a more elaborate writing grew, and full writings of endings like the pronominal suffixes as well as the insertion of pronominal prefixes in the finite verbal forms are characteristics of these texts (cf. the examples above). By completing the writing in this way the scribes probably followed some rules for reciting the Sumerian language as it was taught in the education center, the Eduba, where the instruction, at least in the more advanced classes, seems to have been carried out in Sumerian.[16] It is not impossible that the members of the Eduba knew some rules concerning the grammar and pronunciation of Sumerian, dating back to the time when the language was still spoken, but it is of course not likely that an oral tradition like this could survive the extinction of the spoken language in several hundred years without modifications. Certainly, the recitation and grammatical understanding of the Akkadian scribes during the first half of the 2nd mill. B.C. are in many respects different from that of the original Sumerian speakers, and errors, mistakes and forms influenced by the Akkadian language must be expected.[17] The problem is,

---

16. Cf. Å.W. Sjöberg, 1976 p. 161f. For the teaching of Sumerian in Eduba, see also H.L.J. Vanstiphout, 1979: 'How did they learn Sumerian?' *JCS* 31: 118-126.

17. Uncertainty and irresolution concerning the correct Sumerian form can apparently be seen in the many variants of the literary texts, cf. G.B. Gragg, 1972a: 'Observations on Grammatical Variation in Sumerian Literary Texts', *JAOS* 92: 204-213.

however, that we are not always able to decide whether a form or an expression is originally Sumerian or rather has to be referred to this post-Sumerian stage.

Moreover, mainly for orthographic reasons, we know very little about the Old Sumerian grammar, and, therefore, in many cases we are able to understand the OS texts only when comparing with later grammatical constructions. On the other hand, the Sumerian grammar as it is available in the more comprehensive post-Sumerian textual material is somewhat heterogeneous and partly contradictory, and Akkadian influence can be demonstrated. Finally, many grammatical questions are generally insufficiently attested or occur mostly in fragmentary or very difficult context. We are thus forced to speak about 'good' and 'bad' Sumerian trying to pick out the most reliable grammatical tradition, although the problem is that the 'good' Sumerian cannot be exactly defined, since in practice we know very little about the original Sumerian language in its older stages.

What we should try to do is not to reconstruct the spoken Sumerian, which would be impossible, but to compare the various stages-of the Sumerian written language in order to find out what presumably could be an old grammatical construction, and what is probably a later, secondary form. The grammar as it is expressed in the post-Sumerian texts is not of minor interest and should not be rejected as incorrect or barbarian Sumerian, since it is an interesting testimony of the treatment of the literary language, Sumerian, by the Old Babylonian scholars and scribes[18], and especially because the most important and most extensive text corpus was written in that period.

In the present grammar the language of Gudea is regarded as a sort of standard language representing the best Sumerian that is accessible to us. The reasons for this are: 1. the Gudea text material represents a homogeneous language and grammatical rules are followed rather consistently; 2. although they belong to the NS period when spoken Sumerian was vanishing the Gudea texts are not as influenced by

---

18. The Old Babylonian linguistics can be studied in the grammatical texts: *OBGT*, published in *MSL* IV. Cf. Th. Jacobsen, 'Introduction to the Chicago Grammatical Texts'. *MSL* IV p. 1*-50*; and Th. Jacobsen, 'Very Ancient Texts: Babylonian Grammatical Texts'. In: *Studies in the History of Linguistics. Traditions and Paradigms*. Ed. by Dell Hymes. Bloomington/London 1974; p. 41-62.

Akkadian as the later (and more extensive) OB material; 3. the Gudea
text material is large enough to illustrate most grammatical forms
and constructions.

The Old Sumerian texts, especially those from the first dynasty of
Lagaš, are regarded as reflecting an earlier, more original stage of this
language, but for orthographic reasons less fit for grammatical analysis. The OS inscriptions are occasionally important as a control, sup-
porting (or contradicting) the reliability of some grammatical rules
deduced from later texts.

Strictly speaking only those grammatical rules which are attested
also in the older text material (Old Sumerian and Gudea texts) should
be regarded as reflecting the original Sumerian language, but the literary language of the Old Babylonian period may of course contain
more original material than we are able to discover, even if we always
have to consider if Akkadian influence or secondary scribal practice
could be responsible for any given grammatical construction. In practice it is not possible to check all grammatical forms and consider
their origin and authenticity, although this of course would be the
ideal demand on the grammatical analysis. As presented here, the
Sumerian grammar therefore, quotes the most common forms, leav-
ing out many obscure forms and variants, but, if possible, choosing
the most original forms and rules according to the principles just outlined. I have tried to illustrate the changing of the language by giving
examples from various periods.

Examples of secondary scribal practice which cannot be regarded as an original grammatical rule:

Normally the possessive suffixes /-ani/ 'his/her' and /-bi/ 'its' become -(a-)na
and -ba when followed by the locative postposition /-a/ or by genitive /-ak/,
e.g., šu-na 'in his hand' = /šu-ani-a/. In post-Sumerian texts from the Old
Babylonian period we may, however, have šu-ni-a or ..-bi-a (cf. for instance
Kärki, 1967 p. 25). This is an example of an analytic writing which of course
may render the pronunciation of the Old Babylonian time, but which is certainly not original.

Sometimes we do not know whether a change in scribal practice also reflects
a grammatical change:

In Old Sumerian texts the negation prefix /nu-/ is written with the sign NU
also before the prefixes /ba-/ and /bi-/, whereas later on it is written la-ba-...
(from the end of OS) and li-bí-... (from OB on). This can be interpreted in
two different ways:

1. The change of nu- to la- (or li-) before ba- (and bí-), is not completed
before the end of OS.

2. NU-ba-.. is always to be interpreted as la-ba- (we could then give NU

the value là), the use of NU instead of the phonetic la- is ideographic, NU is not mainly the phonetic value [nu] but contains the meaning: NEGATION.[19]

Bibliography

Miguel Civil, 1973b. 'The Sumerian Writing System: Some Problems'. *OrNS* 42: 21-34.

I.M. Diakonoff, 1976. 'Ancient Writing and Ancient Written Language: Pitfalls and Pecularities in the Study of Sumerian'. *AS* 20: 99-121.

The Textual Material

The textual material forming the basis of the present study of the Sumerian language dates to the period ca. 2500-1600 B.C. Historically it begins with the First Dynasty of Lagaš and ends with the First Dynasty of Babylon. The space of time covered by the Sumerian texts is thus about 900 years which is a rather long period compared to the size of the textual evidence. This means that some periods are not as well attested as others, and that the history of the Sumerian language cannot be described without serious gaps. Moreover, the various text genres are differently preserved: in one period for instance literary sources are almost totally absent, in another royal inscriptions and so on.

For these reasons it is hardly possible to describe the development of Sumerian or to define some linguistic stages of the language, like we are talking about for instance Old Babylonian and Neo-Babylonian. The Sumerian texts are thus first of all classified according to their genre and the date of the literary tradition they are belonging to, and the terms: Old Sumerian, Neo-Sumerian, Old Babylonian therefore reflect the historical periods during which the texts are written down more than the development of the language.

---

19. Similarly the use of HÉ is in some cases probably an ideographic writing of the modal prefix /ha-/, cf. Civil and Biggs, 1966 p. 15.

The distribution of textual material according to historical periods:

	Historical Period	Language Stage	Textual Material
2600 2500 2400	Early Dynastic III or Pre-Sargonic	Old Sumerian	'Archaic' texts from Fara and Abū Ṣalābīkh ca. 2600-2500
			Inscriptions of 1st dynasty of Lagaš ca. 2500-2350
2340	Sargonic or Old Akkadian		Documents and inscriptions
2200 2100	Gutian	Neo-Sumerian	Gudea inscriptions ca. 2140-2120
	3rd dynasty of Ur		Administrative and legal documents ca. 2100-2000
2000 1900 1800 1700 1600	Isin-dyn. Old { Larsa-dyn. Babylonian } 1st dyn. of Babylon	Old Babylonian Sumerian or Post-Sumerian	Royal inscriptions Literary texts

For bibliographical references concerning the textual material cited in the grammar, see Bibliography.

Old Sumerian

Most generally taken the Old Sumerian period includes the oldest intelligible Sumerian texts from about 2600 B.C. until the end of the

Sargonic dynasty ca. 2200 B.C. In a narrower sense, however, the Old Sumerian textual material is the inscriptions dating to the first dynasty of the city-state of Lagaš and contemporary material, ca. 2500-2350. The language of this period has also been called 'classical Sumerian'. The slightly older texts from Fara and Abū Ṣalābīkh (ca. 2600) are difficult and therefore as yet of comparatively little value for the Sumerian grammar.

Written sources from the Sargonic dynasty, on the other hand, i.e. ca. 2340-2200 B.C., are almost exclusively Akkadian, and on the basis of the limited number of Sumerian texts it is difficult to get an exhaustive characterization of the language in order to determine it as Old Sumerian or as an individual stage of the language.

The orthography of the Old Sumerian texts is rather defective: the older the texts the more morphemes are omitted in the writing. This means that the texts generally are difficult to understand and that their value as linguistic sources is reduced. It does not seem possible to describe the Sumerian grammar only on the basis of these texts, but the Old Sumerian material is of importance in order to check and supplement the information of later material. However, apart from the omission of several grammatical elements the orthography in most of the Old Sumerian text material is more or less the same as in the Neo-Sumerian and Old Babylonian literary texts.[20]

Because of the defective orthography it is of course difficult to say exactly how the Old Sumerian grammar possibly differs from that of younger periods. Thus only one characteristic linguistic feature of at least some of the Old Sumerian texts may be cited, namely the so-called vowel harmony: the verbal prefixes /bi/ and /ī/ are written bí- and ì- before morphemes containing the vowels [i] or [u], but bé- and e- before [e] and [a], cf. §§ 7-9. The vowel harmony is not found after the Old Sumerian period and may be used as criterion in order to distinguish this stage of the language.

The Genres of the Old Sumerian Textual Material

The Archaic Texts, ca. 2600-2500: economic, administrative and literary texts, as well as some brief votive inscriptions.

The pre-Sargonic Texts, ca. 2500-2340: first of all the building

---

20. For the UD.GAL.NUN orthography in the Old Sumerian texts, see p. 22.

and votive inscriptions of the First Dynasty of Lagaš. Some of these inscriptions contain rather long narratives like the Stele of the Vultures (= Ean. 1) or the cones of Entemena (= Ent. 28-29). Moreover there are the famous Reform Texts of Uruinimgina (= Ukg. 1-6) which are early law texts or a sort of edict. Finally there are several thousand administrative texts. Literary texts like myths, epics or hymns are few in this period, but cf. Sjöberg, 1969 p. 7 who lists three compositions: a) 'Enlil and Ninhursaĝ' (= *MBI* 1); b) 'Enlil and Iškur' (= Kramer, 1956 p. 280 and 106 fig. 6a); c) 'a mythological text' (= Ukg. 15). These texts are, however, hardly intelligible and therefore not of use for grammatical studies.

The Neo-Sumerian Period: ca. 2200-2000 B.C.

Although the duration of the Neo-Sumerian period is only about 200 years it is necessary to subdivide the text material into two groups:

The Gutian Period, ca. 2200-2100 B.C.: The inscriptions of Gudea, ruler of the city-state Lagaš ca. 2144-2124; most important is the temple hymn describing the building of the Ninĝirsu-temple, Eninnu, inscribed on two clay cylinders (A and B)[21], besides this several inscriptions on statues and other objects, as well as some documents.

In many respects the Gudea texts seem to follow the tradition of the pre-Sargonic Lagaš texts, as regards orthography and linguistic style. The only exceptions are perhaps that there is no vowel harmony (see §§ 7-9) and that the writing is more elaborate.

The Third Dynasty of Ur (= Ur-III): ca. 2100-2000 B.C.: The most extensive textual material from the later part of the Neo-Sumerian period is an enormous number of administrative texts, accounts etc. which are of little use for the grammatical analysis, and therefore not included here. More informative is a considerable number of juridical documents and so-called letter-orders (i.e. administrative and business letters). The language of these texts is rather heterogeneous and clearly differs from the literary style. Generally speaking the texts make the impression of a less careful treatment of the language and

---

21. Cf. Å.W. Sjöberg, 1969 p. 6: 'The Gudea cylinders which represent early examples of the Neo-Sumerian category temple hymns may, when considered in relation to the short temple hymns among the texts from Abū Ṣalābīh, be the climax of a long tradition of 'Old Sumerian' literature.'

in part they seem highly influenced by Akkadian. It is thus hard to imagine the scribes having Sumerian as their mother tongue, at least their Sumerian is rather far from the classical language.[22]

The royal inscriptions are mostly short and uniform in content and style. As far as can be judged, their language is rather close to the Gudea inscriptions.

Literary texts are few and almost all of them are unpublished (cf. Å.W. Sjöberg, 1969 p.7).

The Old Babylonian Period, ca. 2000-1600 B.C.

The historical period which is called Old Babylonian begins after the fall of the Third Dynasty of Ur, i.e. 2003 B.C., and ends with the fall of the First Babylonian dynasty in 1594 B.C. Texts of this period included in the present grammar are best distinguished in two groups according to genre:

Royal inscriptions: The building and votive inscriptions of the rulers of the Isin and Larsa dynasties are exclusively in Sumerian, whereas those of the First Dynasty of Babylon are mostly in Akkadian, some of them with a Sumerian version. Especially the younger part of these inscriptions contain obvious linguistic errors, and in the inscriptions from the Babylonian rulers the Akkadian model is clearly recognizable in the grammar of the Sumerian translation.

Cf. for instance the misunderstood forms of compound verbs: (5) si bí-in-si-sá (Warad-Sin 28, obv. 24); (6) mu-un-ki-ğar (Anam 4, 19); or the confusion of the inanimate and animate possessive suffixes /-bi/ and /-ani/, (see Kärki, 1967 p. 203); incorrect use of cases: terminative for locative, or locative instead of dative: (7) ^{D}Utu lugal-ğá = *a-na* ^{D}*Šamaš be-li-ia* 'for my king Utu' (correct: lugal-ğu$_{10}$-ra; Hammurapi *OECT* I 18 II 19 = *PBS* VII 133 II 4); unusual constructions in Sumerian being directly translated from the Akkadian text: (8) lugal-lugal-e-ne-er lú na-me ba-ra-an-dím-ma = *šar-ru in* LUGAL-*rí ma-na-ma la i-pu-šu* 'which no king among the kings has ever made' (Hammurapi *OECT* I 18 II 16-18 = *PBS* VII 133 II 2-3). The Sumerian text, however, would correctly mean: 'for all the kings no one shall ever make it'. Conversely the Sumerian translation of the Akkadian phrase should be: *lugal-lugal-e.ne-a(loc.) lú na.me nu-un-dím-ma (or nu-mu-na-an-dím-ma) or the like.

Literary Texts: This term includes an extremely varied textual material containing genres like: myths, epics, hymns to gods, hymns to

---

22. Cf. above p. 19 and n. 14 as well as § 343.

kings, prayers, incantations, satirical dialogues, debates, proverbs, and collections of letters.

The literary texts constitute the bulk of the Sumerian linguistic material. At the same time they are practically the only sources to the Sumerian religious and wisdom literature, apart from the few 'forerunners' from ED III or the few NS literary texts (see above). As far as these texts are dated, which is only exceptionally the case, they range from the reign of Rim-Sin of Larsa to that of Ammiṣaduqa of Babylon (i.e. 1822-1626 B.C., cf. A. Falkenstein, 1951 p. 12).

The texts were written and studied in the Old Babylonian school, Eduba, first of all in Nippur, but also in other cities, not only for the purpose of learning to write and read cuneiform, but probably also in order to improve the oral performance of certain literary genres and to compose royal hymns in Sumerian language.

The group of literary texts is very heterogeneous, not only as regards their contents, but also according to the linguistic tradition. The latter probably depends both on the date of origin of the composition as well as on the date and place of the individual duplicate. Since the editions of Sumerian literary texts only exceptionally attempt to classify their texts sources according to linguistic and literary tradition, it is a rather difficult task to point out or to characterize some group of texts or individual school according to authenticity of the language. Generally speaking, however, the texts from Nippur belong to a better tradition than e.g. texts from Ur, and narrative compositions like myths and epics often seem better according to grammar than for instance royal hymns.

The distinction drawn here between literary texts and royal inscriptions is not an absolute one. Some of the inscriptions represent a rather good tradition similar to the best of the literary texts, and some literary texts, on the other hand, are as poor as the latest inscriptions. It is perhaps more justified to say, in very general terms, that, regardless of genre, the younger the date of the origin of the composition, the less correct its grammar, that means that for instance royal hymns and the so-called Eduba compositions like Schooldays and the dialogues certainly created in the Old Babylonian period should contain more errors and secondary forms than epics and myths which probably come from an older, originally oral tradition.

Obviously this is very often the case, but again also the origin of the various text duplicates is of importance.

Bibliography

For the age and history of the Sumerian literary texts, cf.:

A. Falkenstein, 1951. 'Zur Chronologie der sumerischen Literatur'. *CRRAI II* 12-27.

W.W. Hallo, 1963. 'On the Antiquity of Sumerian Literature'. *JAOS* 83, 167-176.

W.W. Hallo, 1976. 'Toward a History of Sumerian Literature'. *AS* 20, 181-203.

For the Old Babylonian School and the oral tradition which was probably somehow continued there, see:

Å.W. Sjöberg, 1976. 'The Old Babylonian Eduba'. *AS* 20, 159-179.

Th. Jacobsen, 1982. 'Oral to Written'. *Studies in Honour of I.M. Diakonoff.* 129-137.

V. Afanasjeva, 1974. 'Mündlich überlieferte Dichtung ('Oral Poetry') und schriftliche Literatur in Mesopotamien'. *Acta Antiqua* 22, 121-135.

B. Alster, 1972a. *Dumuzi's Dream, Aspects of Oral Poetry in a Sumerian Myth.* Copenhagen. (Espec. pp. 9-27.)

For the various literary genres and the content of the individual compositions, see:

J. Krecher, 1978a. 'Sumerische Literatur'. In: *Neues Handbuch der Literaturwissenschaft*. Bd. I: pp. 101-150.

W.H.Ph. Römer, 1974. 'Fünf und zwanzig Jahre der Erforschung sumerischer literarischer Texte'. *BiOr* 31, 207-222.

Sumerian Texts after the Old Babylonian Period

Sumerian texts continued to be written until the Seleucid period (2nd century B.C.), but the greater part of the Sumerian literature known in the Old Babylonian period was not copied after that time. In the later periods the Sumerian texts are: incantations, proverbs, liturgical Emesal texts and laments in Emesal; the only literary compositions that are copied after the Old Babylonian period are An-gim and Lugal-e. These texts represent a continuation of the Old Babylonian literary style, but of course errors and misunderstandings are very frequent, and examples from them are only exceptionally used in the present study to illustrate the Sumerian grammar.

Bibliography (see also above pp. 19-20)

A. Falkenstein, 1953. 'Zur Chronologie der sumerischen Literatur. Die nachalt-babylonische Stufe'. *MDOG* 85, 1-13.

GRAMMAR

PHONETICS

Introduction

§ 1. A satisfactory description of Sumerian phonetics would be possible only together with a detailed study of the writing based on lexical sources, syllabic texts etc. which I have not been able to undertake within the scope of this grammatical study. Therefore, and for the sake of convenience, I have preferred to render the Sumerian phonemes in the traditional way, including, however, the phonemes [dr] and [g̃].

§ 2. The Sumerian phonetic system, as it is traditionally understood, is almost identical to that of Akkadian with two exceptions: 1. that Sumerian has no emphatics (q, ṣ and ṭ), and 2. the Sumerian phonemes [dr] and [g̃]. Since our informations about the pronunciation of Sumerian come from Akkadian sources, this fact is probably the main reason for the seeming conformity with the Akkadian phonological system.[23] Variants, different spellings of certain words, sound changes etc., on the other hand, indicate that the Sumerian phonemes in some respects differ from the Akkadian ones. But as it has been stated above in the chapter 'Writing and Language Reconstructions' the Sumerian writing does not represent a phonetically correct rendering of the language, and it is therefore hardly possible to reconstruct an adequate phonological system of Sumerian.

In the following I have concentrated on the most important observations concerning Sumerian phonemes, especially such which are of importance for the grammar like, e.g., the vowel harmony, contraction and deletion of vowels and consonants, etc. For more detailed studies about Sumerian phonology I shall, however, refer to the bibliography below.

---

23. Cf. A. Falkenstein, 1960 p. 303f., who pointed to the long duration of Sumerian-Akkadian language contact as the cause of this phenomenon.

38

§ 3. Bibliography

A. Cavigneaux, 1976. *Die sumerisch-akkadischen Zeichenlisten. Überlieferungsprobleme*. Diss. München.

M. Civil, 1973a. 'From Enki's Headaches to Phonology'. *JNES* 32: 57-61.

R.R. Jestin, 1965. *Notes de graphie et de phonétique sumériennes.* (*Bibliothèque de l'Ecole des Hautes Etudes, IVe section. Sciences historiques et philologiques, 317*). Paris.

J. Krecher, 1969. 'Verschlußlaute und Betonung im Sumerischen'. *AOAT* 1: 157-197.

S. Parpola, 1975. 'Transliteration of Sumerian: Problems and Prospects'. (*Studia Orientalia 46*) .Helsinki: 239-258.

See also the studies cited in the chapter 'Writing and Language Reconstruction'.

Vowels

§ 4. The vowels clearly distinguished in the writing system are: a, e, i, u. The vowels are probably both short and long. Long vowels are supposed to originate from vowel contraction or from consonant deletion.

Cf. J. Krecher, 1969 p. 169-171; A. Falkenstein, 1960 p. 303.

§ 5. In monosyllabic words of the form CV the vowel is often written double in lexical texts, e.g., ba-a, zi-i, du-ú (Krecher, 1969 p. 170). The importance of this practice is disputed, but some OB lexical texts carefully distinguish writings with and without supplementary vowel which therefore seems to be significant for the pronunciation. A. Falkenstein, 1959a p. 24, denied that such writings indicate primary long vowels. Doubled vowels are rare in words with more than one syllable.

Cf. also Krecher, 1969 p. 169: 'Bei Lehnwörtern im Akkadischen beobachten wir danach eine Tendenz, Langvokale durch Kurzvokale mit folgendem geminierten Konsonanten zu ersetzen.'

§ 6. Nasalized Vowels

A. Falkenstein, 1959a p. 45, assumed that the conjugation prefix ì- represents a nasalized vowel: [ĩ]. Nasalized vowels are apparently not attested elsewhere in Sumerian, but after all nasalization seems to be the only explanation for the changing of [b] to [m] in the following prefix chains:

im-ma- $<$ /ì-ba-/; im-mi- $<$ /ì-bi-/

If, however, the conjugation prefix ì- is a nasalized vowel: [ĩ], then also its allophone e- in the OS texts (see § 7) must be nasalized: [ẽ]. Moreover, provided that the prefix a- is a variant of /ĩ-/ and not an independent prefixe, we also have [ã] (see § 316).

Note that ì- otherwise does not represent [ĩ], but simply [i]; cf. for instance the prefix chain ì-bí- ... $<$ /u-bi-../.

Vowel Harmony

§ 7. The so-called 'vowel harmony' in Sumerian is a phenomenon found exclusively in the OS inscriptions from Lagaš and a few other cities (Umma, Uruk and Ur). It concerns the verbal prefixes /ĩ-/ and /bi-/ only.

These prefixes occur as ì- and bí-, respectively, before verbal stems or prefixes containing the vowels [i] and [u], e.g., ì-zìg, bí-dug₄. Before the vowels [a] and [e] they occur as e- and bé-, e.g., e-ak, e-me-a, e-ma-ni-... $<$ /ĩ-ba-ni../, bé-ĝar.

For further details about variants and exceptions see § 309 and § 339.

§ 8. The principle for the vowel harmony was first worked out by A. Poebel, 1931, where he assumed two groups of vowels: 1. open vowels: a, ĕ, and ŏ; and 2. close vowels: ē, i and u. The prefix /ĩ-/ was thus pronounced with the open vowel ĕ before morphemes containing a vowel of the first group, whereas it was pronounced [i] before a close vowel. S.N. Kramer, 1936, stated the same rule for the prefix /bi-/: bé- before open vowels and bí- before close vowels.

The existence of a six vowel system as suggested by Poebel is, however, rejected by most Sumerologists today, since only 4 vowels, a, e, i and u, seem to be distinguished in the writing. The distinction of two groups of vowels is, however, clear enough, but only in the above mentioned prefixes and only in some part of the textual material. It may, therefore, belong to a certain dialect concentrated in Lagaš.

Most recently S.J. Lieberman, 1979, has taken up the theory of Poebel and with some modifications he argues for a five-vowel system in Sumerian, graphically demonstrated like this (p. 23):

Lieberman bases his assumptions on the pronunciation column in the lexical text Proto-Ea (*MSL* II), where, according to him, ú = [u], but u, ù and u₄ = [o]. This distinction, he assumes, reflects two different Sumerian phonemes. It may as well, however, reflect different Akkadian phonemes and pronunciation, and the existence of a Sumerian phoneme [o] is therefore not beyond doubt.

§ 9. Bibliography

A. Poebel, 1931. *The Sumerian Prefix Forms e- and i- in the Time of the Earlier Princes of Lagaš*. (AS 2). Chicago.

S.N. Kramer, 1936. *The Sumerian Prefix Forms be- and bi- in the Time of the Earlier Princes of Lagaš*. (AS 8). Chicago.

S.J. Lieberman, 1979. 'The Phoneme /o/ in Sumerian'. *Studies in Honor of Tom B. Jones*. (AOAT 203). Neukirchen-Vluyn, pp. 21-28.

Vowel Assimilation

§ 10. Vowel assimilation is found in a number of cases, especially in the prefix chain of the verb. This sort of 'vowel harmony' is based simply on identity with the following vowel. The vowel of the modal prefixes /ha-/, /ša-/, /nu-/ and /u-/ is thus (with some restrictions) assimilated with the vowel of the following conjugation prefix:

Before [i]: hé-bí-, ši-bí-, li-bí- < /nu-bi-/, ì-bí- < /u-bi-/.

Before [a]: ha-ba-, ša-ba-, la-ba- < /nu-ba-/, a-ba- < /u-ba-/ (only OS).

Before [u]: ha-mu- (until OB), hu-mu- (from OB on), ša-mu-, nu-mu-, ù-mu- (see also § 304 'Combinations of Prefixes').

The 'original' vowel of the prefixes /ha-/ and /ša-/ is here assumed to be [a], but it could as well be [e] or [i]. In fact there may be no 'original' vowel, since it simply changes according to the following morpheme.

Vowel assimilation in a nominal, adjectival or verbal stem occurs only exceptionally, for instance in the imperative form of the verb ǧen 'to come': ǧá-na 'come!' < /ǧen + ã/. Since ǦÁ may stand for [ǧe] it is also possible to read ǧe₂₆-na.

§ 11. a > i

The comitative prefix /-da-/ changes to -di-, apparently because of a following -ni-, but also in other cases without obvious reasons, cf. Gragg, *SDI* p. 42ff. and below § 434 'Comitative Prefix'.

§ 12. a > e

The comitative prefix /-da-/occurs also in the form -dè- in OB texts. This form occurs possibly either as a contraction of /-da-/ + /-e-/, or as an assimilation with a preceding -e-: ba-e-dè- < /ba-e-da-/ (cf. Gragg, *SDI* p. 42ff.).

§ 13. e > u

After some verbal roots containing the vowel [u] the [e] of the verbal morpheme /ed/ and of the pronominal suffixes is sometimes changed to [u]: šub-bu-dè < /šub-ed-e/, -šub-bu-uš < /-šub-eš/.

Cf. 'Pronominal Suffixes', 'Writing', § 295.

Vowel Contraction

§ 14. Contracted vowels are assumed to be long, but actually we cannot say for certain whether the vowels are long or short in the examples below:

i + a > a: /-ani-a(loc.)/ or /-ani-a(k)/ > -a-na, /-bi-a/, /-bi-ak/ > -ba

u + a > a: /- g̃u₁₀ -a or -a(k)/ > -g̃á; mu-? (= 1.sg.DAT)/ > ma-

u + e > e: /mu-e-/ > me- (see § 336)

u + e > u: /lú-e(erg.)/ > lú-ú

After verbal stems ending in a vowel the [e] of the verbal morpheme /ed/ and of the pronominal suffixes is either deleted or contracted with the preceding vowel: /-g̃á.g̃á-en/ > -g̃á-g̃á-an, /-du-en/ > -du-un, /g̃á.g̃á-ed-e/ > g̃á-g̃á-dè.

§ 15. In some cases it cannot be decided if a vowel is contracted or simply deleted. For instance is /-bi-e(erg. or loc.t.)/ always written -bi. This writing may represent either [bi] with deletion of /-e/, or it may stand for [bī] with long vowel resulting from the contraction of [i] + [e]; and as a third possibility we may also understand it as -bé = [bē] (or [be]?). Since the correct interpretation is not evident from the writing practice I transliterate -bi throughout without indication of the possible presence of an /-e/.

Consonants

§ 16. The Sumerian consonants which are distinguished in the writing are the following:

b, d, dr, g, g̃, h, k, l, m, n, p, r, s, š, t, z.

Consonants in Final Position

§ 17. Final consonants are often omitted in the writing, e.g.,

é-a $<$ /é-ak/ 'of the house' (never written é-ak)

(9) ù-mu-na-da-ku₄-re $<$ /u-mu-na-da-ku₄.r-en/ 'after you have entered before him with it' (Gudea, cyl. A VII 2)

In some cases the final consonant may actually not have been pronounced, but the omission may also be a purely orthographic phenomenon. The circumstances under which a final consonant is deleted or not are, however, not known in details, since the pronunciation is not rendered explicitly in the writing.

§ 18. As a rule, we may perhaps presume that the final consonant of a verbal stem is dropped in the *marû* reduplication: ku₄-ku₄ from ku₄.r, ǧá-ǧá from ǧar, na₈-na₈ from naǧ. The *marû* form is thus distinguished from the *hamṭu* reduplication ǧar-ǧar, etc. which retains the final consonant. The final consonant of a postposition or of a pronominal element we would assume to be retained, but in fact the writing does not allow us to decide this problem with certainty (cf. the examples in § 17).

A. Falkenstein, 1960, assumed that most consonants could be dropped in final position: 'Im Wort- und Silbenauslaut können alle Konsonanten schwinden, wobei aber der Schwund anscheinend nicht alle Konsonanten in demselben Maße betrifft. Besonders 'anfällig' sind die Nasale, die auch intervokalisch schwinden können.' (p. 305). Cf. also Falkenstein, 1959a p. 29. I.M. Diakonoff, 1976 also stated: 'practically all voiced stops and some other consonants are (as in French) mute in In- and Auslaut' (p. 111). Diakonoff further observed that some consonants are almost invariably retained, others mostly dropped. As reason for this phenomenon he suggested the difference between glottalized and non-glottalized or between palatalized and non-palatalized (p. 111 n. 20). Cf. M. Civil, 1973b, p. 34 n. 13.

§ 19. Because of the uncertainties concerning the actual pronunciation I have, as a principle, rendered the stems with the final consonant: dug₄ (not du₁₁), zid (not zi), níg (not ni) etc. In the *marû* reduplication the short form is given, whereas the *hamṭu* reduplication (which probably does not drop the final consonant, see § 242) is rendered as dug₄-dug₄, ǧar-ǧar etc. as far as the two kinds of reduplication can be distinguished.

The Opposition Voiced: Voiceless

§ 20. The conventional transliterations show a distinction between voiced and voiceless stops in Sumerian, b, d, g : p, t, k. But in fact it is disputed whether this distinction actually existed in Sumerian. First of all the earliest Akkadian system of writing does not distinguish b, d, g and p, t, k and it is most probable that the Akkadians borrowed this custom from the Sumerians. This means that Sumerian originally does not have the opposition voiced: voiceless. Th. Jacobsen, 1957 p. 92 n. 1, thus suggested another opposition: rounded (i.e. pronounced with rounded lips) stops and sibilants: b, d, g, z, š, and unrounded: p, t, k, s.

§ 21. Moreover, Sumerian loanwords adopted in Akkadian before the Old Babylonian period are rendered with p, t, k where the Sumerian word traditionally has b, d, and g, e.g., barag = *parakkum*, é.gal = *ekallum*, dub = *t/ṭuppum*. In loanwords from the Old Babylonian period and later, on the other hand, b = b, d = d, and g = g. A sound shift in Sumerian has therefore been assumed, but other explanations are likewise possible: I.J. Gelb, for instance, suggested two sets of Sumerian consonants, based on the early writing practice and the rendering of loanwords: 'the consonantal pattern of early Sumerian can be reconstructed as containing two contrasting sets of phonemes. One set, written by the signs transliterated with a voiced consonant of the type BA, DA, GA, ZA, expresses phonemes b/p, d/t, g/k, z/s, which sounded like voiceless p, t, k, s to the Akkadians. And another set, written by the signs transliterated with a voiceless consonant of the type PA, TA, KA, SA, expresses perhaps the phonemes p', t', k', s'. Since the Akkadians did not have aspirated stops they expressed Sumerian loan words containing the phonemes p', t', k' simply by their voiceless p, t, k. But they were fully able to express the Sumerian aspirated sibilant s' by their own $š_{1-2}$. (Gelb, 1961 p. 33).

J. Renger, 1971, considered a sound shift in Sumerian very unlikely at a time (namely OB) where Sumerian was no longer spoken. Renger argued for an orthographic reform as the reason for the different renderings of Sumerian loanwords of the Old Akkadian and the Old Babylonian periods.

For further comments on this problem, see J. Krecher, 1969.

§ 22. It is generally assumed that no stem or affix end in one of the phonemes rendered as p, t or k. Actually, if a stem is followed by a suffix with initial vowel, it is always written -ba, -da, -ga (or -bé, -dè, -ge), but not -pa, -ta, -ka etc. The only exceptions are the genitive postposition /-ak/ and the verb ak 'to do': /-ak-a/ > -(Ca)-ka, /-ak-e/ > -(Ca)-ke₄, and the verbal forms ak-ka, ..-ak-ke₄.[24] On the other hand, M. Civil, 1973b, suggests 'the probable existence of a rule that adds a feature + voice to final stops before suffixes with initial vowel' (p. 34), thus KALAG 'strong' = kalak, but kalaga < /kalak.a/.

§ 23. dr

For this phoneme see J. Bauer 1975, 'Zum /dr/-Phonem des Sumerischen', *WO* 8: 1-9. It probably occurs in the following stems: badr(= BAD) 'to be remote', enkudr(= ZAG.HA) 'collector of taxes', gudr(= GUD) 'ox', kešdr(= kéš.dr) 'to bind', kudr(= KUD) 'to cut', padr(= PAD) 'to break', and sudr(= sù.dr), 'to be remote'. When these stems are followed by a morpheme with initial [a] or [e] the ending is written with the sign DU = -rá and -re₆, in contrast to the writings -da, -dè and -ra, -re/-ré.

Initially [dr] may occur in the verb dù 'to build', lit. 'to erect (a building etc.)', cf. the Akkadian loanword *narû* 'stele' = na dù-a 'erected stone'.

§ 24. g

The alternation [g] ~ [b] is found in a few words, especially before [u], for instance buru₄/gu-ru 'raven', abrig/agrig 'steward', see M. Civil, 1973a pp. 59-61 with examples; see also 1973b p. 30, where Civil suggested that this alternation represents either an allophone of [g]: [gʷ] before [u], or a distinct phoneme [gʷ] or [g͡b]. See below [g̃] § 25.

§ 25. g̃

By most scholars this phoneme is described as a velar nasal (so for instance J. Krecher, 1967a p. 87: 'velarer Nasal mit Lippenrundung'; Th. Jacobsen, 1957 p. 92 n.1: 'nasalized labio-velar, approximately c̃ʷ'), but cf. M. Civil, 1973b p. 31: 'several phonetic solutions are likewise possible: /ŋ/, /ŋ͡m/, etc.

See also M. Civil, 1973a p. 61: 'Since /g̃/ is regularly found only before 'front' vowels (the few exceptions can be easily explained), one could wonder

---

24. For the verb ak, see M.A. Powell, 1982, where other readings of this stem are considered.

whether [b] ~ [g] does not represent the allophone of /g̃/ before the 'back' vowel. If /ŋ/ is taken as a narrower definition of /g̃/, then the alternation [b] ~ [g] could represent the labialized velar /ŋʷ/, or if /g̃/ = /ŋ̂m/ (nasal labiovelar), then [b] ~ [g] = /g̃b/ (labiovelar stop)'.

See: R.R. Jestin, 1949. 'Le phonème g̃ en sumérien'. *RA* 43: 41-53. R.R. Jestin, 1950. 'Le phonème g̃ en sumérien. Notes additionnelles'. *RA* 44: 72. J. Krecher, 1978d. 'Das sumerische Phonem |g̃|'. In: B. Hruska und G. Komoróczy (eds.) *Festschrift Lubor Matouš*. Bd. II. (*Assyriologia* V). Budapest, pp. 7-73. (With a list of words with /g̃/, pp. 34-73.)

§ 26. h
The existence of two different h-sounds, one which is retained in final position, another which is dropped, was assumed by I.M. Diakonoff, 1976 p. 111 n. 20 (du$_8$ for duh, but mah).

[h] may alternate with [g] or [k]; for instance the sign HA has also the value ku$_6$ 'fish', and cf. also the modal prefixes /ha-/ and /ga-/ (see § 386), cf. A. Falkenstein, 1959a p. 24.

For [h] cf. also below [r] § 30.

§ 27. l
It has been suggested several times that there are two l-sounds in Sumerian. The reason for this is mainly the different spellings with -la and -lá, respectively, e.g.: ^{D}En.líl-la < /^{D}En.líl-ra/, and ^{D}En.líl-lá < /^{D}En.líl-ak/.

See Th. Jacobsen, 1957 p. 92 n. 1; I.M. Diakonoff, 1976 p. 111 n. 20: 'one of the l-sounds is dropped in Auslaut [e.g. lá for lal, mà for mal, bí for bil, ti for til] the other is retained [in bal, gal, dal, hal, làl, sal].'

§ 28.
[l] and [r] may alternate, cf. A. Falkenstein, 1959a p. 28: rib/lib 'übergroß', kibir(gibir)/gibil; see also A. Cavigneaux, 1976 p. 50: 'Schreibungen mit *l* bzw. *r* sind oft bezeugt; wenn man /r/ als primär ansetzt (...), muß es sich um alveolares /r/ handeln (bei einem velaren /r/ wäre die Verwechslung mit /l/ nicht zu erklären).'

M. Civil, 1973b p. 29: 'The presence of /arganum/ and /argibil/ among words which are expected to include the syllable /al/ in the 'Song of the Hoe', is an indication of an underdifferentiation of /r/ and /l/ in given environments.'

§ 29. *Nasals*

The nasals [m] and [n] may alternate in final position of a stem, thus both alam/alan 'statue', ezem/ezen 'festival', -gim/-gin$_7$ 'like'.

> M. Civil, 1973c p. 174, suggests that the nasal in final position is [n], but changes to [m] before vowel. With -gim/-gin$_7$, however, the opposite seems to be the case, cf. the frequent writing -gin$_7$-nam.

§ 30. r

Two r-sounds have been suggested for different reasons, cf. for instance I.M. Diakonoff, 1976 p. 111 n. 20: 'There were two r-sounds in Sumerian, one of them dropped in Auslaut, as -r(a) of the dative postposition, ku$_4$ for kur$_x$ 'to enter', possibly also in bar and ĝar but not in most other cases'. Å. Sjöberg, 1975 p. 218, suggests that the alternation [h] ~ [r] may point to a different r-sound (for instance ruš/huš = ruššu/huššu 'red' and –suh–re instead of –suh–he or –suh–e).

For [r] see also above [l], § 27.

§ 31. *Sibilants*

In the transliteration we normally distinguish s, š, and z, but the exact character of these sibilants is not clear.

> For a discussion of the Sumerian sibilants in the light of OAkk writing practice and the spelling of Sumerian loanwords, see I.J. Gelb, 1961 p. 34-40. (See also above §§ 20-21).

B. Alster, 1972b p. 352, suggested that [z] may represent [sd], cf. the word ùz 'goat', which, when followed by a vocalic ending is written ùz–da or ùz–dè possibly < /usd–a/, < /usd–e/.

§ 32. Consonant Changes

b > m after the nasalized vowel of the verbal prefix /ĩ-/: /ĩ–ba–/ > im–ma–, /ĩ–bi–/ > im–mi–, see § 6 and §§ 307-308.

n > l before [b]: /nu–ba–/ > la–ba–, /nu–bi–/ > li–bí–, see § 360.

§ 33. At least in one case the voiced labial [b] is inserted between a nasal and [r]: nam.erim$_2$ > nam.ri > /nambri/, written nam–bi–ri, cf.

Sauren, 1969 p. 22f. This is a common phenomenon in many languages, cf. Latin *numerus* > French *nombre*.

§ 34. Phonemic Tones

Because of the great number of homonyms it has been suggested that Sumerian had phonemic tones (cf. A. Falkenstein, 1959a p. 23). This assumption can, however, not be proved, since the writing has no means to show distinctions according to tones.

THE GENERAL STRUCTURE OF SUMERIAN

§ 35. Sumerian is characterized as an agglutinating language. According to J. Lyons. 1968 p. 189, 'determinacy with respect to segmentation into morphs' and 'the one-to-one correspondence between morph and morpheme are characteristic of 'agglutinating' languages'.

A typical Sumerian sentence consists of one or more 'chains', i.e. a nominal or verbal root with some affixes:

> (10) /*ğá*-e *šeš lugal*-ak-ra *é gal*-ani-a ha-mu-na-*ku₄*.r-en/
>   A   B   C   D
> 'I entered indeed before the brother of the king in his big house'

The roots are italicized. A is a pronoun, B and C are nominal chains, and D is a verbal chain or finite verb.

§ 36. Word classes

Nouns. The nominal chain is made up of a nominal root which can be followed by some suffixes denoting possessive, plural and case. The pronouns are similar to the nominal chains, but can be followed by case postpositions only. The suffixes represent one morph or morpheme each: /-ak/ is genitive, /-ene/ is plural, etc.

For the construction of nominal chains, see § 46.

Verbs. The verbal chain, which is the finite construction of the verb, consists of prefixes expressing mood, some uncertain categories, and the direction of the verb, as well as a pronominal prefix and/or suffix denoting the subject and object of the verb. The affixes of the verb have often more than one function, e.g., /-na-/ which denotes the 3. sg. dative.

For the construction of the finite verb, see § 274.

Adjectives. Beside the word classes mentioned above, nouns, pronouns, and verbs, there are adjectives, which are roots standing attributively to nouns, like gal 'big' above. Other adjectives are for instance: tur 'small', dùg 'sweet', kug 'pure', sud.r 'remote', etc. Many of them occur, however, also in finite verbal forms, and it therefore seems most reasonable to classify adjectives as a subclass of the category verb.

§ 37. The Categories Animate and Inanimate

Sumerian has no gender but distinguishes the categories animate and inanimate. Animate are persons. Inanimate are things and animals. This distinction is morphologically carried through in the personal pronouns, the possessive suffixes, the pronominal elements of the finite verb and in the interrogative pronouns. The animate element is generally /n/, the inanimate /b/:

	Animate	Inanimate
Personal Pronouns	/ane/, /ene/ 'he, she'	
Possessive Suffixes	/-ani/ 'his, her'	/-bi/ 'its'
Pronominal Suffixes	/-n-/	/-b-/

In the interrogative pronouns the distribution of /n/ and /b/ is for some obscure reason the opposite: /aba/, animate, 'who?', /ana/, inanimate, 'what?'.

Grammatically the categories animate and inanimate are distinguished too: Only animate beings can be combined with the dative. Exclusively inanimate beings are combined with the locative, ablative and the locative-terminative cases. The plural suffix /-ene/, moreover, occurs with animate nouns only.

§ 38. Sumerian as an Ergative Language

Sumerian is a so-called ergative language. This means that the intransitive subject is treated in the same manner as the transitive object:

/lú-e(erg.) saĝ-Ø(abs.) mu-n-zìg/ 'the man raised the head'
/lú-Ø(abs.) ì-ku₄.r-Ø/ 'the man entered'

The transitive subject is ergative, denoted by /-e/, whereas both intransitive subject and transitive object is in the absolute case which has no postposition. Nouns serving as intransitive and transitive subjects are thus morphologically treated differently, and there are two categories:

1. Intransitive subject and transitive object = absolutive (lú-Ø, saĝ-Ø)
2. Transitive subject = ergative (lú-e)

Whereas nouns distinguish the two categories above, pronouns have one form only:

/zae saĝ-Ø mu-e-zìg/ 'you(sg.) raised the head'
/zae ì-ku₄.r-en/ 'you(sg.) entered'

The transitive and intransitive subjects have here merged into one category: the 'subject case' which corresponds to our nominative.

§ 39. In the Sumerian finite verb the intransitive subject is referred to by means of pronominal suffixes:

/ĝae ì-ku₄.r-en/ 'I entered'

Only the 3.sg. has no suffix: /lú-Ø ì-ku₄.r-Ø/ 'the man entered'.

The transitive, ergative subject in the *hamṭu* conjugation is, as a rule, referred to by a pronominal prefix:

/zae saĝ-Ø mu-e-zìg/ 'you(sg.) raised the head'
/lú-e saĝ-Ø mu-n-zìg/ 'the man raised the head'

§ 40. The object of the transitive verb cannot be expressed by a personal pronoun, but only by a pronominal suffix in the finite verb, provided the verb has no suffix already:

/ane ì-n-tu'd-en/ 'she has born me(or you, sg.)', transitive, *hamṭu* form; /-en/ = 'me/you(sg.)'

These suffixes are identical with the subject elements of the intransitive verb (see above § 39) and in both cases they denote the absolutive. Other pronominal suffixes are: /-enden/ 'we/us', /-enzen/ 'you (pl.)', /-eš/ 'they/them'. The 3.sg. an. and inan. has no pronominal suffix, instead the object is possibly denoted by the prefix /-n-/ or /-b-/.

§ 41. In the transitive *marû* conjugation the subject is denoted by pronominal suffixes, namely the subject suffixes of the intransitive conjugation:

/zae saĝ-Ø mu-zi.zi-en/ 'you(sg.) raise the head'

In the pronominal suffixes the intransitive subject and transitive object have also merged into one category: 'subject case'.

§ 42. On the morphological level Sumerian has thus an ergative system in the nouns and the intransitive vs. the transitive *hamṭu* conjugation, since the intransitive subject and the transitive subject are here clearly distinguished. In pronouns and in the transitive *marû* conjugation vs. the intransitive verb, on the other hand, the system is nominative-accusative, since the intransitive and transitive subject are here treated as one category.

This 'split ergativity' is no uncommon phenomenon, in fact no ergative language is entirely ergative in both syntax and morphology.

In Sumerian the relations between the categories intransitive subject, transitive subject and transitive object, are probably more complicated than outlined here. However, because of the omission of pronominal elements in the writing and many other problems about the correct interpretation of verbal forms the Sumerian split ergative pattern cannot be further elucidated here.

For details about the intransitive and transitive conjugations see §§ 275ff; about the pronominal elements, see §§ 290ff.

§ 43. Bibliography

S. DeLancey, 1981. 'An Interpretation of Split Ergativity and Related Patterns'. *Language* 57: 626-657.

I.M. Diakonoff, 1965. *Semito-Hamitic Languages*. Moscow. (On pp. 15-18 Diakonoff describes the Sumerian ergative construction).

R.M.W. Dixon, 1979. 'Ergativity'. *Language* 55: 59-138.

D.A. Foxvog, 1975. 'The Sumerian Ergative Construction'. *OrNS* 44: 395-425.

P. Michalowski, 1980. 'Sumerian as an Ergative Language, I'. *JCS* 32: 86-103.

Word Order

§ 44. The order of the elements of the nominal chain or of the finite verb is fixed. The order of the various nominal chains (ergative, dative, terminative etc.) in the sentence is, however, rather free, but the verb is always at the end of the sentence.

The usual order of an intransitive sentence is:

    Subject   —   Verb

The usual order of a transitive sentence is:

    Subject   —   Object   —   Verb

Between the intransitive subject and the verb, and between the transitive subject and the object, various dimensional cases may occur. Exceptionally a dimensional case or an adverbial expression may occur between the object and the verb. Conjunctions and interjections are always at the beginning of the sentence, before the subject.

Although these are the most frequent occurring word orders, it is not unusual that a dimensional case stands before the subject. This is for instance almost always the case in votive inscriptions which begin with the dative of the god or goddess to whom the object is dedicated:

(11) ^{D}Nin.ğír.su-ra Gù.dé.a ensi$_2$ Lagaš^{ki}-ke$_4$ É.ninnu mu-na-dù, 'For Ninğirsu Gudea, the ensi of Lagaš, has built the (temple) Eninnu'

In normal narratives it is highly unusual to place the object before the subject. The terminative mostly precedes the ablative, but otherwise the order of the dimensional cases is free.

THE NOMINAL CHAIN

§ 45. The following chart shows the possible nominal constructions with the rank and order of all the nominal affixes in both simple and genitive constructions. The various elements of the chain are of course optional, their choice depends on the sense intended in the text. In the genitive and double genitive constructions all possible elements will never occur at the same time.

Notes to the chart:

The enclitic copula (= COP) which can occur at the end of the chain replaces, so to say, the appropriate case element. For instance the phrase /lugal ki.en.gi.r-ak-m-en/ > lugal ki.en.gi-ra-me-en, can be the virtual ergative subject of the following verb: 'I am the king of the land (and I ....)'.

-àm can, in some rare cases, also occur after the postpositions -šè, -ta and -gin₇. This use of the enclitic copula is probably secondary, caused by the fact that -àm is used as equivalent to the Akkadian emphasizing particle -ma, e.g.,

> (12) ù inim Á.na.na ab.ba-ta-àm Šeš.kal.la-a Nin₉.ab.b[a.n]a b[a]-an-tuku 'and it was at the word of Anana, the father, — Šeškala married Ninabbana' (*NG* nr. 16, 12-14)

§ 46. The Nominal Chain:

Simple construction:

NOUN – ADJ – POSS – PLUR $\left\{{- \text{CAS} \atop (-\text{COP})}\right\}\{(-\text{COP})\}$

/šeš gal-$ŋu_{10}$-ene-ra/ 'for my elder brothers'

Genitive construction:

   [Regens]   [Rectum]   [Rectum's affixes]   [Regens' affixes]

NOUN – ADJ – NOUN – ADJ – POSS – PLUR – GEN – PLUR $\left\{{- \text{CAS} \atop (-\text{COP})}\right\}\{(-\text{COP})\}$

/ki.tuš diŋir gal.gal-ene-ak-a/ = ki.tuš diŋir gal-gal-e-ne-ka 'in the dwelling(s) of the great gods'

/šeš lugal-ŋu-ak-ene-ra/ = šeš lugal-ŋá-ke_4-ne-ra 'for the brothers of my king'

Double genitive construction:

   [Regens 1] [Regens 2] [Rectum 1] [Rectum 1's affixes] [Regens 2's affixes] [Regens 1's affixes]

NOUN – ADJ – NOUN – ADJ – NOUN – ADJ – POSS – PLUR – GEN – PLUR – GEN – PLUR $\left\{{- \text{CAS} \atop (-\text{COP})}\right\}\{(-\text{COP})\}$

/é lugal kalam-ak-ene-ak-a/ = é lugal kalam-ma-ke_4-ne-ka 'in the house of the kings of the land'

/dumu lugal kalam-ak-ene-ra/ = dumu lugal kalam-ma-ke_4-ne-ra 'for the sons of the king of the land'

/dumu ìr lugal-ŋá-ka-ke₄-ne-ra/ = dumu ìr lugal-ŋá-ka-ke_4-ne-ra 'for the sons of the slave of my king'

Nouns

§ 47. Nouns are morphologically not distinguished from adjectives or verbs. The nouns, moreover, have no gender: the categories animate and inanimate are not expressed in the stem, and masculine and feminine nouns cannot be morphologically distinguished either.

§ 48. Compounds

There are no morphological means to derive nouns from verbs or adjectives. Verbal forms can occasionally be used as nouns (see §§ 62-63), but otherwise the only way to make new nouns is constructions of the following kinds:

a) NOUN + NOUN, e.g., an šà 'midst of heaven' (lit.: 'heaven – heart')
b) NOUN + VERB, e.g., di kud.r 'judge' (lit.: 'claim – decide')
c) NOUN + NOUN + VERB, e.g., gaba šu ğar 'adversary' (lit.: 'breast – hand – place' = 'one placing the hand (on) the breast')

(b) and (c) are in fact non-finite forms of the verb, for which see §§ 505-511.

§ 49. Most frequent are compounds with nu, nam and níg, which can be referred to the three above mentioned types: nu+NOUN = (a); nam+NOUN/ADJ/VERB = (a) and (b); níg+(NOUN+)VERB = (b) and (c).

§ 50. *nu + NOUN*

The asyntactical construction of nu + NOUN forms mainly terms of professions. The exact character of /nu/ is not evident; it has been suggested that it is a phonetic variant of lú 'man',[25] or a sort of pronominal prefix (so Edzard, 1963, 111f.).[26]

---

25. For n ~ l, cf. § 32.
26. 'Wir können nu- mit einem der akkadischen Grammatik zu entlehnenden Terminus als Determinativpronomen bezeichnen, müssen aber nachdrücklich betonen, daß es im Gegensatz zum akk. šu 'der des ...' gewöhnlich keinen grammatischen Einfluß auf das folgende Wort ausübt. nu- hat den

§ 51. The constructions with nu- are normally asyntactic, only in one case: nu.^{ĝiš}kiri$_6$, it seems to be a genitive construction; cf. for instance nu.^{ĝiš}kiri$_6$-ke$_4$ (ergative) in *NG* nr. 120b, 4 (see Edzard, 1963, p. 92f.).[27]

§ 52. The compounds with nu- are not very numerous. Terms of professions and the like are the following:

nu.^{ĝiš}kiri$_6$-(a)k 'gardener' (gen. construction, ^{ĝiš}kiri$_6$ = 'garden')
nu.banda$_3$ 'inspector' (banda$_3$ = 'small')
nu.èš (a priest) (èš = 'sanctuary')
nu.gig (a priestess)
nu.saĝ (a priest) (saĝ = 'head')
nu.erim$_2$ 'scoundrel' (erim$_2$ = 'violence')

§ 53. nu- is probably also part of the following divine epithets, the meanings of which are unknown:

^{D}Nu.nam.nir, epithet of Enlil
^{D}Nu.dím.mud, epithet of Enki
^{D}Nu.nir, epithet of Ninurta

§ 54. There are other nouns which may also contain the morpheme /nu/, but their etymology is not quite certain:

nu.mu.su 'widow' (also nu.ma.su and na.ma.su, cf. A. Falkenstein, *GSGL I* p. 40 with n. 1-2)
nu.síg 'orphan'
nu.bar (a priestess)

§ 55. *Bibliography*

D.O. Edzard, 1963. 'Sumerische Komposita mit dem 'Nominalpräfix' nu-'. *ZA* 55: 91-112.
R.R. Jestin, 1973. 'Les noms de profession en nu-'. In: M.A. Beek (e.a.), *Symbolae biblicae et mesopotamicae Francisco Mario Theodoro de Liagre Böhl dedicatae*. Leiden, pp. 211-213.

Charakter eines Präfixes. Es gleicht hierin dem Abstrakta bildenden sächlichen 'Nominalpräfix' nam- (nam-lugal 'Königtum').' (Edzard, 1963 p. 112).

27. nu.^{ĝiš}kiri$_6$ occurs as a loan word in Akkadian: *nukaribbu* or *nukiribbu*. The reason for this different form is not evident.

§ 56. *nam + NOUN/ADJ/VERB*

nam can approximately be translated with 'something' or 'everything that belongs to it'. It is usually regarded as a derivation of the verb me 'to be', either as coming from */ana-àm/ 'what is it?'. (So A. Falkenstein, 1959b p. 101: nam-lugal = *a-na-àm-lugal 'was ist es: der König?' = 'Königtum'.) Or it is understood as derived from a finite form: */na-ĩ-me/ 'it is so' (cf. Oberhuber, 1979 p. 450).

Note that the Emesal form of nam is na.áĝ. The verb me is in Emesal [ĝe].

§ 57. nam+... is a rather 'productive' type of nominal compound.

nam is predominantly combined with nouns denoting animate beings (= type (a) above) and forms abstracts:

nam.dam 'status of a wife'
nam.dumu 'status of a son'
nam.lú.ulu$_3$ 'mankind'
nam.diĝir 'divinity'
nam.ur.saĝ 'heroism'
nam.išib 'craft of the purification priest'

§ 58. nam also occurs with an adjective or a verb (= type (b) and (c) above § 48), but also in these cases the compounds denote abstracts:

nam.mah 'might'
nam.šub 'incantation' (šub = 'to throw', lit.: 'something thrown')
nam.ti(l) 'life'
nam.nir.ĝál 'authority'

§ 59. *níg + (NOUN +) VERB*

níg is a noun = 'thing', 'something'. It is primarily composed with verbal stems and such a compound is thus in fact identical with the non-finite verbal form: N$_1$ R(*hamṭu*) (see § 508), where níg corresponds to N$_1$, i.e. the object of the underlying two-participant verb.

Compound verbs can also be constructed with níg: níg + N$_1$ R(*hamṭu*).

níg.ba 'gift, present' (lit.: 'something — give')
níg.gu$_7$ 'food'
níg.šám 'price'

níg.dirig 'something extra'
níg.á.g̃ar '(act of) violence'
níg.si.sá 'justice'

§ 60. níg with adjectives are: níg.dùg 'something sweet', níg.dag̃al 'something wide .

§ 61. níg can also be part of a subordinate construction (cf. the non-finite N_1 R($hamṭu$)-a, §§ 513-518):

níg dam tag$_4$-a 'the (money) of the divorced wife'
níg mí ús-sa 'something following the bride' = 'wedding present'

Verbal Forms as Nouns

§ 62. Finite verbs can be used as nouns. Such 'frozen' verbal forms are, however, not very frequent, especially not in the older Sumerian texts.

ù.na.a.dug$_4$ 'letter' is originally the introductory formula of letters: /u-ī-na-e-dug$_4$/ 'when you have said it to him'.

(13) ù.na.a.dug$_4$ ì-sar 'you have written a letter' (Dialogue 3 = *UET* VI 150, 19).

Examples of verbal forms used as nouns are collected by W.H.P. Römer, 1970 p. 165.

§ 63. Primarily in lexical and bilingual texts from post-Sumerian times verbal forms with the prefix /ga-/ occur as nouns. ga-an-VERB most often with intransitive verbs, ga-ab-VERB with transitive verbs, e.g.,

ga.an.tuš, lit. 'I will sit', < /ga-ī-n-tuš/ = Akkadian *aššābu* 'tenant, resident' (*MSL* XII 229 iv 22; W.G. Lambert, 1960 p. 241, bilingual proverb).
ga-àm-ku$_4$, lit. 'I will enter', < /ga-ī-m-ku$_4$.r/ = *errebu* 'newcomer, intruder' (*MSL* XIII 164, 103).

J. van Dijk, 1960 p. 139, suggested that ga.an.zé.er = ganzer (IGI. KUR.ZA), the name of the entrance to the Netherworld, also is a verbal form: 'Ich will zerstören' < /ga-ī-n-zé.r/.

For ga- forms, see M. Civil, 1968 p. 10; a lexical list of such nouns is published in *MSL* XIII p. 163-166 (= Izi V).

§ 64. Note that the suffix /-a/ is not used in these cases to make nouns out of verbal forms. This fact is an argument against regarding /-a/ as a nominalization suffix (see below 'The Subordination Suffix /-a/').

Number

§ 65. In indicating number animate and inanimate nouns are treated differently:

	sing.	coll.	plur. (§§ 69-70)	Reduplication: 'totality' (§§ 72-73)	? (ex. 24-26)
animate	lugal 'king'	(lugal?)	lugal-ene 'kings'	lugal-lugal 'all the kings'	lugal-lugal-ene
coll. noun denoting an. beings		eren$_2$ 'troops'		eren$_2$-eren$_2$ 'all the troops'	
inanimate	é 'house'	é 'complex of houses'		é-é 'all the houses'	

§ 66. An inanimate noun can denote both singular and plural, or better collective, just like the English word 'sheep'. é is both 'house' and 'houses' or rather 'complex of houses', gud is 'ox' as well as 'oxen'/ 'herd of oxen'. Inanimate nouns have thus no plural forms, but they can be reduplicated and thus denote a totality: kur-kur 'all the foreign lands'.

§ 67. As regards animate nouns, the single stem may probably also denote collective (see ensi$_2$ in ex. 20), but in general plural is expressed by the suffix /-ene/ (see § 69). Reduplication in the sense of totality occurs also with animate nouns (ex. 20-22), and even reduplication and /-ene/ together (ex. 24-26). The exact meaning of this latter form in contrast to R-ene and R-R is, however, not clear.

> It is, however, also possible that the absence of the plural suffix — at least in some cases -- is an orthographic phenomenon, and that we therefore should restore, e.g., ensi$_2$ kur-kur-ra-⟨ke$_4$-ne⟩ (ex. 20).

§ 68. Collective nouns denoting animate beings, like eren$_2$ 'troops', have normally no plural suffix, but can be subject to a verb in the plural:

(14) eren$_2$-e (...) bí-in-eš, /bi-n-e-eš/ 'the troops have said' (*NG* nr. 215, 1-2)

(15) ^{D}A.nun.na ù di-dè im-ma-šu$_4$-šu$_4$-ge-eš, /ì-ba-šu$_4$.šu$_4$.g-eš/ 'the Anuna Gods stand in admiration' (Gudea, cyl. A XX 23). a.nun-na means litterally 'seed of the prince' and is a name of the great gods. In OB lit. texts, however, often: ^{D}A.nun.na-ke$_4$-ne.

The Plural Suffix /-ene/

§ 69. /-ene/ occurs exclusively with animate nouns. It does not occur after numerals (see § 140).

The suffix is mostly written -e-ne or -Ce-ne; after a vowel it occurs as -ne. Plene writing occurs also: -Ce-e-ne.

The position of the plural suffix is after the adjective or possessive suffix: digir gal.gal-e-ne 'the greatest gods'; ìr-gu$_{10}$-ne 'my slaves', šeš-a-ne-ne < /šeš-ani-ene/ 'his brothers' (Lugalbanda in Hurrumkura 131 = Wilcke, 1969a p. 56).

In genitive constructions: šeš lugal-la-ke$_4$-ne < /šeš lugal-ak-ene/ 'the king's brothers'; é digir gal-gal-e-ne-ka < /é digir gal.gal-ene-ak-a/ 'in the temple of the great gods'.

> A. Poebel, GSG § 135, analysed /-ene/ as the reduplication of the demonstrative /e/, /n/ being 'Hiatustilger'. This explanation was accepted by A. Falkenstein, *GSGL* I p. 73 n.1 and 1959a p. 37; whereas it was rejected by E. Sollberger, 1969a p. 157f.

§ 70. *Examples:*

(16) še gub-ba gudug-ge-ne-ta ka-gur$_7$ e-ta-šub, /še-gub-ba gudug-ene-ak-ta/, 'he removed the master of the storehouse from the barley tax of the *gudug*-priests' (Ukg. 4 VIII 24-27)

(17) mu.ru digir-re-ne-ka, /muru(b) digir-ene-ak-a/, 'in the midst of the gods' (Gudea, cyl. A XXVI 17)

(18) lú.inim.ma-gu$_{10}$-ne (...) ensi$_2$-ra in-na-an-eš-a, /lú.inim. a(k)-gu-ene ensi$_2$-ra ì-na-n-e-eš-a⟨-šè⟩/, '(he declared:)

because my witnesses have said (so and so) to the *ensi*' (*NG* nr. 113, 36-40)

(19) ᴰGilgameš en Kul.aba^ki-ke₄ ur.saĝ-bi-ne-er gù mu-na-dé-e, /ur.saĝ-bi-ene-ra gù mu-na-dé-e/ 'Gilgameš, the *en* of Kulaba, speaks to its (Uruk's) heroes' (Gilgameš and Aka 51-52). Note the sing.dat. -na- of the verb.

Reduplication

§ 71. The reduplication is used with both animate and inanimate nouns, but it is most frequent with the latter.

As mentioned above, reduplication means probably a totality: whereas gud denotes both 'one ox' and 'a herd of oxen', gud-gud is rather 'all the oxen, every single of them'; diĝir-ene means 'the gods', but diĝir-diĝir is 'all the gods'.

Cf. A Falkenstein, *GSGL* II p.47. Falkenstein thought of the reduplication of the adjective as another way to express the plural of the substantive, but I cannot agree with that, see below § 83.

It is probable that the reduplication in post-Sumerian times is used as an ordinary plural corresponding to the Akkadian plural, and without the meaning 'all ...'.

§ 72. Reduplication of the substantive normally does not occur together with reduplicated adjective, only if the adjective is an established part of the expression, e.g., šeš-gal šeš-gal '(all) the elder brothers' (Lugalbanda in Hurrumkura 136, Wilcke 1969a p. 56).

§ 73. *Examples:*

(20) bara₂-bara₂ ki.en.gi ensi₂ kur-kur-ra ki Unug^ki-ge me nam-nun-šè mu-na-TAR-e-ne 'all the sovereigns of Sumer and the *ensi*'s of all the foreign lands ... for him because of the divine rule of princeship in Uruk' (Lugalzagesi, *BE* I 87 II 21-25). Note ensi₂ which is probably a collective form, see above § 67. (For the verb, see H. Steible, 1982 II p. 323.)

Note in the next two examples the contrast between the reduplicated nouns and the plural with /-ene/:

(21) ensi₂-ensi₂ saĝa-e^a-ne sa₁₂.du₅ Gú.eden-na-ke₄-ne nidba

itu-da^b zag mu-bi-im^c si ^{e}àm-ma-sá-e-ne^e (a: om.; b: -dé; c: om.; e-e: àm-sá-⌈e⌉-[) 'all the *ensi*'s, the *sanga*'s and the record-keepers of Guedena prepared the offerings for the new moon and new year ceremony' (Curse of Akkade 51-53)

(22) ab.ba-ab.ba gú.tuku-gin$_7$ bur.šu.ma^a-e-ne gaba.ud.da-zu ^{b}A.HAR^b ud ul.lí^c-a-aš ši-im-dùg-dùg-ge-ne (a: var. om.; b-b: HAR; c: var. om.) 'like all(?) the first old men the old women enjoy your sunshine until distant days ...' (Lugalbanda in Hurrumkura 245-247 = Wilcke, 1969a p. 82)

(23) dar^{mušen}-dar^{mušen} kur-ra su$_6$ ^{na_4}gu[g hé-em-lá] 'may all the francolins(?) of the mountain wear carnelian beards' (Enki and the World Order 228)

§ 74. Occasionally reduplication and /-ene/ occur together in the same word (see above § 67):

(24) lú.éš.gíd gala-mah agrig lú.lunga(KAŠxGAR) ugula-ugula-ne bar sila$_4$ gaba-ka-ka kù bé-ğar-ré-éš 'the surveyor(s), the chief *gala*(s), the steward(s), the brewer(s) and all the foremen paid silver for a ... kid' (Ukg. 4-5 IV 2-8). It is not clear if /-(e)ne/ refers to all the persons mentioned, or if we have to restore /-ene/ after every word. Cf. also sağa-sağa-ne ibid. IV 21. and 23, and V 16.

(25) ^{D}En.líl (...) ab.ba dığir-dığir-ré-ne-ke$_4$ 'Enlil, the father of all the gods' (Ent. 28-29 I 1-3)

(26) ama dumu-dumu-ne, /ama dumu-dumu-ene(-ak)/ '(Ninhursağa), the mother of all children' (Gudea, St. A I 3)

Other examples are for instance: en-en bara$_2$-bara$_2$-gé-ne 'all the *en*'s and all the sovereigns' (Enlil Hymn 81); ur.sağ-ur.sağ-e-ne 'all the heroes' (Keš Hymn 60).

§ 75. *hi-a*

hi-a is originally the subordinate non-finite form of the verb hi (or he) 'to mix', hi-a means then 'mixed', 'various', 'unspecified'. It is found with inanimate nouns, for instance udu hi-a 'various sheep'. In late texts or in ideograms in Akkadian texts hi-a is used simply to denote the plural, but this is not the original function of the word.

(27) 0.0.1. šim ^{ğiš}eren hi-a '1 ban assorted cedar perfumes' (*TCS*
I nr. 263, 14)

(28) 26 udu hi-a 4 ùz-máš hi-a '(concerning) 26 assorted sheep
(and) 4 assorted goats and he-goats' (*NG* nr. 120b 1-2)

-meš

§ 76. /-me-eš/ is the enclitic copula with plural suffix. It is thus no
true plural ending and is not used as such in the oldest texts, but only
in contexts syntactically parallel to, e.g., lugal-me-en 'I, the king':

(29) dumu-banda₂ imin ^DBa.ba₆-me(-eš) bàn-da en ^DNin.ğír.
su-ka-me(-eš) 'they (are) the seven daughters of Baba, the
seven daughters of Ninğirsu' (Gudea, cyl. B XI 11-12).

Especially in Sumerian ideograms in Akkadian context and in late
Sumerian texts /-me-eš/ is used as a sort of plural ending like /-ene/,
but it must be stressed that this is not its original function. Cf. the
following predicative use of the enclitic copula, ex. 30-31 (see also
§§ 541-545).

§ 77. *Examples:*

(30) unu₃ sipa ^DNisaba-ke₄-ne dumu tu-da ama dili-me-eš, tùr
amaš-a á è-a-me-eš 'the cow-herd and shepherd of Nisaba
are sons born of one mother, they grew up in the cattle-pen
and sheepfold' (Enmerkar and Ensuhkešdana 211-213)

(31) lugal-ra lú mu-⟨ši-⟩re₇ᵃ-eš-àmᵇ lú ᶜhi-hi-a-me-ešᶜ (a:
-re₇ʳᵉ-; b: -a for -àm; c-c: hé-a-hé-me-eš) 'the men who
went against the king were a mixed group of men' (Dumuzi's
Dream 110)

§ 78. *Bibliography*

Edmond Sollberger, 1969a. 'Genre et nombre en Sumérien'. *Cahiers Ferdinand
de Saussure* 26: 151-160.

Wolfgang Schramm, 1983. 'Die Pluralbildung der Nomina im Sumerischen'. In:
Althistorische Studien. Hermann Bengtson zum 70. Geburtstag dargebracht
von Kollegen und Schülern. Historia Einzelschriften, 40. Wiesbaden, pp. 1-7.

Adjectives

§ 79. An adjective is a stem standing as attribute to a noun. It stands

64

directly after the noun which it qualifies, and the affixes (possessive suffix, postposition, etc.) come after the adjective: é gal 'the big house', uru kug-ga-ni 'his holy city', é libir-a 'in the old house' etc.

An exception is kug 'holy, pure' which may stand before divine names, e.g., kug ᴰInanna 'holy Inanna', which occurs frequently (but never *ᴰInanna kug).

§ 80. Some adjectives occur always, others occasionally with the suffix /-a/, e.g. ur.saĝ kalag-ga 'the mighty hero', munus šag₅-ga 'the good woman'.

Cf. for instance: sipa zid Gù.dé.a 'the righteous shepherd, Gudea' (Gudea, cyl. A XI 5) and á zid-da lugal-ĝá-ke₄ 'to the right side of my king' (Gudea, cyl. A V 10). J. Krecher, 1978c p. 382ff., suggested that the form with /-a/ denotes the determination of the main word: 'á zi-da unterscheidet sich hinsichtlich des Attributs von sipa zi durch die Determinierung: gemeint ist nicht irgend eine 'Güte', sondern diejenige, die mit der 'Rechtsseitigkeit' gegeben ist; gleichzeitig ist auch das Leitwort determiniert, und zwar eben durch dieses Attribut: nicht *irgend eine* 'gute Seite', sondern *die* 'gute Seite' (also nicht die linke Seite).' (p. 383).

The number of pairs of adjectives with and without /-a/ seems to be too small to confirm this observation, but if it turns out to be correct, this 'determining' character of /-a/ is probably derived from its subordination function, cf. inim dug₄-ga 'the word which has been spoken', i.e. not any word but this particular word spoken by the god or someone else, see also § 504.

§ 81. Adjectives do not differ morphologically from nominal or verbal stems and there are no morphological means to derive adjectives from other stems.

An adjectival stem is primarily characterized by its syntactic use as described above: adjectives are stems standing attributively after a noun expressing a qualification of that noun, e.g., é gibil 'the new house', eden daĝal 'the wide plain', etc.

There is, however, no clear distinction between adjectives and verbs, since some adjectives are also used as verbs in both finite and non-finite forms, for instance daĝal 'to make wide', dùg 'to make sweet', galam 'to make in an artful fashion', gibil 'to renew'. Adjectives can therefore also be regarded as a subclass of the category verb.

Cf. Gragg, 1968 p. 91: 'the adjective has a prefix-chain in its own right, exactly like any verb. In fact this ability must lead us to conclude that adjective in Sumerian is not an independent category, but a subclass of the category verb, and that it is only in the lexicon that certain verbs will be marked with the feature 'adjectival'.

Reduplication of Adjectives

§ 82. The adjective may, like other stems, be reduplicated. The reduplicated adjective probably expresses superlative, e.g.,

(32) diĝir gal-gal-e-ne 'the greatest gods', this expression is frequently found and refers always to the seven highest gods of the Sumerian pantheon.

(33) uru me kug-kug-ga me-bi šu ba-ab-bal 'of the city with the purest *me*'s its *me*'s were overturned' (Eridu Lamentation 132)

Reduplication does not occur with all adjectives, most common is gal-gal, and also kal-kal 'most precious', dirig-dirig 'excessive, extra', whereas mah 'great, exalted' and nun 'princely' are never reduplicated.

Other adjectives like bar_6-bar_6 'white, lighting', di_4-di_4.l 'small' and ku_7-ku_7.d 'sweet' are always found in the reduplicated form.

Reduplication of the adjective cannot cooccur with the reduplication of the noun which is qualified by the adjective.

§ 83. A. Falkenstein, *GSGL* I p. 72, explained the reduplication of adjectives denoting dimensions (like gal, šár 'numerous', dirig and kal) as a way to express the plurality of the substantive, whereas the reduplication of adjectives denoting colours or light (like bar_6-bar_6, dadag (= UD.UD-g) etc.) has an intensive character (cf. *GSGL* II, p. 47).

To my opinion it seems most likely that the reduplication expresses the superlative or has an intensive meaning, whereas the plural of the noun is either expressed by /-ene/ or it is not expressed at all, but the single nominal stem is understood as collective (see § 71). Cf. the expression: diĝir gal-gal-e-ne 'the greatest gods' of which the suffix /-ene/ denotes the plural and the reduplicated gal, therefore, most likely denotes something different, namely the superlative. It is, however, also possible that the reduplication may denote different things with different adjectives, cf. 'Verbal Reduplication' §§ 248-249.

Adverbial Expressions

§ 84. Adjectives are used in adverbial expressions. There are three ways of constructing 'adverbs': with /-eš/, with /-bi/, and with both /-bi/ and /-eš/. The semantic distinctions between the three types are not clear.

The affix /-eš/ is probably the terminative element /-eše/. Note, however, that in the function described here, it is never included in the prefix chain of the verb.

§ 85. a) ADJ + /-eš/

For instance: da-ré-eš 'for ever', gal-le-eš 'greatly', kug-ge-eš 'in a pure way'.

(34) An kug-ge zid-dè-éš mu-ğar 'pure An has faithfully placed it (there)' (Gudea, cyl. B XII 26)

(35) nin-ğu$_{10}$ an.šà-šè^a dùg-ge-eš hu-mu-un-ğá-ğá (a: -ta) 'may they prepare everything well for my lady, until the midst of heaven' (Iddin-Dagan Hymn A 141)

§ 86. b) ADJ + /-bi/

For instance: dağal-bi 'widely', gal-bi 'greatly', gibil-bi 'anew, in a new way'; gibil-la-bi is also frequently found, cf. J. Krecher, 1966 p. 113.

(36) lú banda$_3$ gibil-bi é dù-gin$_7$ 'like a young man building (his) house anew' (Gudea, cyl. A XIX 22, the same phrase occurs in Curse of Akkade 10)

§ 87. c) ADJ + /-bi/ + /-eš(e)/

For instance: gibil-bi-šè 'in a new way', mah-bi-šè 'in a magnificent way'.

(37) En.an.e.du$_7$ (...)-me-en (...) é-bi gibil-bé-eš hu-mu-tu 'I, Enanedu, (...) have indeed fashioned this house anew' (Rim-Sin 8, 28-33)

§ 88. Adverbial expressions can also be derived from verbal roots plus the subordination suffix /-a/: VERB + /-a/ + /-bi/, e.g. hul-la-bi, 'gladly', ul$_4$-la-bi 'quickly'. The distinction ADJ + /bi/ (see § 86):

VERB + /-a-bi/ is not consistent. Stems which we define as adjectives because they occur rarely as finite verbs may add /-a-bi/: gibil-la-bi 'anew', du₉-na-bi 'humbly'.

(38) 3 udu 1 máš gal ul₄-la-bi ha-mu-na-ab-sum-mu, /ha-mu-na-b-sum-e/ 'let him give him quickly 3 sheep and 1 he-goat' (*TCS* I nr. 9, 3-6).

(39) IR.^{D}ZU.EN (...)-me-en (...) du₉-na-bi ù.gul im-ma-an-ğá-ğá, /ī-ba-n-ğá.ğá/ 'I, Warad-Sin, (...) have prayed humbly' (Warad-Sin 1, 1-13)

§ 89. Even nouns may occur in forms morphologically similar to the adverbial expressions, for instance: ud-dè-eš < /ud-eš(e)/ 'like the day-light', téš-bi 'all together, in harmony'.

(40) ^{D}Na.ra.am.^{D}Suen-e bara₂ kug A.ga.dè^{ki}-ka ud-dè-eš^a ^{b}im-mi-in-è^b (a: -éš; b-b: im-è), /ī-bi-n-è/ 'Naram-Sin let it rise like the day-light on the holy dais of Akkade' (Curse of Akkade 40-41)

Personal Pronouns

§ 90. Pronouns are found for the 1.sg., 2.sg., 3.sg. animate, and the 3.pl. Pronouns for the 1. and 2. plur. seem never to be used, but a form derived from COP + pron. suffix replaces the pronoun in some cases. In *OBGT* I col. VI me-en-dè-en and me-en-zé-en are rendered as equivalent to the Akkadian pronouns *nīnu* and *attunu*, rspectively. Outside the lexical texts such forms are extremely rare, but cf.:

(41) me-en-dè (...) ga-mu-na-dúr-ru-ne-en-dè-e[n], /ga-mu-na-durun-enden/, 'let us sit down before him' (Enmerkar and the Lord of Aratta 371-372). me-en-dè also occurs in Lugalbanda in Hurrumkura 127 (= Wilcke, 1969a p. 56) and Lamentation over Sumer and Ur 237 (= Wilcke, 1969a p. 207).

Cf. Kienast, 1980a p. 56; and J. Bauer, 1982.

For a possible inanimate pronoun, ur₅, see § 100.

§ 91.

	1.sg.	2.sg.	3.sg.	3.pl.
Subject	ǧá.e (me.e)	za.e (ze)	e.ne	e.ne.ne
Dative	ǧá-a-ra ǧá-a-ar (ma-a-ra)	za-a-ra za-a-ar	e.ne-ra	e.ne.ne-ra
Term.	ǧá(-a/e)-šè	za(-a/e)-šè	e.ne-šè	e.ne.ne-šè
Com.	ǧá(-a/e)-da	za(-a/e)-da	e.ne-da	e.ne.ne-da
Equative	ǧá(-a/e)-gin$_7$	za(-a/e)-gin$_7$	e.ne-gin$_7$	e.ne.ne-gin$_7$

In parenthesis Emesal forms.

1.sg.: In the Gudea texts the subject case is: ǧá.
2.sg.: In the OB texts za-a occasionally occurs as a variant of za-e.
  zé(-) instead of za(-) occurs also (cf. ex. 54).
3.sg.: In OS, Gudea and NS texts this pronoun has the form: a.ne.
3.pl.: This form should probably be explained as either /ene+ene(plur.
  suffix)/ or as reduplication of the 3.sg. pron. e.ne.ne.ne can
  also be found (*OBGT* I vi 380 = *šu-nu*; Hendursaǧa Hymn 74).

The locative and ablative cases cannot be used with persons and are
therefore not combined with the personal pronouns.

§ 92. *'Subject Case'*

The case here called 'subject case' is the form of the pronouns when
they act as subjects of one-participant (ex. 44) or two-participant
verbs (ex. 43, 45). This case could also be called nominative (see §§
38ff.).

  The subject form of the pronouns also occurs in non-finite constructions thus corresponding to a noun in the absolute and representing
an underlying ergative:

  (42) ǧá ^{D}Nin.ǧír.su a huš gi$_4$-a 'I, Ningirsu, who keep the wild
    waters back' (Gudea, cyl. A IX 20)

There are no examples of a pronoun occurring in the 'Mes-ane-pada
construction' (see § 514): *N ǧá.e R-a. Forms with possessive suffixes
are preferred instead.

(43) sipa-ĝu$_{10}$ ma.mu-zu ĝá ga-mu-ra-búr-búr 'my shepherd, I myself shall interpret your dream for you' (Gudea, cyl. A V 12)

(44) lú uru-šè ĝá-e ga-ĝen nu-mu-un-na-ab-bé, /nu-mu-na-b-e-e/ 'nobody says to him: 'I indeed will go to the city!'' (Lugalbanda and Enmerkar 272)

(45) nam.tar-ra šà-ge gur$_6$-a-zu ĝá-e ga-mu-ri-ib-tar, /ga-mu-ri-b-tar/ 'I myself will decide the fate for you, whatever you want' (Lugalbanda and Enmerkar 166)

§ 93. *Pronouns as Objects*

As a rule the personal pronouns have no 'object case', but objects may be expressed by the means of pronominal suffixes in the finite verb (see § 294). Sometimes, however, pronouns do act as objects, but this is never the case before Old Babylonian, and it is therefore most probably a secondary use of the pronouns. Examples are:

(46) kilib$_3$ diĝir gal-gal-e-ne (...) e.ne ù numun-a-ni šà kalam-ma-ka nam-mu-ni-íb-ĝá-ĝá-e-ne, /na-mu-ni-b-ĝá.ĝá-ene/ 'All the great gods may not let him and his offspring live in the land' (Warad-Sin 27 II 17 − III 5)

(47) e.ne ga-ba-ab-túm-mu-dè, /ga-ba-b-túm-enden/ 'we will take him/her away' (Inanna's Descent 333 = 343; variants: èn and en for e.ne)

(48) lul-da ĝá-a-ra za.a lú mu-un-gi$_4$ 'with lies he has sent you as messenger to me' (Inanna and Enki II i 26)

Use of Pronouns

§ 94. The personal pronouns are not obligatory in the sentence, neither as a subject nor in any dimensional case, since these functions can be expressed in the verbal form by prefixes or suffixes. When the pronouns occur, therefore, they probably have an emphasizing character or they underline the contrast between for instance the 1. and 3. person (ex. 49).

§ 95. As a rule the pronouns are used only when no appositions follow; otherwise the enclitic copula is used, e.g., lugal-me-en 'I, the king', and ĝá-e lugal-me-en 'I am the king', but not *ĝá-e lugal(-e). Cf. however, ĝá ^{D}Nin.ĝír.su in ex. 42. (See also 'The Enclitic Copula' § 545).

§ 96. *Examples:*

(49) e-ne ǧá-a-ra gú ha-ma-anᵃ-ǧá-ǧá (a: var. om.), /ha-mu-DAT.1.sg.-n-ǧá.ǧá-e/ 'may he submit to me' (Enmerkar and Ensuhkešdana 25)

(50) ᴰInanna (...) saǧ.ki zalag-ga-ni ǧá-aᵃ-šè hu-mu-ši-in-zìg (a: var. omits), /ha-mu-ši-n-zig/ 'towards me indeed Inanna has lifted her bright face' (Išme-Dagan Hymn D 106)

(51) lugal-ǧu₁₀ za-gin₇ a.ba an-ga-kalag a.ba an-ga-a-da-sá, /ã-ga-kalag/, /ã-ga-e.da-sá/ 'as you, my king, who is as mighty as you, who rivals you?' (Šulgi Hymn D 14)

(52) èš É.ninnu dù-ba za-ra ma-ra-an-dug₄, /mu-DAT.2.sg.-n-dug₄/ 'to you he has ordered to build (his) temple, Eninnu' (Gudea, cyl. A V 18)

§ 97. *Personal Pronoun + Enclitic Copula*

The personal pronouns are frequently combined with the enclitic copula: ǧá-e-me-en 'it is me', za-e-me-en 'it is you', e-ne-àm 'it is him/her'. Such forms can be used as predicate as in ex. 53, but they may also act as a sort of emphasizing pronoun, ex. 54-55.

(53) sig-ta igi.nim-šè en gal-bi za-e-me-en ǧá-e ús-sa-zu-me-en 'from below to above their great lord are you (indeed), (and) I am subordinate to you (lit.: your follower)' (Enmerkar and Ensuhkešdana 277)

(54) zé-e-me maškim-a-ni h[é]-me 'may you be his bailiff yourself' (*TCS* I nr. 128, 6-7)

(55) e-ne-àm inim en.nu-ǧá-[ta] ma-an-dab₅, /mu-DAT.1.sg.-n-dab₅/ 'it is he indeed who has captured him for me at the command of the watchman' (*TCS* I nr. 54, 6)

§ 98. *Possessive Pronouns as Predicates*

Possessive pronouns as predicates are PRON + /ak/ + COP: ǧá(-a)-kam 'it is mine', za(-a)-kam 'it is yours'.

(56) Ur.lum.ma ensi₂ Ummaᵏⁱ-ke₄ An.ta.sur.ra ǧá-kam ì-mi-dug₄ 'Urlumma, the *ensi* of Umma, has said: Antasurra is mine' (En. I, *AOAT* 25, p. 38: 81-85)

(57) aga ᵍⁱˢgu.za ᵍⁱˢgidru nam.lugal⟨-la⟩ sum-mu ᴰInanna za-kam 'to give the crown, the throne and the scepter of kingship is yours, Inanna' (Innin 142)

§ 99. Bibliography

B. Kienast, 1980a. 'Probleme der sumerischen Grammatik, 2-3'. *ASJ* 2: 52-66. ('Zu den Personalpronomina' p. 52-58.)

J. Bauer, 1982. 'Das sumerische Pronomen der 2. Ps. Pl.' *Altorientalistische Notizen* (18-20). Höchberg, im Selbstverlag des Verfassers, p. 2-4.

§ 100. ur_5, Inanimate Pronoun

ur_5 serves as an inanimate pronoun: 'it'. It is most frequently found in expressions like: ur_5 hé-(en-)na-nam 'it is/was verily so'; ur_5-gin_7 'like this', e.g.,

(58) ur_5-gin_7 inim mu-na-ab-bé 'he says so to him' (Enmerkar and Ensuhkešdana 39)

Cf. *OBGT* I vi 379ff. where ur_5-meš and ur_5-bi together with e-ne-ne and lú-ù-ne are translated by the Akkadian pronoun *šunu* 'they'.

The Possessive Suffixes

§ 101.

1.sg.	$-\hat{g}u_{10}$ 'my'		1.pl.	-me 'our'
2.sg.	-zu 'your'		2.pl.	-zu.ne.ne, -zu.e.ne.ne,
3.sg.an.	-a.ni 'his, her'			-zu.ne 'your'
3.sg.inan.	-bi 'its'		3.pl.	-a.ne.ne 'their'
				-bi, also 'their' presumably collective.

§ 102. Examples of the singular forms are numerous, but plural forms, especially 1. and 2. person are less frequent. Some examples of plural forms of the possessive suffixes are therefore given here.

1. plur.:

(59) ad_6 šeš-me sig_4 Kul.aba_4[ki]-šè ga-ba-ni-ib-ku_4-re-dè-en[a] (a: var. om.-en), /ga-ba-ni-b-ku_4.r-enden/, /ad_6 šeš-me-ak/ 'We will bring the body of our brother to the brickwork of Kulaba' (Lugalbanda in Hurrumkura 128 = Wilcke, 1969a p. 56)

2. plur.: This suffix, which probably is a combination of the singular suffix /-zu/ and the reduplicated(?) plural element /ene/, is not attested before the Old Babylonian period.

(60) lú.ulu₃ hé-me-en-zé-en nam-zu-ne hé-eb-tar-re, /ha-ī-me-enzen/, /ha-ī-b-tar-e(n)/ 'should you(pl.) be mortal, I will decree your(pl.) fates' (Inanna's Descent 243) (/ga-ī-b-tar/ is expected, cf. the parallel in l. 270: nam ga-mu-ri-ib-tar(-en-zé-en) 'let me decree the fate for you(pl.)')

3. plur.:

(61) uru-šè igi-ne-ne i-im-g̃á-g̃á-ne, /ī-m-g̃á.g̃á-ene/ 'they looked at the city (lit.: placed their eyes upon it)' (Curse of Akkade 226)

§ 103. *Animate /-ani/ vs. inanimate /-bi/*

In older texts, OS, Gudea as well as carefully written OB literary texts, the distinction between /-ani/ and /-bi/ is strictly kept, whereas the suffixes later on frequently are confused, since Akkadian does not have this distinction. See I. Kärki, 1967 p. 203 for examples of confusion from the Isin and Larsa royal inscriptions.

Writing

§ 104.
The initial vowel [a] of /-ani/ and /-anene/ disappears after a vowel, e.g., é-ni < /é-ani/, but dig̃ir-ra-ni < /dig̃ir-ani/. Cf. ex. 61. Especially in post-Sumerian texts plene writings are found: dig̃ir-ra-a-ni.

(62) šeš-a-ne-ne ku.li-ne-ne kug Lugal.bàn.da hur.rumᵃ.kur.ra-kamᵇ ᶜim-ma-an-tag₄-a-ašᶜ (a: -ru-um-; b: -ke₄; c-c: mu-ni-ib-tag₄-a-aš) 'his brothers and his friends left pure Lugalbanda in Hurrumkura' (Lugalbanda in Hurrumkura 131-132 = Wilcke, 1969a p. 56). Note that -(a-)ne-ne comes from /-ani-ene/.

§ 105.
The possessive suffixes can be followed by the enclitic copula, postpositions and by the plural suffix.

The final vowel of the suffixes in the singular is normally deleted before the locative /-a/ and genitive /-ak/:

1.sg.	/-g̃u-ak/	>	-g̃á(-k)
2.sg.	/-zu-ak/	>	-za(-k)
3.sg.	/-ani-ak/	>	-a-na(-k)
inan.	/-bi-ak/	>	-ba(-k)

Unconcentrated forms occur also: bar-g̃u$_{10}$-a (Gudea, cyl. B II 6); é mah-ni-a (Gudea, St. A II 5).

After the plural suffixes the [a] of the postposition /-ak/ is deleted:

1.pl. /-me-ak/   >   -me(-k)
2.pl. /-zunene-ak/ >   -zu-ne-ne(-k)
3.pl. /-anene-ak/   >   -a-ne-ne(-k)

§ 106. Possessive suffixes followed by the dative and the terminative postpositions:

1.sg. /-g̃u-ra/   >   -g̃u$_{10}$-úr   /-g̃u-še/   >   -g̃u$_{10}$-uš
2.sg. /-zu-ra/   >   -zu-úr   /-zu-še/   >   -zu-uš
3.sg. /-ani-ra/ >   -a-ni-ir
inan.   /-bi-še/   >   -biš
                                      (sag̃-biš è-a, Gudea cyl. B II 18)

The postpositions -ra and -šè may also be written in full.

(63) ^{D}Utu lugal-g̃u$_{10}$-úr 'to Utu, my king' (Letter of Sin-iddinam to Utu 1)

§ 107. The postposition /-e/ usually disappears after the vowel of the possessive suffixes: /-ani-e/ > -a-ni. If there is reason to assume the presence of the postposition the possessive suffix is often transliterated as -a-né (or -bé). However, we cannot know whether a pronunciation [ane] actually was opposed to normal [ani] and the transliteration -a-né or -bé is thus merely an aid for the translation. In the present study the suffixes have always been written -a-ni and -bi also in cases where a loc.term. or ergative element probably is present.

§ 108. Possessive suffixes followed by the enclitic copula:

1.sg. /-g̃u-m/   >   -g̃u$_{10}$-um
2.sg. /-zu-m/   >   -zu-um
3.sg. /-ani-m/ >   -a.ni-im
inan. /-bi-m/   >   -bi-im

§ 109. For possessive suffixes followed by the plural suffix /-ene/, see above ex. 62.

§ 110. *Etymology of the Possessive Suffixes*

It is generally assumed that the possessive suffixes actually are the personal pronouns placed after the noun: é-zu thus 'house – you' = 'your house' etc. (so Poebel, *GSG* p. 76f.; A. Falkenstein, 1959a p. 33).

Interrogative Pronouns

§ 111.

Animate interrogative pronoun: a.ba 'who?'
Inanimate interrogative pronoun: a.na 'what?'

It is curious that in the interrogative pronouns the otherwise inanimate /b/ occurs in the animate pronoun and the normally animate /n/ in the inanimate pronoun.

In the OB literary texts there might be some confusion about the correct use of a.na and a.ba, cf. for instance the variant in ex. 66 below, or the expression:

(64) a.ba-àm mu-zu 'what is your name?' (Enlil and Namzitara 23), where the inanimate a.na is expected. (Or is this expression actually to be understood as: 'Who is it? Your name!'?)

§ 112. a.ba and a.na are, like the personal pronouns, combined with postpositions and the enclitic copula. The interrogative pronouns are also combined with possessive suffixes (§§ 115 and 122).

a.ba 'who?'

§ 113. a.ba is the absolutive form of the pronoun, used as intransitive subject or as object (ex. 67-68). As ergative subject serves /aba-e/ > a.ba-a (but also a.ba) (ex. 65-66).

(65) a.ba-a igi im-mi-in-du$_8$-a[a] (a: var. -àm), /í-bi-n-du$_8$-a/ 'who has ever seen?' (Curse of Akkade 95). The same phrase occurs in other literary compositions, for instance Dumuzi's Dream 139; Keš Hymn 20.

(66) amar-ǧu$_{10}$[a] gùd-ba[b] [c]a.ba-a[c] ba-ra-ab[d]-tùm[e] (a: -bi for

-g̃u₁₀ ; b: om.; c-c: a.ba; a.na-a; d: om.; e: tum₄ ; túm), /bara(abl.)-b-tùm/ 'who has taken my young away from its nest?' (Lugalbanda and Enmerkar 88)

(67) munus diš-àm a.ba me-a nu a.ba me-a-ni 'there was one woman, who was she not? who was she?' (Gudea, cyl. A IV 23)

(68) a.ba šeš-g̃u₁₀ -gin₇ 'who is like my brother?' (*TCS* I nr. 131, 8)

§ 114. a.ba can occur with the enclitic copula: a.ba-àm 'who is it?', a.ba-me-en 'who are you?', cf. for instance:

(69) a.ba-me-en za.e (var.: a.ba-en za.e-me-en) 'who are you (sing.)?' (Inanna's Descent 80)

(70) a.ba-àm za.e-me-en-zé-en 'who are you(plur.)?' (Inanna's Descent 240)

§ 115. Occasionally a.ba can occur with the possessive suffix:

(71) dìm.me.er na.me a.ba-zu mu-un-dím-[ma] 'who among the gods is fashioned like you?' (Sjöberg, 1960 p. 167: 23, bilingual šu-íl-la from the first mill. B.C..)

a.na 'what?'

§ 116. The form a.na is the absolutive form; since a.na does not occur as ergative subject it has no subject case like a.ba-a.

(72) g̃á a.na mu-ù-da-zu, /mu-e.da-zu/ 'what do I know from (lit.: 'with') you?' (Gudea, cyl. A IX 4)

(73) dumu-g̃u₁₀ a.na bí-in-ak 'my daughter, what has she done?' (Inanna's Descent 218)

§ 117. a.na is also used, not in an interrogative sense, but as a relative or indefinite pronoun:

(74) má-g̃u₁₀ ᴰŠamaš.ì.⟨lí⟩ in-ku₄ -ku₄ -da ud nu-mu-zal-e níg a.na bí-dug₄ -ga hé-eb-g̃á.g̃á, 'In my boat which Šamaš-ilī will bring, let him place whatever I have said before the day passes' (*TCS* I nr. 109, 17-19)

(75) ud a.na ì-ti-la-ni-a, /ì-ti.l-a-ani-a(loc.)/ 'so long as she lives' (lit.: 'in her days (all) that she lives') (*NG* nr. 7, 4)

a.na with Postpositions

§ 118. *a.na-aš 'why?' a.na-aš-àm 'why (is it that)?'* (lit.: 'to what?')

(76) uru-ta á.áǧ.ǧá a.na-aš mu-e^a-de₆ (a: var. om.) 'Why have you brought a message from the city?' (Lugalbanda and Enmerkar 355)

(77) a.na-áš-àm Puzur₄.ha.ià mu še kur-ra-šè še eštub hé-na-sum 'Why is it that Puzur-Haya has given him *eštub*-barley instead of *kur*-barley?' (*TCS* I nr. 125, 3-6)

§ 119. *a.na-gin₇, a.na-gin₇-nam 'how?'* (lit.: 'like what?')

(78) a.na-gin₇ an-ak 'how does he live (lit.: do)?' (Gilgameš, Enkidu and the Netherworld 255)

(79) a.na-gin₇-nam za.e ^aǧá-da^a mu-da-ab-sá-e^b (a-a: ǧá-e-da; b: -en) 'how can you compare with me?' (Dialogue 1, 75 = Ni 9850, *ISET* I pl. 200, rev. 5 = *SLTNi* 113 rev. 1 = *SEM* 65 rev. 4)

a.na with the Enclitic Copula

§ 120. *a.na-àm 'what is it?', 'why?'*

(80) a.na-àm^a ba-du-un kur nu-gi₄-šè (a: var. omits) 'why have you come to the land of no return?' (Inanna's Descent 83)

§ 121. *a.na me-a-bi 'as many as they are', 'all of it'*

(81) ^ǧiššinig ma.da a.na-me-a-bi ambar-bi-a a íb-nag₈-nag₈, /í-b-nag₈.nag₈/ 'the tamarisks of the land, all of them, drink water of its marsh' (Lugalbanda and Enmerkar 397)

(82) diǧir an-ki-a a.na-m[e]-a-bi šilam gal-bi-me-en 'you are the great cow among the gods of heaven and earth, as many as there are' (Innin 183)

§ 122. *a.na + possessive suffix*

(83) kur-ra a.na-bi-me-en 'what are you to the land?' (lit.: 'of the land its 'what' are you?') (Gilgameš and Huwawa 20)

(84) za.e ǧá.e^a dah-ma^b-ab ǧá.e za.e ga-mu-ra-dah a.na-me lú ba-an-tum₄ (a: ma-e; b: var. has -ba- for -ma-) 'you help

me (and) I shall help you — what can then happen to us?'
(Gilgameš and Huwawa 110)

§ 123. *Emesal Forms of the Interrogative Pronouns*

The Emesal form of a.na is ta, which forms the same constructions as
a.na: ta-àm, ta-gin₇, ta-POSS, etc., e.g.,

(85) [a]e.ne[a] ta-gin₇ [b]nam-ma-ra-ab-zé.èm-en-zé-en[b] (a-a: var.
èn; b-b: [na]m-mi-ni-[..]; [..]-ni-ib-zé-em-X̮-X̮-X̮) 'How
could I turn him over to you(pl.)?' (Inanna's Descent 346)

(86) mu.lu ta-zu mu-un-zu, /mu-n-zu/ 'what can a man know
of you?' (Enlil Hymn, *CT* XV pl. 11f. l. 1)

(87) a.a-ĝu₁₀ ta-àm e-ra-an-dug₄ ta-àm e-ra-an-dah, /ī-ra-n-
dug₄/ 'what did my father say to you, what did he add to
you?' (Inanna and Enki II i 49)

Interrogatives

§ 124. Interrogative expressions are constructed with a stem /me/ or
/men/ and postpositions or the enclitic copula:

§ 125. *me-a 'where?', me-šè 'where to?'*

(88) má an-na me-a sá ba-an-dug₄, /ba-n-dug₄/ 'where has the
boat of heaven got to (now)?' (Inanna and Enki II i 5 and
passim)

(89) nam.kalag-ga-zu me-šè ba-an-de₆ nam.ur.sağ-zu me-a 'to
where has your strength brought it? Where is your heroism?'
(Ninurta and the Turtle 53)

§ 126. *me-na-àm 'when?'*

(90) [a]ĝá-àm[a] [b]me-na-àm[b] šà [D]Šul.gi lugal-ĝu₁₀ [c] ki-bi ha[d]-ma-
gi₄-gi₄ (a-a: ĝá-e; ĝá-a; b-b: me-e-na-àm; me-en-na-a; c:
ĝá; d: omits), /ha-mu-DAT.1.sg.-gi₄.gi₄/ 'as for me — when
will the heart of Šulgi, my king, return to me?' (Letter B 1,
26)

§ 127. Other interrogative expressions are me-na-šè and èn-šè, both
translated *adī matī* 'how long?' (cf. Krecher, 1966 p. 101; 114). Several forms of /me/ and /me-n/ are listed in *OBGT* I col. X (= *MSL* IV
p. 57ff.).

§ 128. Indefinite Pronoun

na.me, which may perhaps be derived from /ana-me/ 'what is it?', serves as indefinite pronoun with both animate and inanimate: 'anyone, anything'; with negative verbal form: 'no one, nothing'.

na.me is most often added to a noun like an adjective: lú na.me, níg na.me, but it is also used alone like in ex. 93. na.me is both ergative (ex. 92, 93) and absolutive (ex. 94).

(91) ki na.me-šè na-an-tùm, /na-ī-n-tùm-e/ 'he must not bring it to any other place' (*TCS* I nr. 77, 5)

(92) lú na.me inim nu-un-g̃á-g̃á, tukum.bi lú na.me inim bí-in-[g̃ar], /nu-ī-n-g̃á.g̃á-e/, /bi-n-g̃ar/ 'no one should lay a claim! If anyone lays a claim' (*TCS* I nr. 80, 6-7)

(93) alan-na-ni me.dím.ša im-mi-in-dirig na.me sag̃ nu-mu-e-sum, /ī-bi-n-dirig/, /nu-mu-e-sum/ 'his body she (= Ninhursag̃) has endowed with beautiful limbs, no one can rush toward him' (Martu Hymn 7)

(94) lú na.me níg na.me ugu-na[a] li-bí-in-tuku (a: ugu-a-na), /nu-bi-n-tuku/ 'no one might have any claim against him' (Letter B 12, 4)

Reflexive Pronouns

§ 129. The noun ní 'self' serves as a reflexive pronoun:

ní-g̃u$_{10}$ 'myself'
ní-zu 'yourself'
ní-te-a.ni (or: ní) 'himself, herself'
ní-bi 'itself' and collective
ní-te-a.ne.ne 'themselves'

1.pl. and 2.pl. are not attested.

§ 130. The reflexive pronoun in this form may serve as the direct, absolutive, object (ex. 95, 96), or it may be followed by a postposition (ex. 97, 98).

(95) ní-te-ne-ne ba-ra-an-sa$_{10}$-áš, /ba-ra(abl.)-n-sa$_{10}$-eš/ 'they have sold themselves' (*TMHNF* I-II 53 = Mendelsohn, 1949 p. 15)

(96) kar.kíd ká éš.dam-ma-na-ka ní ha-ba-ni-ib-lá-e, /ha-ba-ni-b-lá-e/ 'may the prostitute hang herself at the gate of her tavern' (Curse of Akkade 243)

(97) mušen-e ní-bi silim-e-šè[a] iri[b]-in-ga-àm-me (a: -eš for -šè; b: i-rí-) 'The bird praises itself' (Lugalbanda and Enmerkar 97). Here probably ní-bi(-e).

(98) ^{D}Nin.urta ur.sağ šu du$_7$-a ní-zu-šè[a] ğeštug$_2$-zu (a: om.) 'Ninurta, perfect warrior, heed yourself' (lit.: 'your ear to your self') (Angim 81, so the OB dupl., the NA duplicates have: ^{D}Nin.urta ur.sağ-me-en šu du$_7$-me-en ní-zu-šè ğeš= tug$_2$-zu = ^{D}MIN qar-ra-da-at šuk-lu-lat ana ra-ma-ni-ka ú-zu-un-ka).

§ 131. The reflexive pronouns are also found in a genitive form: /ní-ğu-ak/ 'my own', etc.:

(99) é.šà ní-ğá-šè mu-šè-ğen-na-am$_6$, /ní-ğu-ak-šè mu-ši-ğen-am/ 'he has (now) come to my own sanctuary' (Enanatum I = AOAT 25 p. 38: X 86-87). (é.šà is a part of the sanctuary, cf. J. Bauer, AWL p. 192)

(100) Lugal.uru.da šám ní-te-na [š]u-na-a si-ga, /ní-te-ani-ak/ 'his own price was filled in the hand of Lugaluruda' (anticipatory genitive: Lugaluruda has sold himself as a slave) (NG nr. 38, 7-8)

§ 132. Especially frequent is the locative form of the reflexive pronoun denoting 'by one's own accord': ní-ğá 'by myself', ní-za 'by yourself', ní-te-na 'by himself', ní-a 'by itself'.

ní-bi-a or ní-ba 'by itself', 'by themselves' are sometimes parallel to téš-bi-a '(al)together' (cf. Heimpel, 1968 p. 152ff.).

(101) munus-e (...) i.lu é si-ga TUR.TUR-bi ní-te-na mi-ni-ib-bé, /bi-ni-b-e-e/ 'the woman speaks of her own accord the lamentation of the destroyed house' (Ur Lament 86-87)

(102) igi uğ-šè ù-ši-bar-ra-zu ní-a hé-ğál-la-àm 'when you have looked at the people there is abundance by itself' (Gudea, cyl. A III 4)

(103) ^{ğiš}al.ğar kù ^{D}En.ki-ka ní-ba mu-un-na-du$_{12}$, /mu-na-du$_{12}$/ 'Enki's pure alğar-instrument sang for him of its own accord' (Enki's Journey to Nippur 66)

(104) diğir ki[a] ní-ba[b] mu-un[c]-na-gam-e-eš[e] (a: var. probably: [-ke$_4$-n]e; b: -bi; c: om; e: om), /mu-na-gam-eš/ 'the gods of earth bowed down before him on their own accord' (Enlil Hymn 7)

Demonstratives

§ 133. In Sumerian there is a number of demonstrative pronouns and suffixes, but they are not used very often, and the semantic distinctions between the various demonstratives are therefore not clear. ne.en or ne.e, 'this', is perhaps opposed to ri, 'that, yonder', which, however, is limited to fixed literary expressions (see ex. 109). The occurrences of še and -e are doubtful, and -bi which is often used in the sense 'this', is simply the possessive suffix of inanimate and collective.

> Cf. E.I. Gordon, 1958 p. 48: 'the threefold classification of the demonstrative elements -e-/-ne- ('here' near the speaker), -še- ('there', within the view of the speaker) and -ri-/-ri-a- ('elsewhere', outside the view of the speaker).' Cf. *OBGT* Ia i 5-7 (= *MSL* IV p. 62); II obv. 10f., 13f. (= *MSL* IV p. 66).

§ 134. *ne.en, ne(-e)* '*this*'

This demonstrative pronoun is attested already in the Gudea texts, and occurs as well frequently in the OB lit. texts. In bilingual and lexical texts it is translated by Akkadian *annû* 'this, that' (cf. *CAD* A/2 p. 136), and by *kīam* 'thus' (*CAD* K p. 326).

> (105) ud ne-na hé-gaz 'on this day he may be killed' (Gudea, St. B IX 7)
>
> (106) a.da.al ne-e ta-àm mu-da-an-ku₄, /mu-da-n-ku₄/ 'now, why has he made this enter with me?' (or intrans.: 'why did this enter with me?') (Inanna and Enki II vi 54)
>
> (107) lú gùd-ǧá^a ne.en ba-e-a^b-ak-a^c (a: -ǧu₁₀; b: omits; c: -e) 'you who has done this to my nest' (Lugalbanda and Enmerkar 105) (cf. ex. 693)
>
> (108) anše.kur lú u₅-a-ni ù-mu-ni-in-šub, tukumbi gú.un-ǧu₁₀ da.rí-šè ne.en-nam al-sig-en^a-e.še (a: om.) 'the horse, after he had thrown off his rider, said: 'If my burden is always to be this, I shall become weak!' (Proverbs 5.38)

§ 135. *ri* '*that, yonder*'

ri is more remote than ne.en. It is primarily found in the expression below ex. 109: ud ri-a 'in those (far remote) days' which has become a literary topos.

> (109) ud ri-a ud sud-rá, ǧi₆ ri-a ǧi₆ bad-rá ri-a, mu ri-a mu sud-rá ri-a 'in those days, in those distant days, in those nights, in those remote nights, in those years, in those distant years' (Gilgameš, Enkidu and the Netherworld 1-3).

This expression occurs frequently in the beginning of literary compositions, cf. for instance The Instructions of Šuruppak 1-3 and, slightly different, Enki and Ninmah 1-3. It is found already in an Old Sumerian literary text from Fara (ca. 2500 B.C.), *TSŠ* 79 I 1-5 (collated): ud ri ud ri-šè na$_5$-nám, ĝi$_6$ ri ĝi$_6$ ri-šè na$_5$-nám, mu ri mu ri-šè na$_5$-nám. Cf. J. van Dijk, 1964-65 p. 31ff. where this literary motive is discussed.

§ 136. *še* '?'

This morpheme which occurs only in the literary composition 'Gilgameš and Aka', has been interpreted as a deictic element, see W.H.Ph. Römer, 1980 p. 77 with references. In the lexical text, *NBGT* III i 11-15 (= *MSL* IV p. 158f.) unfortunately broken, še is translated by Akkadian *animmamû* 'demonstrative pronoun, meaning uncertain' (*CAD* A/2 p. 122). Th. Jacobsen, 1965 p. 117 n. 55, suggested the meaning 'anyone from here'.

(110) ìr lú še lugal-zu-ù 'slave, is this(?) man your king?' (Gilgameš and Aka 69; also l. 70, 71, 91 and 92). Jacobsen, 1965 p. 117: 'Slave! Is your master anyone from here?'

§ 137. *-e*

A suffix -e seems in some cases to be used in a demonstrative sense, see A. Poebel, *GSG* §§ 223-226; A. Falkenstein, *GSGL* I p. 56 ('Das 'dortdeiktische' Element -e 'da, dort''). However, since there are only few instances of the demonstrative -e, and because of its identity with the erg. and loc. term. postposition it seems desirable to seek another interpretation:

(111) alam na-e mu-tu (Gudea, St. I V 1-2 = P V 1-2), Falkenstein, *GSGL* I p. 56, translates: 'er formte diese Stein-Statue', but 'he made it into a statue of stone(loc.term.)' seems more probable, cf.: alam na-šè mu-tu (Gudea, St. D IV 17)

(112) alam-e ù kug nu za.gìn nu-ga-àm, (Gudea, St. B VII 49-50), here, on the other hand, -e seems to be demonstrative: 'this (?) statue is not of silver, and it is not of lapis lazuli'. Cf. also *OBGT* I 324 and 326: lú-ne-ra: *an-ni-a-am*; lú-e-ra: *an-ni-a-am*, 'this one'.

§ 138. -bi

The suffix -bi is used as demonstrative suffix, e.g., ud-ba < /ud-bi-a/ 'on this/that day', lú-bi 'this/that man', etc. This meaning of -bi must be derived from the possessive suffix -bi, 'its, their' (see § 101).

See for instance A. Falkenstein, *GSGL* II p. 24, for references in the Gudea texts.

Numerals

§ 139.

one:	diš, dili, aš
two:	min
three:	eš$_5$
four:	limmu
five:	iá
six:	àš < *iá + aš (5 + 1)
seven:	imin < *iá-min (5 + 2)
eight:	ussu < *iá-eš$_5$ (5 + 3)
nine:	ilimmu < *iá-limmu (5 + 4)
ten:	u
twenty:	niš
thirty:	ušu$_2$
forty:	nimin, nin$_5$
fifty:	ninnu
sixty:	ǧíš, ǧéš
3600:	šár

The pronunciation of numerals is most often not given. In a Sumerian lexical list from early Sargonic Ebla, the numerals 2-10 is written as follows (in parenthesis the suggested pronunciation, see D.O. Edzard, 1980. 'Sumerisch 1 bis 10 in Ebla'. *Studi Eblaiti* 3: 121-127): 2: me-nu (minu), 3: iš$_{11}$-ša-am (iš or eš), 4: li-mu (limmu), 5: i (ya); 6: a-šu (yâšu ?), 7: ù-me-nu (uminu), 8: u-sa-am (ussa), 9: ì-li-mu (ilim-mu), 10: U$_9$-PI-mu (haw(a)mu or haw(u)mu).

For numerals in Emesal see *MSL* IV p. 39f. (Emesal-Vocabulary).

§ 140. *Cardinal Numbers*

As a rule the numeral stands after the noun, like an adjective. In economic texts, however, the numeral is normally given first, for practical reasons. Sometimes the enclitic copula is added after the numeral.

The plural suffix /-ene/ never occurs after a numeral.

(113) abgal imin-e sig.nim-ta šu [a]mu-ra-ni-in-mú-uš[a] (a-a: mu-ra-ni-uš, mu-ni-in-mú-uš) 'the seven sages have enlarged it for you everywhere(?)' (Temple Hymns 139). Note that the plural suffix is missing.

(114) mu Ur.lugal-ke$_4$ saĝ ki min-na ba-ra-sa$_{10}$-a-šè, /ba-ra(abl.)-(n-)sa$_{10}$-a-šè/ 'because Urlugal has sold the slave on two places (i.e. twice)' (NG nr. 68, 6-7)

(115) kug gín iá-am$_6$ e-ĝá-ĝá-ne 'they pay 5 shekels of silver' (Ukg. 6 I 21-22)

§ 141. *Ordinal Numbers*

Ordinal numbers are genitive constructions without regens, followed by the enclitic copula: /min-ak-am/ > min-(na-)kam 'the second'. The genitive may also occur pleonastically: ud min-kam-ma-ka < /ud min-ak-am-ak-a/ 'on the second day'.

(116) ud u-kam-ma-ka, /ud u-ak-am-ak-a/ 'on the tenth day' (Ukg. 14 II 2)

(117) mìn-kam-ma-šè [a]mušen-e[a] gùd-bi-šè še$_{26}$ un-gi$_4$ (a-a: var. om.) 'As the bird cried to its nest for the second time' (Lugalbanda and Enmerkar 72)

§ 142. Numerals which are not standing attributively to nouns have possessive suffixes, e.g.: mìn-na-ne-ne < /min-anene/ 'both of them' (lit.: 'their two').

Conjunctions

§ 143. /u/ 'and', written ù, is a loanword from Akkadian *u*, 'and'. It is found already in a text from Abū Ṣalābīkh ca. 2500 B.C. (see above p. 16 and Biggs, 1974 p. 32).

ù is used as a conjunction of sentences, but usually not between simple co-ordinate sentences. It is rather used in the sense 'and then ...', 'but', 'moreover', so also in the beginning of a sentence.

When ù is used as conjunction of nouns it has also often an emphasizing character: 'A as well as B'.

(118) ud Ĝeme₂.ᴰLama ba-ug₇-e-da-a, Lú.ᴰBa.ba₆ ìr Dug₄.ga. zi.da-ke₄ ù Ur.ᴰŠul.gi-ke₄ in-ba-a-ne, ù eĝer ab.ba-ne-ne ì-ba-a-ne, /ba-ug₇-ed-a-a(loc.)/, /ì-n-ba-ene/, /ì-ba-ene/ 'when Ĝeme-Lama dies, Lu-Baba, the slave, Duga-zida and Ur-Šulgi shall divide (the inheritance), and also (the estate) after their father they shall divide' (*NG* nr. 7, 15-21)

(119) di.kud ib-dú.ru-né-eš ù a-ne ib-gub, /ì-b-durun-eš/, /ì-b-gub/ 'the judges have sat and he was (also) present (lit.: stood)' (*TCS* I nr. 203, 3-4)

(120) ù ĝá-e ní.te.ĝá-ªĝu₁₀-ušª nam.ti sum-mu-na-ab (a-a: omits) /sum + mu-na-b/, 'and as for me, give me(?) health (lit.: life) for my reverence' (Letter of Sin-iddinam to Utu 45, text has -na- 'for him' but only 'for me' seems to give sense.)

§ 144. -bi-da, literally 'with its ..', is used in the sense 'and' with nouns and without the disjunctive force of ù:
áb amar-bi-da 'the cow with its calf' = 'cow and calf'.

§ 145. tukumbi written ŠU.NÍG.TUR.LAL.BI 'if'. As a rule, the verb after tukumbi is *hamṭu*.

(121) tukumbi nu-ub-sar Ur.me.me-ke₄ íb-su-su, /nu-ì-b-sar/, /ì-b-su.su-e/ 'if they have not written it (on the tablet), Ur-meme will restore it' (*NG* nr. 209, 89-91)

(122) tukumbi lugal-ĝu₁₀ ugnim-ma tuš-ù-bi ab-bé, /ã-b-e-e/ 'if my king promises dwelling-places to the troops' (Letter B 2, 8)

(123) tukumbi lugal-me an-na-kam 'if our king is (indeed) of heaven' (Letter B 11, 8)

§ 146. tukumbi with the enclitic negation ...-nu corresponds to *šumma lā* 'except' (see Sjöberg, 1973a p. 128; von Soden, 1952 § 114i).

(124) tukumbi nam.nar-nu 'except the art of singing' (Father and Son 110)

§ 147. According to B. Alster, 1972a p. 119, tukumbi is also used in the sense 'certainly' (see example 1972a p. 119f.), as well as in 'an elliptic construction to express politeness ('If [you will be so kind ...] —'), approximately corresponding to 'please":

(125) a ub-ta-anª-bal-bal aᵇ tukumbi ᶜga-naĝᶜ, (a: om.; b: om; c-c: -KA-A) 'after you have poured water, water — please — let me drink!' (Dumuzi's Dream 207)

§ 148. ud-da < /ud-a(loc.)/, literally 'on the day', is also used in the sense 'when' and 'if'. As a rule, also after ud-da the verb is *ḫamṭu*.

(126) ud-da gú ma[a]-an-ğar gú na-ma-an-ğar (a: ma-ra-), /mu-DAT.1.sg.-n-ğar/, /na-mu-DAT.1.sg.-n-ğar/ 'when he has submitted to me, he has indeed submitted to me' (Enmerkar and Ensuhkešdana 26)

(127) ud-da uru-šè[a] ì-du-un lú [b]nu-mu-e[b]-da-du-ù[c] (a: -ni; b-b: na-e-; c: om.), /ì-du-en/, /na-mu-e.da-du-ed(?)/ 'if you go to the city, nobody shall go with you' (Lugalbanda and Enmerkar 287)

Modal Adverbs

§ 149. i.gi$_4$.in.zu 'as if' is used in hypothetical comparisons.

C. Wilcke, 1968 p. 238f. suggested the etymology: 'the eye has noticed'. Writings are: igi.zu (Gudea texts), i.gi.in.zu, i.gi$_4$.in.zu, e.gi$_4$.in.zu, i.gi$_4$.zu, igi.su and i.gi$_4$in.ŠUL (see Wilcke, 1968 p. 229; 1969a p. 188 n. 466a).

All references have been collected by C. Wilcke:

Claus Wilcke, 1968. 'Das modale Adverb i-gi$_4$-in-zu im Sumerischen.' *JNES* 27: 229-242. With additions in Wilcke, 1969a p. 188f. n. 466a.

(128) alan igi.zu [D]Nin.ğír.su-ka-kam 'as if it was a statue of Ninğirsu' (Gudea, St. B VII 59)

(129) mušen-e ku$_6$-ra[a] engur-ra igi im-ma-an[b]-du$_8$ ğeštug$_2$ ba-ši-in-gub i.gi$_4$.in.zu a-e ba-da-kar umbin(GAD.ÚR) mu-ni-in-lá (a: -e; b: var. -ni-íb- for -an-), /ì-ba-n-du$_8$/, /ì-ba-ni-b-du$_8$/, /ba-ši-n-gub/, /ba-da-kar/, /mu-ni-n-lá/ 'the bird became aware of the fish in the water, it set the mind to it, as if it would take it out of the water, it stretched the claw into it' (Bird and Fish 116-117 = Wilcke, 1968 p. 233)

§ 150. ì.ge$_{(4)}$.en occurs only a couple of instances in the OB lit. texts. It may be a modal adverb like i.gi$_4$.in.zu or an interjection 'but no!' Cf. C. Wilcke, 1968 p. 239f.

(130) ì.ge$_4$.en mu.lu šà.ab-ğá-kam mu.lu šà.ab-ğá-kam, 'but no! is he the man of my heart? is he the man of my heart?' (Dumuzi and Enkimdu 49)

§ 151. ì.ne.šè, or perhaps better ì.ne.éš, also written ne.éš and e.ne.éš, means 'now', corresponding to Akkadian *inanna*.
For references, see Sjöberg, 1973a p. 131; Krecher, 1967b p. 57.

(131) ì.ne.šè [a]mušen-e[a] [b]gùd-bi-šè[b] še₂₆[c] un-gi₄ (a-a: var.s omit; b-b: U.KI.SÈ-bi-šè; Ú.KI.GA-šè; gùd-ta; c: KAxLI; KAx X; KA), /u-ì-n-gi₄/ 'but now after the bird has cried to its nest' (Lugalbanda and Enmerkar 76)

§ 152. a.da.al or a.da.lam is approximately 'now, but now'. Other writings of this word are probably i.da.al, i.da.lam and i.dal.la. According to *OBGT* Ia rev. I 6ff. a.da.al(.lam) = *i-na-an-na(-a-[ma])* 'now, it is now', whereas i.da.al(-lam) is translated *a-ša-a-a[r(-ma)]* 'right now' (cf. *CAD* A/2 p. 413 with exclusively lexical references). The exact difference between a.da.al and i.da.al — if there is any — is not clear. Also the distinction between a.da.al and ì.ne.šè which are both translated *inanna*, 'now', cannot be stated exactly.

See G. Farber-Flügge, 1973 p. 214; C. Wilcke, 1969a p. 206, 216. J. van Dijk, 1970 p. 305 and n. 2, suggested that i.da.al/a.da.al is 'un nom déverbal', containing the comitative element /-da-/ and possibly the verbal prefix /al-/.

(132) a.da.al kug [D]Inanna-ke₄ igi me[a]-ši-kár-kár (a: mu-e- for me-), /mu-e.ši-kár.kár(-e)/ 'now, holy Inanna is examining you' (Enmerkar and the Lord of Aratta 449)

(133) a.da.lam An-ra [a]dug₄-mu-na-ab[a] An-e[b] [c]mu-e[c]-du₈-e[e] (a-a: ba-an-na-ab-bé(-en); ba-an-na-ab-dug₄; b: An-né; c-c: me-(e-); mu-un-; e: -e-en; -en), /dug₄ + mu-na-b/, /mu-e-du₈-e/ 'say to An: now! — (and) An will release me' (Exaltation of Inanna 76)

Interjections

§ 153. ga.na or ga.nam 'well', 'truly'.
It is not the imperative of the verb g̃en 'to go', as A. Falkenstein presumed (*GSGL* I p. 227), since a form of g̃en should be written g̃á-na (or g̃e₂₆-na). For ga.na cf. C. Wilcke, 1968 p. 204f.

(134) ga.na ga-na-ab-dug₄, /ga-ì-na-b-dug₄/ 'well, I will say it to her' (Gudea, cyl. A I 24 = III 22, 23)

§ 154. me.le.e.a 'alas!', 'woe!'.

(135) me.le.e.a uru₂ mu-da-gul ù é[a] mu-da-gul (a: var. seems to

add -ğu$_{10}$) 'alas! the city has been destroyed, and the house (var. my house) has been destroyed' (Ur Lament 292)

(136) me.le.e.a, dam-ğu$_{10}$ ír-ra[a] dumu-ğu$_{10}$ a.nir-ra (a: var. -àm for -ra) 'woe, my wife — tears, my son — lament' (Ur-Nammu's Death 192)

§ 155. ù-a, ù or a 'woe!'.

For writings, see J. Krecher, 1966 p. 114f.

(137) ù.a erim$_6$-ma-ğu$_{10}$ ù.a erim$_6$-ma-ğu$_{10}$ 'woe, my treasury, woe, my treasury!' (J. Krecher, 1966 p. 54: II 6)

CASES

Introduction

§ 156. Sumerian has ten cases: genitive, absolutive, ergative, dative, locative, comitative, terminative, ablative-instrumental, locative-terminative and equative.

Absolutive is the unmarked case, the other cases are denoted by postpositions, i.e. the case morpheme occurs at the very end of the nominal phrase and no other morpheme can follow. Exception is the genitive which is embedded in the nominal phrase of the *regens* of the genitive construction:

(138) /é gibil-ani-šè/ 'to his new house'
(139) /é ab.ba-ǧu$_{10}$-ak-šè/ 'to the house of my father'

The enclitic copula may occur after a case element, see § 45.

Some cases occur only with animate nouns, others only with inanimate, see below § 157.

§ 157.

	Animate	Inanimate	Prefix Chain
Genitive §§ 161-168	-ak	-ak	
Absolutive § 169	-Ø	-Ø	
Ergative § 173	-e	-e	
Dative §§ 175-179	-ra		-na- etc.
Locative §§ 180-187		-a	-ni-
Comitative §§ 188-194	-da	-da	-da-
Terminative §§ 195-202	-šè	-šè	-ši-
Ablative-Instrumental §§ 203-213		-ta	-ta- and -ra-
Locative-Terminative § 174		-e	-ni-
Equative §§ 214-220	-gin$_7$	-gin$_7$	

§ 158. The cases dative, comitative, terminative, ablative-instrumental and probably also locative are incorporated in the prefix chain of the finite verb. For this and for the relations between cases and certain verbs see 'The Case Elements of the Prefix Chain' §§ 423-482.

§ 159. The meanings of the dimensional cases: locative, terminative and ablative, can be differentiated by adding a genitive compound. Such constructions are especially frequent with animate nouns which normally cannot be constructed with these cases:

Locative:

/ki-POSS-a/ 'with' lit.: 'on (his) place'
/ki-PN-ak-a/ 'with PN' lit.: 'on PN's place'
/šà NOUN-ak-a/ lit.: 'in the heart of ...' or simply: 'in ...'

Terminative:

/eğer-NOUN-ak-šè/ 'after' lit.: 'to the back of ...'
/igi PN(or NOUN)-ak-šè/ lit.: 'to the eyes of ...': 'in front of',
'before', 'in the presence of'
/nam NOUN-ak-šè/ 'because of, 'for the sake of'
/mu NOUN-ak-šè/ 'instead of'

Ablative:

/ki PN-ak-ta/ 'from' lit.: 'from PN's place'
/šu PN-ak-ta/ 'under the authority of PN' lit.: 'from the hand of PN'

In those cases where such constructions replace the more simple and original postpositional expressions, as for instance šà uru-ka 'in the city' instead of uru-a, we may perhaps speak of a first step towards a prepositional system. In these instances the genitive is often omitted, e.g., ki lugal-ta 'from the king', but this development is most probably a post-Sumerian phenomenon.

§ 160. Terminology

The terms of the cases used here are approximately the same as those used by A. Falkenstein, for instance in *Das Sumerische* (p. 38ff.). The only exceptions are 'absolutive' for the unmarked case (intr. subj. and tr. obj.) and 'ergative' for the subject of the transitive verb. These terms are in accordance with the terminology used with other ergative languages.

The terminative has been called 'directive' by other scholars, for instance by G.B. Gragg, *SDI* p. 15ff., which term may well be more justified. Also in the case of the locative-terminative another term would probably be more applicable. However, since many questions about the functions and meanings of the Sumerian cases are still unanswered, especially as regards the last mentioned case, I have chosen to retain the established terminology.

Genitive

§ 161. The genitive postposition is /-ak/, but it is never written with the sign AK. [a] is most often assimilated or deleted after a vowel; [k] is deleted in final position and is only written when followed by a vowel.

(140) ig é-g̃á < /ig é-g̃u-ak/ 'the door of my house'
(141) g̃iš.rab mah an ki-a < /.... ki-ak/ 'the huge neckstock of heaven and earth' (Nungal Hymn 2)
(142) DNin.G̃ír.su < /nin G̃ír.su-ak/ 'the lord of G̃irsu', absolutive, but: DNin.G̃ír.su-ke₄ < /nin G̃ír.su-ak-e/, ergative

For another view of the phonological shape of the genitive postposition see E. Sollberger, 1950 p. 74-77: 'Je pense à mon tour que la forme du suffixe est bien -a; cependant, l'argument des tenants de cette théorie, savoir que le -k- a pour but d'empêcher l'hiatus, ne rend pas exactement compte du phénomène: il s'agit, à mon sens, d'empêcher une superposition par souci de clarté' (p. 75).

Th. Jacobsen, 1973 p. 165, interpreted -ak in the following names as the genitive postposition: DNin.kar.ra.ak, DIn.šu.ši.na.ak, Aš.nun.na.ak. It is, however, not certain that these names are genitive constructions (cf. M.A. Powell, 1982 p. 319).

In the text *BIN* VIII 10, 8: síg SAL.ÙZ ak Sollberger, 1959 p. 115 saw a possible writing AK for the genitive postposition, it is here, however, the verb ak, the whole phrase denoting a quality of wool. (For the phrase síg-(ga-) ZUM-ak, see M. Civil, 1967 p. 210f.).

§ 162. The genitive is used with both animate and inanimate beings.

§ 163. *The Rank of the Genitive Postposition in the Nominal Chain*

The *regens* of the genitive normally stands before the *rectum*:

(143) /é lugal-ak/ 'the house of the king'

The case postposition of the *regens* comes at the end, after the genitive:

(144) /é lugal-ak-a(loc.)/ = é lugal-la-ka 'in the house of the king'

In a double genitive construction both genitive postpositions stand at the end:

(145) /é šeš lugal-ak-ak(-a, loc.)/ = é šeš lugal-la-ka(-ka) '(in) the house of the brother of the king'

In the nominal chain the genitive postposition occurs after the affixes belonging to the *rectum* (poss. suffix and/or /-ene/), but before the affixes belonging to the *regens*:

(146) é šeš-ĝu$_{10}$-e-ne-ka = /é šeš-ĝu-ene-ak-a(loc.)/ 'in the house of my brothers'
(147) šeš ab.ba-na-ke$_4$-ne = /šeš ab.ba-ani-ak-ene/ 'the brothers of his father'
(148) é šeš lugal-la-ke$_4$-ne-ka = /é šeš lugal-ak-ene-a(loc.)/ 'in the house of the brothers of the king'

§ 164. *Anticipatory Genitive*

The word order of the genitive construction can be reversed: the *rectum* is then repeated by a possessive suffix. This is the so-called anticipatory genitive.

(149) lugal-la é-a-ni = /lugal-ak é-ani/ 'of the king — his house'
(150) é-a ig-bi = /é-ak ig-bi/ 'of the house — its door'
(151) Ur.^{ĝiš}tukul-ka gud-a-ni ga-na-ab-zìg, /Ur.^{ĝiš}tukul.ak-ak gud-ani ga-ī-na-b-zìg/ 'let me issue Ur-tukula's ox to him' (*TCS* I nr. 36, 3-4)
(152) é-a me-bi diĝir ság nu-di, /é-ak me-bi/ 'no god scatters the divine rules of the house' (Enlil Hymn 41)

The two members of the anticipatory genitive may be separated by another word:

(153) é-a ^{D}En.ki-ke$_4$ ĝiš.hur-bi si mu-na-sá, /é-a ^{D}En.ki.k-e ĝiš. hur-bi si mu-na(-n)-sá/ 'Enki put the plan of the house in order for him' (Gudea, cyl. A XVII 17)

§ 165. The genitive expresses ownership (/é lugal-ak/ 'the king's house') or relationship (/šeš lugal-ak/ 'the king's brother').

Genitive constructions are rather frequently found, where we use adjectives or adverbs, e.g., /é.gal nam.lugal-ak-ani/ 'his palace of kingship', i.e. 'his royal palace'.

(154) ensi₂ lú ğeštug₂ dağal-kam = /ensi₂ lú ğeštug₂ dağal-ak-am/ 'the *ensi* is the man of the wide ear', i.e. 'is a wise man' (Gudea, cyl. A I 12) (cf. ex. 157)

§ 166. In non-finite verbal constructions the genitive may express the agent, thus replacing the ergative. This is the case only in the following non-finite construction:

(N₃) N₁ R-a N₂-ak (cf. § 514).

(155) En.an.na.túm (...) ga zid gu₇-a ᴰNin.hur.sağ-ka, /ᴰNin.hur. sag.ak-ak/ 'Enanatum (...) fed with the good milk by Ninhursağa(k)' (En.I. = *AOAT* 25 p. 36: ii 8-9)

§ 167. The *regens* of the genitive construction may be missing. This construction is especially frequent with the enclitic copula. It is for instance the regular way to form ordinal numbers: min-(na-)kam < /min-ak-am/ 'the second' (see § 141).

(156) gú-na-kam = /gú-ani-ak-am/ 'it is of his neck' = 'it is his responsibility' (*TCS* I nr. 177, 7)
(157) ğeštug₂ dağal-la-ke₄ = /ğeštug₂ dağal-ak-e(erg.)/ 'of the wide ear', i.e. 'the wise (man)' (Enlil Hymn 11) (cf. ex. 154).

§ 168. *Bibliography*

Th. Jacobsen, 1973. 'Notes on the Sumerian Genitive'. *JNES* 32: 161-166.

§ 169. Absolutive

Absolutive is the unmarked case, i.e. it is the nominal stem alone without any postpositional endings.

It is first of all the case of the intransitive subject and of the transitive object; unmarked are also the vocative and the members of the non-finite asyntactic construction (see § 505).

For the use of the absolutive see also §§ 38-42.

Cases marked with /-e/

§ 170. The postposition /-e/ has two apparently quite different functions: *a.* ergative, denoting the subject of a transitive verb, and *b.* denoting the direction approximately 'near to', the so-called 'locative-terminative'.

As it is difficult to imagine two semantically totally different cases to be morphologically identical, it seems more likely to regard /-e/ as one case with two functions, whose relationship, however, is not entirely clear:

a. Subject of two-participant verbs: *ergative*, with both animate and inanimate.
b. Direction 'near to': *'locative-terminative'*, with inanimate only. This last use of /-e/ seems to be restricted to a rather limited number of verbs which can be said to take loc.term. (see § 174); with animate beings the dative replaces the loc.term. (cf. ex. 167, 174 below).

Unlike the other postpositions /-e/ may thus occur twice in a sentence with different members of the clause, namely both as transitive subject and as locative-terminative direction, cf. ex. 169.

§ 171. In some instances -e is by J. Krecher, 1965 p. 28-29, classified as an independent 'isolating particle' with temporal meaning: 'als, während o.ä.'. According to Krecher this particle is distinguished from the loc.term./erg. postposition by the fact that it is not contracted after a vowel, e.g., húl-la-e, and that the [k] of the genitive postposition is deleted before the 'isolating' -e, e.g., é šà-ba-e < /é šà.b-ak-e/, not é šà-ba-ke₄. The examples of the 'isolating' -e cited by Krecher are comparatively few and many of them come from the partly obscure Emesal and unorthographic texts. To my opinion it seems also possible that these instances of -e are either ergative or locative-terminative, although they are not always quite correct according to the standard grammar and orthography.

(158) ᴰGilgameš en Kul.aba₄ ki(-a)-ke₄ ᴰInanna-ra nir g̃ál-la-e inim ab.ba uruki-na-ke₄ᵃ šà-šè ᵇnu-um-gídᵇ (a: -šè; b-b: nu-mu!-na-gíd), /nu-í-m-gíd/, /nu-mu-na-(n-)gíd/ 'Gilgameš, the *en* of Kulaba, trusting in Inanna, did not bear the word of the elders of his city in mind' (Gilgames and Aka 15-17). J. Krecher, 1965 p. 29, classified nir g̃ál-la-e as the temporal use of -e, but to me it seems more likely to understand -e as the ergative postposition, although this should not be written after the form VERB-a.

(159) ud uru₂ gul-gul-e ud é gul-gul-e ud tùr gul-gul-e ud amaš ᵃgul-gul-eᵃ g̃arza kug-ga šu bí-íb-lá-a-ri (a-a: tab-tab-e), /bi-b-lá-a-ri/ 'the storm,

destroying cities, destroying houses, destroying cattle-pens, destroying sheep-folds, it has bound the holy rites' (Ur Lament 391-393). J.
Krecher, 1965 p. 29, suggested the meaning *'was anbelangt'* of -e in
gul-gul-e, but it can also be ergative.

§ 172. *Morphology*

The postposition /-e/ is most often written -e or -Ce. After a vowel
it may occur as -e, -a or -ù, for instance: ama-a (Gudea, cyl. A XIII
3), nu.bànda-a (*NG* nr. 44, 6); Diğir.šag$_5$.ga-a (*NG* nr. 45, 11); lú-ù
(Gudea, cyl. A XIII 11); dumu-ù (Gudea, cyl. A XIII 4); ..-zu-ù
(Šulgi D 38); ..-ğu$_{10}$-ù (Šulgi D 158, 161, 180), etc.

/-e/ may probably be assimilated or deleted after a vowel, for instance after the possessive suffixes /-ani/ and /-bi/ (cf. however mu-
bi-e in ex. 171). Some scholars write in these cases ...-a-né and ...-bé
in order to elucidate the assumed grammar of a certain phrase. In the
present study I have refrained from this transliteration practice since,
first of all, it is not without doubt that /-ani + e/ > [-ane] and /-bi +
e/ > [-be] and not [-ani] and [-bi]; secondly because it is not always
certain whether we have to restore this postposition, especially in its
locative-terminative function (for this cf. ex. 170 below, where /-e/
is also missing after a consonant: -ğa(k)).

The postposition /-e/ is also deleted after the plural suffix /-ene/.

Occasionally /-e/ may occur after the non-finite form: R-a, cf. ex.
158.

§ 173. Ergative

In the ergative function /-e/ denotes the subject of a transitive or
two-participant verb in a finite clause. In non-finite constructions
/-e/ occurs only together with R(*hamṭu*)-a in the so-called 'mes-ane-
pada' construction, where the underlying subject has the ergative
postposition /-e/, cf. ex. 163 and see § 514 and 517.

The ergative postposition /-e/ is used with both animate and inanimate beings.

Together with personal pronouns the postposition /-e/ denotes
both transitive and intransitive subject. The pronominal forms ğá-e
'I', za-e 'you', a-ne 'she', 'he' and a-ne-ne 'they' which probably
contain the ergative postposition may therefore be called 'subject
case' or 'nominative' (cf. §§ 38; 92).

Examples:

(160) ᴰEn.líl-e en ᴰNin.g̃ír.su-šè igi zid mu-ši-bar, /mu-ši-(n-) bar/ 'Enlil looked faithfully at the lord Ning̃irsu' (Gudea, cyl. A I 3)

(161) é-e guruš ug₅-ga-gin₇ gú ki-šè ᵃba-da-an-láᵃ (a-a: g̃á-g̃á-dé), /ba-ta-n-lá/ 'The house bowed down its neck to the earth like young warriors who have been killed' (Curse of Akkade 120)

(162) ù.ku.kuᵐᵘˢᵉⁿ mušen šà.sìg(-ga)-ke₄ gùd hé(-em)-ma-an-úsᵃ (a: adds -e), /ha-ï-ba-n-ús(-e)/ 'the *ukuku*-bird, the bird of sorrow, shall build (its) nest there' (Curse of Akkade 261)

(163) mes An-né pàd-da, /mes An-e pàd-a/ 'the young man called by An', corresponding to: /An-e mes mu-n-pàd/ 'An has called the young man'

(164) É.ninnu An-né ki g̃ar-ra, /É.ninnu An-e ki(-a, loc.) g̃ar-a/ 'Eninnu founded by An' (Gudea, cyl. A IX 11). This construction corresponds to the finite sentence: /An-e É.ninnu ki-a mu-n-g̃ar/, but cf. ex. 165 where an-né is loc.term.:

(165) é me.lám-bi an-né ús-sa, /é-ak me.lám-bi an-e ús-a/ 'the radiance of the house reaches heaven' (Gudea, cyl. A XVII 18) corresponding to /é-ak me.lám-bi an-e ï-m-ús/. Cf.

(166) me.lám huš-bi an-né im-ús 'its terrible radiance reaches heaven' (Gudea, cyl. A IX 16).

§ 174. Locative-Terminative

The locative-terminative function of the postposition /-e/ occurs with inanimate beings only. Dative with animate beings is often parallel to loc.-term. with inanimate, see the examples below.

The meaning of the locative-terminative is approximately the direction 'near to'. The use of /-e/ in this sense seems to be limited to a rather small number of mostly compound verbs taking loc.term. (or locative) with inanimate beings and dative with animate beings (cf. ex. 167, 174): ki...ág̃ 'to love', gù...dé 'to call, to speak to', mí...dug₄ 'to care for', g̃ál...tag₄ 'to open', kúš.ù 'to be troubled about', sag̃...rig₇ 'to grant', si...sá 'to put in order', si 'to fill', gú...si 'to assemble', te 'to reach', g̃iš...tuku 'to hear', ús 'to follow, to reach', ki...ús 'to found'.

/-e/ is thus in general not used with other verbs in order to denote the direction, in the sense 'to, towards' the terminative is always used. Cf. ex. 172 where kar-..-e is the indirect object of the verb ús, whereas Nina^{ki}-šè denotes the general direction.

The verbs taking loc.term. may have the case prefix -ni-, which probably denotes locative and/or loc.term., see § 471. The verbal prefix /bi-/ seems also to be preferred by these verbs as well as the prefix chain /ba-ni-/ (cf. ex. 170 below).

Examples:

(167) é-e lugal-bi gù ba-dé, /ba-(n-)dé/ 'its king spoke to the house' (Gudea, cyl. A I 10). But cf.:

(168) ur.saĝ šul ^DUtu-ra kug ^DInanna-ke₄ gù mu-un-na-dé-e 'to the hero, the young man, to Utu, holy Inanna speaks' (Gilgameš, Enkidu and the Netherworld 51)

(169) é-e ^DAsar-re šu.si ba-sá, /ba-(n-)sá/ 'Asar put the house in order' (Gudea, cyl. B IV 1)

(170) ki-ba ^DIštaran-gin₇ di uru-ĝá si ba-ni-íb-sá-e, /ba-ni-b-sá-e(n)/ 'at this place like Ištaran I will put the justice of my city in order' (Gudea, cyl. A X 26). Here as in other cases with si...sá the 'second object' (di uru-ĝá) has obviously no postposition, since both /-a/(loc.) and /-e/(loc.term.) should be written after the genitive /di uru-ĝu-ak/.

(171) mu-bi-e an.zag-ta kur-kur-re gú im-ma-si-si, /í-ba-(b-)si.si/ 'all the foreign lands gather around its name from the horizon' (Gudea, cyl. A IX 18)

(172) uru-ni Nina^{ki}-šè kar Sirara^{ki}-na-ke₄ má bí-ús, /bi-(n-)ús/, 'he steered the ship to her city Nina, to the quay of Siraran' (Gudea, cyl. A IV 4). Cf.

(173) kar ^DEn.líl.lá-šè ^DNanna ^DSuen-e ^{ĝiš}má na-ga-àm-mi-in-ús, /na-ga-í-bi-n-ús/ 'Nanna-Suen has indeed also steered the ship to the quay of Enlil' (Nanna-Suen's Journey to Nippur 254-255)

(174) níg.si.sá(-e) ki ha-ba-áĝ-ĝá-àm, níg.erim₂-e ki la-ba-ra-áĝ-àm, /ha-ba-áĝ-a-m/, /nu-ba-ra(abl.)-áĝ-a-m/ 'I love justice, I do not love injustice' (Šulgi Hymn A 23-24). But cf.:

(175) ^aĝá-a-ra^a ki ha-ba-an^b-áĝ (a-a: χ ĝá-e; b: -na? - for -an-) 'she has loved me' (Lugalbanda and Enmerkar 313 = 379)

Dative

§ 175. The dative postposition is /-ra/, written with the sign RA. It may be abbreviated to [r] after a vowel, especially after /-ani/ 'his, her' and the plural suffix /-ene/. e.g.:

(176) lugal-a-ni-ir 'for his king'

(177) diĝir gal-gal-e-ne-er 'for the greatest gods'

In the OS texts the dative postposition is regularly omitted after a vowel, as a rule it occurs only after a consonant; also when this consonant is not explicitly written, e.g.,

(178) ᴰNin.ĝír.su-ra = /Nin Ĝir.su-ak-ra/ 'for Ninĝirsu (lit.: the lord of Ĝirsu)'

but:

(179) lugal-a-ni = /lugal-a.ni-ra/ 'for his king'

§ 176. The dative can be used with animate beings only. With inanimate nouns the locative is used instead, sometimes also the terminative or the locative-terminative (cf. ex. 174 and 175 above).

§ 177. The dative denotes the person for whom or towards whom an action is done, e.g.,

(180) ᴰNin.ĝír.su-ra Gù.dé.a É.ninnu mu-na-dù 'for Ninĝirsu Gudea has built the Eninnu'

(181) en ᴰNin.ĝír.su-ra É.ninnu Anzu₂ᵐᵘˢᵉⁿ bar₆.bar₆-ra mu-na-da-ku₄-ku₄ 'he enters before the lord Ninĝirsu in Eninnu, the white Anzu-bird' (Gudea, cyl. A VII 27-29)

§ 178. Most verbs can take dative, except those verbs denoting an action which cannot be done for an animate being like for instance zu 'to know', or verbs which for some other reason take another case element, for instance terminative (cf. Gragg, *SDI* p. 88).

The categories of verbs taking dative are according to Gragg, *SDI* p. 89ff.: Verbs of giving, verbs of speaking, verbs of motion, verbs of 'action-towards', verbs of emotion, verbs of doing for. (See §§ 438-439).

§ 179. In many cases, but not in all, there is concord of dative postposition and prefix in the verbal form. As Gragg stated, 'for most verbs there seems to be no reason to distinguish between their ability to take a dative complement and their ability to take a dative infix. (...) The fact that a verb can take an adverbial in -ra means that under the appropriate conditions it can also take a dative infix. It remains an open question whether the dative concord is itself an optional rule or whether it should be allowed to take place in every instance, and followed by various obligatory and optional deletion rules' (*SDI* p. 88).

Exception is the verb in-šè...dub 'which regularly occurs with a dative complement but never with a dative infix' (Gragg, *SDI* p. 88).

Locative

§ 180. The locative postposition is /-a/; it is written -a or -Ca.

§ 181. The locative postposition occurs normally with inanimate beings only; if a verb takes dative with animate beings, it takes locative (or sometimes terminative) with inanimate beings, dative and locative can thus be regarded as complementary cases. From NS on the locative sometimes replaces the dative, e.g.,

(182) lugal-g̃á ù-na-dug$_4$ 'say to my king', /lugal-g̃u-a/ instead of /lugal-g̃u-ra/ (Letter B 2: 1).

§ 182. The locative denotes the place 'where': an ki-a 'in heaven (and) on earth', uru-a 'in the city', Nibru^{ki}-a 'in Nippur', etc.

(183) Kèš^{ki} kur-kur-ra sag̃(-g̃á) íl-bi 'when Keš lifted its (head) in (or: among) the foreign lands' (Keš Hymn 8)

(184) šà-ba < /šà-bi-a/, lit. 'in their midst' = 'among them'

§ 183. In a figurative sense the locative denotes 'in the status of', 'in the capacity as':

(185) limmu-bi nam.ìr nam.g̃eme$_2$-a ba-a-gi$_4$ 'these four were returned into their status as slaves and slavegirls' (*NG* nr. 30, 14)

§ 184. Temporally the locative denotes 'at a given time', 'when': ud-ba < /ud-bi-a/ 'at that day, when'. So also in the subordinate clause: ud ... VERB-a(subord.)-a(loc.) (cf. § 489).

(186) bala nam.lugal-la-g̃á = /bala nam-lugal-ak-g̃u-a/ 'during my reign' (Sin-kašid 10, 9)

§ 185. Locative is also used in adverbial phrases like for instance: á huš-na < /á huš-ani-a/ 'in his wild strength', hé.ǧál-la 'in abundance, abundantly', ní-ba < /ní-bi-a/ 'on their own accord' (cf. § 132).

§ 186. Many compound verbs take locative with the 'second object', for instance šu...tag 'to decorate', šu...ùr 'to erase'.

(187) mu.šar.ra-a-ba šu bí-íb-ra-ge⟨-a⟩ 'the one who erases this inscription' (Warad-Sin 28, rev. 53-54)

(188) za.gìn-na šu ù-ma-ni-tag 'when you have decorated it with lapis lazuli' (Gudea, cyl. A VI 19)

§ 187. In the prefix chain of the finite verb the locative case is normally referred to by the prefix -ni- which also corresponds to the locative-terminative and the terminative, see §§ 470-482.

Comitative

§ 188. The comitative postposition is written -da, in OS also -da₅ (= URUDU).

A. Falkenstein, *GSGL* I p. 115, regarded the OS writing -da₅ as the most general form of the comitative in this period. However, as a rule, DA seems to be the most used sign also in the OS texts, cf. E. Sollberger, 1952 p. 97 n. 1, and ex. 189, 190 below.

The writing -dè for the comitative /-da/ occurs in the non-finite form R-a-POSS-dè (see § 521). This seems, however, to be the only case where comitative is written -dè, the examples of -dè after nouns from Gudea and NS texts in Falkenstein, *GSGL* I p. 156 and n. 4 are very doubtful.

§ 189. The comitative element /da/ is etymologically the noun da, 'side' (cf. ex. 196).

Comitative occurs with both animate and inanimate. It is incorporated in the verbal prefix chain as -da- (or -di- and -dè-, see § 441).

§ 190. The basic meaning of the comitative is 'with', 'together with', expressing accompaniment as well as mutual action. In this sense the comitative can be used with almost all verbs (cf. ex. 189, 191, 192).

Some verbs like á...áǧ 'to instruct', ad...gi₄ 'to take counsel', gú...lá 'to embrace', and verbs of emotion like húl 'to rejoice in', šag₅ 'to be pleasing to', ní...ri 'to inspire fear', sağ.ki...gíd 'to be angry at', regularly take comitative prefix and postposition (cf. Gragg, *SDI* p. 62-66 and ex. 193, 194 below; see also §§ 447-449).

§ 191. The occurrences of the postposition -da are more rare than the presence of the comitative in the prefix chain with the above mentioned verbs. In some cases -da may graphically be omitted (ex. 192), in others the noun corresponding to the comitative prefix is expressed by another case, for instance the dative as in ex. 194.

> In the OB texts investigated by Gragg there were only 170 occurrences of -da against 430 of the case prefix, of those no more than 26 were cooccurrences of prefix and postposition. Gragg therefore concluded that 'the comitative infix has a greater independence vis-a-vis the individual verb stem than was the case for the terminative and the ablative-instrumental infixes' (*SDI* p. 53).

For the 'abilitative' meaning of the comitative prefix, see § 448.

§ 192. *Examples:*

(189) É.an.na.túm (...)-ke₄ En.á.kal.le ensi₂ Umma^ki-da ki e-da-sur, /í-da-(n-)sur/ 'Eanatum marked off the boundary with Enakale, the prince of Umma' (Ent. 28 I 32-42)

(190) nam.dag ^DNin.ğír.su-da e-da-ak-ka-am₆, / í-da-(n-)ak-a-m/ 'he is the one who has committed a sin against (lit.: with) Ninğirsu' (Ukg. 16 VIII 1-3)

(191) še dub-ğu₁₀ Ur.^DŠul.pa.è-da in-da-ğál, / í-n.da-ğál/ 'my barley tablet is with Ur-Šulpa'e' (*TCS* I nr. 60, 3) (še dub is probably an asyntactic construction)

(192) balağ (...) ^DNin.ğír.su-ra É.ninnu (...)-a mu-na-da-ku₄-ku₄ 'he enters before Ninğirsu in the Eninnu with the lyre' (Gudea, cyl. A VII 24-29)

(193) ^DNin.sikil.a-da á mu-da-áğ 'he instructed Ninsikila' (Gudea, cyl. A XV 15)

(194) ^DSuen-ra^a ^DEn.líl mu(-un)-da-húl (a: -da), /mu-n.da-húl/ 'Enlil rejoiced over Suen' (Nanna-Suen's Journey to Nippur 319). Cf.:

(195) é-d[a ..] lugal i[m]-da-hú[l] 'the king rejoiced over the temple' (Gudea, cyl. B XX 14)

§ 193. The comitative postposition also occurs in the expression -bi-da 'and', lit.: 'with its':

(196) zì.da-bi da-ba gub-ba-bi ^{íd}Idigna ^{íd}Buranun-bi-da hé.ğál lah₅-àm 'the *zida*-vessel standing at its side is the Tigris and the Euphrates bringing abundance' (Gudea, cyl. B XVII 9-11)

§ 194. NOUN-da nu-me-a 'without'. For a discussion of this expression, see Gragg, 1968 p. 100.

(197) kur gal ^DEn.líl-da nu-me-a uru nu-dù á.dam ki li-bí-ib-ğar, /nu-í-me-a/, /nu-í-dù/, /nu-bi-b-ğar/ 'without the great mountain, Enlil, no city is built, no settlement is founded' (Enlil Hymn 108-109)

Terminative

§ 195. The basic form of the terminative postposition is /eše/, but it is most often written -šè, e.g., é-šè 'to the house', an-šè 'to heaven', etc. Mainly in later periods (i.e. after NS) the postposition can be abbreviated to [š] after a grammatical element ending in a vowel (e.g., -bi, -ğu₁₀, -a, etc.): šu-ğu₁₀-uš 'into my hand', ud ul.lí-a-aš 'for ever' (lit.: 'to remote days' see ex. 210). This happens only exceptionally after a noun or adjective or a verbal stem: níg.ba-aš < /níg.ba-eše/ 'as a gift' (ex. 206), Aratta^{ki}-aš (ex. 231).

§ 196. The terminative is used with both animate and inanimate nouns. In the prefix chain of the verb the terminative occurs as -ši-, see § 451.

§ 197. Terminative denotes the motion towards something:

(198) uru-šè ğá-e ga-ğen 'let me go to the city' (Lugalbanda and Enmerkar 272)

(199) ^DEn.líl-le (...) kur gú-erin₇ ^{ki}-na-šè^a igi-ni^b [b]a-an-íl (a: var. om.; b: -na) 'Enlil lifted his eye towards the hostile country' (Curse of Akkade 153-154)

(200) ki.sur.ra ^DNin.ğír.su-ka-ta a.ab-šè maškim di e-ğál-lam 'from the boundary of Ningirsu until the sea there was a bailiff' (Ukg. 4 VII 12-16)

§ 198. In a non-dimensional sense terminative also means 'to', 'as regards', 'concerning' or 'because of, for the sake of':

(201) lú an-gin₇ ri-ba ki-gin₇ ri-ba-šè (...) šeš-g̃u₁₀ ᴰNin.g̃ír.su
ga-nam-me-àm 'concerning the man as big as heaven, as big
as the earth – it was verily my brother Ning̃irsu' (Gudea,
cyl. A V 13-17)

(202) nam.ti-la-ni-šè mu-na-dù 'he has built it for him for the
sake of his life' (Amar-Sin, Brick E 27-28 = *SAK* p. 198)

(203) a.ra.zu ge-na-g̃u₁₀-šè hu-mu-ši-in-še-ge-eš-a, /ha-mu-ši-n-
še.g-eš-a/ 'when they have allowed me (to do so and so) because of my steadfast prayer' (Sin-iddinam 6 I 26-27)

§ 199. The terminative postposition occurs with verbs denoting 'to
make into', 'to call, to name' and the like:

(204) alam na-šè mu-tu 'he has formed it into a statue of stone'
(Gudea, St. D IV 17)

(205) mu-šè mu-na-sa₄ 'he has called it by the name (...)' (Gudea,
St. D V 8 = E IX 4)

(206) níg.ba-aš ha-ma-an-ba-e, /ha-mu-DAT.1.sg.-n-ba-e/ 'let
her give it to me as a present' (Warad-Sin 5, 17-18)

(207) ud ᴰEn.líl-le ᴰNin.urta ur.sag̃ kalag-ga-ni maškim-šè mu-
ni-in-tuku-a 'When Enlil has let him have Ninurta, his strong
warrior, as bailiff' (Išme-Dagan 3, 3-7)

§ 200. *Temporal Use of the Terminative*

In temporal expressions -šè means 'to, until': ud min-šè 'in 2 days'
or 'for 2 days', but also ud min-àm means 'for 2 days'.

(208) ud-te-ta g̃i₆-ba-šè 'from evening until morning(?)' (*TCS* I
nr. 56, 9)

(209) 20 guruš ud 12-šè 6 guruš ud 6-šè a.šà Lú.ᴰBa.ba₆-ka-kà
gub-ba-aš nu-gi.in 'it was not confirmed that 20 workers in
12 days and 6 workers in 6 days have been working in the
field of Lu-Baba' (*NG* nr. 213, 36-37)

(210) mu-g̃u₁₀ ud ul.lí-a-aš g̃á-g̃á-dè 'that my name shall be established until remote days' (Šulgi Hymn A 36). Cf. ud ul-la-šè
in Ent. 36 III 6.

§ 201. Terminative is moreover found in the following expressions:

nam-bi-šè 'therefore, for that reason'
/mu ... -ak-eše/ 'for, instead of, because of'

/bar ... -ak-eše/ 'because'
/igi ... -ak-eše/ 'before'
a.na-áš-àm 'why?' (see 'Interrogative Pronouns' § 118).
ur₅-šè-àm 'therefore, so' (see § 100).

For terminative in adverbial expressions, see §§ 84-89; in causal clauses, see § 489.

(211) 1 gín kug.babbar-àm mu-g̃u₁₀-šè Ba.šag₅-ga hé-na-ab-sum-mu, /ha-ī-na-b-sum-e/ 'let him give Bašaga 1 shekel silver on my behalf' (*TCS* I nr. 131, 3-6)

(212) a.na-áš-àm Puzur₄.Ha.ià mu še kur-ra-šè še eštub hé-na-sum 'why has Puzur-Haya given him *eštub*-barley instead of *kur*-barley?' (*TCS* I nr. 125, 3-6)

(213) 3 4/5 še g[ur lugal] 1 gín kug.babbar mu sag̃-g̃á-šè A.tu-ra in-na-sum-ma '(he has sworn) that he has given Atu 3 4/5 royal *gur* barley and 1 shekel of silver for the slave' (*NG* nr. 208, 22-25)

§ 202. In the royal inscriptions of the First Babylonian dynasty the terminative often replaces the original dative. This is probably because of the identification of -šè with the Akkadian preposition *ana* 'to, for':

(214) ᴰNin.hur.sag̃-g̃á ama in-dím-en-na-⟨g̃u₁₀⟩-uš, /ī-n-dím-en-a-g̃u-eše/ 'for Ninhursag̃, my mother who created me' (Samsuiluna A 44-45 (*LIH* 98) = *LIH* 97, 42-43 (Akkad. version): *a-na* ᴰ*Nin-mah AMA ba-ni-ti-ia*)

Ablative-Instrumental

§ 203. The ablative-instrumental postposition is /-ta/, normally written with the sign TA.

§ 204. -da may occur where -ta is expected. In some cases this is probably only a phonetic variation, e.g.,

(215) me-e é-g̃u₁₀-da mušen-gin₇ im-ma-ra-dal-en, /ī-ba-ra (abl.)-dal-en/ 'I, like a bird I will fly out of my house' (Iškur Hymn 17). But cf.:

(216) g̃iš-bi-ta na-an-na-ra-ab-dal-en (Enmerkar and the Lord of Aratta 115)

(217) dirig níg ud.bi.da-ka, /níg ud.bi.ta-ak-a/ 'more than before' (Warad-Sin 18 I 13'). Cf.

(218) dirig ud.bi.da-šè (Rim-Sin 10, 43) and

(219) dirig ud.bi.ta-šè (Rim-Sin 11, 30; 15, 33). These examples are probably atypical since -ta here is no usual postposition but part of the derived noun ud.bi.ta 'old days, the past', lit., 'from those days', see ex. 224, 238.

The variation -ta: -da may, however, also be due to confusion of the instrumental and comitative cases, or to uncertainty about the case with some verbs. Cf. for instance the verb šár 'to mix' which occurs with both -ta, -da and -a(loc.):

(220) šár-ra sahar-ra[a] la-ba-an-da-[b]šár-re-eš[c] (a: var. adds -t[a][??]; b: adds -an-[; c:]-šár-šár[!?]-re-eš), /nu-ba-n-da-šár-eš/ 'would not numerous (enemies) be mixed with dust?' (Gilgameš and Aka 77, cf. 1. 95). But cf.:

(221) sahar-ta ba-da-an-šár (*TCL* XV, 1: 27)

(222) sahar-da im-da-ab-šár (Lugale = *BE* XXXI, 32: 14 with dupl. *RA* 11, 82 rev. 3: sahar-ta).

(223) kug šag₅-ga-zu sahar kur-ra-ka nam-ba-da-ab-šár-re, /sahar kur-ak-a na-ba-da-b-šár-en/ 'do not mix your good silver with (lit.: 'in') the dust of the Netherworld!' (Inanna's Descent 44)

This verb probably takes either instrumental ('to mix with') or locative ('to mix in(to)') with the noun, but the prefixes of the verbal form are regularly ba-da- which probably derives from /ba-ta-/, cf. § 449.

I prefer to interpret sahar-ra in ex. 220 as /sahar-a(loc.)/ and not as /sahar-ta/ as Falkenstein did, *GSGL* I p. 116.

§ 205. The ablative-instrumental postposition -ta is used with inanimate beings only. The direction away from a person is expressed with ki: /ki PN-ak-ta/ 'from PN', lit.: 'from the place of PN'.

Cf. also the following compounds with -ta:

/eğer ...-ak-ta/ 'from the back of ...' = 'after, behind'
/ki ...-ak-ta/ 'from the place of ...' = 'from' with animate beings
/šà ...-ak-ta/ 'from the heart of ...' = 'out of, from among'
/šu ...-ak-ta/ 'with the hand of ...' = 'under the authority of'

§ 206. Ablative is the motion away from something, e.g. Unug^{ki}-ta ba-ǧen 'he went from Uruk', but it can be used with every action or state having a starting point both in a local and a temporal sense (for the temporal use of -ta see also below §§ 207-208):

(224) ud ^DNin.ǧír.su (...)-ke₄ šà lú 36000-ta šu-ni e-ma-ta-dab₅ - ba-a nam.tar-ra ud-bi-ta e-šè-ǧar, /ì-ba-ta-(n-)dab₅-a-a/, /ì-ši-(n-)ǧar/ 'after Ninǧirsu has taken his hand out of 36.000 men (i.e. chosen him among 36.000 men), he (Uru- inimgina) re-established the order of former days' (Ukg. 4 VII 29-VIII 9)

(225) tukumbi nu-na-an-sum é-a-ni-ta íb-su-su, /nu-ì-na-n- sum/, /ì-b-su.su-e/ 'if he does not give it to him, he shall re- store it out of his (own) possessions (lit.: house)' (*TCS* I nr. 177, 8-11)

(226) eren₂ gal-ǧu₁₀ sig-ta igi.nim-šè ab-ta kur ^{ǧiš}eren-šè (...) gú ga-mu-ni-íb-ǧar, /ga-mu-ni-b-ǧar/ 'my great army from below to above, from the sea to the cedar mountain, I will let submit to him' (Enmerkar and Ensuhkešdana 159-160)

§ 207. -ta with temporal expressions: ud/mu ...-ta means 'since ...' or '... days/years ago', e.g.,

(227) mu ^DŠu.^DSuen lugal-ta 'since the year Šu-Suen (became) king' (*TCS* I nr. 148, 6)

(228) mu-da-20-ta Az.ǧu₁₀ A.al.la dumu-na in-na-ba-a, /ì-na- (n-)ba-a/ '(they have sworn) that Azǧu has given him (= the slave) to Alla, his son, twenty years ago' (*NG* nr. 31, 10-13). In mu-da-...-ta the element -da- is not clear, see Th. Jacob- sen in: J.B. Siegel, 1947 p. 32 n. 15, and Falkenstein, *NG* III p. 142.

(229) 1 ǧeme₂ iti ^DDumu.zi-ta ud 1-àm ba-ra-zal Á.nin.ǧá.ta ì- dab₅ 'Aninǧata has taken one slave-girl on the first day of the month of Dumuzi (lit.: from the month of Dumuzi one day has passed)' (*TCS* I nr. 297, 3-4)

§ 208. Temporal clauses are: ud ...-a-ta 'after ...' and eǧer ...-a-ta, 'after ...', or simply ...-a-ta (see also § 489):

(230) En.suh.kešda.an.na-ke₄ inim-bi ǧiš ba-an-tuku-a-ta En.me. er.kár-ra lú ^amu-un-ši-in-gi₄-gi₄ ^a (a-a: mu-e-ši-in-gi₄), /mu-n.ši-n-gi₄.gi₄-e/ 'Ensuhkešdana, having heard this

matter, sends a man to Enmerkar' (Enmerkar and Ensuhkešdana 273-274)

(231) Ha.ma.zu hul-a-ta Aratta^{ki}(-aš) bal-a 'When Hamazu had
been destroyed, he crossed over to Aratta' (Enmerkar and
Ensuhkešdana 137)

§ 209. As in other languages the ablative postposition -ta also denotes
the instrument or means:

(232) á ^DNanše-ta á ^DNin.ĝír.su-ka-ta Gù.dé.a ĝidru sum-ma
^DNin.ĝír.su-ka-ra Má.gan^{ki} Me.luh.ha^{ki} Gu.bi^{ki} kur Dil-
mun^{ki} gú ĝiš mu-na-ĝál-la-àm 'by the means of /because of
the strength of Nanše and the strength of Ninĝirsu Magan,
Meluhha, Gubi and the mountain Dilmun submitted to Gudea whom Ninĝirsu has given the sceptre' (Gudea, St. D IV
2-11)

(233) ^DNin.ĝír.su ur.saĝ ^DEn.líl-lá-ke₄ inim si.sá-ni-ta Umma^{ki}-
da dam.ha.ra e-da-ak, /í-da-(n-)ak/ 'Ninĝirsu, the warrior
of Enlil, at his (i.e. Enlil's) righteous word made battle with
Umma' (Ent. 28 I 22-27). inim-(...)-ta is a very commonly
used phrase in the Sumerian royal inscriptions.

(234) ud (...) ^{íd}Idigna íd šà dùg-ga-na usu ma.da-ni-ta im-mi-
in-ba.al-la-a, /í-bi-n-ba.al-a-a/ 'when he has dug the Tigris,
the river of his pleased heart, with the power of his land'
(Sin-iddinam 3, 12-15)

(235) ^{kuš}guru₂₁-bi zú-ni-ta hé-HAR-re 'may he chew its door
straps with his teeth' (Curse of Akkade 255)

§ 210. Similar to the instrumental meaning is the use of -ta with expressions of emotion:

lipiš-ta 'in anger'
šà ge-na-ni-ta 'of one's own accord' (lit.: with one's firm heart')
šà húl-la-ni-ta 'with (his/her) joyful heart'

Cf. Gragg, SDI p. 31 with examples.

§ 211. The postposition -ta also denotes distributive: 'each'.

(236) 4 guruš á-bi 0.0.4.-ta 'four workers — their wages (are) 4
bán each' (TCS I nr. 17, 3)

(237) ud ^{íd}Idigna íd gu-la mu-ba.al-la-a, á lú diš-e še⌈x x⌉-ta

ninda 2 sila$_3$-ta kaš 4 sila$_3$-ta ì 2 gín-ta-àm, ud diš-a ur$_5$-gin$_7$ šu ha-ba-an-ti, /mu-ba.al-a-a/, /ha-ba-n-ti/ 'when I dug the Tigris, the big river, (as) wages each (lit.: one) man (received) ⌜xx⌝ barley, 2 *sila* bread, 4 *sila* beer and 2 shekel oil, daily (lit.: in one day) he received like this' (Sin-iddinam 6 II 16-24)

(238) munus ud.bi.ta-ke$_4$-ne nita 2-ta ì-tuku-àm 'the women of the past married two men each' (Ukg. 6 III 20-22)

§ 212. It has been noted that -ta also may stand for locative, cf. Gragg, *SDI* p. 30 n. 3 and p. 31 (n. 1: 'In those 'locative' uses of the ablative, the -ta- may indicate deixis 'over there'.'); A. Shaffer, 1969, 433-46; A. Falkenstein, *GSGL* II p. 149f.

In most of the examples quoted in these works -ta seems to denote the origin and must thus be regarded as an aspect of the ablative rather than a 'locative use' (ex. 239, 240). In other cases the use of ablative is due to different view of the direction of some verbs, e.g. in Sumerian something is hanging *from* a nail and not *on* a nail (ex. 241).

(239) ^{uru}Ur.su^{ki} hur.saĝ Eb.la-ta ^{ĝiš}Za.ba.lum (...) ad-šè mu-ak-ak 'from Ursu, the mountain Ebla, they made Zabalum-wood to beams' (or perhaps: Z.-wood from Ursu) (*GSGL* II p. 149: 'in Ursu ..') (Gudea, St. B V 53-58)

(240) ká ki lugal ku$_4$-bi-ta hu.rí.in am-šè igi íl-íl-dam 'from the gate where the king is entering the *hurin*-bird is looking for the wild bull' (*GSGL* II p. 150: '*an seinem Tor* ...') (Gudea, cyl A XXV 5-6)

(241) uzu níg.sìg(-ga) ^{ĝiš}kak-ta (igi-ni) lú ^{a}ba-da-an-lá^a (a-a: mu-un-da-lá; ba-an-ta-lá) 'they hung up the corpse on a nail (before her)' (Inanna's Descent 172)

The phrase sahar-ta which frequently occurs with the verb tuš 'to sit, to live', can, however, hardly be interpreted as ablative but denotes apparently the locative: 'to sit in (the) dust':

(242) ^{D}A.nun.na-ke$_4$ sahar-ta im-mi-in-dúr-dúr-ru-ne-eš, /ì-bi-n-dúr.durun-eš/ 'The Anuna Gods sat there in the dust' (Enki and Ninhursaĝ 220)

§ 213. In the prefix chain of the verb the ablative is referred to by the prefixes -ta- and -ra-; the instrumental which occurs less frequently is expressed by -ta-. The other meanings of the postposition -ta, i.e. distributive, emotions, temporal, are not repeated in the prefix chain. For further details see §§ 460-469.

Equative

§ 214. The equative postposition is mostly written with the sign GIM which may be read both -gim and -gin$_7$. Because of the frequent spelling -GIM-nam = equ. + COP and the syllabic writings -gi-in etc. (cf. § 215), -gin$_7$ is perhaps the most probable form of the postposition, but note that -gim-ma-àm is also found (ex. 249), see § 29.

> A. Poebel, *GSG* p. 128f., thought the basic form of the equative to be /gimin/, probably because of the writing -GIM-nam, which he analysed as /-gimin-am/, and the late form e-qi-me (*ASK* 7 obv. 4, corresponding to a-gim 'how'). Poebel interpreted /-gimin/ as gi = '*eins*', min = '*zwei*', i.e. '*eins ist (wie) das andere*' (*GSG* p. 123). This 'basic' form is, however, nowhere attested, and the proposed etymology is rather doubtful.

> The writing of -gé is attested in a NS letter:
>
> (243) a.ba šeš-g̃u$_{10}$-gé 'who is like my brother?' (*TCS* I nr. 143, 8)
>
> The same expression with -gin$_7$ instead of -gé occurs frequently in the NS letters (cf. *TCS* I p. 120). Because of the writing -gé E. Sollberger thought -ge(n) to be the original form of the postposition (*TCS* I p. 120), but to me it seems more likely that -gé is an exception or a mistake.

§ 215. In the unorthographic texts the syllabic writings -gi-in, -ge-en, -gi$_4$-in can be found (cf. Falkenstein, 1959a p. 39f.; Sjöberg, 1960 p. 91): ab.ba-gi.in (= ab.ba-gin$_7$) 'like the sea' (*VS* II 1, 2 = Sjöberg, 1960 p. 89); zi-gi-in (= za-a-gin$_7$) 'like you' (*CT* XV 15, 21); zi-gi$_4$-in (= zì-gin$_7$) 'like flour' (*VS* II 2 iii 28); cf. also ù-ki = ùz-gin$_7$ 'like a goat' (*VS* II 94, 13 and *VS* II 95, 13 = Krecher, 1967b p. 34).

§ 216. /-gin$_7$/ means: 'like', 'as'; it is used in comparisons. /-gin$_7$/ is used with both animate and inanimate nouns.

The comparison may consist of a noun, frequently also of a non-finite verb or of a relative clause; -gin$_7$ stands of course at the end of the whole phrase. The phrase determined by -gin$_7$ stands normally after the word with which it is compared (é hur.sag̃-gin$_7$: 'the house like a mountain', ex. 245).

The enclitic copula is frequently added after the equative postposition (ex. 249); the copula is probably emphatic, since it is often rendered as -ma in Akkadian (cf. Römer, 1980 p. 92).

§ 217.

(244) Zabalam^{ki}-e u$_8$ sila$_4$ gur$_5$ -a-gin$_7$ sig$_4$ mu-da-gi$_4$ -gi$_4$ 'Zabalam cries like an ewe who has been cut off from (its) kid' (Lugalzagesi, *BE* I 87 II 43-45)

(245) é hur.sağ-gin$_7$ im-mú-mú-ne 'they made the house grow like a mountain' (Gudea, cyl. A XXI 19)

(246) u$_4$.sar gibil-gin$_7$ men bí-íl 'he made it (the house) wear a crown like the new moon' (Gudea, cyl. A XXIV 10)

(247) ki-ba ^DIštaran-gin$_7$ di uru-ğá si ba-ni-íb-sá-e 'on this place I, like Ištaran, shall put right the judgement of my city' (Gudea, cyl. A X 26)

(248) a-bi a-gin$_7$ ^amu-e^a-nağ-a^b-gin$_7$ ^amu-e^a-bal-e (a-a: mu-un-; b: om.) 'you have crossed their (= the rivers') water as if you have drunk it' (Lugalbanda and Enmerkar 237)

(249) ğá-nu Lugal.bàn.da-ğu$_{10}$ inim šà-ga sè-ge ur$_5$ -gim-ma-àm, /ğen + í/, /sè.g + í/ 'come, my Lugalbanda, place the word to the heart, so it shall be!' (Lugalbanda and Enmerkar 162-163)

§ 218. -gin$_7$(-nam) may occur after a finite verb, then probably in a temporal sense: 'just as ...' (see Römer, 1980 p. 94).

(250) lú še lugal-ğu$_{10}$ ì-me-a bí-in-dug$_4$ -ga-gin$_7$ -nam, /bi-n-dug$_4$ -a-gin-am/ 'this man is my king! Just as he has said this' (Gilgameš and Aka 91-92)

§ 219. The enclitic copula may alternate with or even replace the equative postposition. -àm is thus also translated by *kīma* 'like' (see W. Heimpel, 1968 p. 24-42 with references and many examples).

§ 220. The equative is not incorporated in the prefix chain of the verb.

THE VERB

§ 221. The Verbal Forms

The Sumerian verb cannot be inflected but its various forms are constructed by adding prefixes and/or affixes of different kinds to the verbal root. These constructions can, both on the morphological and on the syntactic level, be separated into two groups: finite and non-finite verbal forms.

1. Finite constructions serve as the main verb of a sentence. They consist of a prefix chain with 3-4 elements on the average + the verbal root + possibly a pronominal suffix: /mu-na-ni- + ku$_4$.r + -en/ = 'I(-en) have entered(ku$_4$.r) there(-ni-) before him(-na-).'

    For the construction of finite forms and their morphemes, see § 272ff.

2. A non-finite form is either the verbal stem alone, or the stem + a suffix: /-a/, /-e/ or COP. Such forms stand attributively to nouns.

    For the construction of non-finite forms, see §§ 500-527.

For other constructions: imperatives and the rare 'finite' forms without prefix chain, see § 273.

§ 222. The Verbal Stems

The verb has three or four different stems: 1. the *hamṭu* stem, 2. the reduplicated *hamṭu* stem, 3. the *marû* stem, and 4. the stem with the morpheme /ed/ (perhaps denoting the future tense).

According to the shape of the *marû* stem the verbs are divided into four classes: I. Regular Verbs, II. Reduplication Class, III. Alternating Class, and IV. Complementary Verbs.

The regular verbs have no *marû* stem, but only one basic stem, = the *hamṭu* stem. In those forms where the *marû* stem of the other verbal classes occurs, the regular verbs use the *hamṭu* stem (like in /sum + ed/).

	Hamṭu stem/ basic stem	*Hamṭu* redupl./ total redupl. (§§ 242-250)	*Marû* stem	'Future' stem (§§ 252-259)
I Regular Verbs (§§ 224-226)	sum	sum-sum		sum + /ed/
II Reduplication Class (§§ 227-228)	g̃ar	g̃ar-g̃ar	Partial redupl. g̃á-g̃á	g̃á-g̃á + /ed/
III Alternating Class (§ 229)	è	è-è	Alternated stem è-d	è-d + /ed/
IV Complement- ary Verbs (§ 230)	dug₄ de₆	dug₄-dug₄ (?)	Comple- mentary stem e túm	(?) túm + /ed/

For the terms *hamṭu* and *marû* and the functions of these stems, see §§ 231-241.

The Verbal Classes

§ 223. The Sumerian verbs can be classified according to their way of forming the *marû* stem. It is, however, not always without problems to consider the correct *marû* stem of a verb, since the *marû* reduplication can be confused with the reduplication of the *hamṭu* stem. The *marû* stem can most easily be recognized from the non-finite form: VERB-ed-e, but not all Sumerian verbs have by now been classified with certainty. It is of course also possible that some verbs have changed class which could explain some apparently contradicting forms.

M. Yoshikawa, 1968a, was the first to introduce the classification of the Sumerian verbs on the basis of non-finite /ed/-forms. In that study and in his following articles on *hamṭu* and *marû* (1968b and 1974) Yoshikawa classified many of the verbs listed below.

D.O. Edzard, 1971a, 1972 and 1976a, accepted the principle of Yoshikawa's classification, but modified it on some important points (see 1976a, 45-52; 55-59).

The classification presented here differs in some respects from those of both Yoshikawa and Edzard, see below to the individual classes.

I. Class of Regular Verbs

§ 224. The regular verbs are those which have no special *marû* stem at all, but only one basic root = the *hamṭu* stem. These are in fact the majority of the Sumerian verbs, and therefore the term 'regular verbs' is used. *Hamṭu* and *marû* forms of these verbs can thus be distinguished only in the finite transitive verb, whereas intransitive forms can express the *hamṭu* aspect only.

> M. Yoshikawa, 1968a, called this class 'Affixation Group', because he regarded the pronominal suffix /-e/ of the 3.sg. transitive as a *marû* element of this class of verbs, e.g. tar = *hamṭu* : tare = *marû* (see § 233). D.O. Edzard, who did not follow the affixation theory of Yoshikawa called this class *'unveränderliche Klasse'* but used the term *'regelmäßige Verben'* about all verbs except the complementary stems (1976a p. 48).

§ 225. 50-70% of the Sumerian verbs presumably belong to the class 'Regular Verbs'. The verbs listed below are those which almost with certainty can be classified here, but there are no doubt more.

áǧ 'to measure'	dúb 'to heap up'
ak 'to do, to make'	e₁₁.d 'to descend'
ba 'to give'	gam 'to bow down'
bal 'to transfer, to cross'	gi.n 'to be firm'
bar 'to open, to split'	gíd 'to be long'
dab₅ 'to seize'	gu₇ 'to eat'
dah 'to add, to augment'	gub 'to stand (sing.)'
dal 'to fly'	gul 'to destroy'
dé 'to pour'	gur 'to come back'
dib/díb 'to pass'	ǧál 'to be'
dím 'to make, to fashion'	ha.lam 'to destroy'
dù 'to build'	ha.za 'to grasp'
du₈ 'to open, to loosen'	huǧ 'to hire'

húl 'to rejoice'
hu.luh 'to be frightened'
kàm 'to change'
kar 'to go/take away'
kud.r 'to cut'
kúr 'to act as an enemy, to change'
kúš.ù 'to be troubled'
lá 'to carry'
lu.g 'to swarm'
nigin 'to wander'
pad.r 'to break'
pàd 'to call'
peš 'to grow'
ru.gú 'to withstand'
sá 'to be equal to, etc.'
sa$_4$ 'to name'
zar.re.eš...sal 'to heap up'
sar 'to chase'
si.g 'to level'
sì.g 'to place'

sìg 'to beat'
silig 'to cease'
sum 'to give'
še.g 'to obey'
šed$_7$ 'to cool'
šid 'to count'
šub 'to throw'
šúr 'to be enraged'
tab 'to double'
tag 'to touch'
tar 'to cut'
ti.l 'to live (sing.)'
tu$_{10/11}$.b 'to smite'
tuš 'to sit (sing.)'
ul$_4$ 'to hurry'
uru$_4$ 'to plough'
ús 'to follow'
zàh, záh 'to flee'
zal 'to pass'
zi.r 'to tear out'

§ 226. Adjectives which are used as verbs belong, as a rule, to the class of regular verbs, for instance:

dağal 'to be/make wide'
dùg 'to be/make sweet'
dugud 'to be/make heavy'
gal 'to be/make big'
galam 'to be/make artful'
gibil 'to be/make new'
gur$_4$ 'to be/make thick'

kal 'to be/make precious'
kalag 'to be/make strong'
kug 'to be/make clean'
mah 'to be/make magnificent'
sikil 'to be/make pure'
silim 'to be/make healthy'
tur 'to be/make small'

II. Reduplication Class

§ 227. The verbs belonging to this class form the *marû* stem by partial reduplication. *Hamṭu* stems which end in a consonant may regularly lose this, e.g., ğá-ğá from ğar, ku$_4$-ku$_4$ from ku$_4$-r.

In most cases the exact phonetic shape of a reduplicated verb is not known, because the reduplication is simply rendered by doubling the word sign. It must, however, be assumed that some phonetic rules are operating, e.g., $C_1 VC_2 + C_1 VC_2 > C_1 V-C_1 V$, or $C_1 VC_2 - C_1 V$, or $C_1 VC_1 -C_2 V$ etc. (cf. § 243). Of verbs with two syllables there are even more possibilities, but phonetic writings are rare.

In contrast to the partial *marû* reduplication the *hamṭu* reduplication is probably a total reduplication, thus ǧar-ǧar versus ǧá-ǧá, see §§ 242-243. In the case of some verbs, however, the two kinds of reduplication will be identical, e.g., gi₄-gi₄ from the verb gi₄ 'to return'.

§ 228. About 25% of the Sumerian verbs have reduplicated forms which could probably classify them as members of the reduplication class. However, because of the possible confusion with the *hamṭu* reduplication, so far only a minor part can be proved as belonging to this class.

gi₄: gi₄-gi₄ 'to return'
ǧar: ǧá-ǧá 'to place'
he: he-he 'to mix'
kár: KÁR-KÁR, igi...kár 'to examine'
kin: KIN-KIN 'to seek'
ku: ku-ku, ù...ku 'to sleep'
ku₄.r: ku₄-ku₄ 'to enter'
mú: mú-mú 'to grow'
naǧ: na₈-na₈ 'to drink'
ra: ra-ra 'to hit'
si: si-si 'to fill'
sa₁₀: sa₁₀-sa₁₀ 'to buy/sell'

šag₅: ša₆-ša₆ 'to be good, pleasant'
šéš: še₈-še₈ 'to anoint, to shed tears'
šú: šú-šú 'to cover'
tag₄: TAG₄-TAG₄ 'to leave'
tu₅: tu₅-tu₅, a...tu₅ 'to bathe'
tuk₄: TUK₄-TUK₄ 'to tremble'
tuku: TUKU-TUKU 'to have'
ùr: ùr-ùr 'to drag'
zìg: zi-zi 'to rise, to lift'
zu: zu-zu 'to know'

The writings with capital letters indicate that the pronunciation of the reduplicated stem is uncertain.

§ 229. *III. Alternating Class*

This class has only few members, so far three verbs have been classified as such. The verbs in question have both a short and an expanded form serving as *hamṭu* and *marû* stem, respectively.

It is probable that more verbs whose phonetic representation of the different stems is not yet exactly known should be classified here.

M. Yoshikawa treated these verbs and the complementary verbs as one class called 'Alternation Group' (cf. for instance 1968a p. 259ff. and 1968b p. 411ff.). D.O. Edzard, 1976a p. 48, however, argued that verbs like è:è-d and te:te-ǧ should be separated from verbs having two entirely different stems:

'stammverändernde Klasse' and *'Klasse der Komplementärverben'*, respectively. This view has been followed here.

è : è-d 'to go out'
ri : ri.g 'to pour' etc.
te/ti : te/ti-g̃ 'to approach'

§ 230. *IV. Complementary Verbs*

Only a limited number of verbs have two entirely different roots serving as *hamṭu* and *marû* stem. The *marû* stem can in some cases also serve as a plural verb (see § 266).

de$_6$: tùm/túm 'to bring (sing.)'
dug$_4$: e 'to say (sing.)' (with plural erg. subject e is used in both *hamṭu* and *marû* forms)
g̃en : du 'to go (sing.)'
re$_7$: su$_8$-b 'to go (plur.)'
úš : ug$_5$ or ug$_6$ 'to die (sing.)' (with plural abs. subject ug$_{5/6}$ is used in both *hamṭu* and *marû* forms)

The *Hamṭu* and the *Marû* Stem

§ 231. *The Terms Hamṭu and Marû*

The terms *hamṭu* and *marû* are borrowed from the bilingual grammatical and lexical lists. In these texts there are a few instances where the basic stem of a verb (e.g. zu or dug$_4$) is marked as *hamṭu*, lit.: 'quick', and the reduplicated (e.g. zu-zu) or complementary stem (e.g. e) is denoted as *marû*, lit. 'fat' (cf. *CAD* H p. 71 and M/1 p. 306f.).

These terms have been understood as describing different aspects of the Sumerian verb, but in fact it is also possible that they refer to the Akkadian tranlations and not primarily to the meanings of the Sumerian stems.[28] However, the terms *hamṭu* and *marû* have gained access into the Sumerian grammar as the names of the different stems of some verbs (i.e. class II-IV), and it therefore seems most convenient to maintain them here, as long as the exact meanings of the stems in Sumerian are not known, and we therefore cannot give them more appropriate names. It must, however, be noted that our use of the

---

28. Cf. G. Steiner, 1981b p. 10ff.

Akkadian terms probably differs from that of the Akkadian scribes who introduced them.

§ 232. *Morphology*

Hamṭu is the basic stem, whereas the *marû* stem in most cases is an extension of the *hamṭu* stem (class II and III). It is remarkable that the regular verbs (= class I), which comprise 50% or more of all verbs, have no *marû* stem at all but only a basic stem or, in other words, a *hamṭu* stem.

The shape of the *marû* stem of the regular verbs is disputed. M. Yoshikawa, who started the discussion about the *hamṭu* and *marû* stems, argued that the verbs of class I form the *marû* stem through the suffix /-e/, thus for instance /tar/ = *hamṭu*, /tare/ = *marû*. Yoshikawa thus analyses tar-re-da as /tare-d-a/ instead of traditional /tar-ed-a/ (1968a). The transitive 3.sg. form ...-tar-e he analyses as /...-tare-Ø/ instead of traditional /...-tar-e/ where /-e/ is the pronominal suffix of 3.sg. transitive, *marû* (1974 p. 18). Yoshikawa therefore called the class of these verbs for 'Affixation Group'.

D.O. Edzard, on the other hand, 1976a p. 47ff., maintained the view that /-e/ is a pronominal ending and thus no *marû* affix. Therefore according to Edzard the verbs of class I do not change their basic stem, and he named them '*unveränderliche Klasse*'. This view is followed here.

§ 233. *The Affix /-e/: Marû Mark or Pronominal Element?*

The crux of the discussion of the *marû*-conjugation is the analysis of the pronominal suffixes. The traditional view is that /-en/, /-e/, /-en‑den/, /-enzen/ and /-ene/ are the transitive subject elements of the 'present-future' (= the *marû*-conjugation), and that the vowel [e] of these elements disappears after a vowel, e.g., /tar-en/ > -tar-re-en, but /-ǵá.ǵá-en/ > -ǵá-ǵá-an. However, according to Yoshikawa's theory mentioned above (§ 232) [e] will appear only in verbs of class I and not together with the *marû* stems of class II, III and IV: 1.sg.: /-tare-n/, /-ǵá.ǵá-n/, 3.sg.: /-tare-Ø/, /ǵá.ǵá-Ø/, and non-finite: /tare-d-a/, /ǵá.ǵá-d-a/ (see Yoshikawa, 1968a and 1974).

This theory has some obvious advantages: all verbs have then both a *hamṭu* and a *marû* stem to be recognized independent of the occurrence of pronominal elements. However, tempting as this theory is, it can neither be proved nor refuted. That the [e] does not occur after the *marû* stem of the verbs of class II, III and IV can be explained by the vocalic endings of most verbs: /-e/ is then contracted after a vowel. On the other hand there are no clear instances of a verb of class II, III or IV with an [e] after a consonant contradicting Yoshikawa's theory, and whenever such evidence might be found, it could be explained as a late analogy. Therefore, it does not seem that this problem can be easily settled.

I shall, however, refer to one feature of the Sumerian language structure which, I think, speaks against Yoshikawa's theory. Consonantic morphemes seem to be in conflict with the language structure since double consonant in initial or final position of a syllable cannot be expressed, and all other morphological elements of the Sumerian language are either vocalic or can be separated into syllables of the shape CV or VC.[29] If, therefore, the subject elements of the transitive *marû* form are /-n/, /-nden/, /-nzen/, /-ne/, it must also be assumed that this is the phonetic shape of the intransitive subject elements. But in this case there would often have to be double consonants in final position which would be impossible to express in the writing, and which moreover are contrary to the phonetic system of Sumerian. In fact, we have the intransitive form ì-ku₄-re-en 'I entered', showing that at least the intransitive subject element must be /-en/, and not /-n/: /ì-ku₄.r-en/.

§ 234. *Occurrences of Hamṭu and Marû*

Both the *hamṭu* and the *marû* stem occur in finite constructions. The transitive verb distinguishes a *hamṭu* conjugation with pronominal prefixes and a *marû* conjugation with pronominal suffixes, whereas the intransitive verb has only one conjugation with pronominal suffixes for both stems.[30]

Whereas verbs of class II, III and IV are able to distinguish *hamṭu* and *marû* in both intransitive and transitive forms, the regular verbs have no intransitive *marû* forms, but only forms with the *hamṭu* stem.[31]

---

29. The only exceptions are the pronominal elements /-n-/ and /-b-/ which, however, always occur after verbal prefixes or after case elements ending in a vowel.
30. For these conjugations, see §§ 279-282.
31. For the possibility that VERB + /ed/ of the regular verbs replaces the *marû* forms of the intransitive verb, see § 256.

The *hamṭu* stem occurs as a non-finite verb in the asyntactic form, e.g., / g̃ar/, in the subordinate form, e.g., /g̃ar-a/, as well as with the enclitic copula, e.g., /g̃ar-am/. The *marû* stem, on the other hand, apparently does not occur in non-finite constructions, here the 'future' stem is used instead, e.g., /g̃á.g̃á-ed/, /g̃á.g̃á-ed-a/, /g̃á.g̃á-ed-am/.[32] The *hamṭu* stem is moreover obligatory in the imperative.

Some modal prefixes prefer either the *hamṭu* or the *marû* stem, or they have different meanings depending on whether they are combined with *hamṭu* or *marû*: /ga-/, cohortative, has always *hamṭu*; /ha-/ is affirmative with *hamṭu*, precative with *marû*; /na-/ is affirmative with *hamṭu*, prohibitive with *marû*; /bara-/ is negative with *hamṭu*, vetitive with *marû*.

The Meanings of the Hamṭu and the Marû Stem

§ 235. In the *hamṭu-marû* discussion of the last 15 years the morphology of the stems has been discussed in details whereas less attention has been given to the meanings of *hamṭu* versus *marû*. In general some aspectual contrast is assumed, but this has not been systematically investigated.

Lexical and literary texts render the finite *hamṭu* forms mostly with Akkadian preterites, the *marû* forms with the Akkadian present tense. In traditional Sumerian grammars the two transitive conjugations were thus called: preterite (= *hamṭu*) and present-future (= *marû*), cf. for instance A. Poebel, *GSG* p. 173 and A. Falkenstein, 1959a p. 44. The distinction between the tenses was thought to be expressed by the different distribution of the pronominal elements, and the intransitive verb, which apparently does not distinguish tenses, was said to have only one tense or form: 'the normal form' (German: '*Normalform*', cf. Falkenstein, 1959a p. 45).

However, as it was realized that the verb distinguishes different stems, the preterite and the present-future tenses were considered to be replaced by the *hamṭu* and *marû*, which probably expresses aspectual differences: perfective and imperfective, or punctual and durative (see § 237). So M. Yoshikawa, 1968b p. 416: 'Hence it is quite probable that at least the present-future tense, as has been almost universally accepted, is to be replaced preferably by the *marû* aspect, while

---

32. For the probable presence of /ed/ in the asyntactic non-finite form, see § 509.

we are probably to replace the preterit tense with the *hamṭu* aspect. This is to argue that the main axis of the Sumerian verbal system does not consist in the temporal difference, but, mainly, in the aspectual difference.'

D.O. Edzard, on the other hand, argued against the replacement of the categories preterite and present(-future) by *hamṭu* and *marû* (1976a p. 46). In his opinion, apparently, the terms *hamṭu* and *marû* point to the verbal form as a whole and not to the possible aspectual meaning of the stem: 'e = *qabû marû* 'sprechen, fett/langsam' sollte heißen, daß der Verbalstamm e in Zusammenhängen vorkommt wie 'Präsens' oder 'Präteritum Plural'. (...) Es ist demnach wohl berechtigt, die traditionellen Bezeichnungen 'Präteritum', 'Präsens' für das transitive Verbum, 'Normalform' für das intransitive Verbum weiter zu verwenden' (1976a p. 54). However, Edzard did not exclude that various verbal forms might have temporal or aspectual functions, primary as well as secondary (1976a p. 54f.).

§ 236. Although *hamṭu* and *marû* originally might have denoted something different, as already mentioned above, I have here chosen to use the terms in the following cases:

1. As terms for two various manifestations of the verb: *hamṭu* = the basic stem of a verb, *marû* = the, in some way or other, changed stem of verbs belonging to class II, III and IV (see §§ 223-230).

2. The term '*hamṭu* conjugation' is used for the transitive finite form with pronominal prefixes (previously 'preterite'), and the term '*marû* conjugation' for the transitive finite form with pronominal suffixes (previously 'present-future'). See §§ 280-282. Since the transitive conjugations probaly do not express tenses (see §§ 237-240), it seems not justified to me to maintain the old terms 'preterite' and 'present-future'.

§ 237. The question about the meaning of the *hamṭu* and the *marû* has not yet been settled. As a matter of fact some aspectual differences of the Sumerian verb has already long been assumed by some scholars.

For previous theories about *hamṭu* and *marû* 'aspects', see D.O. Edzard 1971a p. 209-212.

A. Falkenstein, *GSGL* II p. 155, described '*Präteritum*' like this 'in der Mehrzahl der Fälle eine in der Vergangenheit abgeschloßene Handlung, die im Akkadischen durch den 'Punktual' (*ikšud*) dargestellt wird. In einigen Fällen entspricht es einem echten Perfekt.' 'Präsens-Futur' was defined as: 'eine in der Gegenwart oder in der Zukunft liegende oder eine zeitlose Handlung.'

Th. Jacobsen, 1956, considered two different distinctions: *hamṭu* : *marû*, and ...-VERB-Ø : ...-VERB-e: 'Tentatively we would suggest that the essence of the distinction [i.e. *marû:hamṭu*] might be one between 'process' and 'event', that the *hamṭu* root presents the underlying notion as a single fact, all of one piece and indivisible, whereas the *marû* root presents it as in process, as a striving toward or as successive attempts at, realizing it.' The distinction V-e : V-Ø 'may be defined roughly as one between unfinished and finished action. More precisely V-e indicates that the carrier of the action(subject) is visualized at a point or over a span of time within the duration of the action while V-Ø indicates that the carrier of the action(Subject of Intransitive or Passive, Object of Transitive Active) is visualized at a point or over a span of time subsequent to the action' (p. 22*). Cf. also Jacobsen, 1965: 'The root has normally punctive, singular force. A few roots differ, however, and are on lexical grounds restricted to durative and/or plural meaning. (...) A special curtailing reduplication in which the root elides its final consonant (e.g. g̃á-g̃á from g̃ar) serves to lend it durative, ingressive force' (p. 96).

M. Yoshikawa, 1968b p. 401 n. 2, mentioned as possible meanings of the *hamṭu* and *marû*: 'completion, incompletion, momentariness and continuation.'

§ 238. What the distinction *hamṭu* : *marû* really denotes is a rather difficult question because of the difficulties of interpreting Sumerian texts. When we choose to render a certain verbal form as, e.g., imperfective or durative our translations may be due exclusively to our subjective interpretation of the text, and not necessarily expressed grammatically in the Sumerian form. However, a context where *hamṭu* and *marû* forms are alternating may give some hints to the direction into which the contrast works. From such instances, I think, the functions of *hamṭu* and *marû* can very tentatively be described as follows:

Hamṭu is used in statements of universal validity, it thus expresses states and results of actions, or actions which have been completed.

Marû, on the other hand, denotes actions which have not yet taken place (ex. 251, 252), or actions which are in progress (ex. 254, 255-258). Perhaps more precisely: actions the completion of which has not yet taken place, without specifying whether the action has already started or is to start in the future. Therefore, the *marû* can be translated as both present, future, imperfective and durative. The most characteristic term for the *marû* forms should perhaps be ingressive or inchoative.

The examples below serve to illustrate some of the differences of meaning probably expressed by changing from *hamṭu* to *marû*.

§ 239. *Examples:*

(251) An.ta.sur.ra-ta é ᴰDimgal.Abzu-ka-šè ní ba-ni-è-dè ì-mi-dug₄, /ba-ni-è.d-en/(*marû*), /ï-bi-(n-)dug₄/(*hamṭu*) 'From Antasura to the temple Dimgal-Abzu I shall exercise control (?) (in the future), he has said' (Ent. 28 IV 30-33, the verb means literally 'let fear(?) go out')

(252) nu.síg nu.ma.{nu}su lú á tuku nu–na–ğá–ğá-a ᴰNin.ğír.su-da Uru.inim.gi.na-ke₄ KA-bi KA e-da-kéš, /nu-ï-na-ğá.ğá-e-a/(*marû*), /ï-da-(n-)kéš.dr/(*hamṭu*) 'Uru-inim-gina has made the agreement with Ninğirsu, that he never will deliver (lit.: place) the orphan and the widow to the mighty man' (Ukg. 4 XII 23-28)

(253) ki.sur.ra ᴰNin.ğír.su-ka-ta a.ab-šè maškim di e-ğál-lam, /ï-ğal-am/(*hamṭu*) '(In the old days) there was a bailiff from the boundary ditch of Ninğirsu until the sea' (Ukg. 4 VII 12-16). Compare *marû*:

(254) maškim lú nu-e, /nu-ï-e-e/, '(now) no man acts (lit.: speaks) (as a) bailiff' (Ukg. 4 IX 25)

(255) má.gur₈-ra-na ğiri₃ nam-mi-gub
uru-ni Ninaᵏⁱ-šè íd Ninaᵏⁱ ğen-a má mu-ni-ri
íd-dè húl-la-e kur.ku₄ ì-si.il-e
/na-ï-bi-(n-)gub/(*hamṭu*), /mu-ni-(n-)ri/(*hamṭu*), /ï-si.il-e/(*marû*) 'he has entered his *magur*-boat (lit.: placed the foot on), he has directed the boat towards her city Nina (following) the canal which leads to Nina, (and) he is (now) splitting the waves-of the canal with joy' (Gudea, cyl. A II 4-6). The passage could perhaps also be interpreted as: 'having entered the boat ... etc. he is now going to split the waves'

(256) min-kam ur.saĝ-ĝá-àm á mu-gur li.um za.gìn šu im-mi-du$_8$, é-a ĝiš.hur-bi im-ĝá-ĝá, /mu-(n-)gur/(hamṭu), /ì-bi-(n-)du$_8$/(hamṭu), /ì-m-ĝá.ĝá-e/(marû) 'a second time there was a hero, he had bent (his) arm, he had a tablet of lapis lazuli in (his) hand, and he was drawing the plan of the house (on it)' (Gudea, cyl. A V 2-4). (Or perhaps: 'he was now going to draw a plan')

(257) Gù.dé.a gal mu-zu gal ì-ga-túm-mu, /mu-(n-)zu/(hamṭu), /ì-ga-túm-e/(marû) 'Gudea has experienced great things, and (now) he is also performing them' (Gudea, cyl. A VII 9-10). (Or: 'he is going to perform them')

In the inscription, Gudea, Statue B, the report about the making of the statue is all over in *hamṭu* forms, then col. VII 21ff. it changes to *marû*:

(258) Gù.dé.a alam-e inim im-ma-sum-mu, /ì-ba-sum-e/(marû) 'Gudea is now giving the (following) order to the statue:'

§ 240. I am well aware of the fact that the description of the *hamṭu* and *marû* forms given here is rather vague. However, the system of the stems as well as that of the various conjugations of the finite verb seem to be highly inconsistent and considering the fact that Sumerian verbal forms generally are badly understood (cf. the insufficient determination of most verbal prefixes or the unclear meaning of many verbs) I think that it is not possible to give a definitive answer to the question of the exact meaning and function of the *hamṭu* and *marû* stems. Moreover, it is very probable that the distinction *hamṭu* : *marû* at least to some extent or in some texts functions as a result of the need for appropriate renderings of the Akkadian 'tenses',[33] and this is not necessarily a particularly late phenomenon since the Sumerian-Akkadian language contact is of older date. It is thus possible

---

33. *Hamṭu* forms are thus translated by Akkadian preterite, *marû* by Akkadian present, e.g. in the Old Babylonian Grammatical Texts : bí-in⌐gu₇⌐ = *īkul* 'he ate', í⌐gu₇⌐-e = *ikkal* 'he eats' (*OBGT* VIII 85, 87 = *MSL* IV p. 103); sá bí-i[n-d]ug₄ = *ikšud* 'he reached', sá an-e = *ikaššad* 'he reaches'; ⌐sá an⌐-e-en = *akaššad* 'I reach' (*OBGT* IX 79, 95-96 = *MSL* IV p. 107). The Akkadian preterite and present could, at least originally, be characterized as punctual and durative, respectively, cf. W. von Soden, 1952 p. 102f., §§ 78-79.

that several different and maybe contradictory grammatical distinctions are expressed, dependent on the linguistic circumstances under which the text was composed or copied.

§ 241. *Bibliography*

D.O. Edzard, 1971a. *'ḫamṭu, marû* und freie Reduplikation beim sumerischen Verbum. I'. *ZA* 61 : 208-232.
—, 1972. *'ḫamṭu, marû* und freie Reduplikation beim sumerischen Verbum. II'. *ZA* 62 :1-34.
—, 1976a. *'ḫamṭu, marû* und freie Reduplikation beim sumerischen Verbum. III'. *ZA* 66: 45-61.
B. Kienast, 1980b. 'Probleme der sumerischen Grammatik. 4'. *ZA* 70 : 1-35. (Comment to the above mentioned articles of D.O. Edzard).
G. Steiner, 1981b. *'Ḫamṭu* und *Marû* als verbale Kategorien im Sumerischen und im Akkadischen'. *RA* 75 :1-14.
M. Yoshikawa, 1968a. 'On the Grammatical Function of -e- of the Sumerian Verbal Suffix -e-dè/-e-da(m)'. *JNES* 27 :251-261.
—, 1968b. 'The *Marû* and *Ḫamṭu* Aspects in the Sumerian Verbal system'. *OrNS* 37 :401-416.
—, 1974. 'The *Marû*-Conjugation in the Sumerian Verbal System'. *OrNS* 43 : 17-39.

Verbal Reduplication

§ 242. Reduplication is an important way of expressing grammatical distinctions in Sumerian (cf. nominal reduplication §§ 71-73; 82). The verbal reduplication seems to have at least two functions which are probably morphologically distinguished: 1. A partial reduplication forming the *marû* stem of verbs belonging to class II (see §§ 227-228); and 2. A probably total reduplication of the *ḫamṭu* stem which can affect all verbs.

§ 243. In many cases it is impossible to distinguish the two kinds of reduplication for morphological or orthographic reasons, since the reduplication is simply expressed by doubling the word sign (cf. the writings DU and DU.DU in §§ 265, 267, 268). This may be a sort of ideographic writing of the partial reduplication as well as a more exact rendering of the reduplicated *ḫamṭu* stem: for instance can TAG_4-TAG_4 be interpreted as the possible *marû* stem ta_x-ta_x or as the *ḫamṭu* reduplication tag_4-tag_4. The exact morphological shape of both *ḫamṭu* and *marû* reduplication is thus not entirely clear. On the

124

basis of the contrast between ǧar-ǧar(*hamṭu*) and ǧá-ǧá(*marû*) it is assumed that the *hamṭu* reduplication renders the verbal root in a fuller form than the reduplicated *marû* stem. However, there are only few instances of syllabic writings, and various phonetic modifications can therefore not be excluded. Moreover, some verbs possibly do not distinguish two sorts of reduplication.

Possible forms are:

$C_1 VC_2 + C_1 VC_2 > C_1 VC_2 - C_1 VC_2$ (ǧar-ǧar), *hamṭu* reduplication

$> C_1 V - C_1 V$ (ǧá-ǧá, ku$_4$-ku$_4$), *marû* reduplication

Marû or *Hamṭu?*

$> C_1 VC_2 - C_1 V$ (hal-ha, te-en-te, Edzard, 1976a, 53, n. 210)

$> C_1 V - C_1 VC_2$ (la-la-ah)

$> C_1 V - C_1 C_2 V$ (tu-ut-ke from tuk$_4$-tuk$_4$)

$C_1 VC_2 VC_3 + C_1 VC_2 VC_3 > C_1 VC_2 - C_1 VC_2 VC_3$ (approximately zalzalag from ZALAG + ZALAG)

$> C_1 V - C_1 VC_2 VC_3$ (ga-ga-la-am from galam)

Phonetic writings of reduplicated forms were collected by A. Poebel, *GSG* §§ 94-95, p. 34f. and p. 323; A. Falkenstein, 1959b p. 99f.; and D.O. Edzard, 1971a p. 227f. Most of these instances, however, come from Emesal and/or unorthographic texts, others occur in late or lexical texts, and it is therefore doubtful whether they can be used as a basis for establishing the phonetic shape of reduplicated verbs in general. They may also reflect a secondary scribal tradition.

Examples are: ba-ad-ba-ad (< bad+bad), ba-ba-r (< bar+bar), bi-bi-z (< bi-z+bi-z), bi-ib-r (< bir+bir), te-ed-mi (< dím+dím), ga-ga-la-am (< galam+galam), ge-en-ge-en (< gi-n+gi-n), gu-ul-gu-ul (< gu-l+gu-l), ǧá-ar-ǧá-ar (< ǧar-ǧar), la-la-ah and la-ah-la-ah (< /lah+lah/), si-is-h (< sùh+sùh), šu-uš-r (< šu-r+šu-r), tu-ut-k (< tuk$_4$+tuk$_4$), ta-at-k (< tak$_4$+tak$_4$), ul-lu-ul (< ul$_4$+ul$_4$), ur-ru-ur (< ur$_4$+ur$_4$). (za-al-zu-le-g < zalag+zalag, see Sjöberg, 1975 p. 238f. = In-nin-šà-gur$_4$-ra 160; za-al-za-le-bi in l. 124 which is variant to zalag-zalag-bi Sjöberg considers as a scribal error for zíl-zíl-bi, 1975 p. 235).

The Hamṭu Reduplication

§ 244. The reduplicated *hamṭu* stem occurs in both *hamṭu* and *marû* conjugation of the finite transitive verb, whereas the reduplicated *marû* stem of verbs belonging to class II is used exclusively in the *marû* conjugation. *Hamṭu* are ex. 259, 261, 262-264, *marû*: ex. 260. The *hamṭu* reduplication cannot occur with the morpheme /ed/.

§ 245. In general the *hamṭu* reduplication seems to express exactly the same as the plural verbs (cf. § 260): a) the plural of the intransitive subject (ex. 259 (zàh-zàh), 260), and, b) the plural of the object of the transitive verb (ex. 259 (dab₅-dab₅), 261, 262), that is in both cases the plural of the absolutive. In this function the *hamṭu* reduplication is probably not obligatory, but merely serves to stress the plurality. It may thus be translated by: 'many, several, all'.

> D.O. Edzard, 1971a, used the term *'freie Reduplikation'*. He described the *hamṭu* reduplication like this : 'Wir dürfen damit rechen, daß im großen Ganzen ein produktives System der Reduplikationsbildung vorliegt — produktiv und frei im Gegensatz zu der von vornherein festgelegten *marû*-Reduplikation' (p. 231).

§ 246. *Examples:*

(259) mu 5-kam-ma dam dumu Ku.li dumu Ba.ba.g̃u₁₀-ke₄-ne ba-an-da-zàh.zàh-éš, dumu Ba.ba.g̃u₁₀-ke₄-ne mu-dab₅- dab₅-bé-eš, /ba-n.da-zàh.zàh-eš/, /mu-(n-)dab₅.dab₅-eš/ 'in the fifth year the wife and daughters of Kuli have run away from the sons of Babag̃u, the sons of Babag̃u have seized them' (*NG* nr. 41, 10-13)[34]

(260) amaš ha-ra-dagal-dagal, /ha-ī-DAT.2.sg.-dagal.dagal/ 'may all the sheepfolds be wide for you' (Išme-Dagan Hymn A 49)

(261) alam-bi ì-gul-gul, /ī-(n-)gul-gul/ 'he destroyed several/all of its statues' (Ukg. 16 IV 3-4 and 9-10)

(262) hur.sag̃ 5 hur.sag̃ 6 hur.sag̃ 7-e im-me-ri-bal-bal, /ī-ba-ra (abl.)-bal.bal/ 'five mountains, six mountains, seven mountains he all crossed' (Enmerkar and the Lord of Aratta 170). For the prefix chain see § 468 to ex. 652.

§ 247. With the so-called compound verbs the *hamṭu* reduplication refers to the plural of the 'dimensional object':

---

34. For further examples of reduplicated dab₅, see P. Steinkeller, 1979 p. 63f.

(263) SAHAR.DUL.TAG$_4$-bi eden-na ki ba-ni-ús-ús, /ba-ni-(n-)
ús.ús/ 'he piled up their many burial mounds in the plain'
(Ent. 28 I 30-31)

(264) níg.mí.ús.sa ^{D}Ba.ba$_6$ nin-a-na-ke$_4$ si ba-ni-sá-sá, /ba-ni-
(n-)sá.sá/ 'he put in order all the wedding presents of Baba,
his lady' (Gudea, St. D II 13-III 2)

§ 248. Other functions of the *hamṭu* reduplication have been suggested, for instance iterative and intensive, but they are difficult to
verify because such meanings are based on the subjective interpretation of the text. In the lexical and bilingual texts the reduplicated
hamṭu stem is translated by Akkadian D-stems (i.e. factitive), by
iterative *tan*-forms, and even by reciprocal *t*-forms or the causative
Š-stem. It must, however, be questioned whether these translations
represent original functions of verbal reduplication in Sumerian. In
some cases at least, they may be secondary, introduced in order to
give Sumerian equivalents to the different Akkadian stems.

For a possible intensive function of the *hamṭu* reduplication, see E. Sollberger, 1952 p. 43. D.O. Edzard, 1971a p. 231, enumerated the following previously suggested functions of the *hamṭu* reduplication: 'a) Betonung der Pluralität oder Totalität des Subjekts; b) Betonung der Pluralität oder Totalität
des direkten oder dimensionalen Objektes; c) Subjekt oder Objekt im Distri-
butivverhältnis; d) Betonung der Größe, Gewaltigkeit, Bedeutung des Objekts;
e) Betonung der zeitlichen Dauer (aber keineswegs 'Präsensreduplikation'!);
f) Detaillierung, Wiederholung der Handlung; g) Betonung des hohen Wirk-
samkeitsgrades, der Reichweite der Handlung'. The examples in Edzard,
1971a, can however, also be explained as denoting the plurality of subject or
object.

§ 249. Chiefly based on the above mentioned Akkadian translations
(§ 248) M. Yoshikawa, 1979b, suggested that verbal reduplication in
Sumerian denotes different things with different verbs. Besides the
marû reduplication he found the following functions of verbal reduplication: a) *piel*-reduplication (i.e. plurality if the object); b) iterative; c) causative; d) reciprocal; e) denominative; f) onomatopoeic
reduplication. '(...) the function of verbal reduplication basically differs from verb to verb, each verb thus being confined to one of the
seven functions (...). It will be observed also that the *marû*, *piel* and

iterative reduplications form paradigmatically primary or major categories, and that the *piel* and iterative reduplications are grammatically, as well as, semantically concerned with the so-called plural expressions in Sumerian verb' (1979b p. 117).

Although it is difficult to prove this theory convincingly, the possibility should not be totally excluded.

> The functions of reduplication in Sumerian can be compared to those in other languages, cf. e.g., the New Guinean language Motu which has two sorts of reduplication: total (*tore* : *toretore*) and partial (*mahuta* : *mamahuta*). Whereas the partial reduplication has almost always the function of pluralization, the total reduplication has various functions: with verbs it denotes depreciation, repetition, continuation, or with some verbs it forms intransitive verbs from transitive, or nouns from verbs; with nouns it most often denotes diminution, with adjectives and adverbs intensification. See A.J. Taylor, 'Reduplication in Motu' (*Pacific Studies in honour of Arthur Capell*. Edited by S.A. Wurm and D.C. Laycock. Canberra 1970. *Pacific Linguistic Series C*, Book 13, 1-2, p. 1235-1245).

§ 250. *Bibliography*

M. Yoshikawa, 1979b. 'Verbal Reduplication in Sumerian'. *ASJ* 1: 99-119.

§ 251. Tripling and Quadrupling of Verbs

The instances of this phenomenon are not numerous. The following verbs are found: di-di-di, dím-dím-dím, du-du-du, du_7-du_7-du_7, gi-gi-gi, gi_4-gi_4-gi_4, ğá-ğá-ğá, KU.KU.KU, lá-lá-lá, mú-mú-mú, ra-ra-ra, sa_4-sa_4-sa_4, sír-sír-sír, su-su-su, šár-šár-šár, šú-šú-šú, zi-zi-zi, and ğar-ğar-ğar-ğar'

> Instances have been collected by A. Falkenstein, *GSGL* II p. 63 n. 1, and D.O. Edzard, 1976a p. 57 n. 225.

Quite a lot of these verbs belong to the Reduplication class (du_7, gi_4, ğar, mú, ra, šú and zi), a fact which could lead to the conclusion that the tripling of the verbal root serves as the '*hamṭu* reduplication' in those cases where the reduplication is reserved for *marû* functions. This theory, however, does not take into account the cases of other verbs which are tripled (di, dím, du, gi, KU, lá, sa_4, sír and šár) of which at least lá, sa_4 and dím belong to the regular verbs. Since the instances are rather few and, moreover, occur in difficult context

(Emesal and unorthographic texts), it is not possible to define the function of tripling and quadrupling further. Intensive or iterative could also be suggested.

(265) dub.lá (...)-zu guruš mah g̃eštin nag̃-a^a-gin$_7$ ki-šè ^{b}hé-g̃á-g̃á-g̃á^b (a: -g̃[á; b-b: hé-em-ta-g̃á-g̃á) 'your gates shall fall on the earth like great men who have drunk wine' (Curse of Akkade 232-233). Or: 'all your gates ...'?

(266) še$_{25}$ gi$_4$-bi(-šè) kur(-ra) LUL.LUL-bi-a ki^a ^{b}mu-un-ra-ra-ra^b (a: kur-kur; b-b: mu-ra-ra) 'Because of its cry the earth trembled in the ... of the mountain' (Lugalbanda and En-merkar 46). (Perhaps 'it trembled constantly/again and again'?)

The Verbal Morpheme /ed/

§ 252. The element /ed/ is closely connected with the verbal root; its position is immediately after this and before any pronominal element or syntactic suffix that may occur. With regular verbs /ed/ is combined with the basic stem (= the *hamṭu* stem), with other verbs it is added to the *marû* stem. VERB + /ed/ is used first of all in non-finite forms but it also occurs in finite forms.

§ 253. The morpheme /ed/ is never written -ed; [e] is, as a rule, written after a consonant, but only exceptionally after a vowel; [d] is only written when followed by a vowel: tar-re < /tar-ed/, hug̃-g̃e$_{26}$-dè < /hug̃-ed-e/, ág̃-e-dè < /ág̃-ed-e/, gi$_4$-gi$_4$-da < /gi$_4$.gi$_4$-ed-a/, è-dè-dam < /è.d-ed-am/ etc. But also writings like ág̃-dam, bal-dè etc. occur.

[e] often but not always changes to [u] after verbs having the vowel [u], e.g., after the verbs: dub, dúb, gub, gu.ul, hur, kud.r, kúr, sum, sur, šub, túm (gub-bu-dè, sum-mu-dè, etc.).

For writings, see for instance Yoshikawa, 1968a p. 256ff.

§ 254. *Analysis of /ed/*

A. Poebel has first defined the morpheme as /ed/ (*GSG* §§ 625-627) and most Sumerologists have followed this view.[35] If, we, however,

---

35. Cf. the outline of earlier treatments of /ed/ in D.O. Edzard, 1967 p. 29-31 and n. 3.

follow the theory of M. Yoshikawa and consider /e/ as a *marû* mark, we consequently have to regard the morpheme as /d/ only (see § 233). Whereas it is of minor importance for the understanding of the non-finite forms whether we analyse, e.g., /kar-ed-e/ or /kare-d-e/, both: 'in order to remove', the analysis and understanding of finite forms are decisively influenced by the choice of *marû* theory. It concerns especially the forms of the 3.sg. A form with the ending -e or -Ce can thus be interpreted differently according to the two theories.

ba-gub-bu is in the traditional theory either = /ba-gub-ed/ 'he will stand', intrans. 3.sg.; or = /ba-gub-e(pron. suffix)/ 'he places', trans. 3.sg., whereas a transitive /-ed/ form would be: ba-gub-bu-dè = /ba-gub-ed-e/. However, if /e/ is a *marû* mark, as according to the theory of Yoshikawa, ba-gub-bu = /ba-gube/ is the normal 3.sg. intransitive *marû* form as well as the transitive *marû* form (the latter possibly with a pronominal prefix), but it could also be an /ed/-form: /ba-gube-d/. The traditional view is followed here.

		Traditional view	Yoshikawa
Intransitive			
3.sg., *hamṭu*	/ba-gub/ = ba-gub	/ba-gub/ = ba-gub
3.sg., *marû*	/ba-gub/ = ba-gub	/ba-gube/ = ba-gub-bu
3.sg., + /ed/	/ba-gub-ed/ = ba-gub-bu	/ba-gube-d/ = ba-gub-bu
Transitive			
3.sg., *hamṭu*	/ba-n-gub/ = ba-an-gub	/ba-n-gub/ = ba-an-gub
3.sg., *marû*	/ba-PRON-gub-e/ = ba-...-gub-bu	/ba-PRON-gube/ = ba-...-gub-bu
3.sg., + /ed/	/ba-PRON-gub-ed-e/ = ba-...-gub-bu-dè	/ba-PRON-gube-d/ = ba-...-gub-bu

The Meaning of /ed/

§ 255. /ed/-forms almost always refer to the future. A no less important function, however, seems to be to denote something that has to be done, an obligation, prospective or the like.[36] So the non-finite forms: ğá-ğá-dè 'in order to place', nu-kur-ru-dam 'which cannot ever be changed', and zi-re-dam 'it has to be destroyed'.

---

36. Modal implications of the future stem is no uncommon phenomenon, cf. for instance the use of *will* and *shall* in English (see J. Lyons, 1968 p. 309ff.).

130

It is noteworthy that /ed/ comparatively rarely occurs in finite forms. The lack of finite examples may of course be due to the difficulties of recognizing this element (cf. § 254), but it is also possible that the function of /ed/ is first of all to express the above mentioned modal implications in non-finite forms, whereas the finite forms will use modal prefixes.

§ 256. In finite forms /ed/ is especially frequent with intransitive verbs. When combined with regular verbs the /ed/ form thus corresponds to the *marû* forms of other verbs, e.g., /ì-zàh-en/ 'I have run away' corresponds to /ì-ku₄.r-en/ 'I have entered', /ì-zàh-ed-en/ 'I (will) run away' to /ì-ku₄.ku₄-en/ 'I (will) enter' (cf. examples in § 258).

Verbs of class II-IV which have a special *marû* stem do not have to be combined with /ed/ in intransitive forms, but actually many of the intransitive /ed/-forms are verbs like gub, du, gi₄ etc. which do have a particular *marû* form.

Cf. D.O. Edzard, 1967 p. 59, where he examines the promissory oath formulas: 'Wenn statt der 'infiniten' Form ein 'finites' Verbum im Präsens-Futur steht, ist /ed/ entbehrlich; ist das 'finite' Verbum intransitiv, steht dagegen /ed/. Dieser Befund liegt nahe, daß /ed/ im promissorischen Eid nur bei transitivem 'finitem' Verbum entbehrlich, sonst aber unvertauschbar war.'

§ 257. Th. Jacobsen, 1965 p. 98, interpreted /ed/ as prospective: '-ed- mark of pre-actional aspect indicating prospectiveness of the action as present at the point in the time the speaker has in mind. Attention is thus not on the action as future but on its prospectiveness as present.'

D.O. Edzard, 1967 p. 62, concluded that the primary function of /ed/ is to specify the tense, namely an action which has not yet taken place. As secondary functions he suggested modal implications: '1) der Ausdruck einer modalen Nuance des Sollens, Verpflichtetseins, die sich unschwer aus dem futurischen Zeitbezug ableiten läßt; 2) bei bestimmten negierten Verbalformen der Ausdruck des Nichtkönnens, wo ebenfalls Rückführung auf den futurischen Zeitbezug logisch plausibel erscheint.' As another secondary function of /ed/ Edzard suggested the ingressive, see 1967 p. 60ff.

§ 258. *Examples:*

(267) mu lugal ud.rá min-ka ì-zàh-dè-na ga-hul bí-in-dug₄, /ì-zàh-ed-en-a/ 'he has sworn by the name of the king: let me die, if I run away a second time!' (*NRVN* I 1, 6-8)

(268) é-g̃u₁₀ lú ì-bùr-dè, /ì-bùr-ed-e/ 'Someone may break into my house' (Codex Lipit-Ištar XIII 26)

(269) ki di.kud-ru-bi-šè diĝir an ki-a im-ši-gam-e-dè-eš, /ì-m-ši-gam-ed-eš/ 'the gods of heaven and earth will bow down to the place where judgement is pronounced' (Nungal 35)

(270) tilla₂ nam-ba-e-gub-bu-dè-en, /na-ba-e-gub-ed-en/ 'may you not stand on the market place!' (Father and Son 29)

(271) é-a-ni dù-da ma-an-dug₄, /dù-ed-a mu-DAT.1.sg.-n-dug₄/ 'he has ordered me to build his house' (Gudea, cyl. A IV 20)

(272) ud-ta ud gur-ra-ka nu-ši-gur-da mu lugal-bi in-pàd-dè-éš, /nu-ì-ši-gur-ed-a/, /ì-n-pàd-eš/ 'they have sworn by the name of the king that they will not return from this day and in the future' (*UET* III, 26: 9-11)

§ 259. *Bibliography*

D.O. Edzard, 1967. 'Das sumerische Verbalmorphem /ed/ in den alt- und neusumerischen Texten'. *HSAO* I: 29-62.

G. Steiner, 1981a. 'The Vocalization of the Sumerian Verbal Morpheme /=ED/ and its Significance'. *JNES* 40: 21-41.

M. Yoshikawa, 1968a. 'On the Grammatical Function of -e- of the Sumerian Verbal Suffix -e-dé/-e-da(m)'. *JNES* 27: 251-261.

Plural Verbs

§ 260. A small number of verbs have two separate roots denoting singular and plural, respectively. The crucial factor is the plurality of the absolutive subject or object. The plural verb is thus used in one-participant forms with plural subject and in two-participant forms with plural object, whereas the singular root is used when the absolutive subject or object is singular. Cf. for instance the following forms of the verb 'to stand', gub (sing.) : su₈.g (plur.):

(273) lugal-ĝu₁₀ ᴰEn.ki ì-gub-bé-en, /ì-gub-en/ 'my king, Enki, I am standing at your service!' (Inanna and Enki I v 16 and passim)

(274) diĝir diĝir A.nun.na (...) á-áĝ-ĝá zi-dè(-eš) (ši-)im-ma-su₈-ge-eš, /ša-ì-ba-su₈.g-eš/ 'the Anuna Gods stand faithfully according to his instruction(s)' (Enlil Hymn 9)

(275) ÌR.ᴰEN.ZU (...) ᵘʳᵘᵈᵘalam gal-gal(-la) (...) bí-in-su₈-ga, /bi-n-su₈.g-a/ 'Warad-Sin who has erected the big statues' (Warad-Sin 8, 18-20)

§ 261. An exception to the above mentioned principle (§ 260) is the verb dug$_4$ (hamṭu) 'to speak'. e is the marû stem of this verb but also the plural verb. As plural verb e occurs with plural ergative subject in transitive forms: bí-in-dug$_4$ = /bi-n-dug$_4$/ 'he has said', but bí-in-eš or bí-né-eš = /bi-n-e-eš/ 'they have said'.[37]

§ 262. The function of the plural verb is thus in general the same as that of the hamṭu reduplication, but the singular and plural verbs can also be reduplicated:

(276) dug$_4$-dug$_4$-ma-ab ga-ra-ab-dug$_4$-dug$_4$ ga-na dug$_4$-ma-ab, /(dug$_4$).dug$_4$ + mu-DAT.1.sg./, /ga-ī-DAT.2.sg.-b-dug$_4$. dug$_4$/ 'tell me everything! — I shall tell you everything — come on, tell me!' (Father and Son 19-21)[38]

(277) dub.lá-bi am-gin$_7$ mu-šu$_4$-šu$_4$, /mu-(n-)šu$_4$.šu$_4$/ 'he erected its gates like (i.e. resembling) wild oxen' (Gudea, cyl. A XXIV 18)

Such instances point to the other suggested functions of the hamṭu reduplication: intensive, iterative, etc. (see §§ 248-249), which, however, for the present cannot be determined with certainty.

The fact that two of the plural verbs, e and ug$_5$/$_7$, also serve as marû stems may indicate some connection between plurality and the marû aspect; cf. the instances where the marû reduplication is identical with the hamṭu reduplication, e.g., gi$_4$-gi$_4$.

§ 263. Until now only seven verbs have been identified as having separate singular and plural roots, but it is possible that more plural verbs are hidden behind different readings of the signs or behind the doubling of word signs in the writing whose exact phonetic representation is not known.

Cf. M. Civil. 1976a p. 150 and n. 44, who suggests that sun$_5$ (= BÚR) is probably the plural of the verb ku$_4$.r 'to enter'. P. Steinkeller, 1979 p. 65: 'it is possible that some of the variant readings assigned in lexical sources to the same sign will eventually turn out to be plural stems (e.g., the value sìm of sum 'to give'?).'

37. Cf. examples in A. Falkenstein, NG III p. 104.
38. D.O. Edzard, 1971a p. 231, classified this instance as 'Detaillierung, Wiederholung der Handlung', and translated 'sage mir alles genau ... ich will dir alles genau sagen' (p. 229).

§ 264. *Bibliography*

J. Krecher, 1968a. 'Die pluralischen Verba für 'gehen' und 'stehen' im Sumerischen'. *WO* 4: 1-11.

P. Steinkeller, 1979. 'Notes on Sumerian Plural Verbs'. *OrNS* 48: 54-67.

M. Yoshikawa, 1981. 'Plural Expressions in Sumerian Verbs'. *ASJ* 3: 111-124.

§ 265. *'to bring'*

	hamṭu	*marû*
sing.	de_6 (= DU)	tùm or túm (= DU) (IV)
plur.	lah_4 (= $\frac{DU}{DU}$)	lah_4 (I)

Cf. *NBGT* II 7-8 (= *MSL* IV p. 148): de-e DU = *ba-ba-lum ha-am-ṭú*, DU = *ba-ba-lum* MEŠ *ma-ru-ú*; Diri II 24: la-ah DU.DU = *ba-ba-lum*, see *CAD* A/I p. 10f., *abālu* A, lexical section.

M. Yoshikawa considered the singular *hamṭu* stem as túm (= DU), the *marû* stem as tùm (cf. 1968a p. 259f.; 1968b p. 413; 1974 p. 35f.). However, according to *NBGT* cited above and to other forms with DU it is more likely that the *hamṭu* stem is de_6; for this problem, see P. Steinkeller, 1979 p. 60f. and n. 11; p. 66f.

For the plural stem lah_4 (= $\frac{DU}{DU}$) or lah_5 (= DU.DU), see the examples in P. Steinkeller, 1979 p. 57ff. Note the non-finite *marû* form la-hi-dam (*NG* nr. 120a, 7; nr. 120b, 23). /lah/ can also be written lah_6 = DU (Steinkeller, 1979 p. 59).

The singular *marû* stem túm is also used as plural stem, cf.: ga-ba-ab-túm-mu-dè-en, /ga-ba-b-túm-enden/ 'we will bring him back' (Inanna's Descent 310).

§ 266. *'to say, to speak'*

	hamṭu	*marû*
sing.	dug_4	e (IV)
plur.	e	e

In contrast to other plural verbs, the plural stem, e, is used with a plural ergative subject: bí-in-né-eš = /bi-n-e-eš/ 'they have said it' (see §§ 260-261).

§ 267. *'to stand, to erect'*

	hamṭu	*marû*
sing.	gub (= DU)	gub (I)
plur.	su₈·g (= $\frac{DU}{DU}$)	su₈·g (also su₈·g-su₈·g) (I or II)
	šu₄·g (Gudea, NS)	

Cf. *NBGT* Il i 5-6 (= *MSL* IV p. 148): gu-ub DU = *ú-zu-uz* DIŠ *ha-am-ṭú*, su-ug $\frac{DU}{DU}$ = *ú-zu-uz* MEŠ *ma-ru-ú*.

The plural verb su₈·g perhaps belongs to the reduplication class, cf. the *marû* form:

(278) nin₉ hé-me-eš téš-bi-da hé-en-da-su₈-su₈-[g]e-eš, /ha-ĩ-n.da-su₈.su₈.g-eš/ 'let (Lahar and Ašnan) be sisters, let them stand together' (Lahar and Ašnan 181 unpubl., cited after Gragg, *SDI* p. 51). Cf. also J. Krecher, 1968a p. 7ff.

§ 268. *'to go'*

	hamṭu	*marû*
sing.	ğen (= DU)	du (IV)
plur.	/(e)re/	su₈·b (= $\frac{DU}{DU}$) (IV)

/(e)re/ is written with the signs $\frac{DU}{DU}$ = re₇, DU-DU = er$_x$, DU = re₆, ir₁₀, er$_x$, or phonetically: er-re. See J. Krecher, 1968a p. 3ff. and P. Steinkeller, 1979 p. 61 for examples.

In *OBGT* plural forms of the verb 'to go' are always written $\frac{DU}{DU}$ = su₈ or re₇. That the *hamṭu* form shall be read re₇ can be seen from *OBGT* VII (*MSL* IV p. 88-99), e.g., l. 284:

(279) ga-àm-ne-$\frac{DU}{DU}$-en-dè-en = *i ni-li-kam šu-nu-ši* 'let us go to them'. Here re₇ seems more justified than su₈ because of the writing of the suffix. Cf. the *marû* form in l. 285:

(280) hé-em-ne-su₈-bé-eš = *li-il-li-ku-nim šu-nu-ši* 'let them go to them'. Cf. also:

(281) lú-ù-ne lú mu-un-dè-re₇^{re}-eš-àm, /mu-n.da-ere-eš-a-m/ 'the men who went with her' (Inanna's Descent 295, text U)

(282) lugal-ra dumu Adab^{ki}-a min-àm mu-(un-)ši-re₇^(re)-eš, /mu-n.ši-ere-eš/ 'the two sons from Adab went to the king' (Dumuzi's Dream 119)

Phonetic writings are:

(283) ì-im-er-re-eš, /ì-m-ere-eš/ 'they went there' (NG nr. 120b, 10)

su₈.b is also found in a reduplicated form, e.g.,

(284) zid-da gùb-bu-zu nam nam.ti-la-šè ud sud-rá-šè hé-em-da-su₈-su₈ ᵃ-bé-eš (a: gloss: su-su), /ha-ì-m-da-su₈.su₈.b-eš/ 'let them go out at your right and left in order (to bring) the fate of life and long days' (UET VI/1, 103: 42-43)

Unfortunately the relevant section in NBGT II (MSL IV p. 148) is partly destroyed: col. I 1-4: [...] = a-la-ku UL₄ (= hamṭu) ⌜šá DIŠ⌝, [...] du = (a-la-ku) šá DIŠ [ma-ru]-⌜ú⌝, [...]$^{DU}_{DU}$ = a-lak MEŠ UL₄, [su₈]-bi = (a-lak) ma-ru-ú.

§ 269. 'to live'

	hamṭu	marû	
sing.	ti.l	ti.l	(I)
plur.	sig₇	sig₇	(I ?)

sig₇ could also be read se₁₂. For references see P. Steinkeller, 1979 p. 55 n. 5, and C. Wilcke, 1969a p. 132 and n. 369, p. 139.

§ 270. 'to sit, to live somewhere', 'to seat'

	hamṭu	marû	
sing.	tuš	tuš	(I)
plur.	durun	durun	(I)

/durun/ is normally written dúr (= TUŠ)-ru-nV/un; in texts earlier than Ur III the plural stems are written TUŠ.TUŠ with the reading durun$_x$, cf. P. Steinkeller, 1979 p. 56f. n. 6.

Cf. also NBGT II 11-12 (= MSL IV p. 148f.): tu-uš TUŠ = a-šab DIŠ ha-am-ṭú, dúr-ru-un = (a-šab) MEŠ ha-am-ṭú u ma-ru-ú.

§ 271. *'to die, to kill'*

	hamṭu	*marû*	
sing.	úš	ug$_5$, ug$_7$	(IV)
plur.	ug$_5$, ug$_7$	ug$_5$, ug$_7$	(I)
	ug$_7$–ug$_7$		

The plural stem is in early texts written ÚŠ.ÚŠ = ug$_x$, or ÚŠ = ug$_7$, cf. J. Bauer, 1970 p. 188f. From OB on it is written ug$_5$ = EZENxÚŠ. In OB, however, the distinction between singular and plural stems is not consistently carried through, cf. P. Steinkeller, 1979 p. 55 n. 4.

THE FINITE VERB

§ 272. A finite form is a verbal construction with a prefix chain and pronominal elements. The finite form may be terminated by the subordination suffix /-a/ (possibly followed by a postposition), or by a syntactic suffix. The construction of finite forms appears from the chart below § 274.

The finite verb has three conjugations: the intransitive conjugation, the transitive *hamṭu* and the transitive *marû* conjugation (see § 275ff.).

In contrast to the finite verbs there are the non-finite forms which have no prefix chain and no pronominal element, but only suffixes (see below § 273).

§ 273. Other verbal constructions which are no real finite constructions, but consist partly of the same grammatical elements are:

Finite Forms Without Prefix Chain: In some rather few cases – only about 30 forms are attested – a verb without a prefix chain but with pronominal suffixes serves as a finite verb, e.g.,

(285) me-a tuš-ù-dè-en me-a gub-bu-dè-en, /tuš-ed-en/, /gub-ed-en/, 'where shall I sit, where shall I stand?' (Ur Lament 294)

In this case rather the forms ba-tuš-ù-de-en and ba-gub-bu-dè-en are expected.

Both intransitive and transitive forms without prefix chain are attested, and syntactically they do not differ from ordinary finite forms. The phenomenon does not occur before OB and is found in literary texts only, mostly in hymns and laments. Because of the few instances it is not possible to give any rules or explanation of the deletion of the prefix chain.

For examples, see W.H.P. Römer, *SKIZ* p. 220-223. See also W.R. Sladek, 1974 p. 193f., who suggests that the metrical accent may have something to do with the absence of the prefix chain.

Imperatives: The imperative must be called a finite form since it has a prefix chain. The chain, however, is placed after the verbal root, e.g., gi$_4$-mu-un = /gi$_4$ + mu-n/ 'return it'. The 'prefix' chain of the imperative is most often comparatively short.

For further details, see §§ 495-499. The construction of the imperative is not included in the chart below § 274.

§ 274. Construction of Finite Forms

Modal Prefixes §§ 359-422	Conjugation Prefixes §§ 305-352	Case Prefixes §§ 423-482	Pronominal Prefixes §§ 290-293	Verbal Root §§ 231-250	Future (?) Element §§ 252-259	Pronominal Suffixes §§ 294-301	Syntactic Suffixes	Postpositions
nu bara na ga ha ša u iri nuš	$\{\tilde{\imath}/a\}$-$\{ga^{a}\}$- $\begin{Bmatrix} m^{a)} \\ mu \\ ba \\ bi \end{Bmatrix}$	-DAT-da-$\begin{Bmatrix} \check{s}i \\ tab \\ ra \end{Bmatrix}$$\begin{Bmatrix} mi \\ ri \end{Bmatrix}$	$\begin{Bmatrix} e/a \\ n \\ b \end{Bmatrix}$	$\begin{Bmatrix} R(mar\hat{u}) \\ R \\ R\text{-}R \end{Bmatrix}$	ed^{c}	en e enden enzen eš ene	-a$^{d)}$ eše ĝišen COP	e ra a še ta da -ak- $\begin{Bmatrix} gin \\ ri \end{Bmatrix}$

al — (§§ 353-358)

a) /-ga-/ and /-m-/ cannot begin the prefix chain, but are always preceded by /ĩ-/.
b) -ra-ta- and -ta-ra- are also found, see § 467.
c) /-ed-/ can be combined with the *marû* stem only, with regular verbs, however, with the basic stem.
d) /-a-/ is obligatory before postpositions, see §§ 483-493.

The Intransitive and Transitive Conjugations

§ 275. Both on the syntactic, grammatical and on the morphological level the intransitive and transitive finite constructions can be distinguished:

A. intrans.: SUBJ-∅(abs.) PREF-VERB-PRON
/lugal ba-ĝen/ 'the king came', /ì-ku₄.r-en/ 'I entered'
B. trans.: SUBJ-e(erg.) OBJ-∅(abs.) PREF-PRON-VERB, or PREF-(PRON-)VERB-PRON:
/lugal-e é mu-n-dù/ 'the king has built the house'
/ĝá-e é mu-dù-en/ 'I build the house' (cf. é-zu ma-ra-dù-e 'I shall build your house for you' Gudea, cyl. A VIII 18).

(The occurrences of the pronominal elements (= PRON) are here very simplified).

The means to distinguish these types of verbal constructions is first of all the pronominal elements (= PRON) (perhaps to some extent also the conjugation prefixes, cf. § 345), and it must therefore be noted that on the morphological level this distinction is possible in the finite verb only.

There are two series of pronominal elements indicating the above mentioned distinction: (a) Pronominal suffixes, (b) pronominal prefixes. Intransitive forms have only pronominal suffixes and never prefixes, whereas transitive forms have either prefixes or suffixes or both.

§ 276. The Sumerian verbal root is in principle neither transitive nor intransitive but neutral in this respect. The root ku₄.r can thus mean both 'to enter' (intrans.) and 'to bring in, to make enter' (trans.), the root sum both 'to be given' (intrans.) and 'to give':

(286) ᴰIsimu-dè (...) lú ki.sikil Abzu Eriduᵏⁱ-šè im-ma-ni-in-ku₄-ku₄ (...) lú ki.sikil Abzu Eriduᵏⁱ-šè um-ma-ku₄-ra-ta, /ì-ba-ni-n-ku₄.ku₄/, /u-ì-ba-ku₄.r-a-ta/ 'Isimud makes the girl enter Abzu-Eridu, (..) the girl having entered Abzu-Eridu' (Inanna and Enki I ii 16-20)

(287) eĝer-a-ni ù dam dumu-ni dumu Ba.ba.ĝu₁₀-ke₄-ne ba-ne-sum-ma, /ba-ne-sum-a/ 'that his estate and his wife and children were given to the sons of Babaĝu' (NG nr. 41, 6-8)

(288) é-ĝu₁₀ dù-da ĝiskim-bi ga-ra-ab-sum, /ga-ra-b-sum/ 'I will give you a sign about the building of my house' (Gudea, cyl. A IX 9)

No verb seems to have the lexical restriction that it occurs exclusively as either transitive or intransitive. In practice some verbs may be used primarily in the intransitive, others in the transitive form, but theoretically any verb can be found in both constructions.

§ 277. *Terminology*

In the traditional grammars verbs like gub 'to stand', ğen 'to go' and ku$_4$.r 'to enter' are called 'basically intransitive', whereas verbs like gu$_7$ 'to eat', dím 'to fashion' and sum 'to give' are called 'basically transitive' (cf. for instance A. Falkenstein, *GSGL* II p. 59). J.N. Postgate, 1974 p. 26, rightly pointed to the inconsistency of this classification and instead suggested the following terminology applying to all categories of verbs: one-participant construction = 'he went' or 'it was given'; two-participant construction = 'he gave it' or 'he made him enter'; three-participant construction = 'x causes y to destroy z'.

In the present study 'one-participant' and 'two-participant' are used as the most general terms for the clauses of type A and B, respectively. The terms 'intransitive' and 'transitive' are, however, also used in their traditional sense: intrans. = lugal in-ku$_4$ 'the king entered', trans. = lugal-e é mu-un-dù 'the king has built the house' (but še ba-de$_6$ 'the barley was bought', is one-participant).

§ 278. The intransitive/one-part. finite verb has only one conjugation: I (§ 279) with both *hamṭu* and *marû* stem. The transitive/two-part. verb has two conjugations: II and III. When the verb has a special *marû* stem this is applied in III. The future stem with /ed/ is conjugated like the *marû* stem, the reduplicated *hamṭu* stem like the single *hamṭu* stem.

...- denotes the prefix chain consisting of modal, conjugation and case prefixes, except the pronominal prefixes. PRON means the pronominal prefixes /-b-/ and /-n-/ which may occur as transitive or object marks.

For writing and occurrences of the prefixes and suffixes, see §§ 287-301.

§ 279. *I. Intransitive/One-Participant Conjugation*

In the intransitive conjugation the pronominal suffixes denote the subject:

Hamṭu: 'I entered', etc.

1.sg.	...-VERB-en	ĝá-e i-ku$_4$-re-en
2.sg.	...-VERB-en	za-e i-ku$_4$-re-en
3.sg.	...-VERB	a.ne i-ku$_4$ 'he entered'
		lú i-ku$_4$ 'the man entered'
1.pl.	...-VERB-enden	me.en.dè.en i-ku$_4$-re-en-dè-en
2.pl.	...-VERB-enzen	me.en.zé.en i-ku$_4$-re-en-zé-en
3.pl.	...-VERB-eš	a.ne.ne i-ku$_4$-re-eš
		lú-e-ne i-ku$_4$-re-eš

The *marû* forms have the same endings: i-ku$_4$-ku$_4$-en 'I enter', etc.

The pronominal prefixes /-n-/ and /-b-/ may exceptionally occur in intransitive/one-part. forms. Such occurrences must surely be regarded as scribal errors or mistakes.

ba-VERB is very common as the 3.sg. form, but /ba-/ is not exclusively an intrans./one-part. prefix, see §§ 341-352.

For the suffixes, their writing and occurrences, see §§ 294-301.

§ 280. *II. Transitive/Two-Participant Conjugation: Hamṭu*

In this conjugation the subject is denoted by pronominal prefixes (2. sg., 3.sg. an. and inan.), or by a combination of prefix and suffix (3. pl. and perhaps also 2.pl., see below). The 1.sg. has no subject mark, and the 1.pl. has only a suffix.

In those forms which have no prefix referring to the subject a pronominal element, /-b-/ or /-n-/ (= PRON), may occur, which refers to the object (see §§ 281, 282).

1.sg.	...(-PRON)-VERB	ĝá-e saĝ i-(b-)zìg 'I raised the head'
2.sg.	...-e-VERB	za-e saĝ mu-e-zìg 'you raised the head'
3.sg.an.	...-n-VERB	a-ne saĝ in-zìg 'he raised the head'
		lú-e saĝ in-zìg 'the man raised the head'
inan.	...-b-VERB	gud-e saĝ íb-zìg 'the ox raised the head'

1.pl.	...(-PRON)-VERB-enden	ˌme.en.dè.enˌ sg̃ ì-(bˍ-)z̀ig-gˌe-en-dè-enˌ
2.pl.	...-e-VERB-enzen	ˌme.en.zé.enˌ sg̃ mu-e-zìg-gˌe-en-zé-enˌ
3.pl.	...-n-VERB-eš	ˌa.ne.neˌsg̃ in-zìg-gˌe-ešˌ
		ˌlú-e-neˌsg̃ in-zìg-gˌe-ešˌ

In the 1.sg. and pl. forms /ī-/ alone would be written ì-, /ī-b-/ = ìb-.

The prefix /mu-/ is predominant before the pronominal element /-e-/ for the 2. person. In the earlier stages of Sumerian it was perhaps obligatory.

The 1.pl. form is identical with the 1.pl. of the *marû* conjugation, unless the verb clearly distinguishes *hamṭu* and *marû*.

Poebel, *GSG* p. 176, reconstructed the 1.pl. preterite *ì-me-dím, 'we have made', but such forms are not attested (cf. § 290). Since the cohortative ga-forms, which are *hamṭu*, have /-enden/ as subject element (cf. § 389 and Falkenstein, 1939), it is here assumed that other *hamṭu* forms, without ga-, have this ending too. Cf. also: ì-sum-mu-un-dè-en, 'we have given it (to them 15 years ago)' (*HSM* 1384, 7 = Edzard, 1976b p. 160, a document dating to the reign of Enlil-bani of Isin, 1860-1837 B.C.).

The 2. pl. is uncertain. The form rendered here is based on forms like nu-mu-e-sum-mu-un-zé-en, 'you(pl.) have not given it (to me)' (*HSM* 1384, 11 = Edzard, 1976b p. 160), see also § 291.

§ 281. The singular forms of the transitive *hamṭu* conjugation may add a pronominal suffix denoting the object: /-en/ 'me, you(sg.)', /-enden/ 'us', /-enzen/ 'you(pl.)', and /-eš/ 'them'.[39] Such forms are ambiguous unless the verb clearly distinguishes *hamṭu* and *marû* stem. /ī-n-tud-en/ can thus theoretically be both 'I (or you, sg.) bear her' and 'she has born me (or you, sg.)' (cf. D.O. Edzard, 1959 p. 243f.).

§ 282. *III. Transitive/Two-Participant Conjugation: Marû*

The subject of the transitive *marû* form is marked with pronominal

---

39. For the 3.sg. an. and inan. object, see § 282.

144

suffixes, just like the intransitive subject. Only the 3.sg. and pl. differ from the corresponding intransitive forms. The 3.sg. subject is thus unmarked in the intransitive verb: /lú ì-ku$_4$.r/, but the transitive subject is in the *marû* conjugation marked by /-e/.[40] The 3.pl. subject of the transitive *marû* conjugation is denoted by the suffix /-ene/ which is identical with the plural suffix of animate nouns. The suffix /-eš/, on the other hand, is the suffix of 3.pl. in both intransitive forms and the transitive *hamṭu* conjugation.

The transitive *marû* forms have no pronominal suffixes denoting the direct object since the suffixes already refer to the subject, but a pronominal prefix (= PRON), /-b-/ or /-n-/, most often occurs immediately before the verbal root. These prefixes probably denote inanimate and animate object, respectively, or they have simply the notion 'transitive' in order to distinguish the form from the intransitive conjugation.[41]

1.sg.	...-PRON-VERB-en	g̃á-e̞ s̯ag̃ íb-zi-zi-e̞n̞
2.sg.	...-PRON-VERB-en	za-e̞ s̯ag̃ íb-zi-zi-e̞n̞
3.sg. an. and inan.	...-PRON-VERB-e	a-ne̞ sag̃ íb-zi-zi(-e), lú-e̞ sag̃ íb-zi-zi(-e)
1.pl.	...-PRON-VERB-enden	me.en.dè.en̞ sag̃ íb-zi-zi-e̞n-dè-en̞
2.pl.	...-PRON-VERB-enzen	me.en.zé.en̞ s̯ag̃ íb-zi-zi-e̞n-zé-en̞
3.pl.	...-PRON-VERB-ene	a.ne.ne̞ sag̃ íb-zi-zi-n̞e̞
		lú-e-ne̞ sag̃ íb-zi-zi-n̞e̞

§ 283. *Problems Concerning the Reconstruction of the Conjugations*

It is very difficult to reconstruct the system of the pronominal elements especially as regards the two-part. conjugations, since texts earlier than the Old Babylonian Period contain only little evidence. This is first of all due to the older scribal practice of omitting several grammatical elements for the sake of convenience, and because 3. person forms predominate whereas 1. and 2. person forms are rather

---

40. For the suffix /-e/, see § 233.
41. For the variation of /-b-/ and /-n-/, see Gragg, 1972a.

scarce. A complete system must therefore be based primarily on the Old Babylonian literary texts, that means on texts written by Akkadian speaking scribes at a time when Sumerian was already a dead language. The many variants in the various duplicates of the literary texts belonging to this period demonstrate that there was no agreement as to the insertion of these elements, and as a fact no exact rules can be given for the occurrences of the pronominal elements. The paradigms thus merely give the major trends in relation to which most forms can be explained.

The question whether the system as stated here also existed in the older language although it was not explicitly written can hardly be answered with certainty, since we have no texts to compare with. The most reliable Sumerian text material, the Gudea texts, contain only few pronominal elements, but on the other hand the Old Babylonian literary texts seem to follow a literary and grammatical tradition which can be traced back to the Gudea texts.

Causative Constructions

§ 284. In principal real causatives are three-participant constructions like (a) 'x caused y to destroy z', whereas two-participant constructions like (b) 'x caused y to go' are to be compared with usual transitive forms. In Sumerian both types are constructed like two-participant verbs.

Of the causative construction (a) there is an underlying two-participant sentence: 'y destroyed z', y is thus called the underlying subject or the second subject of clause (a). In the causative verb this underlying or second subject is in general indicated by a dative prefix or by –ni– for 3.sg., –ri– for 2.sg.[42]

> This causative function of -ni- can be illustrated by forms in the Old Babylonian Grammatical Texts where -ni- corresponds to -š- of the Akkadian causative Š-stem (for instance *OBGT* VI and IX).

§ 285. *Examples:*

(289) kur-re gaba.šu.ğar nam–mu–ri[a]–in–[b]tuku-un[b] (a: –ni– for

---

42. For a possible instance of terminative instead of -ni- or dative, see Wilcke, 1969a p. 140 and n. 386: ki-gub-bi in-ne-pàd, with var. im-mu-e-ši-in-pàd, / ĩ-ne-n-pàd /, / ĩ-mu-e-ši-n-pàd /, 'he let them find their places' (Bird and Fish 20).

-ri-; b-b: -tuku-tuku), /na-mu-ri-n-tuku-en/ 'I will not let you have a counterpart in the mountains' (Lugalbanda and Enmerkar 109)

(290) [^{D}E]n.líl-le [gaba.š]u.g̃ar nu-mu-ni-tuku, /nu-mu-ni-(n-)tuku/ 'Enlil did not let him have a counterpart' (Lugalzagesi, *BE* I 87 II 14-16)

(291) za-e-me-en inim-g̃u$_{10}$ an.ki-a gaba.ri la-ba-e-ni-tuku, /nu-ba-e-ni-tuku/ 'you did not let my word have a counterpart in heaven and earth' (Inanna and Ebih 66 = UET VI/1 14, 17). -e- is apparently the pronominal prefix of 2.sg. subj., here applied before the case prefix.

For the underlying transitive sentences of ex. 289-291, cf.:

(292) inim ^{D}En.líl-lá-ta gaba.šu.g̃ar nu-mu-un-tuku, /nu-mu-n-tuku/ 'at the word of Enlil he has no counterpart' (Išme-Dagan Hymn A 57)

(293) ká é.gal-šè mu lugal pàd-mu-ni-ib, /pàd + mu-ni-b/ 'make him swear (lit.: call the king's name) at the Palace Gate' (*TCS* I nr. 39,9) Cf.:

(294) mu lugal-bi in-pàd-dè-eš, /ì-n-pàd-eš/ 'they have sworn by the name of the king' (*NG* nr. 99, 46; cf. also *NG* III p. 142)

(295) igi-bi-šè mu lugal ba-pàd, /ba-pàd/ 'the name of the king was called before them' (*NG* I p. 102: L 11004: 11)

(296) amar gàm.gàm^{mušen} gùd-ba^a tuš-a-gin$_7$ mu-ni-ib-gu$_7$-ù-ne mu-ni-ib-na$_8$-na$_8$-ne^b (a: -bi; b: -e for -ne), /mu-ni-b-gu$_7$-ene/, /mu-ni-b-na$_8$.na$_8$-ene/ 'like a young of a *gam-gam*-bird sitting in its nest they let him eat, they let him drink' (Lugalbanda and Enmerkar 248-249)

§ 286. In sentences of the type 'x caused y to go', y is the direct, absolutive object of the two-participant verb 'to cause to go', and the verb is constructed like a normal transitive verb. Such constructions may, however, also contain the prefix -ni- as in the examples below, but note that -ni- also can be explained as referring to the locative.

(297) É.an.na.túm (...-e) e-bi Íd.nun-ta Gú.eden.na-šè íb-ta-ni-è, /ì-b.ta-ni-(n-)è/ 'Eanatum let its ditch go out from Idnun to Gu-edena' (Ent. 28 I 32-II 3). But cf. the same verb without -ni-:

(298) Gù.dé.a é ^{D}Nin.g̃ír.su-ka ^{D}Utu-gin$_7$ dugud-ta ba-ta-è,

/ba-ta-(n-)è/ 'Gudea let the house of Ninĝirsu go out/rise like the Sun-god from the clouds' (Gudea, cyl. A XXIV 13-14)

(299) ^{D}Ĝá.tùm.dùg-ke$_4$ sig$_4$-bi kur.ku$_4$-a mu-ni-ku$_4$, /mu-ni-(n-)ku$_4$.r/ 'Ĝatumdug brought the brick into ...' (Gudea, cyl. A XX 17-18) But intrans. with -ni-:

(300) é-a húl-la ì-na-ni-ku$_4$, /ì-na-ni-ku$_4$.r/ 'he has happily entered the house' (Gudea, cyl. A VII 30)

The Pronominal Elements

§ 287. The pronominal elements of the finite verbal form refer to the persons involved in the verbal action. There are two main series with different ranks: the prefixes and the suffixes. A verbal form can have at most one prefix immediately before the verbal root and one suffix after the root (or, if present, after /ed/), both referring to subject and/or object. The prefixes are identical with the pronominal elements which under some conditions occur together with case prefixes (see § 428).

For the different functions of the pronominal elements, cf. for instance:

(301) mu-e-ši-in-gi$_4$-nam =
/mu – e – ši – n – gi$_4$ – en – am/
PREF – 'you' – term. – 'he' – VERB – 'me' – COP
'It is (my king) who has sent me to you' (Enmerkar and the Lord of Aratta 176)

§ 288. In the standard grammars of Sumerian other terms have been used, for instance: 'Subjektselemente', 'akkusativische Personalelemente' (A. Poebel, *GSG* p. 173; 206); 'Personenzeichen', 'Akkusativinfixe und -suffixe' (A. Falkenstein, 1959a p. 44, 47); 'Subject and Direct-Object Elements' (Th. Jacobsen, 1968 p. 99).

However, since their functions are very complex, I shall prefer 'pronominal elements' as the more neutral term here. Moreover, it must be stressed that the term 'infix' should be used only about morphemes inserted in the root or stem, and not about the elements of the prefix chain.

§ 289. In the older stages of the Sumerian language the pronominal elements belong to the grammatical elements which are frequently omitted in the writing, and their use before at least the Neo-Sumerian period can hardly be described. The following remarks on these elements are based largely on the occurrences in the Old Babylonian literary texts, in these texts, however, there seems to be many inconsistencies and, moreover, the various duplicates of a literary composition may render the verbal forms rather differently especially as regards the prefixes /-n-/ and /-b-/.

Cf. § 283 and G.B. Gragg, 1972a. 'Observations on Grammatical Variation in Sumerian Literary Texts.' *JAOS* 92: 204-213.

The Pronominal Prefixes

§ 290. According to earlier theories there exists a series of pronominal prefixes for all persons:

1.sg.	-?-	1.pl.	-me-
2.sg.	-e-	2.pl.	-e-ene-
3.sg.an.	-n-	3.pl.	-ene-
inanimate	-b-		

Thus A. Falkenstein, 1959a p. 47, when the prefixes are used before case elements; A. Poebel. *GSG* p. 188ff., has for the 1.sg.: -'-, for the 2.pl.: -ene-; when the prefixes serve as subject marks in the transitive 'preterite' (i.e. *hamṭu*), Falkenstein renders the 2.pl. as -e-...-a-(e)ne, the 3.pl. as -n-...-eš (1959a p.44), Poebel has -ene-... and -n-...-eš (*GSG* p. 173).

In the texts, however, only three different prefixes are actually written, namely: /-e-/ (also rendered as -ù- and -a-), /-n-/ and /-b-/, and it does not seem justified to try to reconstruct prefixes for the other persons. The plural prefixes /-me-/ and /-ene-/ (or better /-ne-/) are used as dative elements only ('for us' and 'for them', respectively, see § 435; § 437), and it is thus more probable that they are case elements than pronominal elements.[43] The 2.pl. is so rarely attested that nothing can be said with certainty about a pronominal prefix for this person, cf. §§ 281 and 291.

The conclusion must be that there are three pronominal prefixes

---

43. In *NBGT* I me is translated by *ni-nu* AN.TA = 'we, prefix' (l. 125), and e-ne = *at-tu-nu* KI.TA = 'you(pl.) suffix' (l. 146). Cf. D.O. Edzard, 1976b, p. 165 n. 14: 'Die von A. Poebel, *GSG* § 453, rekonstruierte Form *ì-me-dím 'wir haben gemacht' (...) ist m.W. bis heute nicht bestätigt worden.' See also § 280 above.

only for three different 'classes': a) /-e-/ for 2. person (and perhaps also for 1. person), b) /-n-/ for animate; and c) /-b-/ for inanimate.

The Pronominal Prefix /-e-/

§ 291. *Writing*: Before the Old Babylonian period there are only few instances of this pronominal prefix. In the Gudea texts it is written -ù- after /mu-/, and -a- after /ba-/ (see *GSGL* I p. 161); in the OB texts it is most often written -e-, but also mu-u₈- occurs.[44]

The main function of /-e-/ is to denote the 2. person:
a) As subject mark of the 2.sg. in transitive *hamṭu* forms, e.g.,

(302) mu-e-íl 'you have lifted' (Angim 9)
(303) mu-e-sum 'you have given' (Gilgameš and Aka 104)

b) Together with the pronominal suffix /-enzen/, /-e-/ may serve as subject mark of the 2.pl. in transitive *hamṭu* forms as contrasting to *marû* forms which have only /-enzen/, e.g.,

(304) nu-mu-e-sum-mu-un-zé-en = /nu-mu-e-sum-enzen/ 'you (pl.) have not given it (to me)' (HSM 1384, 11 = D.O. Edzard, 1976b p. 160, 165)
(305) ǧiš ba-e-šub-bu-za-na-gin₇, /ba-e-šub-enzen-a-gin₇/ 'as you (pl.) have thrown the lot' (Lugale = *SEM* 32 III 15 and dupls., cf. A. Falkenstein, 1950b p. 65)

c) Before case prefixes referring to 2.sg., e.g.,

(306) igi-bi mu-e-ši-ǧál 'they look upon you' (Iddin-Dagan Hymn B 59)

A vocalic element, perhaps identical with this /-e-/, may in a few cases refer to the 1.sg., thus for instance as a subject mark in transitive *hamṭu* forms:

(307) šu zid ma-ra-a-ǧar (= /mu-DAT.2.sg.-e(?)-ǧar/) 'I have faithfully performed it for you' (Gudea, cyl. B II 20)

or before case prefixes:

(308) á še mu-e-da-a-a-áǧ (= /mu-e.da-e-áǧ/) 'you have instructed me(-e.da-)' (Letter, A 1, 8)[45]

---

44. Cf. also pa bí-i-è 'you have made resplendent', si bí-i-sá 'you have made straight' (Iddin-Dagan Hymn B 27 and 30).
45. The subject mark -e- in preradical position has changed to -a- because of the

/-e-/ occurs also rather frequently in contexts where it cannot denote the 2. person, for instance:

(309) me.lám-bi (...) Aratta^{ki}-a túg-gin$_7$ ^{a}ba-e-dul^a gada-gin$_7$ ba-e-búr (a-a: bí-in-dul) 'Its radiance covered Aratta like a garment, enveloped it like linen' (Enmerkar and Ensuhkešdana 13)

A rule for these occurrences cannot be given. ba-e-VERB is especially frequent and probably mostly intransitive.

/-e-/ probably indicating 2.sg. trans. subject, seems to occur not only in preradical position, but also before case elements, e.g.

(310) la-ba-e-ni-tuku, /nu-ba-e-ni-tuku/ 'you did not let it have (a counterpart)' (Inanna and Ebih 66 = UET VI/1, 14: 17)

The Pronominal Prefix /-n-/

§ 292. /-n-/ denotes the 3. sg. animate. It is probably the same morpheme as in /-ani/ 'his, her' and /ane/, /ene/ 'he, she'.
The functions of /-n-/ are:
a) As subject mark of 3.sg. animate it occurs very frequently in transitive *hamṭu* forms, e.g. bí-in-dug$_4$ = /bi-n-dug$_4$/ 'he has spoken', mu-na-an-sum = /mu-na-n-sum/ 'he has given it to him', etc.
b) Together with the pronominal suffix /-eš/, /-n-/ denotes 3.pl. animate subject of transitive *hamṭu* forms, e.g., mu-na-an-sum-mu-uš = /mu-na-n-sum-eš/ 'they have given it to him'.
c) Before case elements referring to a person, e.g.,

(311) á mu-un-da-an-áĝ = /mu-n.da-n-áĝ/ 'he has instructed him' (Iškur Hymn 15)

d) More rarely /-n-/ may denote the 3.sg. animate object. As a rule this can only be the case in *marû* forms which have no pronominal prefix as subject mark, e.g.,

(312) nu-um-ma-ši-in-gi$_4$-gi$_4$ = /nu-ī-ba-ši-n-gi$_4$.gi$_4$-e/ 'He sends out no other (god)' (Angim 95)[46]

---

preceding -da-; the second -a- probably denotes some sort of transition between the pronominal prefix and the initial vowel of the verb, cf. Gragg, *SDI* p. 85.

46. Cf. A. Salonen and P. Siro, 1958 p. 13.

In the OB texts /-n-/ occurs in many instances where none of the functions (a-d) can be ascribed to it, for instance in intransitive forms or in transitive forms with 1. or 2. person as subjects and with inanimate object, e.g.,

(313) e.ne (...) hu-mu-da-an-ti 'may he dwell with her', ğá.e (..) mu-da-an-ti-(e-)en 'I will dwell with her' (Enmerkar and Ensuhkešdana 27-28 and 58-59; we would expect /ha-mu-n.da-ti/ and /mu-n.da-ti-en/)

(314) ÌR.^DEN.ZU (...)-me-en (...) ù.gul im-ma-an-ğá-ğá 'I, Warad-Sin, pray' (Warad-Sin 1, 13, /ì-ba-ğá.ğá-en/ is expected).[47]

The reasons for these occurrences of /-n-/ are not evident.

The Pronominal Prefix /-b-/

§ 293. /-b-/ denotes inanimate, and is probably the same morpheme as in the poss. suffix /-bi/ 'its'.

The functions of /-b-/ are:

a) Analogous to the function (a) of the pronominal prefix /-n-/, also /-b-/ should be expected to occur as subject mark in transitive *hamṭu* forms. Such forms are, however, comparatively rare.

(315) amar-bi (...) gù nu-um-ma-ni-ib-gi₄, /nu-ì-ba-ni-b-gi₄/ 'Its young did not answer' (Lugalbanda and Enmerkar 77)

b) /-b-/ may also refer to a 3.pl. subject in transitive *hamṭu* forms; such instances can be found especially in the NS juridical texts, e.g.

(316) nam.erim₂-bi íb-kud 'they have sworn' (*NG* nr. 40, 8 and passim).

These forms have no pronominal plural suffix.

c) Most often /-b-/ occurs in transitive *marû* forms, probably referring to the inanimate direct object, e.g.,

(317) ensi₂-ra ^DNanše mu-na-ni-íb-gi₄-gi₄ 'Nanše answers u'·' *ensi*' (Gudea, cyl. A V 11)

(318) ku.li-zu-ne-er nam-mu-ni-ib-bé(-en), /na-mu-ni-b-e-en/ 'do not say it to your friends!' (Lugalbanda and Enmerkar 214)

---

47. For more such instances in the Isin-Larsa inscriptions, see Kärki, 1967 p. 120f.

Numerous examples of this occurrence of /-b-/ can be found.

Moreover, /-b-/ occurs comparatively often in the cohortative /ga-/ forms, e.g.,

(319) me šu ga-mu-ra-ab-du$_7$, /ga-mu-DAT.2.sg.-b-du$_7$/ 'I will make the *me*'s perfect for you' (Gudea, cyl. A II 15)

(320) ga-àm-mi-íb-gu-ul, /ga-ī-bi-b-gu.ul/ 'I will destroy it' (Šulgi Hymn D 219)

d) /-b-/ may also occur before case prefixes referring to inanimate,

(321) á šed$_{10}$-bi-šè ní hé-eb-ši-te-en-te(-en), /ha-ī-b.ši-te.en.te (.en-e)/ 'let him refresh himself in its cool arm(s)' (Šulgi Hymn A 33)

Also /ba-/ and /-m-/ are used before case prefixes referring to inanimate, see §§ 329; 342.

The Pronominal Suffixes

§ 294.

	A	B
1.sg.	-en	-en
2.sg.	-en	-en
3.sg.	-Ø	-e
1.pl.	-enden	-enden
2.pl.	-enzen	-enzen
3.pl.	-eš	-ene

The suffixes of series A indicate the subject of the intransitive verb (cf. § 279). In this respect the suffixes of series A are absolutive elements and may therefore also indicate the direct object of a transitive verb (see § 281). The instances of suffixes acting as object elements are, however, comparatively rare.

/-eš/ is also used in two-part. * hamṭu* forms together with the prefix /-n-/ to denote the 3.pl. ergative subject, e.g.: mu-na-an-sum-mu-uš < /mu-na-n-sum-eš/ 'they have given it to him'.

The suffixes of series A are moreover found after the enclitic copula: e.g., lugal-me-en 'I am (the) king' (or: 'you are (the) king') (see § 541).

The series B — which differs from A in the 3. person only — serves as subject marks of the two-part. *marû* conjugation (see § 282): mu-ĝá-ĝá-an < /mu-ĝá.ĝá-en/ 'I place it'.

Note, however, that the suffix /-enden/ also occurs as 1.pl. subject element in two-part *hamṭu* forms. Also /-enzen/ is perhaps used as subject element for the 2.pl. in two-part. *hamṭu* forms together with the prefix /-e-/ (see § 291).

/-enzen/ is added at the end of imperatives to denote the 2.pl., e.g.,

(322) sum-mu-na-ab-zé-en < /sum + mu-na-b + enzen/ 'give it to him!' (Nanna-Suen's Journey to Nippur 320-321)

(323) DU-mu-un-zé-en < /DU + mu + enzen/ 'bring it!' (Dumuzi's Dream 19) (see § 499)

Writing

§ 295. The initial [e] of the suffixes may be changed to [u] under the influence of the vowel of the verbal root, e.g., -šub-bu-uš = /-šub-eš/. Other such verbs are: gub, hur, kúr, sum, sur, túm, gu-ul, gur; with the same verbs writings with [e] can also be found.

If the verbal stem ends in a vowel the [e] is contracted, e.g., -du-un < /-du-(e)n/, -ǧá-ǧá-an < /-ǧá.ǧá-(e)n/.

§ 296. /-en/ In the NS texts it may be written -èn or -en₆, otherwise it is written -en. After a verb ending in a vowel it is written -an or -un. The suffix is hardly attested before the NS period. In the Gudea texts the writing -e or -Ce represents /-en/, and only if followed by another suffix like -a or -àm, is it explicitly attested, e.g.,

(324) ma-dù-na = /mu-DAT.1.sg.-dù-en-a/ '(the house) which you build for me' (Gudea, cyl. A IX 8), but cf.:

(325) ma-ra-dù-e = /mu-DAT.2.sg.-dù-e(n)/ 'I will build it for you' (Gudea, cyl. A XII 1).

§ 297. /-enden/ is written -(e)n-dè-en or -dè-en, e.g.,

(326) ga-ba-ab-túm-mu-dè-en (var.: ba-ab-túm-dè-en), /ga-ba-b-túm-enden/ 'we will bring him back' (Inanna's Descent 310)

(327) gú nam-ba-an-ǧá-ǧá-an-dè-en = /na-ba-n(?)-ǧá.ǧá-enden/ 'let us not submit' (Gilgameš and Aka 8)

§ 298. /-enzen/ This suffix is normally written -en-zé-en; before the subordination suffix /-a/ we have the writings: -(en)-za-na, e.g.,

(328) ì-su₈-ge-en-za-na = /ì-su₈.g-enzen-a/ 'you who are standing here' (Enki's Journey to Nippur 118)

§ 299. /-eš/ is in the older periods written -éš, later on -eš (or after
verbs with the vowel [u]: -uš).

§ 300. /-e/ is written -e or -Ce (or -Cu, cf. above). This suffix is in
most cases altogether omitted after a verb ending in a vowel, and it is
thus most frequently found with regular verbs.
It is also attested in the OS texts.

§ 301. /-ene/ is written -e-ne or -Ce-ne, or simply -ne after verbs
ending in a vowel.

THE PREFIX CHAIN AND ITS ELEMENTS

§ 302. 'Prefix chain' is the name of the elements of the finite verb standing to the left of the verbal stem, e.g. mu-na-an- of the form mu-na-an-dù 'he has built for him'. There are four categories of elements in the prefix chain: 1) Modal prefixes (e.g. nu-), 2) Conjugation prefixes (e.g. mu-), 3) Case prefixes (e.g. -na-), 4) Pronominal prefixes (e.g. -n-).

In a finite form at least one conjugation prefix is obligatory, but the number of elements of the chain may vary from only one conjugation prefix to more complex chains like for instance: ha-mu-na-ab-sum-mu = /ha-mu-na-b-sum-e/ 'let him give it (-b-) to him (-na-)', or ga-àm-ma-da-ra-ab-e₁₁-dè-en-dè-en = /ga-ī-ba-da-ra-b-e₁₁.d-enden/ 'let us make them (-b-) descend from there (-ra-) together (-da-)' (Lahar and Ašnan 40 = *UET* VI/1, 33: 37 and dupls.). As an average the prefix chain consists of two or three elements. The older texts (OS) have in general fewer elements, but this may be due to abbreviation and not represent the actual spoken form.

Possible combinations of the members of the prefix chain can be seen in § 274 and § 304.

§ 303. The Verbal Prefixes

The verbal prefixes proper are those elements of the prefix chain which are able to initiate the finite form. They are subdivided into three groups according to their rank:

A. Conjugation Prefixes: /ī (or ã), -ga-, -m-, mu, ba, bi/

At least one of the conjugation prefixes /ī, mu, ba, bi/ is compulsory in every finite form. /mu, ba, bi/ mutually exclude each other but can be combined with /ī/.

/-ga-/ and /-m-/ cannot initiate the finite form and occur always with /ī/ (or /ã/). They are therefore strictly speaking not real conjugation prefixes.

The term 'conjugation prefix' is a traditional one and here used merely for practical reasons. I have been unable to find a new and more suitable name, since the meaning of the prefixes belonging to this category only approximately can be established.

Note that A. Falkenstein used the term 'Konjugationspräfixe' for ì-, mu- and al-, whereas ba- and bí- were called simply 'Präfixe', (1959a p. 45f.; *GSGL* I pp. 179-183; *GSGL* II pp. 158-190).

B. The Prefix /al-/

This prefix must be listed apart, since, in principle, it is never combined with other prefixes, neither verbal prefixes nor case and pronominal elements. /al-/ stands always immediately before the verbal root. Its meaning is not known.

A. Falkenstein classified /al-/ as 'Konjugationspräfix' (1959a p. 46).

C. Modal Prefixes: /nu, bara, na, ga, ha, ša, u, iri, nuš/

The modal prefixes mutually exclude each other; their rank is before the conjugation prefixes. The modal prefixes express the mood, e.g., negative, prohibitive, vetitive, precative, etc., but the meaning of some of the prefixes cannot be established with certainty. A modal prefix is not obligatory in the finite verb.

The modal prefixes were named 'Präformative' by A. Falkenstein (1959a pp. 49-51; *GSGL* I pp. 217-227; *GSGL* II pp. 209-217).

§ 304. Combinations of Verbal Prefixes

All theoretically possible combinations are listed below. If no example is given, the form is not necessarily ungrammatical, but it is not attested as far as I know.

The Conjugation Prefixes:

/ì + ga/   >   e-ga- (OS), ì-ga- (Gudea), in-ga- (OB)
/ì + ga + mu/
   /ì + ga + mu + DAT.1.sg./   >   e-ga-ma- (OS)
/ì + ga + ba/
/ì + ga + bi/
/ì + m/   >   im- (Gudea, NS, IL, OB), ì-im- (Gudea, NS, OB)
/ì + mu/   >   im-mu- (OB)

/ī + ba/	> e-ma-, ì-ma- (OS), im-ma- (Gudea, and later)
/ī + bi/	> ì-mi- (OS), im-mi- (Gudea and later)[48]
/ī + b(PRON)/	> íb- (all periods), ì-íb- (Gudea, NS)
/ī + n(PRON)/	> in- (all periods), ì-in- (NS)
/ã + ga/	> an-ga-
/ã + m/	> àm- (NS, OB)
/ã + mu/	> àm-mu- (OB)
/ã + ba/	> àm-ma- (OB)
/ã + bi/	> àm-mi- (OB)
/ã + b(PRON)/	> ab- (OB: a-ab-)
/ã + n(PRON)/	> an-

Modal Prefixes and Conjugation Prefixes:

/nu + ī/	> nu-
/nu + ī + ga/	> nu-ga- (Gudea)
/nu + ī + ga + mu/	
/nu + ī + ga + ba/	
/nu + ī + ga + bi/	
/nu + ī + m/	> nu-um- (Gudea, NS, OB)
/nu + ī + mu/	
/nu + ī + ba/	> nu-ma- (Gudea), nu-um-ma- (OB)
/nu + ī + bi/	> nu-mi- (Gudea, NS), nu-um-mi- (OB)
/nu + mu/	> nu-mu- (all periods)
/nu + mu + DAT.1.sg./	> nu-ma- (NS)
/nu + ba/	> nu-ba- (OS, Gudea), la-ba- ((OS), Gudea and later)
/nu + bi/	> nu-bí- (Gudea), li-bí- (NS and later)
/bara + ī/	> ba-ra-
/bara + ī + ga/	
/bara + ī + ga + mu/	
/bara + ī + ga + ba/	
/bara + ī + ga + bi/	
/bara + ī + m/	
/bara + ī + mu/	

---

48. im-me- is either a writing for im-mi- < /ī-bi-/, or comes from im-mu-e- < /ī-mu-e-/.

/bara + ī + ba/
/bara + ī + bi/
/bara + mu/   > ba-ra-mu- (OS, NS)
  /bara + mu + DAT.1.sg./
/bara + ba/   > ba-ra-ba-
/bara + bi/   > ba-ra-bí- (IL)

/na + ī/   > na-
/na + ī + ga/
/na + ī + ga + mu/ > na-ga-mu- (OS), nam-ga-mu- (OB)
/na + ī + ga + ba/
/na + ī + ga + bi/
/na + ī + m/   > nam- (Gudea, OB)
/na + ī + mu/   (see /na + mu/)
/na + ī + ba/[49]   > nam-ma- (OS, OB)
/na + ī + bi/   > nam-mi- (OS, Gudea, OB), na-mi- (NS, IL)
/na + mu/   > nam-mu- (IL, OB), na-àm-mu- (OB), na-mu- (Gudea, OB)
  /na + mu + DAT.1.sg./ > na-ma- (NS), nam-ma- (OB)
/na + ba/   > na-ba- (NS)
/na + bi/   > na-bí- (NS)

/ga + ī/   > ga-
/ga + ī + ga/
/ga + ī + ga + mu/
/ga + ī + ga + ba/
/ga + ī + ga + bi/
/ga + ī + m/   > ga-àm- (OB)
/ga + ī + mu/   (see /ga + mu/)
/ga + ī + ba/   > ga-àm-ma- (OB)
/ga + ī + bi/   > ga-àm-mi- (OB)
/ga + mu/   > ga-mu-
  /ga + mu + DAT.1.sg./ > ga-ma- (Gudea)
/ga + ba/   > ga-ba-
/ga + bi/

---

49. It is not clear whether nam-ba- and nam-bí- (which occur in NS and OB) come from /na-ba-/ and /na-bi-/ or /na-ī-ba-/ and /na-ī-bi-/.

/ha + ī/	> { ha- (before -a-, -b-, -n-, -na-, -ni- and -ra-) hé- (before -a-, -b-, -n-, -da-, -ne-, -ni-, -ri-, -šè, -ši-) }
/ha + ī + ga/	> hé-en-ga- (OB)
/ha + ī + ga + mu/	> hé-en-ga-mu- (OB)
/ha + ī + ga + ba/	
/ha + ī + ga + bi/	
/ha + ī + m/	> hé-em- (Gudea, NS, IL, OB), ha-àm- (NS)
/ha + ī + mu/	(see /ha + mu/)
/ha + ī + ba/	> hé-ma- (Gudea), hé-em-ma- (Gudea, NS, IL, OB)
/ha + ī + bi/	> { hé-mi- (OS, Gudea, IL, OB), hé-em-mi- (IL, OB) hé-me- (OB) }
/ha + mu/	> ha-mu- (OS, Gudea, NS), hu-mu- (IL, OB)
/ha + mu + DAT.1.sg./	> ha-ma- (Gudea, IL, OB), hé-ma- (NS)
/ha + ba/	> ha-ba- (Gudea, NS, IL, OB), hé-ba- (NS)
/ha + bi/	> hé-bé- (OS), hé-bí- (NS, IL, OB), (ha-bí-, NS)
/ša + ī/	> ša- (OB), note ši-in- < /ša-ī-n-/, OB
/ša + ī + ga/	> ši-in-ga- (OB), ši-ga- (OB)
/ša + ī + ga + mu/	
/ša + ī + ga + ba/	
/ša + ī + ga + bi/	
/ša + ī + m/	> ši-im- (OB)
/ša + ī + mu/	> ši-mu-[50] (see also /ša +mu/)
/ša + ī + ba/	> šè-ma- (OS), ši-im-ma- (OB)
/ša + ī + bi/	> ši-im-mi- (OB), ši-mi- (OB)
/ša + mu/	> ša-mu- (OB), šu-mu- (OB)
/ša + ba/	> ša-ba- (OB)
/ša + bi/	> ši-bí- (IL, OB)
/u + ī/	> ù- (all periods)
/u + ī + n/	> un-
/u + ī + ga/	

---

50. ši-mu- is perhaps = /ša-mu-/.

/u + ī + ga + mu/
/u + ī + ga + ba/
/u + ī + ga + bi/
/u + ī + m/   >   um- (Gudea, OB)
/u + ī + mu/
/u + ī + ba/   >   ù-ma- (Gudea), um-ma- (OB)
/u + ī + bi/   >   ù-mi- (Gudea, NS), um-mi- (IL)
/u + mu/   >   ù-mu- (OS, Gudea, NS, IL, OB)
   /u + mu + DAT.1.sg./
/u + ba/   >   a-ba- (OS), ù-ba- (OB)
/u + bi/   >   ì-bí- (Gudea), ù-bí- (IL)

/iri + ī/   >   iri-, i-ri-, i-rí-
/iri + ī + ga/   >   iri-in-ga-

/nuš + ī/   >   nu-uš-, ni-iš-, (cf. also na-aš-an-da-ab-
                                p. 212 n. 95)
/nuš + ī + ga/   >   nu-uš-in-ga-
/nuš + ī + ga + mu/
/nuš + ī + ga + ba/
/nuš + ī + ga + bi/
/nuš + ī + m/
/nuš + ī + mu/
/nuš + ī + ba/
/nuš + ī + bi/   (see /nuš + bi/)
/nuš + mu/   >   nu-uš-mu-
   /nuš + mu + DAT.1.sg./   >   nu-uš-ma-, nu-uš-mu-e-a-
/nuš + ba/   >   nu-uš-ba-
/nuš + bi/   >   nu-uš-bí-, ni-ìš-mi-ni-[51]

---

51. This form may also come from /nuš-ī-bi-/.

THE CONJUGATION PREFIXES

The Order of the Conjugation Prefixes

§ 305. The mutual order of the conjugation prefixes and their possible combinations have often been discussed, and there is no consensus about it among the Sumerologists.[52]

In the present study it is assumed that /ĭ-/ has a rank of its own before the other conjugation prefixes, and that /mu-, -m-, ba-, bi-/ constitute another rank together. /ã-/ is in most cases taken as a variant of /ĭ-/, and /-ga-/ is assumed to be merely an addition to /ĭ-/ (or /ã-/) being able to occur before /mu-, ba-/ and /bi-/. /-m-/ apparently has the same rank as /mu-, ba-, bi-/, since it cannot be used together with these prefixes. /-m-/ differs, however, in that it cannot begin the prefix chain, but must always be combined with /ĭ-/.

§ 306. This system as outlined above can be questioned on various points. The most important problem is the rank of /mu-/. Falkenstein, to example, classified /ĭ-/ and /mu-/ as one group: 'Konjugationspräfixe', whereas /ba-/ and /bi-/ belonged to another group.[53] In the light of the cases where mu–VERB and ba–VERB are contrasting (see §§ 341-345) it seems, however, more likely to rank /mu-/ together with /ba-/ and /bi-/ than with /ĭ-/. On the other hand, while it seems rather certain that im–ma- and im–mi- can be derived from /ĭ-ba-/ and /ĭ-bi-/,[54] it is not completely clear whether /ĭ-/ is compatible with /mu-/. As a fact, im–mu- is first found in literary and

---

52. Cf. for instance the charts in Jacobsen, 1965 p. 102; and Gragg, *SDI* p. 8.
53. See A. Falkenstein, 1959a p. 58-60; he regarded /ĭ-/ and /mu-/as mutually interchangeable: /ĭ-/ being obligatory before a case element of the 3.sg.inan. (except -ni-), /mu-/ obligatory before case elements of the 1. person. Th. Jacobsen, on the other hand, regarded /mu-, ba-, bi-/ as belonging to the same rank, but /ĭ-/ to a different rank, before /mu-/, etc. (see 1965 p. 102). The question of rank is discussed in details in J.N. Postgate, 1974 p. 16-26.
54. This is for instance the view of Postgate, 1974 p. 19ff. Falkenstein, on the

162

lexical texts from the Old Babylonian period, but if it is correct to analyse /ï-ga-/ > in-ga-, then /ï-/, when combined with /-ga-/, may occur before /mu-/, cf. for example the Old Sumerian form na-ga-mu-zu 'he knows also' = /na-ï-ga-mu-zu/ (Ean. 1 rev. I 32).

J.N. Postgate (1974 p. 24 n. 18) suggested that the prefix chains im- and i-im-, which occur in all periods, might represent /ï + mu/. Referring to *OBGT* VII (*MSL* IV p. 88-89) where im-mu-e-ši- is contrasting with im-ši- and i-im-ši- he concludes: 'it seems at least worth suggesting, therefore, that forms like i-im-gin (l. 74) or i-im-ši-gin (l. 77) are for *i.mu.ši.gin, so that after /i/ the /u/ of the prefix mu- drops out if in an open syllable followed by a consonant, but is retained before a vowel.' There may be such instances where im- is parallel to im-mu-. As a rule, however, im- seems rather to be in contrast to mu- before case elements, (see §§ 329-332), and i-im- mostly occurs in contexts totally different from that of the prefix mu- (see § 333). Therefore, I do not think it likely that /-m-/ in these cases could be derived from /mu-/. It is not excluded that there exists some relationship between /mu-/ and /-m-/, but since there is considerable uncertainty as regards both the meanings and functions of the conjugation prefixes I will leave the question open for the present.

The Conjugation Prefix /ï-/

§ 307. The prefix is normally written with the sign NI = ì; in IL and OB also the sign I = i- may be found. When /ï-/ occurs together with pronominal elements we have the writings in- and íb-: in-dù-a = /ï-n-dù-a/ 'who has built' (= ex. 332), in-na-an-sum = /ï-na-n-sum/ 'he has given it to him' (passim), íb-zi-re-a = /ï-b-zi.r-e-a/ 'who destroys it' (Gudea, St. B. VIII 10). Before other conjugation prefixes /ï-/ is written ì- (and e-), in OS, or im- and in-: ì-ma-, e-ma- (OS), im-ma- < /ï-ba-/, ì-mi- (OS), im-mi- < /ï-bi-/; ì-im-, im- < /ï-m-/; im-mu- < /ï-mu-/; ì-ga- (OS and Gudea), in-ga- < /ï-ga-/, see the examples below and the chart § 304.

_____

other hand, analyses im-ma- as /i-b-a-/, /-b-/ being the inanimate pronominal element, /a/ the locative element (see *GSGL* II p. 168); Gragg, *SDI* p. 8, does not analyse them further but renders them as imma and immi. The forms bí-dug₄ and ì-mi-dug₄ (En. I = *AOAT* 25 p. 38, 75 and 85), šu bí-dug₈-a : šu im-mi-du₈, and bí-ğál-la-a : im-mi-ğál (Gudea, cyl. A V 22; IV 25; V 23; IV 26), where bí- and im-mi- occur in exactly parallel contexts, seem to be a strong argument for deriving ì-mi- and im-mi- from /ï-bi-/ (see § 313).

§ 308. /ĭ-/ is considered a nasalized vowel because ĭ- + ba-/bí- becomes im-ma- and im-mi-. This fact may also explain why the prefix is written with the sign NI (= ì) and not with ordinary I (= i).[55]

§ 309. In the Old Sumerian texts from Lagaš, Uruk, Ur and Umma /ĭ/ has the variant /ē/, written ì- and e-, respectively. ì- is used immediately before verbal roots containing the vowels [i] and [u] (e.g., ì-gíd, ì-zìg, ì-si, ì-dù, ì-dug₄, ì-gu₇, ì-šub, etc.) and sometimes also before verbs with the vowel [a] (e.g., ì-bal, ì-gaz, ì-pàd). Further, /ĭ/ is used before the case element -ni-. /ĭ-bi-/ becomes ì-mi-; occasionally also /ĭ-ba-/ is written ì-ma- instead of the more common e-ma-, for instance: nam ì-ma-ni-tar-re₆ = /ĭ-ba-ni-tar-e/ (Ean. 1 rev. V 32). e- is used immediately before verbal roots containing the vowels [a] and [e] (e.g., e-ak, e-ğar, e-lá, e-me-a) and before the case elements -da-, -na-, -ne-, -šè- and -ta-. Furthermore, /ĭ + ba/ = e-ma-, /ĭ + ga/ = e-ga-.

> In the OS texts we also have the writing e-me- for /ĭ + bi/: e-me-ğar 'he has placed' (*AWL* nr. 90, 5, p. 281); e-me-sar-sar 'he has inscribed (numerous steles)' (Ent. 28 II 5); and e-ni- for /ĭ + ni/: e-ni-ba-e 'he will give' (*AWL* nr. 68, 4, p. 231); e-ni-sa₄-a-ni 'she has named' (Ean. 1 V 25).

The contrast ì- : e- is not found in the OS texts from Adab, Fara, Nippur and Isin, which have only ì-, and e- is no longer written in the Old Akkadian period.

The same 'vowel harmony' is found in the OS writings of the conjugation prefix /bi-/, see §§ 7-9; § 339.

§ 310. *Bibliography*

A. Poebel, 1931. *The Sumerian Prefix Forms e- and i- in the Time of the Earlier Princes of Lagaš*. Chicago, *AS* 2.

§ 311. *The Meaning of the Prefix /ĭ-/*

It is difficult to attribute any characteristic function or meaning to the prefix /ĭ-/. It seems to be the most neutral prefix, used where the other presumably more specific conjugation prefixes are not necessary. When /ĭ-/ begins the prefix chain, and when it is not followed by another conjugation prefix, it stands in most cases immediately

---

55. ì = ĭ, so also Falkenstein, 1959a p. 45.

before the verb in the Gudea texts and in the OB literary texts, whereas the OS texts have many instances of /ī-/ before case elements.

§ 312. *Examples:*

(329) lú Umma^{ki}-ra É.an.na.túm-me sa.šuš gal ^{D}En.líl-lá e-na-sum, /ī-na-(n-)sum/ 'Eanatum has given the big net of Enlil to the man of Umma' (Ean. 1 XVI 12-16)

(330) uru-šè ì-du-e, /ī-du-en/ 'I will go to the city' (Gudea, cyl. A III 18)

(331) ensi$_2$ lú ğeštug$_2$ dağal-kam ğeštug$_2$ ì-ğá-ğá, /ī-ğá.ğá-e/ 'the *ensi* is a wise man, he will set his ear to it' (Gudea, cyl. A I 12)

(332) ^{D}Nin.ğiš.zi.da diğir-ra-ni Gù.dé.a ensi$_2$ Lagaš^{ki} lú É.ninnu ^{D}Nin.ğír.su-ka in-dù-a é Ğír.su^{ki}-ka-ni mu-na-dù, /ī-n-dù-a/, /mu-na-(n-)dù/ 'for Ninğišzida, his god, Gudea, the *ensi* of Lagaš who has built the Eninnu of Ninğirsu, has built his Ğirsu house for him' (Gudea, Brick D) Note the change from /ī-/ to /mu-/.

(333) ud-dam ì-è an.ú.sa$_{11}$.an-na-àm ì-gi$_4$-gi$_4$, /ī-è/, /ī-gi$_4$.gi$_4$/ 'by day he goes out, in the evening he comes back' (Enmerkar and Ensuhkešdana 41)

(334) é kug-ga i-ni-in-dù na$_4$-za.gìn-na i-ni-in-gùn, gal-le-eš KUG.GI-ga^{56} šu tag ba-ni-in-dug$_4$, /ī-ni-n-dù/, /ī-ni-n-gùn/, /ba-ni-n-dug$_4$/ 'he built the house of silver, he made it colourful with lapis lazuli, he decorated it with gold in a great way' (Enki's Journey to Nippur 11-12)

§ 313.
The meaning of /ī-/ when it precedes the prefixes /ba-/ and /bi-/ (or /mu-/), is equally difficult to define. Cf. the following examples where /bi-/ and /ī-bi-/ are found in parallel contexts:

(335) munus (...) gi dub-ba kug-NE-a šu im-mi-du$_8$, dub mul an dùg-ga im-mi-ğál, ad im-da-gi$_4$-gi$_4$, /ī-bi-(n-)du$_8$/, /ī-bi-(n-)ğál/, /ī-m-da-gi$_4$.gi$_4$-e/ 'a woman (...) held a stylus of ...-metal in her hand, she placed a tablet ..., she was taking counsel with it' (Gudea, cyl. A IV 23-V 1) In this passage Gudea describes his dream. When later on the goddess Nanše

---

56. For a possible reading kù.sig$_{17}$ instead of traditional guškin, see M. Civil, 1976c p. 183f.

explains the dream to Gudea, she uses forms without /ĭ-/:
šu bí-du$_8$-a 'the woman who held in her hand', bí-ğál-la-a
'who placed', but ad im-da-gi$_4$-a 'who has taken counsel
with it' (cyl. A V 22-24)

(336) Ur.lum.ma (-..-e) e.ki.sur.ra ^{D}Nin.ğír.su-ka-ke$_4$ e-ma-bal,
An.ta.sur.ra ğá-kam (...) bí-dug$_4$, /ĭ-ba-bal/, /bi-(n-)dug$_4$/
'Urlumma crossed the boundary ditch of Ninğirsu and said:
Antasurra is mine!' (En. I 66-75 = *AOAT* 25 p. 37f.). Cf.
the following passage where Ninğirsu describes the event:

(337) Ur.lum.ma(-..-e) An.ta.sur.ra ğá-kam i-mi-dug$_4$, /ĭ-bi-(n-)
dug$_4$/ '(Ninğirsu said:) 'Urlumma has said: Antasurra is
mine!' (ibid. l. 81-85)

(338) mušen-e gùd-bi-šè še$_{26}$ un-gi$_4$ amar-bi gùd-bi-ta gù nu-
um-ma-ni-ib-gi$_4$, /nu-ĭ-ba-ni-b-gi$_4$/ 'after the bird has cried
to its nest, its young did not answer from its nest' (Lugalbanda and Enmerkar 70-71) Compare the form without /ĭ-/ before /ba-/: ud na-an-ga-ma mušen-e gùd-bi-šè še$_{26}$ un-gi$_4$
amar-bi gùd-bi-ta gù ba-ni-ib-gi$_4$-gi$_4$, /ba-ni-b-gi$_4$.gi$_4$-e/
'usually when the bird has cried to its nest, its young answers
from its nest' (ibid. 74-75)

§ 314. *Earlier Theories About ĭ-*

Th. Jacobsen, 1965 p. 76, described the prefix /ĭ-/ as follows: 'mark
of transitory, nonconditioning aspect. The prefix i/e- presents the
occurrence denoted by the verb as touching on the subject without
inwardly conditioning him in any lasting manner.'

M. Yoshikawa, 1979a, regarded /mu-/ and /ĭ-/ as standing in opposition to each other: 'Topical mu-, a) absolute expression: mu- topicalises the high social status of agent in the absolute action. Yet the
selection of mu- is never compulsory' (p. 186). 'b) relative expression: mu- topicalises the action of person(s) of lower social standing,
including for instance, the action of a king towards a god' (p. 187).
'Non-topical ì-, a) absolute expression: ì- denotes the absolute action performed by person(s) of lower social standing, inimical per-
son(s), inanimate things, without respect to other person(s). ì- is also
used to denote the absolute action of a god, ensi, person of high social standing, in cases where it is not worthy of topicalization' (p.
188f.). 'b) relative expression: ì- also denotes the relative action of

person(s) of high social status towards person(s) of lower social status, including, for instance, the action of a god towards a king' (p. 190).

See further E. Sollberger, 1952 p. 120ff., for discussion of other theories of /ī-/ and /mu-/.

§ 315. *ī- after Modal Prefixes*

If a modal prefix begins the prefix chain the presence of /ī-/ can be established with certainty only if followed by /ba-/ or /bi-/: /ha-ī-ba-/ > hé-em-ma-, /na-ī-bi-/ > nam-mi-, etc. In forms like ga-na-dug₄ 'I will tell him', which constitute almost half of the forms with modal prefixes, we cannot say for certain whether the forms should be analysed /ga-ī-na-dug₄/ or /ga-na-dug₄/, in other words whether a conjugation prefix is always compulsory even if preceded by a modal prefix. In this study it is assumed that ī- always has to be present when no other conjugation prefix occurs, and although not explicitly written in the texts, it is here always inserted in the morphemic analysis in such cases, thus: /ga-ī-na-dug₄/ etc.

The Conjugation Prefix /ã-/

§ 316. Occurrences of a prefix /ã-/ are comparatively rare. It is attested already in the OS texts in a few cases in the forms: a-VERB and an-VERB (ex. 339 below). In the OAkk and NS period the prefix chains an-na-, an-ne-, an-ta-, an-da-, ab-, ab-ši- can also be found. The OB literary texts, on the other hand, seem to prefer the forms àm-, àm-ma-, àm-mi- and àm-mu-, whereas the occurrences of a-, ab- or an- are rather few.

Since the combinations /ã/ + /ba/ and /ã/ + /bi/ have become àm-ma- and àm-mi-, /ã/ must be regarded as a nasalized vowel just as it is the case with the prefix /ī/.

§ 317. *Examples:*

(339) kug šà-g̃á a-šag₅-ga, /kug šà-g̃u-a(loc.) ã-šag₅-a/ 'the silver that is good for my heart' (i.e. 'the price that I want') (Ukg. 4 XI 26)

(340) tukumbi dur (a-)ab-tu.lu, /ã-b-tu.lu/ 'if the rope is loose' (Georgica 54 = *UET* VI/2 172 II 16 = *OECT* I pl. 34 III 3) The -b- is not correct, since the verb is intransitive.

(341) ud-bi-a ^{D}Gilgameš$_2$ en Kul.aba$_4$^{ki}-ke$_4$ inim guruš uru-na-šè^a šà-ga-ni an-húl ur$_5$-ra-ni ba-an-zalag (a: -ka), /ã-n(?)-húl/ 'on that day Gilgamesh, the lord of Kulaba, — his heart was glad because of the word of his young men — he was in high spirits' (Gilgamesh and Aka 40-41) The grammar is corrupt: Gilgameš-...ke$_4$ is ergative, but an-húl must be an intransitive verb. For an- as a sort of stative prefix, see § 319. ur$_5$-ra-ni ba-an-zalag is also rather expected to be an intransitive clause: 'his spirits were bright' than a transitive form.

(342) ^{D}Utu uru-ǧu$_{10}$^{a} Kul.aba$_4$^{ki}-šè^b àm^c-ku$_4$-ku$_4$-dè-ne-a (a: -ǧá; b: -a; c: var. om.), /ã-m-ku$_4$.ku$_4$-ed-en-e-a/ 'when Utu will let me enter my city Kulaba' (Lugalbanda and Enmerkar 178) The analysis of the verbal form is not clear, ...-en-e is unusual.

(343) é ^{D}En.líl-lá-šè àm-ma-da-an-ku$_4$-ku$_4$, /ã-ba-da-n-ku$_4$.ku$_4$/ '(Ninurta) entered the temple of Enlil' (Angim 101) /-n-/ is not correct, since the verb is intransitive.

(344) nin$_9$ ki šeš àm-mu-un-pàd-dè-a, /ã-mu-n-pàd-e-a/ 'a sister who reveals the (hiding) place of (her) brother' (Dumuzi's Dream 138)

Is /ã-/ an independent prefix?

§ 318. Because of the limited use of /ã-/ in all periods it has been regarded by some scholars as a variant of /ï-/,[57] although there does not seem to be any phonetic rule according to which /ï-/ changes into /ã-/.

It must be admitted that in many cases it seems rather fruitless to try to establish a separate meaning of /ã-/ in contrast to that of /ï-/, but there are indeed other important indications in favor of regarding

---

57. Cf. for instance A. Falkenstein, *GSGL* I p. 180 n. 4; see E. Sollberger, 1952 p. 118f., for references to older treatments of /ã-/. Th. Jacobsen, 1965 p. 76, regards /ã-/ as a 'mark of persistence': 'The prefix a- presents the occurrence denoted by the verb as persisting in the subject, who is dominated and lastingly conditioned by it. Accordingly forms with a- denoting past action are regularly translated into Akkadian as permansives, not preterits.'

/ā-/ as an independent prefix. In Sumerian texts from Nippur dating in the Old Akkadian period forms with a- and ì-, respectively, seem to contrast in the following way: /ā-/ is used in sentences where the agent is not mentioned, i.e. impersonal forms, whereas /ī-/ occurs in normal transitive forms:[58]

(345) 135 še líd.ga lunga-ne an-ne-áǧ, /ā-ne-áǧ/ '135 líd.ga of barley were measured out to the brewers' (*TMH* V 129: 1-3 = *ECTJ* p. 68)

(346) ᵐLugal.sipa dumu Lugal.lá ᵐUr.ᴰEn.líl šeš-ni an-ne-sum, /ā-ne-sum/ '(the field) was given to Lugal-sipa, the son of Lugal-la, and to Ur-Enlila, his brother' (*SR* nr. 21, 6-10)

(347) 10 še líd.g[a] É.ki.gal.l[a] dumu Ur.ᴰEN.TI É.lú Lugal.an. né-bì-da ì-ne-sum, /ī-ne-(n-)sum/ 'Ekigala, the son of Ur-ᵈEN.TI, has given 10 líd.ga barley to Elu and Lugalane' (*SR* nr. 36, 5-11)

§ 319. It is not possible to confirm this meaning of the prefix because the instances of /ā/ are rather few. It must be noted, however, that the Old Babylonian Grammatical Texts seem to treat the prefix in a similar way translating forms with a- and an- most often with stative or the passive N-stem. At least some forms with a- in literary texts may also be interpreted as equivalents to the Akkadian stative, cf. e.g. ex. 340 and 341.

Cf. e.g. *OBGT* VI 97: ab-ǧar = ša-ki-in (Stative, G-stem)
OBGT VI 85: an-da-ǧar = ša-ki-iš-šu (do.)
OBGT VI 91: an-na-ǧar = ša-ki-iš-šum (do.)
OBGT VI 94: an-na-ni-íb-ǧar = šu-uš-ku-un-šum (do.)
OBGT VI 221: ab-ǧar-re = iš-ša-ak-ka-an (Present N-stem)

Note that the last form is corrupt: in Sumerian texts the verb ǧar cannot have the *marû* ending -e, the *marû* form of ǧar is ǧá-ǧá. In other cases /ā/ and /ī/-forms are translated in the same way, e.g., *OBGT* VII 34 and 40: both ì-du and an-du = i-il-lak 'he goes'.

Sometimes the use of an- in the Old Babylonian texts and in *OBGT* gives the

---

58. See A. Westenholz, *ECTJ* p. 8: 'the Nippur tablets often employ verbal forms with a prefix a-, (...) such forms of transitive verbs are clearly to be translated in the passive. (...) The distinction between ì- and a- is consistently kept only with the dative infix in transitive verbs; in other forms, the meaning of the prefix a- is less clear, and in some cases it alternates with ì-.'

impression of it being regarded as one single morpheme /an/ not to be analysed as prefix + pronominal element. Whereas the Old Sumerian form an-ne-sum is analysed as /ã-ne-sum/, no pronominal element is justified in the intransitive forms an-húl (ex. 341 above), an-du, sá an-e 'he arrives' or sá an-e-en 'I arrive' (*OBGT* IX 95-96). The writing an- may perhaps simply render the nasalized vowel [ã].

§ 320. In the cases of àm-, àm-ma- and àm-mi- it is also very difficult to find any semantic or grammatical distinction between these forms and forms with the prefixes im-, im-ma- and im-mi-. The prefix chains àm-, àm-ma-, àm-mi- and àm-mu- are found only in OB literary texts or texts from later periods.

(348) É.gal.mah ki.tuš nam.lugal-(la-)ka im-ma-da-an-ku₄-k[u₄], /ĩ-ba-da-n-ku₄.ku₄/ 'he enters (with gifts) the Egalmah, the royal residence' (Išme-Dagan Hymn A 59)

(349) é ᴰEn.líl-lá-šè àm-ma-da-an-ku₄-ku₄, /ã-ba-da-n-ku₄.ku₄/ 'he enters (with gifts) the house of Enlil' (Angim 101) For ku₄.r with -da- see Gragg, *SDI* p. 60: 'entry into a place as suppliant or votary'. The verbal forms should perhaps be interpreted as transitive forms with *hamṭu* reduplication: 'he brought (several gifts) into the temple'.

§ 321. Many imperative forms have the prefix /ã-/, but it is not clear whether it in these cases shall be interpreted as the independent prefix /ã-/ or as a variant of /ĩ-/ under the special circumstances of the enclitic position of the prefix chain in the imperative.[59]

(350) é-a-ni gul-a, /gul + ã/ 'destroy his house!' (*TCS* I nr. 142, 9)

(351) dub-g̃u₁₀ zi-ra-ab, /zi.r + ã-b-/ 'cancel (lit.: break) my tablet!' (*NG* nr. 208, 17)

(352) siskur še nu-nir-ra dug₄-ga-ab, /dug₄ + ã-b-/ 'say a prayer for the ... barley!' (Georgica 100 = *UET* VI/2 172 IV 4 = *OECT* I pl. 35 IV 24)

The Conjugation Prefix /-ga-/

§ 322. /ga/ is always combined with the prefix /ĩ/, and cannot itself

---

59. Cf. Th. Jacobsen, 1965 p. 76: 'The preference [of a- in imperative] is a natural one since the prefix presents the action as conditioning and compelling for the subject'. For another view of the [a] of imperatives see M. Yoshikawa, 1980 p. 167.

be in initial position of the prefix chain. It is thus no real conjugation prefix but rather a sort of addition to /ĭ/ with the meaning 'also' or 'and then'.

§ 323. In texts older than OB the prefix is always written -ga-: OS: e-ga- = /ĭ-ga/, na-ga- = /na-ĭ-ga-/, OAkk and Gudea: ì-ga- = /ĭ-ga/, nu-ga- = /nu-ĭ-ga/. In OB literary texts and later it is normally written in-ga- = /ĭ-ga/; after modal prefixes we have e.g.: na-an-ga-, or nam-ga- = /na-ĭ-ga/, ši-in-ga- = /ša-ĭ-ga/, iri-in-ga- = /iri-ĭ-ga/ and nu-uš-in-ga- = /nuš-ĭ-ga/, hé-in-ga- = /ha-ĭ-ga/.

The form of this prefix is normally considered to be /inga/ or /nga/.[60] However, since the vowel is always [i] in initial position and with the modal prefixes /ha/, /ša/, and /nuš/, I prefer to analyse /ĭ + ga/ in which case the spellings -in-ga- or -n-ga- are due to the nasalization of /ĭ/. This analysis seems to be supported by the older writings e-ga- and ì-ga-.

It should be noted that /-ga-/ has nothing to do with the modal prefix /ga-/.

§ 324. In some rare cases the writing im-ga- can be found for /ĭ-ga-/ (e.g. J. Krecher, 1966 p. 60: SK 25 VII 29: im-ga-du = /(igi) ĭ-ga-du₈/ 'she also looked'). For the writing nam-ga- for /na-ĭ-ga-/, see § 325. I do not think it possible that /-m-/ here is the conjugation prefix /-m-/ (see § 329ff.); im-ga- is probably only a variant to in-ga-.

§ 325. *Rank and Combinations of /-ga-/*

/ĭ + ga/ may precede /m/, /mu/, /ba/ and /bi/, but in most cases /ĭ + ga/ are the only verbal prefixes of the chain.

The modal prefixes /nu/, /na/(affirm.), /ha/, /ša/, /iri/ and /nuš/ occur with /ĭ + ga/, the combination /na-ĭ-ga-/ is the most frequent. In the latter case both the writings na-an-ga- and nam-ga- occur. Since the prefix /m/ cannot be expected at this place, nam-ga must be considered a simple scribal variant of na-an-ga-.[61]

---

60. Cf. A Falkenstein, *GSGL* I p. 218: i(n)ga-; E. Sollberger, 1952 p. 172: ega-; A. Poebel, *GSG* p. 148: -nga- and -(n)ga-; Th. Jacobsen, 1965 p. 77: -n-ga-, -m-ga-.

61. Th. Jacobsen, 1965 p. 77, treats -n-ga- and -m-ga- as two independent prefixes: 'n-ga, mark of general conjunctivity, 'also'; (...) m-ga, mark of specified contemporaneity, 'at this (just specified) time.'

Difficult forms are also na–an–ga–àm–ma– and na–an–ga–àm–mi–. According to the principle of rank we expect /na–ī–ga–ba–/ = na–an–ga–ba–, and /na–ī–ga–bi–/ = na–an–ga–bí–, which do occur:

(353) nam–ga–bí–íb–gul–en[a] (a: -e for -en) 'I shall indeed destroy it too' (Enmerkar and the Lord of Aratta 120)

Since /na–ī–ga–ī–ba(or -bi)–/ seems impossible, I shall tentatively suggest that na–an–ga–àm–ma/mi– are secondary forms, that na–an–ga– in these cases is considered an independent prefix: /nanga–ī–ba (or bi)–/.[62] At any rate, /ba/ and /bi/ are otherwise extremely rare after /ī + ga/.[63]

§ 326. *Functions of /-ga-/*

The basic meaning of /ga/ is 'also'. A sequence of clauses with the negative /nu-/ and /nu–ī–ga–/ means 'neither ... nor ...' (cf. ex. 356). Whereas /ī + ga/ and /nu–ī–ga/ connect two sentences (ex. 355, 356), /na–ī–ga/ very often occurs at the beginning of a composition or introduces a new section (ex. 358), in which cases it must be translated 'and then ...', or 'and now ...'.

/ga/ occurs frequently together with -gin₇ 'like', and in this case it has the meaning 'as well as', e.g.,

(354) g̃á-e ᴰUtu-gin₇ in–ga–dím–me–en, /ī–ga–dím–en/ 'I am also created like Utu', i.e. 'I am as good as Utu' (*PAPS* 107 nr. 1, 17), cf. ex. 357.[64]

§ 327. *Examples:*

(355) sipa zid Gù.dé.a gal mu-zu gaḷ ì–ga–túm–mu, /ī–ga–túm–e/ 'the good shepherd Gudea has experienced great things and he is also going to carry them out' (Gudea, cyl. A VII 9-10)

(356) alam-e ù kug-nu za.g̃ìn nu–ga–àm, /nu–ī–ga–me/ 'this statue

---

62. A. Falkenstein gave i(n)ga- the rank before /ī/, since it precedes /mu/ which, according to Falkenstein, has the same rank as /ī/. ì-ga-túm-mu he thus analyses: i(n)ga-i-túmu(-e) (*GSGL* I p. 219).

63. It cannot, however, be excluded that /ga/ or perhaps /nga/ at least in OB is an element without a specific rank that can be added also to the affirmative prefix /na/, na–an–ga–àm–ma– thus = /na–nga–ī–ba/.

64. Cf. W.W. Hallo and J. van Dijk, 1968 p. 79: 'inga-/iga 'again, equally''; and p. 57: 'the force of the verbal prefix i(n)-ga-, with or without the corresponding nominal postposition -gim, is precisely that of comparative.'

is neither of silver nor is it made of lapis lazuli' (Gudea, St. B VII 49)

(357) Kéš^{ki}-gin₇ rib-ba lú ši-in-ga-an-túm-mu
ur.saĝ-bi ^{D(aš)}Aš₇.gi₄-gin₇ rib-ba ama ši-in-ga-an-ù-tu
/ša-ī-ga-n-túm-e/, /ša-ī-ga-n-ù.tu-e/
'what man will (ever) bring forth something as great as Keš?'
'what mother will (ever) bear someone as great as its hero Ašgi?'
(Keš Hymn 18-19)

(358) en-e níg.ul-e pa na-an-ga-àm-mi-in-è
en nam.tar-ra-na šu nu-bal-e-dam
^DEn.líl numun kalam-ma ⌜x⌝-ta è-dè
an ki-ta bad-e-dè saĝ-na na-an-ga-àm-ma-an-sum
ki an-ta bad-e-dè saĝ-na na-an-ga-ma-an-sum
/nanga-ī-bi-n-è/, /nanga-ī-ba-n-sum/
'And then the lord let everything come forth
the lord whose decision cannot be changed,
Enlil, the seed of the land coming out of ...,
hastened to separate heaven from earth,
hastened to separate earth from heaven.'
(Hymn to the Hoe 1-5 = *SRT* 19, 1-5. Note that nanga-...
here is used at the beginning of the composition.)

§ 328. *Bibliography:*

R.R. Jestin, 1967. 'Sur les particules verbales sumériennes'. *RA* 61: 45-50. (p. 48f. Elément préfixé ga- (ṅa)).

The Conjugation Prefix /–m–/

§ 329. The morpheme /–m–/ cannot occur together with the prefixes /mu-/, /ba-/, and /bi-/, and is thus said to have the same rank as these. However, since /–m–/ is not able to begin the prefix chain, but has always to be preceded by /ī-/, it is no true conjugation prefix.

/–m–/ occurs in some specific contexts: either immediately before the verbal root or before one of the case elements -da-, -ši- or -ta- referring to inanimate. /ī-m-/ can be preceded by a modal prefix.

/–m–/ is also found in the prefix chain ì-im-, occurring mostly immediately before the verb, but also, especially in OB, before case elements. ì-im- has often been regarded as a variant to im-, but there are strong arguments that it should be analysed differently and that it has a grammatical function of its own (see below § 333).

§ 330. The morpheme /-m-/ has been explained in different ways, and as is the case with most of the verbal prefixes it is not easy to confirm any characteristic meaning or function of it. The theory which has most arguments in its favour, I think, is that /-m-/ is a ventive element (this was put forward by M. Yoshikawa, see bibliography § 335). It may be possible that /-m-/ in some way is related to /-mu-/, although I do not think it likely that im- is the same as /ī-mu-/, since im- rather must be said to be in opposition to mu-, at least in some cases.

§ 331. *Earlier Theories about /-m-/*

A. Falkenstein regarded /-m-/ as derived from /-b-/, the inanimate pronominal element (1959a p. 48-49). There is, however, no cogent reason for assuming a phonetic rule b > m, since we have also íb-ta-, íb-ši-, íb-da- and íb-VERB.

Th. Jacobsen, 1965 p. 77f. and n. 8, regarded /-m-/ as an independent morpheme: 'm#, mark of propinquity to (zero mark for collative) the area of the speech situation (m). The prefix is neutral as to direction (...) of motion'.

Also M. Yoshikawa regarded /-m-/ as an independent morpheme denoting ventive, occurring as -m- or -im- and in opposition to /-b-/ denoting ientive (i.e. 'spatial and emotional movement away from the speaker', 1978 p. 461). ì- denotes 'non-topicality (peripheral topic)' in opposition to mu- denoting 'topicality (central topic)' (1979a p. 206).

J.N. Postgate, 1974 p. 24 n. 18, suggested that /-m-/ might be derived from /mu-/ (cf. § 306). im- is, however, used before case elements referring to inanimate and thus in opposition to mu- which occurs before animate (see §§ 341-346).

§ 332. *Examples:*

(359) é-a ğiš.hur-bi im-ğá-ğá, /ī-m-ğá.ğá-e/ 'he places the plan of the house on it' (Gudea, cyl. A V 4)

(360) ud ᴰNin.ğír.su-ke₄ uru-ni-šè igi zid im-ši-bar-ra, /ī-m-ši-(n-)bar-a/ 'as Ningirsu has looked faithfully upon his city' (Gudea, St. B III 6)

(361) 10 eren$_2$ É.lugal.la^{ki} 20 eren$_2$ Ga.eš$_5$^{ki} kaskal-šè-àm hé-em-gi$_4$-gi$_4$, /ha-ì-m-gi$_4$.gi$_4$-e/ 'let him return ten soldiers from Elugala and twenty soldiers from Gaeš for the expedition' (*TCS* I nr. 95, 3-6)

(362) [^{D}A.nu]n.na ^{a}digir [še]š-ğu$_{10}$-ne^a hé-em-ši-gúr-e-dè-eš (a-a: dig̃ir gal-gal-e-ne), /ha-ì-m-ši-gúr-ed-eš/ 'let the Anuna Gods, my brothers (or: the great gods), bow down there' (Angim 174)

(363) šà ^{D}En.líl-lá-ke$_4$ ^{id}Idigna-àm a dùg-ga nam-de$_6$, /na-ì-m-de$_6$/ 'the flood (lit.: heart) of Enlil — it is the Tigris — has indeed brought sweet water' (Gudea, cyl. A I 9)

(364) lú na.me inim nu-um-g̃á-g̃á, /nu-ì-m-g̃á.g̃á-e/ 'no one shall claim (lit.: place a word)' (*UET* III 51 rev. 7)

The Prefix Chain ì-im- (or i-im-)

§ 333. ì-im- is in NS texts found exclusively with the verb g̃en 'to go, to come' and almost always immediately before the verbal root.

(365) ud ^{D}Íd.lú.ru.gú-ta ì-im-e-re-éš-ša-a, /ì-i(?)-m-ere-eš-a/ 'when they came here(?) from the ordeal river' (*TDr* 85, 4-5) (ere is the plural *ham̧tu* stem of g̃en)

(366) ì-im-g̃en, /ì-i(?)-m-g̃en/ 'he has come here'[65]

In the OB literary texts i-im- is combined with several different verbs and in most cases a ventive element must not necessarily be ascribed to the forms:[66]

(367) kur-kur ú.sal-la i-im-ná, /ì-i(?)-m-ná/ 'the mountain people lie on the meadows' (Curse of Akkade 38)

(368) ki.en.gi.ra níg-ga ní-ba-ta ^{giš}má i-im-da-gíd-da^a (a: -dè), /ì-i(?)-m-da-gíd-a/ 'in Sumer the ships sail with goods on their own account' (Curse of Akkade 45)

§ 334. Similarly the prefix chains ì-in- and ì-íb-, containing the pronominal elements -n- and -b-, also occur in the NS texts, always

---

65. Examples have been collected by M. Yoshikawa, 1977b p. 231f. Note also that the paradigm of the verb g̃en in *OBGT* VII is the only paradigm in *OBGT* which has the prefix ì-im-. Does this mean that this tablet of *OBGT* follows an older grammatical tradition?

66. Cf. also the examples in M. Yoshikawa, 1977b p. 233ff.

immediately before the verbal root and combined with various verbs.[67] They are not found in later texts (see Yoshikawa, 1977b p. 223). These writings have mostly been regarded as simple variants to im-, in- and íb-, but M. Yoshikawa, 1977b p. 223-236, has argued for a locative-terminative morpheme /i/[68] in these prefixes, and the -m- of ì-im- he interprets as the ventive element.[69]

Although this interpretation may be possible, it cannot be definitely confirmed. It is too easy to apply a locative meaning to any verb, and there may also be other possible solutions to this. However, I think M. Yoshikawa is right in his assumption that ì-in- etc. have distinctive grammatical functions of their own.

§ 335. Bibliography

M. Yoshikawa, 1977b. 'On the Sumerian Verbal Prefix Chains ì-in-, ì-íb-, and ì-im-'. *JCS* 29: 223-236.

M. Yoshikawa, 1978. 'Sumerian Ventive and Ientive'. *OrNS* 47: 461-482.

M. Yoshikawa, 1979a. 'The Sumerian Verbal Prefixes mu-, ì- and Topicality'. *OrNS* 48: 185-206.

§ 336. The Conjugation Prefix /mu-/

In the form [mu] the prefix is always written with the sign MU = mu. /mu + DAT. 1.sg./ > ma-, e.g., Ma.an.sum = /mu-DAT.1.sg.- n-sum/, 'he has given to me' (very often used as personal name);

(369) ha-ma-an-pàd-dè = /ha-mu-DAT.1.sg.-n-pàd-e/ 'may he tell me (the place)' (Lugalbanda and Enmerkar 26)

Together with modal prefixes note the contrast between the forms with dat.1.sg.: nu-ma-, na-ma-, ha-ma-, *ša-ma-, *ù-ma- and the combinations MOD+ī+ba: nu-(um-)ma, nam-ma-, hé-em-ma-, ši-im-ma-, um-ma- (and ù-ma-) (see § 304). This distinction is, however, not always carried through in the writing.

---

67. Examples, see Yoshikawa 1977b p. 223-230.

68. According to M. Yoshikawa, 1977b p. 230, this /i/ might originate from the locative -a-: 'it might be appropriate to think, if only tentatively, that /i/-/i/- has its origin in *ì-a-.'

69. Yoshikawa admits that it is a difficulty that a case element should precede the ventive /-m-/: 'Metathesis or analogy is a possible solution, but in the latter case the chronological relation between ì-im- and ì-in-/ì-íb- must be taken into consideration' (1977b p. 236). 'An interpretation is that ì-im-developed by analogy to ì-in- and ì-íb-; this presupposes that ì-in- and ì-íb- appeared earlier than ì-im-' (p. 236 n. 32).

/mu + 2.sg.dat/ > ma-ra-, the analysis is questionable: /mu-a-ra-/ or /mu-ra-/, /mu-a-r-a-/.[70] Examples:

(370) ^DNin.ǧír.su é-zu ma-ra-dù-e, /mu-ra-dù-en/ 'Ninǧirsu, I shall build your house for you!' (Gudea, cyl. A VIII 18).

After the modal prefixes /nu-/, /ga-/, /ha-/, and /ša/ the form -mu- is retained before the 2.dat. -ra-, e.g.:

(371) ma.mu-zu ǧá ga-mu-ra-búr-búr, /ga-mu-ra-búr.búr/ 'let me interpret your dreams for you' (Gudea, cyl. A V 12)

(372) ^DŠu.ì.lí.šu zi sù.ud nam.ti-bi-šè èš É.meš.lam-ma ul-⟨šè⟩ šu ša-mu-ra-ab-mú-mú, /ša-mu-ra-b-mú.mú-e/ 'Šu-ilišu will pray to you for ever in Emešlam for a long life and vitality' (the verb means literally 'to let the hand grow') (Šu-ilišu Hymn A 66)

/mu/ and /e/ (pron. element of 2.sg.), is often written -me- if following a modal prefix; this writing does not occur before OB literary texts.

(373) a.da.al kug ^DInanna-ke₄ igi me^a-ši-kár-kár (a: mu-e-), /mu-e.ši-kár.kár-e/ 'Now, holy Inanna examines you' (Enmerkar and the Lord of Aratta 449)

(374) ku₆-ǧu₁₀ ku₆ he-a hé-en^a-ga-me-da-an-ku₄-ku₄ (a: var. om.), /ha-ï-ga-mu-e.da-n-ku₄.ku₄/ 'My fish, may all kinds of fish enter with you' (the pronominal element -n- is not correct since the verb is intransitive) (Home of the Fish 68)

For the functions of /mu-/, see below §§ 341-347.

§ 337. The Conjugation Prefix /ba-/

The prefix is always written with the sign BA = ba, except after /ï-/: /ï-ba-/ > ì-ma-, e-ma- (OS), and im-ma-, e.g.,

(375) im-ma-ǧen = /ï-ba-ǧen/ 'he went (to the house)' (Gudea, cyl. A XVIII 8)

According to A. Falkenstein, 1959a p. 46, the prefix may also exceptionally be written PA = bà, but he gives no references.

---

70. Cf. Gragg, *SDI* p. 84f., see for further details the section Case Elements, below.

For the functions of /ba-/, see below §§ 341-352.

The Conjugation Prefix /bi-/

§ 338. The prefix is normally written NE = bí.

PI = bì is found for instance in IL:

(376) hé-bì-kin-kin (Warad-Sin 28 rev. 20), and in OS:
(377) 1 gud (...) lugal-le gal-banšur-šè g̃iš bì-tag 'the king sacrificed an ox to
...' (*UET* II Suppl. nr. 15, 1-5)

/í-bi-/ changes to ì-mi- (OS; Gudea), and im-mi- (NS; OB). After
modal prefixes: /nu-í-bi-/ > nu-(um)-mi-; /na-í-bi-/ > nam-mi-
and na-mi-; /ga-í-bi-/ > ga-àm-mi-; /ha-í-bi-/ > hé-(em-)mi-;
/ša-í-bi-/ > ši-im-mi-.

Before the case prefix -ni- /bi-/ changes to mi-, e.g., na gal-gal-bi
lagab-ba mi-ni-de₆, /bi-ni-(n-)de₆/ 'he has brought large stones in
blocks' (Gudea, cyl. A XVI 6).

A. Falkenstein considered mi-ni- as a variant to mu-ni- (*GSGL* I p. 184f.) but
as Postgate stated in 1974 p. 21f., there are heavy arguments for mi-ni- representing /bi + ni/: Although im-mi-ni- = /í-bi-ni-/ occurs rather frequently, we
never have *bí-ni-, but the occurrences of mi-ni- would exactly serve as the
missing *bí-ni- forms; moreover, mi-ni- can be found with verbs often occurring with /bi-/ alone. An argument against mi-ni- < /bi-ni-/ is perhaps that
ba-ni- does not change to *ma-ni-.

(378) gi-diš-ninda éš.gana₂ za.gìn šu mi-ni-in-du₈, /bi-ni-n-du₈/
'he held the ... in (his) hand' (Inanna's Descent 25) (Variants to the verbal form are: ba-ni-in-du₈, and [b]a-an-du₈)
(379) a.tu-e šibir šu bí-in-du₈, /bi-n-du₈/ 'the *atu*-priest held the
staff in (his) hand' (Keš Hymn 109)

I can give no reason for why -ni- is employed in the first example,
but not in the second.

§ 339. In OS we can observe the 'vowel harmony' in the writing of
/bi-/ similar to the conjugation prefix /í-/ (see § 309): bé- (= BI)
and e-me- are found before verbs having the vowels [a] or [i], e.g.,
bé-g̃ar-re-eš (Ukg. 4-5 IV 1); bé-gi₄ (Ean. 2 VI 8); hé-bé-lá (Ean. 1
VII 22); e-me-sar-sar (Ent. 28-29 II 5).

bí-, e-mi-, ì-mi-, hé-mi- and nam-mi-, on the other hand, are found with verbs containing the vowel [u] (e.g., dù, dub, dug$_4$, šu$_4$, šuš and tuku), but also with verbs with [i], like gi$_4$, sì and zìg. See also §§ 7-9.

§ 340. The only case prefix which can occur with /bi-/ is -ni-.

The Functions of /mu-/, /ba-/ and /bi-/

§ 341. The functions of /mu-/ and /ba-/ can best be illustrated in the light of their contrasting uses. It seems as if the choice of either /mu-/ or /ba-/ is primarily decided by the element immediately following:

/mu-/, /ba-/ and /bi-/ before Case Prefixes

§ 342. /mu-/ is preferred before case prefixes referring to animate beings. In the cases where a modal prefix begins the verbal form, /mu-/ is often missing although it is followed by a case prefix with animate reference, e.g., ga-ra-ab-sum 'I will give it to you' (Gudea, cyl. A IX 9), instead of the expected ga-mu-ra-ab-sum. In these cases we will here assume that /mu-/ is replaced by /ĩ-/ and analyse: /ga-ĩ-ra(dat.)-b-sum/ (cf. § 315).

/ba-/ is preferred before case prefixes referring to inanimate beings, places, etc.

Examples:

(380) ^{D}En.líl-e en ^{D}Nin.ğír.su-šè igi zid mu-ši-bar, /mu-ši-(n-)bar/ 'Enlil looked faithfully on the lord Ninğirsu' (Gudea, cyl. A I 3), cf.:

(381) KA.AL-bi-šè igi zid ba-ši-bar, /ba-ši-(n-)bar/ 'he looked faithfully on its ...' (Gudea, cyl. A XIII 18)

For more examples with /mu-/, see *GSGL* I p. 186:

(382) ma-a-dug$_4$, /mu-DAT.1.sg.-(n-)dug$_4$/ 'you have spoken to me'

(383) gù ma-ra-a-dé, /mu-DAT.2.sg.-(n-)dé/ 'she has spoken to you'

(384) ha-mu-da-gub, /ha-mu-da-gub/ 'may she stand with me'

(385) inim dug$_4$-ga ^{D}Nin.ğír.su-ka-šè sağ sig ba-ši-ğar, /ba-ši-(n-)ğar/ 'to the word of Ninğirsu he bent his head' (Gudea, cyl. A XII 14-15)

(386) inim nin–a–na–šè ğeštug₂ ba–ši–in–gub, /ba–ši–n–gub/ 'to
the word of her mistress she set her mind' (Inanna's Descent
175)

§ 343. This rule is followed rather consistently in the Gudea texts,
and, to a somewhat lesser extent, also in the OB lit. texts. Especially
in the NS juridical texts and letter orders exceptions can frequently
be found. In these texts /ba-/ seems first of all to indicate a one-participant verb with non-agentive subject (cf. § 345), even if it is followed by a case prefix:

(387) Ba.zi–(...)–ra Lú.Hu.wa.wa nam.ğeme₂–ni–šè ba–an–na–sum,
/ba–na–sum/ 'Lu-Huwawa was given to Bazi as his slave-girl'
(NG nr. 126, 12-13); but cf.:
(388) ᵐDŠara.ì.šag₅ (...) Ma.ma ù Da.da dumu–ni A.tu–ra in–na–
sum, /ì–na–(n–)sum/ 'Šara-išag has given his children, Mama
and Dada, to Atu' (YOS IV 2: 1-4)
(389) igi–bi⟨–šè⟩ sağ ba–sum, /ba–sum/ 'Before these (witnesses)
the slave was given (i.e. sold)' (UET III 14: 21)

§ 344. /ba-/ alone may also occur as a sort of case prefix with inanimate or plural (i.e. collective) reference, parallel to the dative mu-
na-... or mu-ne-... with animate reference. This function of /ba-/
seems to be a later phenomenon, occurring in the NS documents and
in the literary texts from the OB period on.

(390) an–né ba–te (...) ki–a ba–te (...) gud–e ba–te (...) guruš–ra
mu–na–te (...) [ki].sikil–ra mu–na–te 'it approaches heaven ...,
it approaches earth ..., it approaches oxen ..., it approaches
the young man ..., it approaches the young girl' (TCL XVI
89, 3-9) Inanimate + locative (or locative-terminative) corresponds here to animate + dative[71]

§ 345. *When the Prefix Chain Contains no Case Prefixes:*

/mu-/ is preferred with animate and agentive subjects, that means
that /mu-/ occurs mostly in transitive forms.

/ba-/ is preferred when the subject is inanimate and/or non-agentive, i.e. most often in intransitive/one-participant verbal forms.

Note, however, the distinction between /ì-/ and /ā-/ in OS texts,
see § 318.

---

71. Cf. A. Falkenstein, 1933 p. 304.

Examples:

(391) sig$_4$ mu-íl ug̃-g̃á-na mu-de$_6$, /mu-(n-)íl/, /mu-(n-)de$_6$/ 'he lifted the brick and brought it before his people' (Gudea, cyl. A XIX 15)

(392) máš bar$_6$-bar$_6$-ra šu mu-gíd-dè máš-a šu ì-gíd máš-a-ni ì-šag$_5$, /mu-gíd-e/, /ì-gíd/, /ì-šag$_5$/ 'He is examining the white offering animal; the animal was examined: his omen was favourable' (Gudea, cyl. A XII 16-17) Note the change from /mu-/ to / ì-/ with the verb šu...gíd.

The most frequently quoted examples of this distinction of /mu-/ and /ba-/ are the year formulas of the NS kings;[72] e.g., the third year of Amar-Suen:

(393) mu ^{D}Amar.^{D}Suen-ke$_4$ Ur.bi.lum^{ki} mu-hul, /mu-(n-)hul (-a)/ 'The year in which Amar-Suen destroyed Urbilum' or: mu Ur.bi.lum^{ki} ba-hul, /ba-hul(-a)/ 'The year in which Urbilum was destroyed'[73]

(394) sá-dug$_4$ ba-g̃ál-la-àm, /ba-g̃ál-am/ 'this is the sá.dug$_4$-offering' (Gudea, St. B I 12)

(395) ù-te-àm é libir-ra-áš rá-zu-a ba-g̃en, /ba-g̃en/ 'in the evening he went to the old temple in prayer' (Gudea, cyl. A XVII 29)

(396) šu si-sá-a-g̃u$_{10}$ an kug-ge ù-a ba-zìg-ge, /ba-zìg-ed/ 'that which my hand had arranged shall raise in a flood to the holy Heaven' (Gudea, cyl. A X 9)

(397) ug̃-e zi-šà-g̃ál ù-ma-sum, /u-ì-ba-sum/ 'when life has been given to the people' (ug̃-e is the loc.-term.) (Gudea, cyl. A XI 24)

(398) dusu kug mu-íl ù.šub-e im-ma-g̃en, /mu-n-íl/, /ì-ba-g̃en/ 'he lifted the holy basket and went to the brick form' (Gudea, cyl. A XVIII 23)

---

72. The latest study of these year-names is: M.J.A. Horsnell, 1977. 'The Grammar and Syntax of the Year-Names of the First Dynasty of Babylon'. *JNES* 36: 277-285, where Horsnell comes to another conclusion, namely that the verb in both cases has to be interpreted as transitive.

73. For the NS year-names, see N. Schneider, 1936. *Die Zeitbestimmungen der Wirtschaftsurkunden von Ur III.* (*AnOr* 13) Rome.

(399) mu-bi-e an.zag-ta kur-kur-re gú im-ma-si-si, /í-ba-(b-)si. si/ 'at its name all foreign lands assemble from the borders of heaven' (Gudea, cyl. A IX 18)

(400) é-e lugal-bi-ir ği₆-a ár im-ma-ab-de₆ dùg-bi mu-un-ğá-ğá, /í-ba-b-de₆/, /mu-n-ğá.ğá(-e)/ 'the house praised its lord during the night, it makes everything good (for him)' (Enki's Journey to Nippur 17) The distinction between /ba-/ and /mu-/ is not quite clear in this case

(401) mu-un-dù-a-ba mu-un-dù-a-ba (72)
Eriduᵏⁱ ᴰEn.ki-ke₄ im-ma-an-íl-la-ba (73)
hur.sağ galam kad₅-dam a-e ba-dirig (74)
zag-ga-a-ni ğiš.gi-a ba-an-KU (75)
ğⁱˢkiri₆ šag₅-ga gurun íl-la-a-ba, mušen-e haš-bi mu-un-
ğá-ğá (76-77)
/mu-n-dù-a-bi-a/, /í-ba-n-íl-a-bi-a/, /ba-dirig/, /ba-n-KU/, /mu-n-ğá.ğá/
'After he has built it, after he has built it,
after Enki has lifted up Eridu,
the mountain which is built in an artful fashion floats on
the water,
he founded(?) his shrine in the cane-brake,
the birds brood(?) in its pleasant garden which carries fruit'
(Enki's Journey to Nippur, 72-77) The verbs in l. 73 and 75 have /ba-/ although being transitive, which is against the rule outlined above; /ba-/ in l. 75 may be explained as referring to the locative ğiš.gi-a. It is possible that /í-ba-/ acts differently from /ba-/

(402) ᴰIsimu-dè sig₄-e gù ba-an-sum, /ba-n-sum/ 'Isimud talked to the brick' (lit.: 'gave voice to it') (Enki's Journey to Nippur 70)

§ 346. However, the distinction of /mu-/ and /ba-/ illustrated in the examples above is only one aspect of their functions, since both of them can be replaced by /í-/ (or by /í-m-/). It is not possible to decide why /í-/ is in some cases chosen rather than /mu-/ or /ba-/, just as the contrast between /í + ba/ and /ba-/ alone cannot be explained satisfactorily.

For examples with im-CASE-... with inanimate reference, see § 332. Cf. also the examples with /í-/ in § 312.

Note that /mu-/ is often deleted or replaced by /ī-/ after a modal prefix, although a case prefix with animate reference follows. This is probably in order to avoid a too long prefix chain, see § 315.

§ 347. *Various Theories about the Meaning of /mu-/*

/mu-/ has very often been regarded as in contrast/opposition to /ī-/, /mu-/ and /ī-/ being a sort of prefix 'pair'. See for instance the account of earlier theories in Sollberger, 1952 p. 120-121, and cf. A. Falkenstein, 1959a p. 58f.: 'Die Setzung von i- ist verpflichtend, wenn dem Konjugationspräfix unmittelbar ein dimensionales Infix der 3.sg. 'sächl.' – abgesehen vom Lokativ-Terminativinfix der 3.sg. 'sächl.' – folgt. Umgekehrt ist mu- verpflichtend vor den dimensionalen Infixen der 1.sg. und pl. In den übrigen Fällen (...) ist grundsätzlich sowohl i- als auch mu- möglich. (...) i- ist das Konjugationspräfix der neutralen Diktion. Der betonte Hinweis auf ein (..) richtungsbestimmtes Wort der Personenklasse im nominalen Satzteil verbindet sich mit dem Konjugationspräfix mu-.'

To this cf. J.N. Postgate, 1974 p. 24f. n. 19: 'We would agree that in these terms, i- is neutral, since it belongs to a different rank from mu-/ba-, of which the first refers to an animate noun, and the second to an inanimate or to no noun; i- has no place in the opposition between mu- and ba-.'

E. Sollberger, on the other hand, concluded: 'Lorsque l'objet du verbe (principalement le datif) appartient à la classe animée, et que l'on veut mettre en évidence le fait que le verbe a un objet appartenant à la classe animée, on emploie le préfixe mu-; si, en revanche, l'objet du verbe appartient à la classe inanimée, ou si on ne juge pas utile de souligner le fait que le verbe a un objet appartenant à la classe animée, on emploie le préfixe e-' (1952 p. 122).

Th. Jacobsen, 1965 p. 79, described the meaning of mu- as follows: 'mark of location of the occurrence denoted by the verb on the inside border (.u) of the area of the speech situation (m.). This is typically the place of the two participants, speaker and addressee, so that depending upon which of them the speaker has in mind mu- locates approximately as Latin *hic* and *iste*. It adds to this implications of emotional involvement of the speaker, of his being personally engaged.'

The latest study of /mu-/ and /ī-/ is M. Yoshikawa, 1979a. 'The Sumerian Verbal Prefixes mu-, ì- and Topicality'. *OrNS* 48: 185-206, where it is concluded: 'The possible factors determining the selection of mu- and ì- are the social status of the agent in correlation with that of the beneficiary, the direct objects, the localistic elements (locative, ablative, directive, terminative), the action or event as a whole, and others' (p. 206).

See also R.R. Jestin, 1976. 'Quelques notes complémentaires sur le système préfixal sumérien'. *AOAT* 25 pp. 261-263.

§ 348. *Various Theories about the Meaning of /ba-/*

/ba-/ has been called a 'passive prefix' because of its frequent occurrence in one-participant forms. As explained above this use of /ba-/ depends on its inanimate/non-agentive reference, and it has nothing to do with the category 'passive', see § 345.

In bilingual literary texts from the Old Babylonian period Sumerian ba-forms (ba-VERB and im–ma-VERB < /ī-ba-VERB/) very often correspond to the Akkadian *t*-perfect. This indicates a temporal function of ba- which might explain those occurrences which do not follow the rules outlined above. How such a function may harmonize with the other functions of ba- is not evident, and I follow Falkenstein in the opinion that this is a later development which cannot be observed in the Gudea texts (*GSGL* II p. 185f. n. 3). Cf. von Soden, 1965, for a different view.

The Functions of /ba-/ and /bi-/

§ 349. It is generally assumed that /ba-/ and /bi-/ contain the pronominal element /b/ for inanimate plus a case element, i.e. locative /a/ and locative-terminative /i/, respectively.

Cf. for instance A. Falkenstein, 1959a p. 46; *GSGL* I p. 190 and 192. Th. Jacobsen, 1965 p. 82 describes /ba-/: 'mark of location of the occurrence denoted by the verb inside relevant area, not that of speech situation'; /bi-/ he describes: 'mark of location of the occurrence denoted by the verb outside, on the outside border of, the relevant area, not that of the speech situation' (p. 84). But cf. the opinion of M. Civil cited by Postgate, 1974 p. 20 n. 11: 'I am grateful to Prof. M. Civil for allowing me to quote his opinion that while the prefix ba- has no connection with a locative element /a/, bí- represents the prefix ba- with the addition of a 'locative-terminative' /i/ or /e/.'

§ 350. The relation of /ba-/ to the inanimate element /b/ is justified, not only for morphological reasons, but also because of the use of

/ba-/ in contrast to /mu-/ as described above. The locative reference of /ba-/, on the other hand, may seem reasonable in the light of the instances where ba- corresponds to mu-na- (ex. 390), but in most of the occurrences of /ba-/ this locative sense cannot be found.

§ 351. The loc.-term. sense of /bi-/ can be claimed in those cases where it occurs with a verb, for instance a compound verb, which takes loc.-term. (ex. 406-407). But /bi-/ occurs with many other verbs and very often without a loc.-term. noun, e.g., the frequent phrase bí-in-dug₄ 'he said'. In other cases /bi-/ occurs with a noun in the locative (ex. 408), or in forms which could be interpreted as causatives (ex. 409). This use of /bi-/ resembles that of the case prefix -ni- (see §§ 470-482), and to some extent also that of the conjugation prefix /ba-/. The semantic and grammatical distinctions between /ba-/, /bi-/ and -ni-, and between /ba-ni-/ and /bi-ni-/ are far from evident (cf. ex. 406-412).

The prefix /bi-/ is most probably not automatically employed for the reason of concord with a loc.-term. or loc. noun, but it rather serves the semantic differentiation of the verb. It seems to be used with certain verbs or in a specific sense of the verb and regularly occurs with šu...dug₈ 'to hold in the hand', túg-gin₇...dul 'to cover like a garment', pa...è 'to make resplendent', and si...sá 'to put in order, to prepare', to mention some of the most frequent verbs with /bi-/.

Since /bi-/ cannot occur with case prefixes other than -ni-, it can only be used when the presence of such other case prefix is not necessary. A verbal form with /bi-/ may thus possibly have a more general meaning, as the semantic differentiation of the case prefix is annulled. For instance, the verb ad...gi₄ 'to take counsel' normally takes -da- referring to the person with whom counsel is taken, e.g.,

(403) ad ši-mu-da-an-gi₄-gi₄, /ša-mu-da-n-gi₄.gi₄-e/ 'she takes counsel with you' (Enlil Hymn 160)

Without -da- the verb has a reflective sense according to Gragg, *SDI* p. 62. When -da- does not occur, the verb can (or must) have /bi-/:

(404) ní-zu ad li-bí-gi₄, /nu-bi-(e-)gi₄/ 'you did not take counsel with yourself' (Bird and Fish 89, *SDI* p. 62)

(405) íd-dè lugal-bi-ir ad im-mi-ib-gi₄-gi₄, /ì-bi-b-gi₄.gi₄-e/ 'the river takes counsel (with itself) for its king' (Enki's Journey to Nippur 91)

§ 352. *The Use of /ba-/ and /bi-/: Examples*

(406) gud du$_7$ máš du$_7$-re$_6$ ĝiš bí-tag, /bi-(n-)tag/ 'he sacrificed perfect oxen and perfect goats' (Gudea, cyl. A XVIII 7)

(407) kar Sirara^{ki}-na-ke$_4$ má bí-ús, /bi-(n-)ús/ 'he directed the ship to the quay of Siraran' (Gudea, cyl. A IV 4)

(408) é (...) muš.huš-gin$_7$ ki šúr-ra bí-dù, /bi-(n-)dù/ 'he has built the house like a dragon in a terrible place' (Gudea, cyl. A X 19-20)

(409) ke.en.gi ki.uri gú bí-(i-)zìg, /bi-e-zìg/ 'you have made Sumer and Akkad raise the neck' (Iddin-Dagan Hymn B 29)

(410) šu.luh si bí-sá, /bi-(n-)sá/ 'he prepared the handwashing (ritual)' (Gudea, cyl. A X 8)

(411) ki-ba ^{D}Ištaran-gin$_7$ di uru-ĝá si ba-ni-íb-sá-e, /ba-ni-b-sá-en/ 'on this place like Ištaran I shall prepare the judgements of my city' (Gudea, cyl. A X 26)

(412) šà ní-ba-ka ad ha-ba-ni-ib-ša$_4$ (...) tigi imin-e ad hé-em-mi-ib-ša$_4$, /ha-ba-ni-b-ša$_4$/, /ha-í-bi-b-ša$_4$/ 'he made them (the musical instruments) resound by themselves (...), he made the *tigi*-drum resound' (Enki's Journey to Nippur 65-67) In this example there seems to be a clear relationship between ba-ni- and the locative ša-ní-ba-ka, and between /bi-/ and the loc.-term. tigi imin-e

THE PREFIX /al-/

§ 353. The Prefix /al-/ must be listed separately since it cannot normally occur with other verbal prefixes, modal prefixes, case elements or pronominal elements.[74] With very few exceptions (cf. § 354) /al-/ is written with the sign AL and occurs always immediately before the verbal root: al-ĝen, al-til, etc.

§ 354. /al-/ with Other Prefixes

In Neo-Sumerian texts /u-al-/ can be found a couple of times:

(413) šuku-bi ù-ul-gíd, /u-al-gíd/ 'after their food portions have been measured out' (NG nr. 215, 3)

(414) šuku Lú.ša.lim.ma šuku lú 1-a-gin₇ ù-ul-dím dirig-bi eren₂-e ba-ab-tùm, /u-al-dím/, /ba-b-tùm/ 'after the food portion of Lu-šalim has been made like the food portion of one man the troops have taken the rest away' (NG nr. 215, 19-21)

(415) dub-bi ú.gu ba-an-dé ù-ul-pàd zi-re-dam, /u-al-pàd/ 'its tablet has disappeared, when it has been found it must be destroyed' (Or 47-49, nr. 411, 7-10) Cf.:

(416) dub-ba-ne-ne ú.gu ba-dé al-pàd zi-re-dam (TMH NF I-II 47, 10-13)

In lexical texts we also find /nu-al-/ which probably is a secondary development since it does not occur elsewhere: di-bi al-til = di-in-šu ga-m[i-ir] 'its judgement has been pronounced' (lit.: completed), di-bi nu-al-til = di-in-šu la ga-mi-[ir] 'its judgement has not been pronounced' (Ana ittišu VII i 31-32).

The form al-bí-in-e₁₁-dè = i-tel-li (BL pl. VIII 8-9), quoted by Th. Jacobsen, 1965 p. 78 n. 9, is late and probably misunderstood (Jacobsen: 'reading and analysis of the form are not very clear').

---

74. A. Falkenstein, 1959a p. 46 and 59, classified /al-/ as 'Konjugationspräfix', i.e. the same category as /ĩ-/ and /mu-/. So also G.B. Gragg, SDI p. 8 and 1968 p. 107 n. 8: 'The prefix al- corresponds structurally to this conjugation class'.

§ 355. /al-/ is a rather infrequently used prefix but it can neverthe-less be found in most periods and text genres, only in the Gudea text corpus it does not occur at all.

§ 356. In almost all cases al-VERB is an intransitive form, and it is thus often translated with an Akkadian stative. The exact meaning of /al-/ or the difference between al-VERB and intransitive forms with other prefixes can, however, not be determined.

It is generally agreed that the meaning of /al-/ is approximately that of the stative, cf. E. Sollberger, 1952 p. 174: /al-/ 'semble avoir, entre autres, une valeur de duratif ou de statif'; A. Falkenstein, 1959a p. 59: /al-/ 'bildet meist stativische Formen (...), jedoch auch fientische Formen in Verbindung mit dem transitiven Präsens-Futur oder der intransitiven Normalform'. Th. Jacobsen, 1965 p. 78, sug-gested a different meaning of /al-/: 'The point referred to by l#- is rarely specified; usually it is rather an ideal point, an implied goal or fulfillment point of the action as such. 'Goal-aimed aspect' describes perhaps the function of the prefix best.'

§ 357. It cannot be excluded that there is some connection between /al-/ and /ã-/. In the very few Old Sumerian examples /al-/ and /ã-/ occur in the same context and in the OB literary texts an- or ab- are occasionally found as variants to al-.

(417) nam-[ur]-zag-bi pad-da ğeštug$_2$-ni al-zu-zu-a
mu-sar-ra-bi ab-ta-ğír-a ğeštug$_2$-ni al-zu-zu-a
izi ba-sum-mu ğeštug$_2$-ni [al-zu-zu-a]
[...] m[u-...] ğešt[ug$_2$-ni] al-zu-zu-a
igi ^{D}Nanše-šè diğir-ra-ni na-dib-bé a-ne na-dib-bé
'its destroyed ..., his ear ...; its inscription which has been ..., his ear ...; it is given to the fire, his ear ..., [...], his ear ...; be-fore Nanše, his god, he shall not pass, he indeed shall not pass' (Ean. 62 IV 1 - V 7) The meaning of this passage is very obscure. Cf. the translation of Sollberger, 1952 p. 175: '(celui qui) pour détruire son ... – c'est ce que son esprit doit savoir! – pour effacer son inscription, – c'est ce que son esprit doit savoir! – y mettrait le feu, – c'est ce que son esprit doit savoir! – y ... – c'est ce que son esprit doit sa-voir! – devant Nanše son dieu le prendra! lui-même il le prendra!'

(418) an en-nam šul-le-šè al-DU, an ki téš-ba sig$_4$ an-gi$_4$-gi$_4$ 'An is the lord – he is standing (or going?) like a young hero, heaven and earth are shouting together' (Ukg. 15 II 1-2) The translation is uncertain, cf. J. van Dijk, 1964-65 p. 40: 'An, comme En, se dressa comme un jeune héros, An et Ki échangeaient des cris l'un avec l'autre'; E. Sollberger, 1952 p. 174: 'le dieu est le seigneur: il alla vers le jeune homme'.

(419) bar 9 iku ^{m}Ur.èš [...] {^{D}Íd-da} Šeš.banda nu.èš-ra ^{D}Íd-da an-na-e$_{11}$ Lugal.ra maškim-bi
bar gana$_2$ ^{m}LUL.KA lú.u$_5$ ^{m}Ur.^{D}Nusku dumu [Š]eš.banda ^{D}[Íd]-šè al-DU.DU Ur.^{D}Gú.lá sagi maškim-bi
'Because of 9 iku field is Ur-eš, [the ...], descended into the river for Šeš-banda, the nu.èš-priest. Lugal-ra was the bailiff. Because of a field have LUL.KA, the ..., and Ur-Nusku, son of Šeš-banda, gone to the river. Ur-Gula, the cupbearer, was the bailiff'. (*TMH* V 159 IV 16 - V 18, translation and transliteration in D.O. Edzard, *SR* p. 156, and A. Westenholz, *ECTJ* p. 80). This text from Nippur, dating to the Akkade period, contains 17 river ordeal protocols. The act is expressed either by the verb e$_{11}$ 'to descend' or by the form al-DU.DU, which may stand for al-su$_8$.b 'they went' or for al-lah$_5$ 'they were brought'. In the context, however, we would expect a plural form with the ending -eš.

§ 358. *Examples:*

(420) En.an.e.du$_7$ (...) nun ní-tuku du$_8$ mah é lugal-la-na-šè šu.luh.ha-ta al-gub-bu-a, /al-gub-e-a/ 'Enane-du (...), the respectful princess, who stands at the lofty platform of the temple of her king with the handwashing (ritual)' (Rim-Sin 8, 1 and 9)

(421) si-a ^{D}Inanna me kur-ra-ke$_4$ šu al-du$_7$-du$_7$ 'be satisfied, Inanna! The divine rules of the netherworld are fulfilled' (Inanna's Descent 132)

(422) é al-dù giri$_{17}$.zal-bi al-dùg 'the temple is built, its splendour is good' (Keš Hymn 118)

(423) diĝir ĝìr kù ^{D}Nun.gal-la-ke$_4$ ní silim-šè al-e 'the strong goddess, the holy Nungal, praises herself' (Nungal 63)

(424) eren$_2$-bi al-tur a-ga-bi-ta al-bir-re 'their army is small, and afterwards it is dispersed' (Gilgameš and Aka 38)

(425) gud su$_7$(!)-ta kar-ra-gin$_7$ lul al^a-si-ge (a: 2 texts have al-, 2 texts have ab-) 'like an ox which has escaped from the threshing-floor, he is filled with falsehood' (Proverb 2.85)

THE MODAL PREFIXES

The Modal Prefix /nu-/, Negative

§ 359. The negative prefix is /nu-/ which may occur before all conjugation prefixes as well as in non-finite forms. Moreover, /nu/ is used in enclitic position after nouns (see § 363).

§ 360. The negation is normally written NU = nu. Before the prefixes /ba-/ and /bi-/ it is changed to la- and li-, respectively.

In OS and Gudea texts the writings nu-ba- and la-ba- are both found; in these texts also nu-bí- is written, whereas li-bí- occurs from the Neo-Sumerian period on. It is possible that nu- in nu-ba- and nu-bí- shall be understood as a sort of logogram = 'negation', and not necessarily as denoting a pronunciation nu-ba/bi-. Cf. the examples:

(426) ku$_6$-bi lú nu-ba-da$_5$-kar-ré, /nu-ba-da-kar-e/ 'a man shall not carry their fish away' (i.e. 'nobody shall ...') (Ukg. 6 III 9)

(427) á bad-a-ǧu$_{10}$ lú la-ba-ta-è, /nu-ba-ta-è/ 'nobody shall escape my wide arm' (Gudea, cyl. A IX 26)

(428) ír nu-bí-dug$_4$, /nu-bi-(n-)dug$_4$/ 'she did not wail' (lit.: 'said a lamentation') (Gudea, St. B V 4)

(429) ki-bi li-bí-gi$_4$⟨-a⟩, /nu-bi-(b?-)gi$_4$/ '(the temple) which they have not restored' (Sin-iddinam 2, 11)

§ 361. *Examples:*

(430) ìr Ur.^{D}Sahar.^{D}Ba.ba$_6$-ka nu-ù-me-en, /nu-ĩ-me-en/ 'I am not the slave of Ur-Sahar-Baba' (*NG* nr. 32, 3) It is not certain what -ù- represents; the writing occurs frequently in the Neo-Sumerian texts, cf.:

(431) nu-ù-gub-ba-šè 'because he was not present' (lit.: 'he did not stay (there)') (*NG* nr. 84, 15)

(432) mu ibila nu–ù–tuku–a–šè 'because he has no heir' (*NG* nr. 183, 13)

(433) nu–ù–zu 'that he does not know it' (*NG* nr. 137,5; also nr. 89, 12: 'they did not know')

(434) nu–ù–zu–bi 'without their knowing it' (*NG* nr. 15, 13)

(435) kug ^{D}Inanna–ke$_4$ ù nu–um–ši–ku–ku, /nu–ī–m–ši–ku.ku-e/ 'holy Inanna does not go to sleep' (Curse of Akkade 24) Cf. Gudea, cyl. A VI 11:

(436) é dú–dè igi–zu ù dùg–ga nu–ši–ku$_4$–ku$_4$, /nu–ī–ši–ku$_4$.ku$_4$-en/ 'in order to build the house you will not let your eyes sleep'

(437) Šà.nin.ğá–ke$_4$ gud lá–dè nu–un–huğ, /nu–ī–n–huğ/ 'Šaninğa did not rent an ox to yoke' (*TCS* I nr. 129, 3-5)

(438) ki.sikil ^{D}Inanna za–e a–na–aš nu–ub–še–ge–en, /nu–ī–b–še.g-en/ 'virgin, Inanna, why do you not obey?' (Dumuzi and Enkimdu 13)

(439) lú inim šà–ga–na–ke$_4$ nu–um–mi–íb–sè–sè–ge, /nu–ī–bi–b–sè.sè.g-e/ 'nobody has placed there the words of his heart' (i.e.: 'none gave him the idea') (Lugalbanda and Enmerkar 6)

(440) šà–bi nu–mu–ù–da–zu, /nu–mu–e.da–zu/ 'I do not know its meaning (lit.: 'its heart')' (Gudea, cyl. A VIII 22)

§ 362. /nu-/ can also negate the non-finite verbal forms:

(441) ur.sağ (...) gaba.šu.ğar nu–tuku 'the hero who has no adversary' (Gudea, cyl. A II 10)

(442) kur ^{giš}eren–na lú nu–ku$_4$–ku$_4$–da, /nu–ku$_4$.ku$_4$–ed-a/ 'the cedar mountain which no man can enter' (Gudea, cyl. A XV 19)

(443) ad.da a dam–ğu$_{10}$ nu–di–dè dam bànda úr–ra nu–húl–le–dè, /nu–di–ed-e/, /nu–húl–ed-e/ 'that the father says nots 'Oh my wife', that the young wife rejoice not in (his) lap' (Lamentation over Sumer and Ur 13-14 = *UET* VI/2, 124: 13-14)

(444) nu–zu–a–ğu$_{10}$–dè 'Without my knowing it' (Enmerkar and Ensuhkešdana 255)

§ 363. /nu-/, and probably also /ha-/ (cf. § 402), are the only verbal prefixes which are able to occur alone without a verb. In this function nu serves as a negative counterpart to the enclitic copula with the meaning 'it is not'. Examples of /nu/ in this construction is found already in OS texts:

(445) na.rú-a mu-bi lú-a nu, /na.rú.a-ak mu-bi lú-ak nu/ 'the name of the stele is not that of a man' (Ean. 1 rev. X 23-25)

(446) alam-e ù kug nu za.gìn nu-ga-àm ù urudu nu ù an.na nu za-bar nu (...) na₄esi-àm 'this statue is neither (made of) silver nor of lapis lazuli, and it is not (made of) copper, of pewter or of bronze (...) — it is of diorite' (Gudea, St. B VII 49-54)

(447) munus diš-àm a.ba me-a-nu a.ba me-a-ni 'there is a single woman — who can it be?' (Gudea, cyl. A IV 23) (lit.: who is it not — who is it?)[75]

(448) uru nu 'it is not a city' (Proverb 2.118)

/nu/ after an adjective:

(449) me-a mu-zu x mah nu 'Where is your name not great?' (Innin 187)

§ 364. The same function as the enclitic /nu/ has /PREF + nu/ in OB literary texts and later on:

(450) šu peš-da-bi ba-nu 'there was no fishing' (Proverb 1.109)

(451) lú bí-in-nu 'there is nothing man(-like) about it' (Proverb 1.37)

(452) in-nu(-ù) 'there is not'[76]

(453) lú še lugal-ĝu₁₀ in-nu 'this man is not my king' (Gilgameš and Aka 70), cf.: lú še lugal-ĝu₁₀ ì-me-a 'this man is my king' in line 92.

§ 365. The form nu-a 'without' is apparently analogous with the non-finite verbal form R-a:

(454) ùz máš nu-a 'goat without kid' (TDr 26, 9)[77]

---

75. For this construction see A. Falkenstein, GSGL I p. 150, where it is compared with the pronominal conjugation.

76. Cf. the examples in C. Wilcke, 1969b p. 83 and n. 78; D.O. Edzard, 1972 p. 19; W.H.P. Römer, 1980 p. 78; Å.W. Sjöberg, 1973a p. 127.

77. For further examples, see D.O. Edzard, 1976a p. 61.

The Modal Prefix /bara-/: Vetitive and Negative Affirmative

§ 366. /bara-/ is always written ba-ra-. The prefix is found in all periods except in the Gudea texts.

(455) lú á dah ba-ra-bí-tuku, /bara-bi-(n-)tuku/ 'nobody had too much wages' (Sin-iddinam 6 II 26-27)

§ 367. /bara-/ occurs before the conjugation prefixes /ï-/, /mu-/, /ba-/ and /bi-/, but not before im-ma- and im-mi-.

§ 368. /bara-/ is found with all persons; forms with the 1.sg. are the most frequent.

/bara-/ with *marû* denotes vetitive, /bara-/ with *hamṭu* negative affirmative. Forms with /bara-/ thus correspond to positive forms with /ha-/:
Vetitive:

(456) di ba-ra-a-da-ab-bé-en$_6$, /bara-ï-e.da-b-e-en/ 'I will not carry on a lawsuit against you' (*NG* nr. 20, 8). Cf. precative:

(457) hé-na-bé, /ha-ï-na-b-e-e/ 'let him tell him' (*TCS* I nr. 129, 10)

Negative affirmative:

(458) ba-ra-ra-dug$_4$, /bara-ï-ra(dat.)-dug$_4$/ 'I have never said to you' (Father and Son 77). Cf. affirmative:

(459) ha-ra-ab-dug$_4$, /ha-ï-ra-b-dug$_4$/ 'they have indeed said (prayers) for you' (Georgica 87 = *OECT* I pl. 35 iv 10)

§ 369. *Examples:*

/bara-/ is not particularly frequent, most often it occurs in promissory oaths, especially in the Neo-Sumerian juridical documents:

(460) ki-sur-ra ^{D}Nin.ǧír.su-ka-ke$_4$ ba-ra-mu-bal-e e-pa$_5$-bi šu bal ba-ra-ak-ke$_4$ na.rú.a-bi ba-ra-pad-re$_6$, /bara-mu-bal-e/, /bara-ï-ak-e/, /bara-ï-pad.r-e/ 'he shall not transgress the boundary ditch of Ninǧirsu, he shall not change the ditch and the canal, he shall not destroy the stele' (Ean. 1 XX 17 - XXI 3) It is also possible to understand the passage as the direct speech of the oath of the Ummaite: 'I will not transgress etc.' /bara-mu-bal-en/.

(461) mí.ús.sá–zu mí.ús.sá–ğu$_{10}$ ba–ra–me, /bara–ī–me/ 'your son-in-law shall not be my son-in-law!' (*NG* nr. 18, 24)

(462) ba–ra–ab–gi$_4$–gi$_4$–dè, /bara–ī–b–gi$_4$.gi$_4$–ed–en/ 'I will not return (with this claim)' (*NG* nr. 164, I 3)

(463) ki–ni ba–ra–zu, /bara–ī–zu/ 'I really do not know his place' (Dumuzi's Dream 144)

§ 370. *Bibliography*

For /bara-/ with *marû* and *hamṭu*, see D.O. Edzard, 1971a p. 216-219.

The Modal Prefix /na-/: Prohibitive and Affirmative

§ 371. The prefix /na-/ is written na- or, if it precedes /ī–m-/, /ī–ba-/, /ī–bi-/, nam-, e.g.,

(464) na–an–mú–mú–un, /na–ī–n–mú.mú–en/ 'do not start a quarrel' (*PAPS* 107 nr. 1, 7-9)

(465) ud na–bí–zal–e, /na–bi–zal–e/ 'the day must not pass' (*TCS* I nr. 25, 7a)

(466) nam–ta–è, /na–ī–m–ta–è/ 'he went out' (Gudea, cyl. A VIII 1)

(467) nam–mi–gul–e, /na–ī–bi–gul–e/ 'no one shall destroy it' (Gudea, St. B VII 57)

§ 372. In OB literary texts nam-ba-... and nam-bí-... occur as well as the writings nam-ma-... and nam-mi-..., but it is not completely clear whether nam-ba/bí- represents /na-ī-ba(bi)/ or rather /na-ba(bi)/ and thus, in the latter case, replace na-ba-... and na-bí-...[78]
Cf. for instance:

(468) nam–mi–in–hu.luh–[...] with the variants: nam–mi–ib– and nam–bí–in-, 'do not frighten' (Angim 87)

(469) gú nam–ba–(an–)ğá–ğá–an–dè–en (variants: ba–an–ğar–re–en–dè–en, nam–ba–an–ğar–re–en–zé–en, nam–ba–an–ğar–re–en–dè–en) 'let us not submit' (Gilgameš and Aka 8)

---

78. Because of the writings nam-ba- etc. I.M. Diakonoff has assumed the form nã- for the prohibitive/affirmative prefix, see D.O. Edzard, 1971a p. 219 n. 32.

§ 373. When /na-/ precedes /ī-ga-/ the prefix chain is written either na-an-ga- or nam-ga-, in OS na-ga-, e.g.,

(470) É.an.na.túm-me gal na-ga-mu-zu, /na-ī-ga-mu-(n-)zu/ 'Eanatum knows also great things' (Ean. 1 rev. I 31-32)

(471) ki šà-ğu$_{10}$ ^{a}na-an-ga^a-ma-ab-bé-e-a (a-a: na-ga-, an-ga-), /na-ī-ga-mu-DAT.1.sg.-b-e-e-a/ 'on the place which my heart chooses (lit.: says) for me' (Lugalbanda and Enmerkar 177)

(472) ki nam-ga-bí-ib-gul-en^a (a: -e for -en), /na-ī-ga-bi-b-gul-en/ 'I shall indeed destroy it too' (Enmerkar and the Lord of Aratta 120)

§ 374. The prefix /na-/ has two different meanings dependent on the aspect of the verb: na + *marû* = prohibitive:

(473) na-(ab-)pàd-dè, /na-ī-b-pàd-en/ 'do not tell (where I am)' (Dumuzi's Dream 92)

na + *hamṭu* = affirmative:

(474) nam-mi-gub, /na-ī-bi-gub/ 'he set indeed (his foot on the ship)' (Gudea, cyl. A II 4 and IV 3)

This pattern seems to be relatively well established. However, in some cases /na-/ has the *marû* stem with, apparently, affirmative meaning: na-ri-bé, /na-ī-ri-b-e-e/ 'they sing for you', na-mu-un-e, /na-mu-n-e/ 'she says', na-e, /na-ī-e-e/ 'she says', na-ur$_4$-ur$_4$-re, /na-ī-ur$_4$.ur$_4$-e/ 'she collects', na-ğá-ğá, /na-ī-ğá.ğá-e/ 'she places'.[79] It is striking that most instances have the verb e 'to say' and, moreover, that all are from OB literary texts, very often in difficult context. We might, therefore, leave these examples out of account and at least state that *generally marû* = prohibitive, and *hamṭu* = affirmative.

§ 375. The prohibitive /na-/ forms are the negative counterpart to the imperative and to the precative forms with /ha-/. Prohibitive is found with the 2. and 3. person, whereas the 1. person occurs with /bara-/ in vetitive forms. /na-/ with 1.pl. is, however, attested:

(475) gù nam-ba-(an-)ğá-ğá-an-dè-en, /na-(ī?-)ba-(n-)ğá.ğá-en-den/ 'let us not submit' and

79. The examples are from A. Falkenstein, 1942 p. 201 nr. 25; p. 204f. nr. 1-5; p. 219 nr. 3; p. 217 nr. 13; cf. also D.O. Edzard, 1971a p. 221 and note 36.

(476) ^{ğiš}tukul nam-ba-an-sìg-ge-en-dè-en, /na-(ì?-)ba-n-sìg-en-
den/ 'let us not smite it with weapons' (Gilgameš and Aka 8
and 14) (cf. the parallel, positive forms in the same context:
gú ga-àm-ğá-ğá-an-dè-en 'let us submit', ^{ğiš}tukul ga-àm-
sìg-sìg-en-dè-en 'let us smite it with weapons', l. 14 and 8)

§ 376. The affirmative /na-/ is used with all persons; for 1.pl., cf.:

(477) na-an-dúr-ru-ne-en-dè-en 'we lived there' (Enlil and Ninlil
1-3)

The term 'affirmative' is not very precise, and it may well be asked
how /na-/ differs in meaning from other modal prefixes (/ha-/ and
/ša-/) which are also called affirmative. For the present, however, it
seems impossible to solve this problem, since the contexts in which
these forms occur give almost no opportunity to compare the various
uses of the prefixes in question.

§ 377. Th. Jacobsen regarded the affirmative /na-/ as etymologically
different from the prohibitive prefix, cf. 1965 p. 73 n. 4: 'From
these data [*MSL* IV 194: 163: na-a = NA = *šu-u*; p. 194: 105: né-e
= NA = *šu-u* and others] it seems possible to conclude that na- varied
in pronunciation toward ne- — possibly in differentiation from vetitive na- — and that it has third-person reference to subject (*šū*) or object (*šuāti*). This seems confirmed in some measure by its etymology
since it would appear to consist of a third-person pronominal element
-n- 'he', 'she', 'it'(?), and a relater -a 'in', 'for'.

According to this analysis Th. Jacobsen gave a more precise formu-
lation of the meaning of /na-/: 'As actually used (...) na-, 'within him',
seems to present an act not objectively, in itself, 'he did', but subjec-
tively, in its psychological matrix of impulse, inner urge, decision to
act, in the subject, 'he saw fit to do'" (1965 p. 74 n. 4).

A. Falkenstein also quotes a dative prefix /na-/ which in his opinion
is identical with the case element -na- 'for him/her'. There is, however, hardly any evidence for this prefix. Falkenstein himself gives
only two rather uncertain examples which in my opinion may as well
be interpreted as affirmative na-forms: na-gu-ul-gu-ul 'he made indeed (the presents) great' (Gudea, cyl. B II 12-13).

(478) é ur₅-gin₇ dím-ma ensi₂ aš-e ^DNin.ğír.su-ra nu-na-dù na-
mu-dù 'a temple made like this has no *ensi* ever built for

Ningirsu, (but) he indeed has built it' (Gudea, St. B VI 77 -
VII 4). Cf. A. Falkenstein, *GSGL* I p. 189; II 182; 1959a p.
46.

§ 378. /na/- is always used in the introductory formula of Sumerian
letters. If this /na/- has to be interpreted as the affirmative prefix, we
would expect a *hamṭu* form, but this is never the case.

(479) Lú.en.na saĝa ^{D}Nin.MAR.KI-ka-ke$_4$ na-e-a, [En].e.tar.zid
[saĝa] ^{D}Nin.[ĝír.]su-[ka]-ra [dug$_4$]-ga-n[a], /na-ï-e-e-a/,
/dug$_4$ + ï-na/ 'this is what Luenna, the *saĝa* of Nin-MAR.KI
says — say it to Enetarzid, the *saĝa* of Ningirsu' (Enz. 1 I
1-6)

(480) lugal-e na-ab-bé-a Ur.^{D}Li$_9$.si$_4$-na-ra ù-na-a-dug$_4$, /na-ï-
b-e-e-a/, /u-ï-na-e-dug$_4$/ 'this is what the king says —
when you have said it to Ur-Lisina' (*TCS* I nr. 1, 1-4)

(481) ^{m}^{D}I.bí.^{D}EN.ZU lugal-ĝu$_{10}$-ra ù-na-a-dug$_4$, ^{m}Puzur$_4$.Šulgi
ensi$_2$ Ka.zal.lu^{ki} ìr-zu na-ab-bé-a, /na-ï-b-e-e-a/ 'When
you have said it to my king, Ibbi-Sin, that is what Puzur-
Šulgi, the *ensi* of Kazallu, your servant, says' (Letter A 3, 1-3)

§ 379. A morpheme /na/ occurs in forms of the verb me 'to be': na-
nam, ga-nam-me-àm, both = 'it is indeed', and (ur$_5$) hé-na-nam(-
ma-àm) 'it is so', 'may it be so'. Although the meaning of these
phrases may well be described as affirmative, it is not beyond doubt
whether /na/ shall be regarded as identical with the affirmative modal
prefix /na-/, since it is here preceded by the prefixes /ga-/ and /ha-/
which is otherwise not the case, and the analysis of all forms is rather
problematic.

na-nam seems to be a fixed term to which the prefix /ha-/ is
added in either an affirmative or precative sense, cf. also the very late
form in-ga-na-nam (*BL* 16, 1) 'it is also'.

A. Falkenstein regarded na- of these phrases as the affirmative prefix and analysed /ga-na-i-me-àm/; he saw ga- as a variant to hé-.[80]

Note that nam-me is the prohibitive form of the verb me: 'may it/
he/she not be':

(482) sipa engar nam-me 'the shepherd shall not be a farmer'
(Proverb 1.100)

---

80. See *GSGL* I p. 220; and 1942 p. 186 n. 1.

§ 380. *Examples:* /na-/, *Affirmative, with me 'to be':*

(483) (lú ...) šeš-g̃u₁₀ ᴰNin.g̃ír.su ga-nam-me-àm '(the man who ...) is indeed my brother Ning̃irsu' (Gudea, cyl. A V 17, cf. also A V 25 and VI 8)

(484) 1-kam-ma Maš.gu.la mu-ni hé-en-na-nam 'of the first his name is indeed Mašgula' (Enmerkar and Ensuhkešdana 214)

(485) ì-ne-šè ᴰUtu ud-dè-e-a ur₅ ᵃhé-en-na-nam-ma-àmᵃ (a-a: hé-na-nam) 'and now, when Utu lets the day begin, so may it be!' (Curse of Akkade 274)

(486) ud-bi-a imin hé-ne-me-eš imin hé-na-me-eš 'on that day they were indeed seven, they were indeed seven' (Lugalbanda in Hurrumkura 57, see Cl. Wilcke, 1969a p. 49f.)

(487) a nam-de₆ a zal-le na-nam kurun₂-bi na-dùg-ge, še nam-de₆ še gu.nu na-nam ùg̃-e na-kú-e 'he has brought water — it is indeed everflowing water, he makes its wine good (or: as good as wine?), he has brought grain — it is indeed ...-grain, the people eat it' (Enki and the World Order 259-260) (na-dùg-ge and na-kú-e are *marû* forms and should, therefore, be prohibitive, but this does not seem to make sense in the context)

(488) ki-ág̃-bi na-nam ki-ág̃-bi na-nam en É.kur-ra ki-ág̃-bi na-nam 'he is indeed its beloved, he is indeed its beloved, he is indeed the beloved lord of Ekur' (Nanna-Suen Hymn A 21-22)

For na-nam and the affirmative /na-/ together:

(489) uruᵏⁱ na-nam ᵃna-anᵃ-dúr-ru-ne-en-dè-en (a-a: àm-, na-àm-), /na-ì-n-durun-enden/ 'this is the city, and we live there indeed' (Enlil and Ninlil 1-3)

§ 381. *Examples:* /na-/, *Prohibitive*

(490) ud nu-šè-sa₁₀-sa₁₀-a-a ugula lipiš-bi na-na-tag-ge, /nu-ì-ši-sa₁₀-sa₁₀-e-a-a-/, /na-ì-na-tag-e/ 'if he does not buy it, the overseer must not be angry with him' (Ukg. 4 XI 29-31)

(491) ᴰInanna (...) g̃ⁱˢgu.za gub-ba-na suhuš-bi na-an-ge-né nu. mun-a-ni hé-til, /na-ì-n-ge.n-e/, /ha-ì-til/ 'may Inanna (...) not make the foundation of his throne firm, may his off-spring come to an end' (Gudea, St. C IV 9-16)

(492) kilib₃ dig̃ir gal-gal-e-ne (...) e-ne ù numun-a-ni šà kalam-ma-ka nam-mu-ni-íb-g̃á-g̃á-e-ne, /na-mu-ni-b-g̃á.g̃á-ene/

'may all the great gods not let him and his seed stay in the land' (Warad-Sin 27 II 17 - III 5)

(493) ì dùg-ga bur-ra na-an-še$_{22}$-še$_{22}$(-en), ir.si.im-bi-šè ^{a}nam-mu(-e)^a-niĝin-ne-eš (a-a: ba-e-dé-), /na-ī-n-še$_{22}$.še$_{22}$-en/, /na-mu-e-niĝin-eš/ (= *ša-man pu-ú-ri ṭa-a-ba la tap-pa-ši-iš*, *a-na i-ri-ši-šu i-pah-hu-ru-ka*) 'do not rub yourself with fine oil of the jar, (then) they will indeed gather about you at its fragrance' (Gilgameš, Enkidu and the Netherworld 187-188) The first form is prohibitive, the second affirmative; for other such pairs, see ibid. l. 185-199.

§ 382. *Examples: /na-/, Affirmative*

(494) [an-gal]-ta ki-gal-šè ĝeštug$_2$-ga-ni na-an-gub, /na-ī-n-gub/ 'from the great heaven she set her mind to the great earth (i.e. the Netherworld)' (Inanna's Descent 1)

(495) hur-sag daĝal téš-bi nam-ta-an-e$_{11}$, /na-ī-m-ta-n-e$_{11}$/ '(Enlil) brought (Gutium) the wide mountain in its whole down (into Sumer)' (Curse of Akkade 155)

§ 383. *Bibliography*

A. Falkenstein, 1942. 'Untersuchungen zur sumerischen Grammatik: Das affirmative Präformativ na-'. *ZA* 47: 181-223.

The Modal Prefix /ga-/: Cohortative

§ 384. This prefix is written ga- before all conjugation prefixes and case elements. The vowel is normally not subject to change, unlike the prefixes ha-/hé-/hu- and ša-/ši-/šu-. Only exceptionally do forms like the following turn up:

(496) gú-mu-ra-ra-ba.al = /ga-mu-ra(DAT.2.sg.)-ra(abl.)-ba.al/ 'I will return it to you' (*NG* nr. 132, 5)

(497) saĝ-šè gú-mu-ni-rig$_7$ = /ga-mu-ni-rig$_7$/ 'I will give as a gift' (Šulgi Hymn D 210)

(498) gi$_4$-bí-íb-gu$_7$ = /ga-bi-b-gu$_7$/ 'I will let them eat' (Šulgi Hymn D 176)[81]

81. More forms occur in Šulgi Hymn D: gi$_4$-ni-in-ug$_7$ (l. 156); gi$_4$-ni-in-šú (l. 169); gi$_4$-bí-ni-mú (l. 222); gi$_4$-ni-íb-bal-bal (l. 225); gi$_4$-rí-íb-tar^{ar} (l. 384); gú-mu-rí-íb-tar^{ar} (l. 384-387); cf. also ge$_4$-me-e-da-LI-na (= /ga-mu-e.da-LI-?/?/) in the difficult syllabic Dumuzi-lament *VS* II 2 iii 2.

§ 385. In Emesal context the cohortative prefix has the form da- or du$_5$ -:

(499) da-an-u$_5$ 'I will board the ship' (*VS* X 199 iv 13)

(500) ír-ra da-mar-re-en 'I will set up a lament' (*SBH* 14, 18)[82], other examples are:

(501) i.lu (...) du$_5$ -mu-ri-ib-dug$_4$, /ga-mu-ri-b-dug$_4$/ 'let me say a lamentation for you' (Inanna and Bilulu 165)

(502) [Abzu Uru].zé.eb^{ki}-šè me-e mí du$_5$ -mu-na-ab-dug$_4$, /ga-mu-na-b-dug$_4$/ 'let me take care of Abzu-Eridu' (Inanna and Enki I i 25)

In Emesal da-, dè- and du$_5$ - are also used for the precative /ha-/ (see § 395). Cohortative and precative are thus morphologically the same category in Emesal.

§ 386. In some cases ha- is used for ga-:

(503) ha-a-tuku = /ga-ī-a-tuku/ 'I will marry her' (*NG* nr. 16, 6; 15, 6: ha-tuku)

(504) ha-a-me-en = /ga-ī-me-en/ 'I will be (the slave-girl of PN)' (Sollberger, 1976 p. 441 nr. 6, 9)[83]

The writing ha- instead of ga- may suggest that /ga-/ and /ha-/ phonetically are rather similar, cf. the Emesal forms da- etc. which are both cohortative and precative (see § 385).[84]

§ 387. The cohortative /ga-/ is found in the first person only, both singular and plural. Instances of the 1.pl. occur exclusively in the literary texts from the Old Babylonian period and later (cf. § 392).

§ 388. Singular cohortative forms have always the *hamṭu* stem of the verb, and normally there is no subject mark in the 1.sg., neither in transitive nor in intransitive forms (see examples in § 391). Exceptions do of course occur:

---

82. /ga-ī-n-u$_5$/ and /ga-ī-gar-en/ are not grammatically correct. We would expect /ga-ī-u$_5$/ and /ga-ī-g̃ar/.

83. The -a- may represent the transitive *hamṭu* subject element for the 1.sg. (see § 291). In ha-a-me-en, however, -a- cannot be explained in this way, since the form is intransitive.

84. Cf. also J. van Dijk, 1967 p. 256f. The basic form of the word hé-du$_7$, 'architrave', is probably *hin-du$_7$ because of the Akkadian rendering *hittu*. The readings hé and gan of the sign HÉ are therefore possibly only 'Ablaut'.

(505) ga–na–ab–bé–en, /ga–ī–na–b–e–en/ 'let me tell it to her'
(Iddin-Dagan Hymn A 1ff.); cf.

(506) ga–na–ga–na–ab–dug₄ (Gudea, cyl. A I 24). Cf. also the Neo-
Sumerian forms ha-a-tuku and ha-a-me-en mentioned
above (§ 386) and ex. 516.

Reduplicated forms can be understood as plural verbs denoting the
plurality of the object:

(507) ma.mu-zu ǧá ga–mu–ra–búr–búr, /ga–mu–DAT.2.sg.-búr.
búr/ 'let me interpret your dreams' (Gudea, cyl. A V 12)

(508) ǧiš tur–tur–bi úr–ba ga–mu–bù–bù, /ga–mu–bù.bù/ 'let me
tear out its small trees in their roots' (Šulgi Hymn D 223)

§ 389. The plural cohortative forms, on the other hand, always have
the ending /-enden/ together with the plural stem (ex. 517-519) or
the reduplicated verb; in ex. 520 the *marû* form is used.

The pronominal suffix may also be missing, cf.

(509) me.en.dè (...) e.ne.sù.ud ga–da–e 'let us copulate' (*PAPS* 107
nr. 4, 20)

§ 390. A special expression with the prefix /ga-/ is: ga-nam-me-àm
'it is indeed', where /ga-/ is rather affirmative, similar to /ha-/.

§ 391. *Examples: 1.sg.*

(510) na ga–ri na.ri–ǧu₁₀ hé–dab₅, /ga–ī–ri/, /ha–ī–dab₅/ 'let me
give (you) instructions — may my instructions be followed!'
(Gudea, cyl. A VI 14). In OB literary texts the phrase goes
like this:

(511) na ga–e–ri na.ri–ǧu₁₀ hé–e–dab₅, /ga–ī–e–ri/, ha–ī–e–dab₅/
(Enmerkar and the Lord of Aratta 69). -e- is in both forms
incorrect; 'may you follow my instructions' should be:
*/ha–ī–b–dab₅ –en/

(512) šu zid ga–mu–ra–ab–ǧar, /ga–mu–ra–b–ǧar/ 'let me carry it
out for you steadily', (lit.: 'place the hand ...') (Gudea. cyl.
A II 13)

(513) ugula–ni ga–šè–sa₁₀ ù–na–dug₄, /ga–ī–ši–sa₁₀/ 'When the
foreman has said: 'I will buy it'' (Ukg. 4 XI 23-24)

(514) ǧá–e Ak–kà–šè ga–àm–ši–ǧenᵃ (a: var. ga–ǧen), /ga–ī–m–ši–
ǧen/ 'I will go to Aka' (Gilgameš and Aka 57)

(515) uru–bi–a ga–tuš bí–in–dug₄–ga, /ga–ī–tuš/ 'the one who has
said: let me live in this city' (Curse of Akkade 272)

Wrong, or at least unusual, is the ending /-en/:

(516) inim–inim–ma nam.dumu.é.dub.ba–a–ke₄–ne ga–ab–šid–dè-
en, /ga-ī-b-šid-en/ 'I will recite the words of the school-
boys' (Dialogue 1, 7-8 = Ni 9581, *ISET* I pl. 205, 3-4 = Ni
9715, *ISET* II pl. 84, 7-8)

§ 392. *Examples: 1.pl.*

(517) ku.li–ni–ir ga–an–ši–re₇–en–dè–en, /ga-ī-n.ši-ere-enden/ 'let
us go to his friend' (Dumuzi's Dream 140)
(518) ga–ba–húl–húl–le–en–dè–en, /ga-ba-húl.húl-enden/ 'let us
rejoice' (Ni 2461, 12 = *ISET* I pl. 90, love song)
(519) ᴰInanna inim–gin₇ ga–àm–me–en–dè–en, /ga-ī-m-e-enden/
'Inanna, let us talk about it' (*PAPS* 107 nr. 1, 8)
(520) gú ga–àm–g̃á–g̃á–an–dè–en, /ga-ī-m-g̃á.g̃á-enden/ 'let us submit' (Gilgameš and Aka 14, text C)

§ 393. *Bibliography*

A. Falkenstein, 1939. 'Untersuchungen zur sumerischen Grammatik: Der Plural
des Kohortativs'. *ZA* 45: 169-180.
D.O. Edzard, 1971a, p. 222-225.

The Modal Prefix /ha-/: Precative and Affirmative

§ 394. *Writing*

The precative and affirmative prefix is written either ha-, hé- or hu-
depending on which prefix is following. The basic form is here assumed to be /ha-/, but it could as well be /he-/ (see § 401). hu- is
not used before the Old Babylonian period.

/ha-/ can occur before all conjugation prefixes. Generally, ha- is
written before prefixes containing the vowel [a], i.e.: ba-, ma- <
/mu-DAT.1.sg.-/, -ra-(DAT.2.sg.), etc., and until the Old Babylonian
period also before /mu-/. hé-, on the other hand, is written before
/ī-/ and /bi-/. hu- is in the Isin-Larsa inscriptions and in the Old
Babylonian literary texts found before /mu-/.

ha-		hé-		hu-	
ha-ba-	< /ha-ba-/	hé-en-	< /ha-ĭ-n-/	hu-mu-	< /ha-mu-/
ha-ma-	< /ha-mu-DAT.1.sg.-/	hé-eb-	< /ha-ĭ-b-/		
ha-ra-	< /ha-ĭ-DAT.2.sg.-/	hé-em-	< /ha-ĭ-m-/		
ha-mu-	< /ha-mu-/	hé-	< /ha-ĭ-/		
(before the OB period)		hé-CASE-	< /ha-ĭ-CASE-/		
		hé-em-ma-	< /ha-ĭ-ba-/		
		hé-em-mi-	< /ha-ĭ-bi-/		

Exceptions to these rules are numerous in the NS texts, but can also be found in the Old Babylonian texts:

(521) šu ha-bar-re, /ha-ĭ-bar-e/ 'let him release' (*TCS* I nr. 46, 4)[85]

(522) šu-na ha-ab-ši-ib-gi₄-gi₄, /ha-ĭ-b.ši-b-gi₄.gi₄-e/ 'let him return it' (*TCS* I nr. 116, 6)

(523) ha-bí-íb-da-e, /ha-bi-b-da-e/ 'let him ...' (*TCS* I nr. 77, 4)

(524) ha-àm-DU, /ha-ĭ-m-DU/ 'let them go' (*TCS* I 113, 7)[86]

(525) ha-na-ab-bal-e, /ha-ĭ-na-bal-e/ 'let him turn it over to him' (*TCS* I nr. 162, 9) Since -na- refers to a person ha-mu-na-bal-e is expected.

(526) hé-an-ši-dab₅, /ha-ĭ-n.ši-dab₅/ 'let him take' (*TCS* I nr. 112, 5)

(527) hé-ba-ab-sum-mu, /ha-ba-b-sum-e/ 'let him give it to them' (*TCS* I nr. 151, 7)

(528) hé-mu-na-ab-sum-mu, /ha-mu-na-b-sum-e/ 'let him give it to him' (*TCS* I nr. 89, 6)

(529) ^{D}Inanna ur₅-re hé-mu-e-húl-e, /ha-mu-e-húl-e/ (the analysis of the form is not very clear) 'Inanna, may you rejoice!' (Išme-Dagan Hymn K 10, cf. the var. in YBC 4609, 10 = Hallo, 1966 p. 244: ga-mu-u₈-húl-l[e] 'I will rejoice'). Note that hé- regularly occurs before mu-e:

(530) hé-mu-e-te-ğál (Iddin-Dagan Hymn B 46, cf. the var.: hu-mu-te-ğál)

(531) hé-mu-e-dù (Dialogue 1, 143 = *UET* VI 156 rev. 13)

ha-ni- is found in OS and Gudea texts although we would expect /ha-ĭ-ni-/ > hé-ni-, e.g.:

---

85. Cf. hé-ab-bar-re in *TCS* I nr. 67, 5.
86. Cf. kas₄ hé-àm-e in *TCS* I nr. 252.

(532) ha-ni-gaz-e 'let him be killed' (Ent. 28 VI 40)

(533) ha-ni-ku$_4$-ku$_4$ 'may you enter there' (Gudea, cyl. B II 22)

hé-ni- is, however, used regularly in the Old Babylonian period (cf. the instances in Gragg, *SDI* p. 70)

§ 395. In Emesal texts the prefix is written as either da-, dè- or du$_5$-, e.g.[87]

(534) é-a ur dè-en-ku$_4$ dè-en-ná, /ha-ī-n-ku$_4$/, /ha-ī-n-ná/ 'let the ... enter the house, let him lie in the house' (*STVC* 83 II 6, see Krecher, 1966 p. 143) The verbs are intransitive and /-n-/ is thus not correct.

§ 396. Like the prefix /na-/ (cf. § 374), also /ha-/ has different meanings dependent on the aspect of the verb: ha+*marû* is precative, ha+*hamṭu* is affirmative. (See D.O. Edzard, 1971a p. 213-216, and M. Yoshikawa, 1968b).

To this rule there is the following restriction: in some apparently intransitive forms the verb is *hamṭu* although the meaning must be precative:

(535) ensi$_2$ inim bí-íb-gi$_4$-gi$_4$-a me ^{D}Nin.ğír.su-ka ba-ni-íb-lá-a sá.dug$_4$-na é ^{D}Nin.ğír.su-ka-ta inim hé-eb-gi$_4$ inim ka-ni hé-kéš 'the *ensi* who calls back the word or who diminishes the *me* of Ningirsu — may his offerings be called back from the house of Ningirsu, may his word become invalid(?)'[88] (Gudea, St. B I 13-20) hé-eb-gi$_4$ is *hamṭu*: /ha-ī-b-gi$_4$/, /-b-/ is not correct, since the verb is intransitive.

§ 397. Intransitive/one-participant forms of regular verbs cannot differentiate precative and affirmative, since they have only one form with the basic stem:

(536) nam.tar-ra-ni hé-da-kúr-ne gud-gin$_7$ ud-dè-na hé-gaz am-gin$_7$ á huš-na hé-dab$_5$, /ha-ī-da-kúr-ene/ = trans., *marû*; /ha-ī-gaz/ and /ha-ī-dab$_5$/ = intrans., basic stem of regular verbs, 'may (the gods) change his lot, may he be slaughtered

---

87. Th. Jacobsen, 1965 p. 72f., regarded de-/da-/du- as an independent prefix denoting 'jussive': 'be it that'. Cf. also § 385.

88. KA...kéš means 'to make an agreement' ot 'to have a structure', with -ta- 'to become undone' (cf. Gragg, *SDI* p. 36).

like an ox on his ..., may he be caught in his fierce arm like a bull' (Gudea, St. B IX 5-9)

(537) na ga-ri na.ri-g̃u₁₀ hé-dab₅, /ha-ï-dab₅/ 'let me give instructions, may my instructions be followed' (Gudea, cyl. A VI 14, see ex. 510 above)

(538) uru-g̃u₁₀ ki ma.al-ba hé-en-ga-mu-daᵃ-gul (a: -dè- for -da-), /ha-ï-ga-mu-da-gul/ 'my city was indeed destroyed on its foundation' (Ur Lament 108)

§ 398. *Examples: /ha-/, Precative*

(539) šà-bi ha-ma-pàd-dè, /ha-mu+DAT.1.sg.-pàd-e/ 'may she reveal to me its meaning' (Gudea, cyl. A II 3), cf.

(540) nam hé-ma-kud-e, /ha-ï-ba-kud-e/ 'may she curse him' (Gudea, St. C IV 12)

(541) níg-ak-ak-da-g̃á ᴰNanna en an-ki hu-mu-húl-le(-en), /ha-mu-húl-en/ 'may you, Nanna, the lord of heaven and earth, rejoice in my deeds' (Warad-Sin 10, 45-47)

§ 399. *Examples: /ha-/, Affirmative*

(542) zi lugal g̃á-e-me ha-na-sum, /ha-ï-na-sum/ 'by the king's life, it is indeed I who did give it to him' (*TCS* I nr. 81, 5-7) An affirmative form in the first person is uncommon. Cf. also:

(543) ki-bi(-šè) hé-em-mi-gi₄, /ha-ï-bi-gi₄/ 'I have indeed restored it' (Warad-Sin 7, 22; 17 II 9; 11, 39)

(544) a.ra.zu ge-na-g̃u₁₀-šè hu-mu-ši-in-še-ge-eš, /ha-mu-ši-n-še.g-eš/ 'at my persistent prayer they have indeed granted it' (Sin-iddinam 6 I 26-27)

(545) ku.li-g̃u₁₀ sag̃ ú-a hé-en-šub, /ha-ï-n-šub/ 'my friend has indeed ducked down his head in the grass' (Dumuzi's Dream 144)

§ 400. */ha-/ with the verb me 'to be':*

(546) uru-g̃u₁₀ du₆ hé-a g̃á-e šika-bi hé-me-en, /ha-ï-m-en/ 'let my city become a mound, let me become its sherds' (Enmerkar and Ensuhkešdana 133)

hé-àm 'so be it', can be used as a noun, = *annu* 'consent, approval':

(547) hé-àm-zu hé-àm gul-lu [x (x x)] gul-lu 'your 'so be it' *is* 'so

be it', to(?) destroy ... destroy' (Innin 204) For hé-àm-bi
see Römer, *SKIZ* p. 225)

§ 401. */ha-/ without a finite verb:*

It is possible that /ha-/ in the affirmative sense, like /nu-/, can occur
with non-finite verbs, cf. the forms quoted by J. Krecher, 1978c p.
402f.: ki hé-ús-sa-àm, šu hé-tag-ga-àm, etc. It is of course possible
to analyse /ha-ī-../, which would explain the writing hé-. On the
other hand, if these forms are non-finite, they argue for the basic
form of this prefix being /he-/.

§ 402. /ha-/ seems to share another characteristic with the prefix
/nu-/: also /ha-/ can be used alone without a verb, however, not in
the form ha, but as hé:

(548) lú Umma^{ki} hé lú kur-ra hé ^DEn.líl-le hé-ha-lam-me, /ha-ī-
ha.lam-e/ 'Whether he is a man from Umma or a man from
the mountains, may Enlil destroy him!' (Ent. 28 VI 29-32)
The same construction is found in Ukg. 1 IV 26-29.

E. Sollberger, 1952 p. 224, understands hé in these cases as an abbreviated form of /ha/ + the verb me, 'to be'.
For /nu-/, see § 363.

§ 403. *Bibliography*

N. Schneider, 1946. 'Die Wunschpartikel ha-, hé- und hu- in der Ur III-Texten'.
OrNS 15: 89-94.

The Modal Prefix /ša-/

§ 404. In the Old Sumerian texts there are a few instances of this
prefix written šè- or ši-. Otherwise it is attested in the Old Babylonian period only — there are no instances at all in the Gudea texts. In
the Old Babylonian texts the prefix is written ša- before prefixes
containing the vowel [a] (ba-, -ra-),[89] and before /mu-/; ši- before
the prefixes /ī-/ and /bí-/; šu- is rare, but can be found before /mu-/,
see A. Falkenstein, 1944 p. 71. In late texts šà- may occur, see Falkenstein, 1944 p. 73.

---

89. Note that ša- is used although we would expect ši-ra- < /ša-ī-ra-/, like ši-im-
ma- < /ša-ī-ba-/. Cf. ha-ra- in § 394.

§ 405. /ša-/ is found before all conjugation prefixes.[90]
/ša-/ can be used with both *hamṭu* and *marû* stem of the verb (cf.
D.O. Edzard, 1971a p. 222).

§ 406. The exact meaning of /ša-/ can for the present not be established. Many of the instances are in hymns to gods or royal hymns.
Falkenstein called the prefix /ša-/ 'affirmative' (see for instance
1959a p. 50), which is a rather vague description. Moreover, no distinction can be drawn between /ša-/ and the other so-called 'affirmative prefixes' like /ha-/ (with *hamṭu*) and na- (with *hamṭu*).
Th. Jacobsen, 1965 p. 73, suggested that /ša-/ is 'contrapunctive'
meaning 'correspondingly', 'he on his part': 'the profix ši- indicates
that the speaker presents the occurrence denoted by the verb as a
parallel, corresponding counterpart occurrence to something else.'
Cf. 1965 n.3 p. 73: 'We base our suggestions about the meaning of
the profix on the remarkable frequency with which two entities are
found in counterpart relation with each other in these examples.'

§ 407. *Examples*

The Old Sumerian instances, all in rather difficult contexts, are the
following:

(549) ^{D}En.ki g̃iš BULUG̃$_3$ šè-šub '...' (Urn. 49 III 6-7) (Cf. M.
    Civil, 1967 p. 211 n. 33: giš-bu$_x$ šè-šub 'Enki will put you
    in a magic circle')
(550) na.rú-a mu-bi lú-a nu mu-bi ši-e 'the name of the stele is
    not the name of a man, its name is:' (Ean. 1 rev. X 23-25)
(551) SAR-àm te-me-nam ki bùr a šè-ma-si 'it is a ... it is a foundation – ... it is filled with water (?)' (Ukg. 15 I 4-5)

Old Babylonian examples:

(552) kur sukud-rá-gin$_7$ su.lim-ma ši-bí-in-íl, /ša-bi-n-íl/ 'I have
    made it (= the temple) rise in awe like a high mountain'
    (Warad-Sin 6, 21)
(553) ur.sag̃ $^{D(aš)}$AŠ$_7$.gi$_4$-gin$_7$ rib-ba ama ši-in-ga^a-ù.tu^b (a: var.

---

90. A. Falkenstein quotes an instance of /ša-/ before the affirmative prefix /na-/
    (1944 p. 118 = Enlil and Ninlil 13). This form must, however, be read: ša
    na-mu-un-ri-ri, it is the Emesal form of the verb na...ri, 'to give counsel',
    where ša is the Emesal form of the noun na.

-an-; b: ši-in-ga-an-u₈-du₈), /ša-ī-ga(-)-ù.tu-e/ 'one great
as its hero Ašgi — what mother will (ever) bear someone
(like him)?' (Keš Hymn 19)

(554) ğá-e ud-ba ša-ba-na-gam-e-dè-en
e.ne nam.mah-a-ni ši-im-ma-an-zu-zu-un[a]
uru-gin₇ nam.dumu-ğá[b] gú ši-im-ma-ğá-ğá-an[c] e.ne-ra
dug₄-mu-na-ab
(a: var. om.; b: -ğu₁₀; c: var. om), /ša-ba-na-gam-ed-en/,
/ša-ī-ba-n-zu.zu-en/, /ša-ī-ba-ğá.ğá-en/, /dug₄ + mu-na-
b/ 'I (on my part?) shall then bow down to him, and he (on
his part?) shall make known his superiority, like the city I
shall submit (to him) like a son — say so to him!' (Enmerkar
and the Lord of Aratta 291-293)

(555) sipa zid lú i.lu dùg-ga-ke₄
ur₅!-ša₄ i.lu ša-ra-ni-ib-bé
in.nin níg.nam-ma níg.ku₇.ku₇-da
ᴰInanna šà-zu hé-mu-e-húl-le
in.nin tùr-ra ku₄-ra-zu-dè
ᴰInanna tùr ša-mu-u₈-{mu-}da-húl-e
/ša-ī-ra-ni-b-e-e/, /ha-mu-e-húl-e/, /ša-mu-e.da-húl-e/
'The good shepherd, the man of the sweet cry, will shout to
you; lady, Inanna — with everything, with everything sweet,
may he please your heart! Lady, when you enter the sheep-
fold, the sheepfold will rejoice in you, Inanna!' (Išme-Dagan
Hymn K 11-16)

§ 408. *Bibliography*

A. Falkenstein, 1944. 'Untersuchungen zur sumerischen Grammatik. 4: Das affirmative Präformativ ši-/ša-'. *ZA* 48: 69-118.

The Modal Prefix /u-/: Prospective

§ 409. The prospective prefix most often occurs as ù-, in OB literary
texts and later also as u-. When the prefix is followed by the pronominal elements /-n-/ and /-b-/ or by /-m-/ it is written un-, ub-
or um-.

In the older periods [u] can change to [a] or [i] under the influence of the following vowel: /u-ba/ > a-ba- (Old Sumerian), /u-bi/
> i-bí- (Gudea texts), see ex. 558.

§ 410. /u-/ may precede all conjugation prefixes; /ĭ/ is, however, always completely deleted. In the Neo-Sumerian texts there are some few examples of /u+al/, see § 354.

§ 411. /u-/ denotes prospective or a condition.[91] As a rule the prefix occurs in *hamṭu* forms only, whereas the following clause most often has a *marû* form, cf. the ex. 557, 559, 561. In some cases the /u-/ form is followed by a *hamṭu* form, e.g. an affirmative form with /ha-/, cf. ex. 560.

> Cf. Gragg, 1973a p. 131: 'The basic function of ù- is to designate the first of a succession of events, without a great deal of precision as to the exact way in which the point of time designated by the ù- clauses relates to the time of the main clause. It is thus similar to the 'conjunctive' or 'gerund' constructions known in a fairly wide variety of languages, especially of the Subject Object Verb Order type. In many contexts the relation between the ù- clause and the main clause can be rendered by a simple 'and then'.

§ 412. In imperatives the enclitic prefix chain is occasionally written -ù, e.g., i.lu ĝar-ù 'set up a lament!' (Dumuzi's Dream 5), é ĝál-ùᵃ (a: -lu) 'open up!' (Inanna's Descent 76). It is, however, not likely that these forms should contain the prospective prefix, since the modal prefixes otherwise do not occur in the imperative. -ù, -lu etc. must therefore represent the conjugation prefix /ĭ/ which, in the enclitic position, is changed to [u].[92]

§ 413. The prospective form with /u-/ is used in the introductory passage of letters:

(556) PN₁ na-bé-a PN₂-ra ù-na-a-dug₄, /na-ĭ-b-e-e-a/, /u-ĭ-na-e-dug₄/ 'this is what PN₁ (= the sender) says — after you (= the messenger) have said it to PN₂ (= the addressee) (he may do so and so)'[93]

In the Old Sumerian letter, Enz. 1, the imperative dug₄-ga-na =

---

91. Gragg, 1968 p. 107 n. 8, calls it 'subordinating prefix', cf. further: 'ù is probably to be considered not a member of Mdl [= Modal prefixes], but a sentence-initial element which gets shifted to prefix position.'

92. Th. Jacobsen, 1965 p. 75, regards this /u/ as an independent prefix occurring exclusively in imperatives: 'mark of limited persistence'.

93. Instances of these introductory passages can be found in E. Sollberger, *TCS* I, and Ali, 1964.

/dug$_4$ + ī-na-/ 'say it to him' replaces the /u-/ form; in Akkadian letters the imperative *qibīma* 'say it' is always used. Note also that 2.sg. forms with /u-/ in late texts are translated by Akkadian imperatives (see A. Poebel, *GSG* § 412 p. 152).

Cf. Falkenstein, *GSGL* II p. 213: 'Da mit u- Formen aller Personen gebildet werden können, ist die übliche akkadische Wiedergabe der am häufigsten belegten 2.ps.sg. durch den Imperativ + satzverbindendes -*ma* 'und dann' als eine idiomatische Darstellung des sumerischen Satzverbandes zu erkennen, die es nicht gestattet, das Präformativ u- als Wunschpartikel oder Imperativzeichen zu werten.'

§ 414. *Examples:*

(557) dumu-uku$_2$-rá-ke$_4$ HAR.SAĜxHA-na ù-ak ku$_6$-bi lú nu-ba-da$_5$-kar-ré, /u-ī-(n-)ak/, /nu-ba-ta-kar-e/ 'provided a *dumu-uku* has made a fish pond(?), no one shall take its fish away' (Ukg. 6 III 6-9)

(558) Ĝír.su^{ki} é saĝ ki Lagaš^{ki}-šè ĝiri$_3$-zu ki ì-bí-ús, é-níg-ga-⟨ra-⟩za kišib ù-mi-kúr, ĝiš ù-ma-ta-ĝar (... ...) tur dug$_4$-ga-zu mah dug$_4$-ga-àm šu ba-a-ši-íb-ti, /u-bi-(n-)ús/, /u-ī-bi-(n-)kúr/, /u-ī-ba-ta-(n-)ĝar/, /ba-e.ši-b-ti(.ĝ+e?)/ '(the goddess Nanše speaks:) When you have reached Ĝirsu, the chief temple of Lagaš (lit.: when your foot has reached), when you have broken the seal of your treasury, when you have brought forth the wood from it (...), then he will receive from you your little word as a great word'

(...) ĝiš-hur é-a-na ma-ra-pàd-pàd-dè /mu-DAT.2.sg.-pàd. pàd-e/ 'then he will let you know all the plans of his house' (Gudea, cyl. A VI 15 - VII 6)

(559) ^{m}Úr.níg.dùg ìr É.lú-ta ù-mu-du$_8$, ba-ra-ba-g[i$_4$-gi$_4$-d]è, /u-mu-(e-)du$_8$/, /bara-ba-gi$_4$.gi$_4$-ed-en/ 'when you have released Urnigdug, the slave, from Elu, I shall indeed never return (in this case)' (*NG* nr. 28, 9-10)

(560) ^{íd}Idigna íd ĝál-la ^{D}Utu-ke$_4$ ù.ma-ĝu$_{10}$-ta gal-bi hé-em-mi-ba.al

ki.sur.ra.in.dub libir-ra ka-bi um-mi-tum$_4$

a.gam.ma-bi-šè si gal hé-em-mi-sá

/ha-ī-bi-ba.al/, /u-ī-bi-tum$_4$/, /ha-ī-bi-sá/ 'I dug the Tigris, the wide river of Utu, in my triumph in a great way, (and) after having led its mouth into the old river bed, I made it straight into the marsh in a splendid way' (Sin-iddinam 6 II 4-11)

(561) šà im ugu abzu-ka ù-mu-e-ni-in-šár, sig₇-en-sig₇-dùg im mu-e-kìr-kìr-re-ne, /u-mu-e-ni-n-šár/, /mu-e-kìr.kìr-ene/ 'when you have kneaded the heart of the clay of Abzu, Sig-en and Sig-dug will nip the clay off' (Enki and Ninmah 3-4) Both verbal forms do not fit our pattern, we would expect: /u-mu-ni-e-šár/ and /mu-(b-)kìr.kìr-ene/.

The Modal Prefix /iri-/

§ 415. *Meaning and Occurrences*

The instances of this prefix are rather few and almost all from the Old Babylonian literary texts or later.[94] /iri-/ occurs in *marû* forms of the compound verb mí...dug₄ 'to praise', and it is not possible to define the meaning of the prefix.

It is written i-ri- or i-rí-, and iri- (= URU).

§ 416. *Examples:*

(562) mí zid iri-ga-àm-e, /iri-ì-ga-m-e-e/ 'he praises' (Ur III: 6 N-T 547 IV 9-10, cited by Sjöberg, 1973b p. 43 and Römer, 1975 p. 4)

(563) nin-e ní-te-a-ni mí zid iri-in-ga-àm-me, /iri-ì-ga-m-e-e/ 'The lady praises herself' (Nungal Hymn 62)

(564) Lugal.bàn-da ... mušen-e mí iri-im-me, (var: i-ri-in-), /iri-ì-m-e-e/ 'Lugalbanda praises the bird' (Lugalbanda and En-merkar 111-113)

§ 417. *Bibliography*

Instances of /iri-/ are listed in:

W.H.Ph. Römer, 1975. 'Kleine Beiträge zur Grammatik des Sumerischen. Das präfigierende Element iri-'. *BiOr* 32: 3-5.

---

94. Two occurrences of ere- (written URU) in OS may be understood either as /iri-/ or as /ì-ri-/, the latter containing the 2.sg. locative-terminative element. Because of the difficult context and considering that neither iri- nor -ri- oc-cur elsewhere in the OS texts, it seems, however, impossible to determine it further. Ean. 1 VII 7-11: ⌜á⌝ zi-da⌜za⌝ ᴰUtu ere-è sag-ki-za NE.DU.GI.UŠ ere-kéš 'at your right Utu will rise for you, at your forehead he will tie ...' (for the translation, see Th. Jacobsen, 1976b p. 253 and note 28).

The Modal Prefix /nuš-/

§ 418. Normally this prefix is written nu-uš- before /ī-/, /mu-/, /ba-/ and /bi-/ (ex. 567-568). Less common are the writings ni-iš- or ni-iš-:[95]

(565) ni-iš-ku-le (Jacobsen, 1954 p. 82: I 6, Emesal)
(566) ni-iš-mi-ni-ğál (*CT* XV pl. 14 rev. 12, Emesal) Cf. nu-uš-bí-in-tuku in the same line.

§ 419. /nuš-/ occurs exclusively in literary texts from the Old Babylonian period or later. It can be combined with all conjugation prefixes except /-m-/. Both *hamṭu* and *marû* forms are attested. It seems to occur exclusively in direct speech.

§ 420. /nuš-/ seems, at least in some cases, to denote a hypothetical wish: 'if only ...', 'were it but that ...'. Since the prefix occurs in about thirty forms only, most of them in very difficult context, there is some uncertainty as to the exact meaning and analysis of it. It is thus not clear whether /nuš-/ contains the negative prefix /nu-/, as suggested by the translation, admittedly rather late, in *NBGT* II 15-16: nu-uš = *lu-ma-an* AN.TA ('now! — prefix'), = *ú-ul* AN.TA ('not — prefix'). If /nuš-/ does contain the negative /nu-/, ex. 568 may be translated 'couldn't you tell me ...', but in other cases a negative translation does not make sense.

> Römer, 1976 p. 377, suggests both a positive and a negative meaning of /nuš-/, but states: 'Es läßt sich meistens auch nicht sicher entscheiden, ob die Bedeutung(snüance) 'Wäre (usw.) doch ...!' oder 'Leider ... nicht!' vorliegt.'

§ 421. *Examples:*

(567) ud-ba ^{giš}ellag-ğu$_{10}$ é nagar-ra-ka nu-uš-ma-da-ğál-àm, /nuš-mu-DAT.1.sg.-da-ğál-am/ 'if only my *ellag* were left in the house of the carpenter' (Gilgameš, Enkidu and the Netherworld 172, the Akkadian text has: u_4-*ma pu-uk-ku ina bīt* ^{lú}*naggāri lu-ú e-z*[*ib*])
(568) nu-uš-ma-ab-bé-en, /nuš-mu-DAT.1.sg.-b-e-en/ 'if only

---

95. In Exaltation of Inanna 55: munus-bi dam-a-ni-ta šag$_5$-ga nam-da-ab-bé 'its woman shall talk pleasantly with her husband', a variant has: na-aš-an-da-ab-bé. However, since the following parallel lines have the prohibitive /na-/ prefix, it seems rather doubtful whether na-aš- here represents /nuš-/.

you could tell me' (Gilgameš, Enkidu and the Netherworld 247, the Akkadian text has: *ul a-qab-ba-ku* 'I cannot tell you')

§ 422. *Bibliography*

W.H.Ph. Römer, 1976. 'Kleine Beiträge zur Grammatik des Sumerischen: 1. Das modale grammatische Element nu-uš-'. *AOAT* 25 p. 371-378. (Contains a rather complete collection of the instances of nuš- and a summary of earlier treatments of the prefix.)
A. Shaffer, 1963. *Sumerian Sources of Tablet XII of the Epic of Gilgameš*. Philadelphia, p. 145.

THE CASE ELEMENTS OF THE PREFIX CHAIN

Introduction

§ 423. Some cases, the so-called dimensional cases, can be incorporated in the prefix chain of finite verbal forms. These cases are: dative, comitative, terminative, ablative, and locative. In principle the case elements have the same shape as the corresponding postpositions and only minor changes in writing and pronunciation occur.

The rank of the case elements in the prefix chain is between the conjugation prefixes and the pronominal element serving as subject/object mark; for the order of the case elements see § 427.

In this section the morphology and syntax of the case elements are dealt with as well as their relations to specific verbs. For the meaning of the cases in general, see Cases, §§ 156-220.

§ 424. *Terminology*

The case elements of the prefix chain are most often called 'infixes' or 'dimensional infixes' by the sumerologists. However, since they do not act as infixes in the stem but merely as members of the chain of grammatical elements preceding the verbal root, 'case elements' or 'case prefixes' are used here as the most appropriate terms.

Rules for the occurrence of the case prefixes

§ 425. The occurrences of the case elements in the prefix chain have mostly been regarded as more or less due to simple concord between the postpositions of the nouns in the sentence and the prefixes in the chain.

> Cf. Sollberger, 1952 p. 61f.: 'L'une des particularités du sumérien consiste à reprendre dans le complexe verbal les relations grammaticales déjà exprimées dans le complexe nominal' (...). 'Ce procédé donne au complexe verbal le caractère d'un véritable résumé de la phrase entière.' (...) 'l'emploi de l'incorporation est loin d'être obligatoire, et bien souvent le complexe verbal apparaît sans aucun élément incorporé. Il semble bien que le choix entre les deux

procédés ressortisse à la stylistique, l'emploi de l'incorporation correspondant généralement à la mise en relief des relations grammaticales ainsi reprises dans le complexe verbal.'

Falkenstein, *GSGL* II: 'Die Setzung der Infixe (...) hängt in erster Linie vom Nachdruck ab, der auf den durch sie aufgenommenen Gliedern des nominalen Satzteils ruht. Eine Rolle spielt dabei noch die Stärke der verbalen Rection in dem Sinne, daß unmittelbar vom Verbum regierte Kasus wesentlich häufiger aufgenommen werden als Fälle, in denen keine direkte verbale Rection vorliegt.' (...) 'Erstarrter Gebrauch' der dimensionalen Infixe liegt in Fällen vor, in denen Infixe gesetzt sind, ohne daß im nominalen Satzteil eine entsprechende dimensionale Bestimmung vorausgeht' (p. 191). 'Unstimmigkeiten zwischen nominalen Satzteil und den darauf verweisenden dimensionalen Infixen ergaben sich infolge von Konstruktionsänderungen im nominalen Teil, wenn sich im Infixbestand noch die alte Konstruktion erhalten hat' (p. 192).

In his study of the case elements in the OB literary texts: *Sumerian Dimensional Infixes*, G.B. Gragg has shown that the independence between postpositions and case prefixes is greater than hitherto assumed:

'while concord does play a part in the placing of infixes (especially the dative and locative), the infixes also function independently of concord to a much greater extent than has been recognized by current theories. In this latter role it will be shown that infixes often function either as quasi-autonomous units or, more frequently, the semantic differentiation of different individual verbal stems' (*SDI* p. 10).

Although Gragg based his investigation almost exclusively on OB literary texts, his conclusions appear to be valid for earlier texts as well. In fact the system of case prefixes seems to work much the same way in all periods, even if the rection of certain verbs may have changed. In the present study I shall therefore follow the view of Gragg as outlined in the quotation above. Also the statements given below according to the semantic range of the various case prefixes are based on his work.

§ 426. A case element occurs in the prefix chain under the following circumstances, cf. G.B. Gragg, *SDI* p. 13:

a) as a result of concord with Noun + Postposition in the sentence. In this way the dative and locative prefixes are used, e.g., (e.ne-ra) mu–na–an–sum 'he has given it to him' (the pronoun is mostly deleted, cf. § 94), lugal-ra mu-na-an-sum 'he has given it to the king'.

b) serving semantic differentiation of the verb: especially ablative and terminative belong to this category and are often used in order to stress the orientation or motion of the verb. There may be concord between prefix and noun complement, but the presence of one (postposition or prefix) does not necessarily imply the presence of the other.

> dal 'to fly', with -ši- 'to fly towards' (*SDI* p. 24)
>
> gi$_4$ has the basic meaning 'to return', with -ni- 'to answer', with -ši- 'to send' (*SDI* p. 25)
>
> igi...bar, often with NOUN+šè but without -ši-: 'to look at', with -ši-: 'to gaze at some object in a certain manner' (*SDI* p. 20f.).

c) as an independent unit which could occur with all verbs, e.g. -da- 'to be able'. There is no concord (cf. *SDI* p. 53ff.):

> (569) kin.gi$_4$a ka-ni dugud šu nu-mu-un-da-an-gi$_4$-gi$_4$ 'The messenger whose mouth is heavy is not able to repeat it' (Enmerkar and the Lord of Aratta 501)

§ 427. *The Order of the Case Elements*

The order of the case elements in the prefix chain is the following:

$$\text{MOD} - \text{CONJ} - \text{Dative} - \begin{Bmatrix} \text{da}^{a)} \\ \text{(com.)} \end{Bmatrix} - \begin{Bmatrix} \text{ši} \\ \text{(term.)} \\ \text{ta}^{b)} \\ \text{(abl.)} \end{Bmatrix} - \begin{Bmatrix} \text{ni}^{c)} \\ \text{(loc.)} \end{Bmatrix} - \text{PRON} - \text{VERB}$$

a)   /-da-ni-/ > -di-ni- (cf. § 441).

b)   Ablative occurs also as -ra-, -ta-ra- and -da-ra-ta-, see below §§ 465-467.

c)   In OB -ri- occurs for 2.sg. (§ 478).

Terminative and ablative mutually exclude each other.

As can be seen from the chart a verbal form may theoretically have at the most four case prefixes but normally there are only one or two. Three or four case elements in the prefix chain are exceptions, cf. for instance:

> (570) e-na-ta-ni-è 'he let go out for him from there' (Ent. 41 IV 2)

(571) mu–na–ra–ni–è–eš 'they came out for him from there' (*NG* nr. 127, 16)

§ 428. *The Pronominal Reference of the Case Prefixes*

According to A. Poebel and A. Falkenstein the reference of the case prefixes is denoted by a pronominal element preceding the case element, and they assumed individual pronominal elements for all persons: –?–, –e–, –n–, –b–, –me–, –e-ene–, –ene– (see Poebel, *GSG* p. 188f., Falkenstein, 1959a p. 47). It was, however, demonstrated above (§ 290) that only three pronominal prefixes do exist, namely:

(a) /-e-/, denoting the 2.sg., e.g.,

(572) za–a–da ša–mu–e–da–ǧál, /ša–mu–e.da–ǧál/ 'it is with you' (Šu–ilišu Hymn A 20)

Sometimes /-e-/ is used for the 1.sg. too:

(573) á še mu–e–da–a–a–áǧ, /mu–e.da–e–áǧ/ 'you have instructed me' (Letter A 1, 8)

For the writing of /-e-/, see § 291.

(b) /-n-/, animate. 3.sg.:

(574) ᴰEn.líl–le igi zid mu–un–ši–in–bar, /mu–n.ši–n–bar/ 'Enlil has looked faithfully upon him' (Iddin-Dagan Hymn B 5)

(c) /-b-/, inanimate:

(575) lú É.an.na–ta íb–ta–ab–è–è–a, /í–b.ta–b–è.è–e–a/ 'the man who takes it out of Eanna' (Gudea, St. C IV 5-6)

im-CASE-... has been regarded as coming from /í-b-CASE/ (cf. for instance A. Falkenstein, *GSGL* I p. 195), but /-m-/ is apparently an independent morpheme, see § 329ff. above.

Comitative and terminative occur with all pronominal prefixes. Ablative-instrumental, however, only with /-b-/, since this case has inanimate reference only.

The dative prefix is the only case prefix which distinguishes all persons by different morphemes (see § 431). The 3.sg.an. -na-, probably contains the pronominal element /-n-/.

The case prefixes -ni-, locative, and -ra-, ablative, do not occur with the pronominal prefixes, but -ni- has a special 2.sg. form, -ri-, in the Old Babylonian literary texts (see § 478).

Case prefixes referring to the 1., 2. and 3. person plural are extremely rare. /-me-/ which Poebel and Falkenstein classified as the pronominal element for the 1.pl., seems to occur as the 1.pl. dative prefix exclusively, cf., however,

(576) á ba–me–da–an–áĝ, /ba-me.da-n-áĝ/ 'he has instructed us' (Samsuiluna C 78 = Sollberger, 1969b p. 35; the Akkadian text has: *ú–wa–'è–ra–an–ni–a–ti*)

The pronominal elements are often omitted in the writing, especially in the earlier stages of the language, and even in the Old Babylonian literary texts they are not written in all cases where they are expected to occur, cf. § 289. We cannot say whether this is due simply to the scribal usage and for the sake of convenience or whether it has some semantic or grammatical significance when the pronominal elements are omitted or not. It seems most logical to assume that the pronominal element is always present, even if it is not written. The choice of the conjugation prefix immediately preceding the case prefix may, however, to some extent replace the the pronominal element, cf. the next paragraph.

Conjugation Prefixes Before Case Elements

§ 429. The reference of the case prefix is important for the choice of the conjugation prefix immediately preceding the case prefix. Thus /mu-/ occurs before prefixes referring to a person, /ba-/ before case prefixes with inanimate reference. This rule is rather consistently carried through in the Gudea texts and to some extent also in the OB literary texts.

The prefix /ī-/ can also be used before both animate and inanimate reference, and the difference between for instance mu–na–an–sum and in–na–an–sum, both 'he has given it to him', is not evident.

The conjugation prefix /-m-/ may occur immediately before –da–, -ši-, or -ta-, but not before any other case prefix. /-m-/ seems to occur exclusively or predominantly before case prefixes with inanimate reference.

Whereas /mu-/ and /ba-/ stand before the pronominal element of the case prefix, /-m-/ cannot occur with a pronominal element, but rather replaces it.

The meaning of /-m-/ is not entirely clear, but it probably denotes ventive (cf. §§ 330-331). /–m–/ with case prefix may thus emphasize the direction, whereas /–b–CASE+/ and /ba–CASE–/ only denote inanimate reference.

§ 430. *Examples:*

(577) á šed$_{10}$–bi-šè ní hé-eb-ši-te-en-te(-en), /ha-ī-b.ši-te.en.te (.en-e)/ 'let him relax in its cool arms' (Šulgi Hymn A 33)

(578) Ak.kà-šè ga-àm-ši-DU, /ga-ī-m-ši-DU/ 'I will send him to Aka' (Gilgameš and Aka 54)

(579) ki di.kud-ru-bi-šè diĝir an-ki-a im-ši-gaṁ-e-dè-eš, /ī-m-ši-gam-ed-eš/ 'the gods of heaven and earth will bow down to the place where judgement is pronounced' (Nungal 35)

(580) gal$_5$.lá-zu im-ši-re$_7$-eš, /ī-m-ši-re$_7$-eš/ 'your demons are coming here (or: towards you ?)' (Dumuzi's Dream 90)

(581) inim nin-a-na-šè saĝ kéš ba-ši-[in-ak], /ba-ši-n-ak/ 'he paid attention to the words of his mistress' (Inanna's Descent 124)

Dative

§ 431. The dative is the only case prefix which has different prefixes for every person. According to the traditional theory (cf. § 428), these prefixes are expected to consist of a pronominal element and the case element. The latter seems here to be /–a–/, probably identical with the locative postposition which serves as dative prefix instead of the postposition -ra. The 3.sg. an. -na- can thus be analysed /–n–a–/, and the 1.sg. ma- is simply the conjugation prefix /mu–/ + /–a–/, since the 1.sg. has no special pronominal element. The other prefixes can, however, not be explained within this pattern.

Cf. Gragg, *SDI* p. 84f.

1.sg.	ma- < /mu-a-/	1.pl.	-me-
2.sg.	-ra-	2.pl.	?
3.sg.an.	-na- < /-n-a-/	3.pl.	-ne-

§ 432. *1.sg.*: ma-. The conjugation prefix /mu–/ is obligatory before the dative of the 1.sg., and it always occurs in the form ma-. If it is preceded by a modal prefix, it may be confused with /ī-ba-/ > im-ma-, e.g., nu-ma-... can be both /nu-mu-DAT.1.sg.-/ and /nu-ī-ba-/ (cf. § 304).

ma-an-dug₄ , /mu-DAT.1.sg.-n-dug₄/ 'he has spoken to me'

§ 433. *2.sg.*: -ra-. It is striking that this prefix is identical with the dative postposition -ra, but this is probably incidental. According to the traditional theory the original form of this prefix is */-e-a-/, and Falkenstein, *GSGL* I p. 200, explained [r] as 'Hiatustilger'. Gragg, *SDI* p. 84, on the other hand, interprets [r] as the pronominal element for the 2.sg., which is also found in the case prefix -ri- (see below § 478). Gragg moreover suggested that this element could be connected with the deictic element /-r-/ in -ri.

If no modal prefix occurs in the verbal form, /mu-/ is obligatory before -ra- and always changed to ma- in the Gudea texts. In OB lit. texts both ma-ra- and mu-ra- can be found:

(582) ma-ra-an-dug₄ = /mu-ra-n-dug₄/ 'he has spoken to you' (e.g. Gudea, cyl. A V 18)

(583) gù zid mu-ra-an-dé = /mu-ra-n-dé/ 'he has spoken faithfully to you' (Iddin-Dagan Hymn B 6)

After a modal prefix mu- is often deleted and probably replaced by the prefix /ī-/, e.g.,

(584) ha-ra-ab-sum-mu = /ha-ī-ra-b-sum-e/ 'may he give it to you'[95a]

/mu-/ is dropped in both Gudea and OB lit. texts.

The prefix -ri-, which occurs in OB lit. texts only, is most probably the 2.sg. counterpart to the locative prefix -ni-. In some cases, however, it occurs parallel to dative, cf. § 478.

§ 434. *3.sg.an.*: -na-. This prefix may change to -ne- in some instances according to vowel harmony, but, as it seems, only in OB and later texts, e.g.,

(585) ù-ne-dè-dah = /u-ī-na-da-e-dah/ 'when you have added to him' (Letter to Nanna 7). Also ù-na-dè-dah is found, for instance Enmerkar and the Lord of Aratta 243, cf. Gragg, *SDI* p. 82.

95a. We would expect hé- before the prefix /ī/, cf. hé-da-du = /ha-ī-da-du/ 'let it come with it' (Gudea, cyl. A XI 11); nam hé-ma-kud-e = /ha-ī-ba-kud-e/ 'may she curse him' (Gudea, Stat. C IV 12), but hé-ra-... is never found. Is this an indication therefore that a conjugation prefix may be altogether missing and should the form be analysed /ha-ra-b-sum-e/?

§ 435. *1.pl.*: -me-. This prefix was previously understood as the pronominal element for 1.pl. The dative prefix was thus expected to be */-me-a-/, 'for us'. -me- is infrequently attested, but almost always as a dative prefix:

(586) sum-me-eb, /sum + (mu-)me-b/ 'give it to us' (Inanna's Descent 248 = 275 = 278; var. sum-me-ab)

(587) hé-me-ús, /ha-ī-me-ús/ 'let him follow us' (Dialogue 2, 187, var.: hé-mi-in-, cf. Gragg, *SDI* p. 84)

–me– as a pronominal element occurs, however, in: á ba-me-da-an-áǧ 'he has instructed us' (= ex. 576 above, Samsuilune C 78), but this text is a rather late royal inscription.

Note that –me– also may stand for /mu-e(2.sg.)-/, cf. above § 336.

§ 436. *2.pl.* ? No independent prefix of the 2.pl. dative is attested. When it is supposed to occur, either the singular form is used or a combination of prefix and the suffix /-enzen/. It is uncertain whether this is the original form of this prefix or whether it is a device of the Old Babylonian scribes. The inconsistencies of the form argue for the latter possibility, but the instances are too few to settle this problem.

(588) diǧir hé-me-en-zé-en inim ga-mu-ra-an-dug$_4$, /ha-ī-me-enzen/, /ga-mu-ra(dat.2.sg.)-n-dug$_4$/ 'if you(pl.) are gods, I will say you something' (Inanna's Descent 242 = 1. 269 with the variants: [ga]-mu-ri-d[ug$_4$]; ga-mu-ra-an-dug$_4$-en-zé-en) Cf. 1. 246 and 247:

(589) a íd-bi [a]mu-un-na-ba-e-ne[a] (a-a: ma-ra-ba(-ne)) 'if they offer you(pl.) a river as a drink'

(590) uzu níg-sìg-ga [ǧiš]kak-ta lá-a im-ma-da-ab-sum-mu-zé-en, /ī-ba-ta-b-sum-enzen/ 'they (or she?) will give you(pl.) the corpse that is hanging on the hook' (Inanna's Descent 251)

(591) e-ne[a] ta-gin$_7$ [b]nam-ma-ra-ab-zé-èm-e[n-zé-en][b] (a: en; b-b: nam-mi-ni-zé-èm-[zé-en]), /na-mu-ra(dat.)-b-sum-enzen/, /na-ī-bi-ni-sum-enzen/ 'how could I give her to you?' (Inanna's Descent 327, this line is repeated in 337 and 346 with the following variants: nam-ma-ra-ni-ib-zé-èm-mèn (= 337), nam-ma-ra-ab-zé-èm-zé-en (= 346) It is also possible to read ta-gin$_7$-nam ma-ra-ab-zé-èm-en-zé-en = /mu-DAT.2.sg.-b-sum-enzen/, see D.O. Edzard, 1976b p. 162 + n. 8)

§ 437. *3.pl.*: -ne-. The 3.pl. dative prefix occurs always as -ne-. According to the traditional theory the original form was */-ene-a-/, but such a form is not attested (cf. *GSGL* I p. 200).

(592) mu-ne-ni-dù, /mu-ne-ni-n-dù/ 'he has built it there for them' (Ukg. 1 II 14)

(593) diĝir-re-e-ne-er mu-ne-gub-bu-nam, /mu-ne-gub-en-am/ 'I have been standing before the gods' (Ur-Nammu's Death 156)

(594) nam hé-en-ne-éb-tar-re, /ha-ï-ne-b-tar-e/ 'may she decide the fate for them' (Rim-Sin 4, 28)

The Use of the Dative Prefix

§ 438. The dative prefix can be used with a large group of verbs, namely all verbs denoting an action which can be done for or in favor of somebody. According to Gragg, *SDI* p. 81-92, there are the following verbs with dative:

Verbs of giving, e.g., sum 'to give', ba 'to give as a ration'.

Verbs of speaking; e.g., dug$_4$ 'to speak', gi$_4$ 'to answer', dah 'to add'.

Verbs of motion, e.g., è 'to go out', ku$_4$.r 'to enter'.

Verbs of 'action-towards', e.g., gam 'to bow down'.

Verbs of emotion, e.g., šag$_5$ 'to be pleasing for', gig 'to pain'.

Verbs of doing for (ethical dative) and verbs signifying 'a consciously undertaken, goal-directed activity' (Gragg, *SDI* p. 91).

Verbs which cannot take dative prefix are either verbs denoting an action which cannot be done for somebody like zu 'to know', or verbs taking another case prefix, e.g., -ni-, even if the nominal complement has dative postposition. For instance: nam...tar 'to decide the fate', saĝ-e-eš....rig$_7$ 'to grant' (see Gragg, *SDI* p. 88).

§ 439. The dative prefix is, like the dative postposition -ra, restricted to animate beings. An inanimate 'goal' has mostly locative or terminative, cf. for instance:

(595) e-[ne-]ra nam-uru$_2$-na mu(-un)-na-te, /mu-na-te/ 'she approached him for the sake of his city' (Ur Lament 82), but:

(596) Aratta^{ki}-aš ba-te 'he approached Aratta' (Enmerkar and the Lord of Aratta 171)

(597) ^{D}En.líl lugal kur-kur-ra-ra Nibru^{ki}-šè hé-na-ab-de$_6$, /ha-
ï-na-b-de$_6$/ '(the boat) has indeed brought it to Enlil, the
king of all the foreign lands, to Nippur' (Enki and the World
Order 130) Note that the terminative is not incorporated in
the prefix chain in these cases.

§ 440. *Bibliography*

D.O. Edzard, 1976b. "Du hast mir gegeben', 'ich habe dir gegeben'. Über das sumerische Verbum sum'. *WO* 8: 159-177. (About the dative prefixes with the
verb sum).

Comitative

§ 441. The basic form of the comitative prefix is /-da-/, identical
with the comitative postposition. In the prefix chain it may change
to -dè- or -di- (see also Gragg, *SDI* p. 40ff.):

/da/ is assimilated to the vowel of the following prefix:

/-da-ni-/ > -dì-ni- or -di-ni-. This alternation occurs already in OS
(for instance šu nu-dì-ni-bal-e, Ukg. 34, 1).
/-da-e-/ > -dè- and -de$_4$- (OB lit. texts).

(598) ù-na^a-dè-dah (a: -ne-), /u-ï-na-da-e-dah/ 'when you have
added to him' (Enmerkar and the Lord of Aratta 114)

/da/ may also be assimilated to the vowel of the preceding prefix, but
this is less common:

/ba-e.da-/ > ba-e-da-, ba-e-dè-, ba-e-di- (OB lit.). According to the
rules for the occurrence of the conjugation prefixes /ba-/ should
not occur before a case prefix referring to an animate being, and
ba-e-da- is thus not found in older texts.
/mu-e.da-/ > mu-ù-da- (Gudea), mu-e/u$_8$-da-, mu-e/u$_8$-dè- (OB).

(599) nir hu-mu-u$_8$-dè-ğál, /ha-mu-e.da-ğál/ 'you have indeed
authority' (Šu-ilišu Hymn A 33)
(600) mu-e-dè-zu-un, /mu-e.da-zu-en/ 'she will learn it from
you' (Dumuzi's Dream 13, /-en/ seems unexplicable)

In some cases there seems to be no reason for the change -da- > -dè-:

(601) mu-un-dè^a-ğen (a: -da-), /mu-n.da-ğen/ 'he travelled with

him' (Enmerkar and the Lord of Aratta 162). See Gragg, *SDI* p. 46 for further examples.

§ 442. *1.sg.*: /mu-da-/. In OB literary texts -e-da- may also be used for the 1.sg. (ex. 603).

(602) ha-mu-da-gub, /ha-mu-da-gub/ 'may she stand by me' (Gudea, cyl. A III 24 and I 25)

(603) á-še mu-e-da-a-a-áǧ, /mu-e.da-e-áǧ/ 'you have instructed me' (Letter A 1, 8)

§ 443. *2.sg.*: /-e.da-/. Cf. above § 441 for possible phonetic alternations.

(604) nu-mu-ù-da-zu, /nu-mu-e.da-zu/ 'I have not learned it from you' (Gudea, cyl. A VIII 22)

(605) amaš ša-mu-u₈-da-húl-e, /ša-mu-e.da-húl-e/ 'the sheep-fold rejoices over you' (Išme-Dagan Hymn K 18)

(606) ka.aš bar-re-da za-a-da ša-mu-e-da-ǧál, /ša-mu-e.da-ǧál/ 'to make decisions is with you' (Šu-ilišu Hymn A 20)

§ 444. *3.sg.an.*: /-n.da-/

(607) mu-un-da-gu₇-e, /mu-n.da-gu₇-en/ 'you will eat it together with him' (Dumuzi and Enkimdu 18)

(608) mu-un-dèª-re₇ᵇ-eš-àmᶜ (a: -da-, -ši-; b: -re₇ʳᵉ-; c: -a), /mu-n.da-ere-eš-am/ 'they who went with him' (Gilgameš, Enkidu and the Netherworld 145)

(609) di in-da-an-dug₄, /ī-n.da-n-dug₄/ 'he was involved in a lawsuit with him' (*NG* nr. 77, 16)

§ 445. *Inanimate*: /(ba)-da-/, /-m-da-/, /-b.da-/

(610) ad im-da-gi₄-gi₄, /ī-m-da-gi₄.gi₄-e/ 'he takes counsel with it' (Gudea, cyl. A V 1)

(611) enkar šibir ᵍⁱˢmá.nu nam.sipa-da zag-da hé-em-dè-gub, /ha-ī-m-da-e-gub/ 'you have indeed placed by your side the *šibir*-weapon and the *manu*-staff of the shepherds' (Enki and the World Order 431)

(612) šu-zuª ka-zu nu-ub-da-sá (a: var. om.), /nu-ī-b.da-sá/ 'your hand is not equal to your mouth' (Dialogue 1, 53 = *CT* XLII nr. 47 obv. II 9 = *SLTNi* 116 obv. 2)

For ba-da- see § 449.

1. and 2.plural are not attested.

§ 446. *3.pl.*: –PI–. In the Old Sumerian economic texts there are a few instances of a prefix –PI–, apparently denoting comitative 3.pl.:

(613) En.ig.gal nu.banda šu-HA ab-ba-ke₄-ne é.mí-a dub-bi e-PI-bal gú-ne-ne-a e-ne-ğar, /ï-PI-(n-)bal/, /ï-ne-(n-)ğar/ 'En-iggal, the inspector, went over the account with the salt-water fishermen in the *é.mí* and placed it on their neck (i.e. 'on their account')'[96] (*DP* 278 VII 5-11)

Compare the form with singular case prefix:

(614) En.ig.gal nu.banda dub-bi e-da-bal gú-na e-ni-ğar (*AWL* nr. 184 II 5 - III 3)

Other forms are: e-PI-ğál, ì-PI-ğál, ba-PI-lá and na ba-PI-ri; possibly also the personal name e-PI-tuš. For references see A. Poebel, 1931 p. 16f.; p. 19 with n.1; E. Sollberger 1952 p. 100f.

Poebel, 1931 p. 16ff., suggested a reading –be– < /-be-d-/ < /-bi-da-/ for –PI–, and Falkenstein, 1957-58 p. 94f., –neda– < /-ene-da-/. None of these proposals harmonize with the system of the pronominal elements outlined here. However, because of lack of evidence the reading of –PI– cannot be established.[97]

The Use of the Comitative Prefix

§ 447. The comitative prefix is more frequent than the postposition. Cooccurrences of prefix and postposition are rare (cf. § 191 and Gragg, *SDI* p. 53). Most verbs which can denote actions performed together with somebody can take comitative prefix, see for instance ex. 601, 602, 607. Other verbs are: a.da.mìn...ak 'to compete with', du₁₄...ak 'to quarrel with', dug₄ 'to speak with, to converse', sá 'to compete with, to be equal to' (ex. 612).

---

96. For the meaning of dub-bi...bal with comitative, see Westenholz, *ECTJ* p. 50f.

97. Note that –PI– and –da– alternate in another context in Sumerian texts from Old Akkadian Nippur: su-PI-um and su-DA-um which seems to be a title of some sort. (*SR* nr. 56 IV 4; nr. 85 rev. 7; *BIN* VIII 203, 9. Cf. Edzard, 1964 p. 276.)

Verbs of emotion also take comitative prefix, for instance: saǧ.ki...gíd 'to be angry with', húl 'to rejoice over' (ex. 605), šà...kúš.ù 'to soothe the heart', ní...ri 'to be afraid of something/somebody', saǧ...sìg 'to tremble', šag₅ 'to be pleasing to', ní...te 'to be afraid of', su...zìg 'to be afraid of'.

    Cf. Gragg, *SDI* p. 62-64.

Other verbs which regularly take /-da-/ are: á...áǧ 'to instruct' (ex. 603), ság...dug₄ 'to scatter', ad...gi₄ 'to take counsel' (ex. 610), nir...ǧál 'to have authority' (ex. 599), mú 'to grow', si 'to fill with', zu 'to know from' (ex. 604).

For the uses of –da– see also Gragg, *SDI* p. 53-66.

§ 448. The comitative prefix is moreover used in the sense 'to be able to' (cf. Gragg, *SDI* p. 53-55):

    1.sg.   /mu-da-.../ 'I am able to'
    2.sg.   /...-e-da-.../ 'you are able to'
    3.sg.an.   /...-n-da-.../ 'he/she is able to'

Cf. *NBGT* I 399-402 (= *MSL* IV p. 145): da = *le-e-ú* 'to be able to', mu-da = *e-li-i* 'I am able to', e-da = *te-li-i* 'you are able to', an-da = *i-li-i* 'he is able to'.

    (615) é mu-da-ba-e-e[n], /mu-da-ba-en/ 'I can divide the estate' (Dialogue 3, 29 = *UET* VI/2, 150: 29)

    (616) é nu-mu-(e-)da-ba-e-en, /nu-mu-e.da-ba-en/ 'you cannot divide the estate' (Dialogue 3, 21 = *UET* VI/2, 150: 21, unpublished dupl. has -e-da-, cf. Gragg, *SDI* p. 54)

    (617) kin.gi₄.a (...) šu nu-mu-un-da-an-gi₄-gi₄, /nu-mu-n.da-gi₄.gi₄(-e)/ 'the messenger cannot repeat it' (Enmerkar and the Lord of Aratta 501)

§ 449. In some cases –da– occurs where –ta– is expected, or –da– and –ta– may alternate. For instance with the verbs ud...zal 'to pass the day', kar 'to flee' and kud 'to cut':

    (618) ud 2 ud 3 nu-ma-da-ab-zal, /nu-ï-ba-ta-b-zal/ 'he did not let two nor three days pass' (Gudea, cyl. A XXIII 2)

    (619) ud im-di-ni-ib-zal-e, /ï-m-ta-ni-b-zal-e/ 'he spends the days' (Enki and the World Order 30)

(620) ud 3 ği₆ 3 ᵃum-taᵃ-zal-la-ta, (a-a: ba-), /u-ī-m-ta-zal-a-ta/ 'after three days and three nights had passed' (Inanna's Descent 173)

(621) gal₅.lá-ğu₁₀ ga-ba-da-kar, /ga-ba-ta-kar/ 'let me escape my demons' (Inanna's Descent 375)

(622) še ba-da-an-kud, /ba-ta-n-kud/ 'he cut the grain' (Curse of Akkade 126), but:

(623) á-ni hé-eb-ta-kud, /ha-ī-b.ta-kud/ 'may his strength be cut off' (Curse of Akkade 248)

These occurrences of -da- instead of expected -ta- can be regarded as graphic or phonetic variants (cf. A. Falkenstein, *GSGL* I p. 215), or as expression of a different understanding of the verb. See D.O. Edzard, *SR* p. 138, who interpreted zàh 'to run away' with -da- as: '(sich) mit/bei jemanden (befinden und von ihm) weglaufen'.

Gene B. Gragg, *SDI* p. 47ff., observed that there are very few instances of ba-ta-... in the Old Babylonian literary texts, whereas ba-da-... occurs frequently and often where /-ta-/ is expected. He therefore concluded that ba-da- comes from /ba-ta-/, and that ba-da- < /ba-da-/ does not occur, at least only exceptionally. In the Gudea texts, on the contrary, forms with ba-ta- are more numerous than ba-da-... It thus seems that /ba-/ can precede the ablative /-ta-/, but not, or rarely, the comitative /-da-/. Both ba-da- and ba-ta- may therefore stand for /ba-ta-/. At least some of the unexpected instances of -da- in the examples above can be explained according to this theory.

§ 450. *Bibliography*

I.T. Kaneva, 1982. 'Notes on Sumerian Grammar'. In: J.N. Postgate (ed.), *Societies and Languages of the Ancient Near East. Studies in Honour of I.M. Diakonoff*. Warminster, p. 160-164.

Terminative

§ 451. In the OS texts the terminative prefix is orthographically identical with the postposition namely written -šè-, with the exception of a few cases where it is written -ši-. After the Old Sumerian period it is always written -ši-.

§ 452. *1.sg.:* /mu-ši-/

(624) saǧ.ki zalag-ga-ni ǧá(-a)-šè hu-mu-ši-in-zìg, /ha-mu-ši-n-zìg/ 'she has indeed lifted her bright face toward me' (Išme-Dagan Hymn D 106)

§ 453. *2.sg.:* /-e.ši-/

(625) tur dug₄-ga-zu mah dùg-ga-àm šu ba-a-ši-íb-ti, /ba-e.ši-b-ti(-e)/ 'he will receive from you your little word like a great word' (Gudea, cyl. A VII 3) We would expect /mu-e-ši-/; but that ba-a-ši- here means 'to you' can be seen from the parallel form:

(626) siskur-rá-zu-ni Gù.dé.a-áš en ᴰNin.ǧír.su-ke₄ šu ba-ši-ti, /ba-(n.)ši-(n-)ti/ 'the lord Ninǧirsu has received his offerings from Gudea' (Gudea, cyl. A II 21-22)

(627) ᴰUtu igi húl-la hé-mu-e-ši-bar-re, /ha-mu-e.ši-bar-e/ 'may Utu look upon you in joy' (Enmerkar and the Lord of Aratta 95)

§ 454. *3.sg.an.:* /-n.ši-/

Although /-n.ši-/ certainly refers to an animate being the corresponding noun is often in the dative:

(628) lugal-ra dumu Adabᵏⁱ(-a) min-àm mu-(un-)ši-re₇⁽ʳᵉ⁾-eš, /mu-n-ši-ere-eš/ 'the two sons of Adab moved against the king' (Dumuzi's Dream 119) Cf. also:

(629) ku.li-ni-ir ga-an-ši-re₇-en-dè-en, /ga-ĩ-n.ši-ere-enden/ 'let us go to his friend' (Dumuzi's Dream 140)

(630) ama dumu-ni(-ir) igi nu-mu-un-ši-bar-re, /nu-mu-n.ši-bar-e/ 'the mother does not look at her child' (Nisaba Hymn 41). Cf. ex. 627.

See also ex. 626 above.

§ 455. *Inanimate:* /ba-ši-/, /-m-ši-/, /-b.ši-/

(631) ud ᴰNin.ǧír.su-ke₄ uru-ni-šè igi zid im-ši-bar-ra, /ĩ-m-ši-(n-)bar-a/ 'when Ninǧirsu has looked faithfully on his city' (Gudea, St. B III 6-7)

(632) en-e inim kug ᴰInanna-ka-šè saǧ-kéš ba-ši-in-akᵃ (a: ǧar for ak), /ba-ši-n-ak/ 'the lord gave heed to the word of Inanna' (Enmerkar and the Lord of Aratta 105)

(633) á.šed$_{10}$-bi-šè ní hé-eb-ši-te-en-te(-en), /ha-ï-b.ši-te.en.te(. en-e)/ 'let him refresh himself in its cool arm(s)' (Šulgi Hymn A 33)

§ 456. The terminative prefix with plural reference is not attested as far as I know.

The Use of the Terminative Prefix

§ 457. The basic meaning of the terminative is the direction towards someone or something, and /-ši-/ is thus used most typically with verbs of motion. The direction can be denoted by NOUN-šè and the terminative prefix serves to emphasize the direction or to differenti-ate the meaning of the verb:

ku$_4$.r without -ši-, but occasionally with NOUN-šè, means simply 'to enter'. ku$_4$.r with -ši- means 'to enter in the presence of some-one'.

de$_6$ without -ši- is simply 'to carry', but with -ši- it means 'to bring in'.

gi$_4$ without -ši-, but with dative prefix or with -ni-, means 'to answer', with -ši-, however, it means 'to send back'.

For these and other references, see Gragg, *SDI* p. 23-26.

§ 458. The terminative prefix is frequently used with verbs of atten-tion, i.e. typically compounds with igi and ğeštug$_2$. Cf. Gragg, *SDI* p. 22: 'In the compounds with gizzal, sag-kéš, and geštú (...) the pres-ence or absence of the terminative infix seems to correspond to the placing or not placing of emphasis on the object of the attention':

igi...bar with -ši-: 'to look upon in a certain manner'. The verb oc-curs also without -ši-, apparently in a more neutral meaning: 'to see, to look at', then often with -ni-:

(634) en Aratta^{ki}-ke$_4$ im-ma igi i-ni-in-bar, /ï-ni-n-bar/ 'the lord of Aratta looked at the tablet' (Enmerkar and the Lord of Aratta 540) (Gragg, *SDI* p. 21). Cf. ex. 627 and 630.

igi...íl occurs both with and without -ši-. Cf. Gragg, *SDI* p. 21: 'the distinction here seems to be that with -ši-, igi-íl means to look at some specific object, usually an individual thing; without it however it means rather to look over (perhaps usually a multitude)'.

Other verbs are: igi...dù 'to set the eyes on', igi...ğar 'to place the eyes', igi...kár 'to look upon', gizzal...ak 'to listen to', ĝeštug₂...gub 'to set the mind to', ĝeštug₂...ĝar 'to give thought to', and saĝ-kéš... ak 'to pay attention to' (ex. 632).

§ 459. Verbs which take terminative prefix are moreover: (ki...)kin 'to seek for', ù...ku 'to sleep', gú...šub 'to be lax with respect', ní...te 'to relax, to cool off' (ex. 633).

(635) lú (...) ki mu-(un-)ši-kin-kin, /mu-n.ši-kin.kin(-e)/ 'he looks for a man' (Lugalbanda and Enmerkar 270). Cf. kin without -ši-:

(636) ᴰDumu.zi(-dè) saĝ ú-a mu-ni-(in-)kin-kin-ne, /mu-ni-(n-) kin.kin-ene/ 'they look for the head of Dumuzi in the grass' (Dumuzi's Dream 145 = 147 = 149). The difference between kin with -ši- and kin without -ši- is not evident to me.

Further examples in Gragg, *SDI* p. 26f.

šu...ti 'to take from, to receive from' is lit.: 'to approach the hand to'. The person from whom the object is received is in the terminative, whereas the object to be received is in the locative-terminative, cf. ex. 625, 626. Without -ši-, šu...ti simply means 'to take' (cf. Gragg, *SDI* p. 26):

(637) ᴰnin.ninni₂ ᵐᵘˢᵉⁿ.ta-e ĝá udu-ka sila₄ šu ba-ni-ib-ti, /ba-ni-b-ti/ 'the ...-bird took a lamb in the house of the sheep' (Dumuzi's Dream 35 = 60)

Ablative-Instrumental: -ta-

§ 460. The ablative-instrumental prefix -ta- is identical with the ablative-instrumental postposition -ta.

/ba-ta-/ is written ba-ta- in OS and Gudea texts but later on ba-ta- is rare and perhaps replaced by ba-da- or ba-ra- (see § 449 and 465).

§ 461. The ablative-instrumental prefix -ta- has inanimate reference only. It can be preceded by the conjugation prefixes /ì-/, /-m-/ and /ba-/ and by the pronominal element /-b-/.

(638) É.an.na.túm (...)-e (...) e-bi Íd.nun-ta Gú.eden.na-šè íb-ta-ni-è, /ĩ-b.ta-ni-(n-)è/ 'Eanatum (...) let the boundary ditch go out from Idnun to Gu-edena' (Ent. 28 I 32 - II 3)

(639) Gù.dé.a é ᴰNin.ĝír.su-ka ᴰUtu-gin₇ dugud-ta ba-ta-è, /ba-ta-(n-)è/ 'Gudea let the house of Ningirsu go out of the clouds like Utu' (Gudea, cyl. A XXIV 13-14)

(640) lú É.ninnu-ta im-ta-ab-è-è-a mu.sar.ra-bi šu íb-ta-ab-ùr-a, /ĩ-m-ta-b-è.è-(e-)a/, /ĩ-b-ta-b-ùr-(e-)a/ 'the man who removes it from Eninnu and erases its inscription' (Gudea, St. B VIII 6-9) Cf. íb-ta-ab-è-è-a in the parallel context St. C IV 5-6.

The Use of the Ablative-Instrumental Prefix

§ 462. /-ta-/ in the instrumental sense is not frequent, but cf.:

(641) ᵍⁱˢšinig ᵍⁱˢŠEĜ₉ An ù.tu-ta É.ninnu im-ta-sikil-e-ne im-ta-dadag-ge-éš, /ĩ-m-ta-sikil-ene/, /ĩ-m-ta-(n-)dadag-eš/ 'they cleaned Eninnu with tamarisk and ..., they made it clean with it' (Gudea, cyl. B IV 10-12), see also Gragg, *SDI* p. 36.

For examples with NOUN-ta(instr.) without concord in the verb, see Gragg, *SDI* p. 31.

§ 463. -ta- in the ablative sense denotes the direction from, out of something. It occurs with verbs of motion, most often è 'to go out', e₁₁.d 'to go down', ĝen 'to go, to come', sar 'to chase away', zìg 'to rise up from'.

ĝar with -ta- means 'to remove', without -ta- it means simply 'to place'.

Other verbs which take ablative -ta- are lá 'to hang from' and zal 'to pass (said about time)'.

§ 464. *Examples:*

(642) é zag uru-ka-ta En.ig.gal nu.banda Ú.ú saĝa é-gal-ra (...) mu-na-ta-ĝar, /mu-na-ta-(n-)ĝar/ 'En-iggal, the inspector, has removed it (= various objects of wood) from the house outside the city for U-u, the steward of the palace' (*AWL* nr. 76 III-IV)

(643) an-ta hé.ĝál ha-mu-ra-ta-du, /ha-mu-DAT.2.sg.-ta-du-e/

'may abundance come from heaven for you' (Gudea, cyl. A XI 8)

(644) [ud e]š₅ ǧi₆ eš₅ (-àm) ᵃum-taᵃ-zal-la-ta (a-a: ba-), /u-ï-m-ta-zal-a-ta/ 'after three days and three nights have passed' (Inanna's Descent 173)

(645) é-e guruš ug₅-ga-gin₇ gú ki-šè ba-da-an-lá, /ba-ta-n-lá/ 'the house let the neck hang from there to the earth like young warriors who have been killed' (Curse of Akkade 120)

Ablative: -ra-

§ 465. Ablative reference is also expressed by the prefix -ra-. This prefix occurs already in the Gudea texts and is frequent in the OB literary texts.[98]

-ra- has, like -ta-, inanimate reference only. However, it cannot occur after /-b-/ and /-m-/, but only after /ba-/ — or after another case prefix. It has the same rank as -ta- and is used with the same verbs. -ra- and -ta- are thus practically identical with the exception that -ra-does not denote instrumental, but the reason for the use of -ra- instead of -ta-is not clear. Since ba-ra- occurs whereas ba-ta-does not (at least not in the OB period, see § 449), ba-ra- may simply stand for ba-ta-, but phonetic reasons for a change ba-ta- > ba-ra- cannot be given.

> A. Falkenstein, 1939 p. 194, hesitated to identify -ra- and -ta-. Cf. also Gragg, SDI p. 98: 'While clear criteria cannot be set up for identifying -ra- and -ta-, no clear rationale can be found either for establishing them as syntactically distinct in the periods of Sumerian over which we have any control. Accordingly we operate with a single ablative infix which may be realized as either /ta/ or /ra/. If they are not to be taken as phonologically conditioned alternates, one might hypothesize as follows: Of two (perhaps originally distinct) infixes, -ra- and -ta-, the latter, for whatever reason could not appear in certain positions (especially after ba-). In these positions it came to be replaced by -ra- (and in some instances by -da-), which in these instances took over the syntactic functions of -ta-.'

§ 466. *Examples:*

(646) min-[a.ne.n]e ᵐBa.al.lí ᵐUr.ᴰSuen lú inim-ma sağ sa₁₀-a-šè mu-ne-ra-è, /mu-ne-ra(abl.)-è(-eš)/ 'against these two

---

98. In Gragg's material there are 80 instances of -ra- compared with 100 instances of -ta-, SDI p. 96 and p. 30.

(persons) Balli and Ur-Suen appeared (lit.: went out) as witnesses concerning the slave who has been sold' (*NG* nr. 51, 12-15) Cf. the same verb with -ta-:

(647) igi di.kud-ne-šè Ur.gu.la (...) Nam.mah (...) Á. lu₅.lu₅ nam. lú.inim.ma.bi-šè im-ta-è-eš, /ì-m-ta-è-eš/ 'Urgula, Nammah and Alulu appeared before the judges as witnesses' (*NG* nr. 99, 23-27)

(648) eden-šè ba-ra-è, /ba-ra(abl.)-è/ 'he went out from there to the plain' (Dumuzi's Dream 1)

(649) Me.luh.ha^{ki} lú kur g̃i₆-ga-kam^a níg.šu ^{b}kur-kur-ra^b mu-un-na-ra-ab-e₁₁-dè (a: -ke₄; b-b: kúr-kúr-ra), /mu-na-ra (abl.)-b-e₁₁.d-e/ 'Meluhha, the people of the black mountain, brings down from there goods of the mountains to her' (Curse of Akkade 48-49)

§ 467. In a few cases the sequences -da-ra-, -ta-ra-, -da-ra-ta- or -da-ra-da- probably denote an ablative element /-dara-/ or /-tara-/, or perhaps /-dra-/ or /-tra-/, cf. Gragg, *SDI* p. 97 and 98 n. 1.

(650) ^{D}Nin.g̃iš.zid.da Utu-gin₇ ki.ša-ra ma-ra-da-ra-ta-è, /mu-DAT.2.sg.-da.ra.ta-è/ 'Ning̃išzida rose for you from the horizon like the sun' (Gudea, cyl. A V 20) Cf.:

(651) uru-e ^{D}Utu-gin₇ ki.ša-ra im-ma-ta-a-è, /ì-ba-ta-a(?)-è/ 'the city rose from the horizon like the sun' (Gudea, cyl. B XVIII 12-13)

§ 468. *The Variant -ri-*

The rather uncommon prefix -ri- in the OB literary texts represents the ablative in a few cases. Why -ri- is used rather than -ra- cannot be explained. (See Gragg, *SDI* p. 100.)

(652) hur.sag̃ ía hur.sag̃ àš hur.sag̃ imin-e im-me-ri-bal-bal, /ì-ba-ra(abl.)-bal.bal/ 'he crossed five mountains, six mountains, seven mountains' (Enmerkar and the Lord of Aratta 170) The analysis of the verbal form is problematic. In other cases me- comes from /mu-e-/, but here no 2. person reference is possible. im-me- must be analysed /ì-ba-/ rather than /ì-bi-/ since no case prefix except -ni- can follow /bi-/. bal 'to cross' is intransitive and normally takes ablative, but in this case locative-terminative. Cf. the parallel phrase:

(653) muš.zar.ra-gin$_7$ [a] hur.sağ-ta[b] im-me-ri-bal-bal (a: -ta; b: -gin$_7$) 'they crossed the mountains like a ...-snake' (Lugalbanda and Enmerkar 252). bal with -ta-:

(654) e ki.sur.ra ^{D}Nin.ğír.su-ka-ka e-ma-ta-bal, /ī-ba-ta-bal/ 'he crossed the boundary ditch of Ningirsu' (Ent. 28 III 2-4). For further references, see Wilcke, 1969a p. 163f. and n. 432.

Other occurrences of ablative -ri- in Gragg, *SDI* p. 99f. For the prefix -ri- as referring to 2.sg., see § 478.

§ 469. *Bibliography*

A. Falkenstein, 1939. 'Untersuchungen zur sumerischen Grammatik: 2. Das richtungsanzeigende Infix -ra-'. *ZA* 45: 180-194.

The Locative Prefix

§ 470. The locative prefix is the last case prefix of the chain; only the pronominal elements /-n-/ and /-b-/ can occur after it before the verbal stem.

The pronominal element /-e-/ is never written after the locative prefix; it is either assimilated or deleted, or it may, in the OB literary texts, be inserted before the locative prefix:

(655) šu-ğu$_{10}$ šu maš.dà (ù-)mu-e-ni-sè, /(u-)mu-e-ni-sè/ 'when you have changed my hands into the hands of a gazelle' (Dumuzi's Dream 170 = 197 = 232 with the variant ù-mu-ni-in-sè) We expect */u-mu-ni-e-sè/.

(656) šà im ugu Abzu-ka ù-mu-e-ni-in-šár, /u-mu-e-ni-n-šár/ 'when you have kneaded the heart of the clay that is in Abzu' (Enki and Ninmah 3) We expect: */u-mu-ni-e-šár/.

In the following example /-e-/ probably refers to 2.sg. object:

(657) lú hul.ğál-e i.zi-a ^{a}im-mu-e-ni^a-dab$_5$-bé (a-a: im-me-ni-), /ī-mu-e-ni-dab$_5$-e/ 'the evil man catches you in the ...' (Dumuzi's Dream 51)

The locative prefix most frequently occurs as -ni-, but has also the form -ri- (see § 478), and the conjugation prefix /bi-/ has probably (at least in parts) the same functions as -ni- (see § 474).

'Locative' is here meant in a very general sense. In fact the prefix is used in three different functions which are also morphologically distinct: 1. Locative. 2. Denoting the 'second object' with compound verbs. 3. Causative.

§ 471. *1. Locative.* In the locative function the prefix occurs as -ni-. G.B. Gragg, *SDI* p. 71, found a very high percentage (40%) of concord between -ni- and the locative postposition /-a/. This fact together with the circumstance that -ni- may occur with practically any verb leads to the conclusion that -ni- refers to the locative, but in a more general sense than the postpositions which distinguish locative (-a), locative-terminative (-e) and terminative (-šè).

> Cf. Gragg, *SDI* p. 78:-ni- 'adds the semantic feature of local determinacy to the features already defining the verb. This notion of local determinacy is usually further specified elsewhere in the verb phrase by an adverbial complement [i.e., by /-a/, /-e/ or /-šè/]. Now in Sumerian nominal postposition system the most general, i.e., unmarked, category for spatial orientation is the locative. And, as a matter of fact, it is with the locative postposition that what we have called the locative infix [i.e., -ni-] chiefly occurs. Since, within the system of infixes, there is no element which exactly covers the semantic properties of the locative-terminative, this function also is taken over by the locative infix. Moreover, as we have just seen, even when more differentiated (more marked) indicators of spatial orientation are used in the adverbial complement, this can be indicated on the verb by the less specific 'locative' infix. When more differentiation is desired in the verb, then, depending on various syntactic and semantic features of the verb, a more 'marked' infix can be used, sometimes, as we have seen, with semantic specialization of the verb'.

In the locative function as described here, the prefix occurs as -ni-. Examples are for instance:

(658) igi-ba šembi ba-ni-ğar, /ba-ni-(n-)ğar/ 'he placed kohl on their eyes' (Ean. 1 XVIII 3)

(659) sig₄ ù.šub-ba mu-ni-ğar-ra-ni ᴰUtu im-da-húl, /mu-ni-(n-)ğar-a-ani(-da), /ī-m-da-húl/ 'Utu rejoiced over his brick that he has laid in the brick form' (Gudea, cyl. A XIX 8-9)

(660) Gù.dé.a (...-e) é-a dusu-bi men kug sağ-ğá mu-ni-ğál, /mu-ni-(n-)ğál/ 'Gudea placed the basket of the house, the holy crown, on (his) head' (Gudea, cyl. A XX 24-25)

(661) ^DNin.ǧír.su-ke₄ èš numun i-a šà-ge ba-ni-pàd, /ba-ni-(n-)
pàd/ 'Ninǧirsu has called into (his) heart the shrine which let
the seed go out' (Gudea, cyl. B XIII 6)

Examples of verbs with -ni- corresponding to nouns in the locative
or locative-terminative can moreover be found in Gragg, *SDI* p. 73-
76.

§ 472. Traditionally -ni- is regarded as consisting of a pronominal
element and the locative-terminative element /e/ > /i/. According to
this we would expect /-n-i-/ > -ni-, animate, and /-b-i-/ > -bi-,
inanimate, but in fact only -ni- occurs and most often with inanimate
reference. A. Falkenstein, *GSGL* I p. 205, considered that the basic
form *-b-i- changed to -mi- after /ī-/ (im-mi-ak), and in other
cases to -ni- by dissimilation (ba-ni-dug₄) or assimilation (ì-na-ni-
ku₄). But the reasons for the phonetic change: /-b-i-/ > -ni- are not
clear, and an analysis of the prefix -ni- can for the present not be given.

The circumstances under which *-b-e- is changed to -ni- are given in Falkenstein, *GSGL* I p. 205-208; for a discussion of this see Gragg, *SDI* p. 68-73.

§ 473. With the other case prefixes the choice of conjugation prefix
depended on the animate or inanimate reference of the prefix
immediately following (see § 429). In the case of -ni- this rule is not
always followed, no reason can thus be given for the form mu-ni-
VERB in ex. 659 and 660 in contrast to ba-ni-VERB in ex. 658 and
661.

§ 474. -ni- is the only case prefix which can occur with the conjugation prefix /bi-/: /bi-ni-/ > mi-ni-. /bi-/ is also analysed as /b-e-/,
containing the locative-terminative element /e/ (cf. §§ 349-351 and
for instance Falkenstein, *GSGL* I p. 192), but the relationship
between /bi-/ and -ni- is far from evident. Moreover the meaning of
/bi-ni-/ or /bi-/ in contrast to /ba-ni-/ and /mu-ni-/ is not clear. Cf.
for instance mí ba-ni-dug₄ and mí mi-ni-dug₄ (ex. 681, 682) and igi
mu-ni-in-du₈, igi im-mi-in-du₈-a and igi im-ma-ni-in-du₈ (ex.
675-678).

See also the examples in Gragg, *SDI* p. 72f. for parallels between
-ni-, im-mi- and bí-.

§ 475. The locative prefix -ni- can occur together with the dative,

the comitative and the terminative prefix. In the Old Sumerian texts
-ni- also appears after ablative -ta-, but not in the Old Babylonian
texts (cf. Gragg, *SDI* p. 67).

(662) íb-ta-ni-è, /ī-b-ta-ni-(n-)è/ 'he let it go out from there'
(Ent. 28 II 3)
(663) e-na-ta-ni-è, /ī-na-ta-ni-(n-)è/ "he let it go out from there
for him' (Ent. 41 IV 2)

§ 476. *2. Denoting the 'Second Object' with Compound Verbs.* The
locative prefix is especially frequent with compound verbs and this
use is certainly related to the locative function described above. With
compound verbs the prefix may correspond to a noun in the locative,
locative-terminative or in the dative.

In contrast to the function of the prefix described in the preceding
section, where -ni- always refers to the place where something happens, the prefix with compound verbs can refer to a place or to persons and animals.

1.sg.	/mu-DAT.1.sg.-ni-/ > ma-ni-	1.pl.		?
2.sg.	/mu-ri-/, /(MOD-)ī-ri-/	2.pl.	/-ri-...-enzen/(?)	
3.sg.an.	/mu-ni-/	3.pl.		?
Inanimate	/ba-ni-/, /bi-ni-/ > mi-ni-			

§ 477. *1.sg.:*

(664) ᴰNisaba-ke₄ ĝeštug₂ gizzal(-la) šu daĝal(-la) ᵃma-ni-in-
dug₄ᵃ (a-a: ma-ra-an-dug₄), /mu-DAT.1.sg.-ni-n-dug₄/
'Nisaba has generously provided me with intelligence and
wisdom' (Šulgi Hymn B 18-19)
(665) ud (...) ĝá-ra saĝ-e-eš-e ma-ni-in-rig₇-eš-a, /mu-DAT.1.sg.-
ni-n-rig₇-eš-a/ 'as they have granted it to me' (Sin-iddinam
6 I 10-14)

§ 478. *2. sg.*, -ri- is not attested before the Old Babylonian period:[99]

(666) igi dùg(-zu) hu-mu-ri-(in-)du₈, /ha-mu-ri-n-du₈/ 'he has

---

99. A. Poebel, 1925 p. 5ff., understood the Old Sumerian forms ere-è and ere-
kéš (Ean. 1 VII 8, 11) as containing the 2.sg. -ri-: /ī-ri-/ but ere- could also
be the modal prefix /iri-/ (see §§ 415-417). Considering the difficult contents of the text the problem cannot be settled, cf. W.H.Ph. Römer, 1975 p.
3ff.

indeed looked kindly at you' (Iddin-Dagan Hymn B 63) Cf. ex. 678.

(667) ᴰEn.líl-le saĝ-e-eš mu-ri-in-rig₇, /mu-ri-n-rig₇/ 'Enlil has granted it to you' (Nergal Hymn 13) Cf. mi-ni-rig₈ in ex. 679.

(668) An-né ki mah-a-ni-a nam gal mu-ri-in-tar, /mu-ri-n-tar/ 'An has decreed a good fate for you on his exalted place' (Iddin-Dagan Hymn B 1).

(669) lugal nam gi₄-rí-íb-tarᵃʳ nam dùg gú-mu-rí-íb-tarᵃʳ, /ga-í-ri-b-tar/, /ga-mu-ri-b-tar/ 'king, let me decree the fate for you, let me decree a good fate for you' (Šulgi Hymn D 384)

In some cases -ri- seems to stand for *-ra(DAT.2.sg.)-ni-. This can for instance be observed in *OBGT* IX, and in fact G.B. Gragg derived -ri- from -ra-ni-: 2 + Loc → ra + (n)i → ri (*SDI* p. 105). The form *-ra-ni- is thus exactly parallel to the 1.sg. ma-ni-.

-e- before -ri- in ex. 670-671 is probably the pleonastically applied pronominal element of the second person.

(670) ud-da ᴰMu.ul.líl e.ne.èm-ba ᵃnu-ri-gubᵃ (a-a: nu-mu-e-ri-gub), /nu-í-ra-ni-gub/ 'if Enlil does not stand by you in this matter' (Inanna's Descent 48) gub with dative prefix means 'to stand by', the locative prefix refers to e.ne.èm-ba

(671) kur-kur(-re) ú.sal-la mu-e-ri-ná, /mu-ra-ni-ná/ 'all the foreign lands will lay down in the meadow for you' (Iddin-Dagan Hymn B 56) ná with dative prefix means 'to lie before someone', the locative prefix refers to ú.sal-la.

However, -ra-ni- is also found:

(672) ur.saĝ-e me-ni gal-gal-la-àm šu ma-ra-ni-íb-mú-mú, /mu-DAT.2.sg.-ni-b-mú.mú-e/ 'the hero — his divine power is the greatest — will let it expand for you' (Gudea, cyl. A VII 8)

(673) ᴰEn.líl-le saĝ-e-eš mu-ri-in-rig₇ nam tar-re-dè šu-za ma-ra-ni-in-ge.en, /mu-ri-n-rig₇/, /mu-DAT.2.sg.-ni-n-ge.n/ 'Enlil has given it to you, to decide the fates he has made firm for you in your hand' (Nergal Hymn 13-14 = 18-19)

§ 479. *3.sg., animate:*

(674) lugal-ni-ir ud-dè maš.ĝi₆-ka Gù.dé.a en ᴰNin.ĝír.su-ra igi

mu-ni-du$_8$-àm, /mu-ni-(n-)du$_8$-a-m/ 'on this day Gudea saw his king, the lord Ninĝirsu, in a dream' (Gudea, cyl. A I 17-18) Compare the following forms with igi...du$_8$ and with various conjugation prefixes:

(675) nin-bi ^{D}Nin.tu-gin$_7$ rib-ba-ra a.ba-a igi mu-ni-in-du$_8$, /mu-ni-n-du$_8$/ 'who has ever seen someone as great as its queen Nintu?' (Keš Hymn 20)

(676) a.ba-a igi im-mi-in-du$_8$-a, /ī-bi-n-du$_8$-a/ 'who has seen (a king)' (Curse of Akkade 95)

(677) Ak.kà igi im-ma-ni-in-du$_8$, /ī-ba-ni-n-du$_8$/ 'Aka saw him' (Gilgameš and Aka 67)

(678) igi dùg hu-mu-ni-du$_8$, /ha-mu-ni-du$_8$(-en)/ 'may you look kindly at him' (Ninurta Hymn 24 and 25) Cf. ex. 666

(679) ^{D}Nin.ĝír.su-ra Lum.ma.gin$_7$.dùg mu-na-ús saĝ-šè mi-ni-rig$_8$, /bi-ni-(n-)rig$_8$/ 'he ... (the canal) Lummagindug for Ninĝirsu and dedicated it to him' (Ean. 2 VII 3-6)

(680) Gù.dé.a en ^{D}Nin.ĝír.su-ke$_4$ nam dùg mu-ni-tar, /mu-ni-(n-)tar/ 'the lord Ninĝirsu has decided a good fate for Gudea' (Gudea, cyl. A XXIV 1-2)

§ 480. *Inanimate:*

(681) ^{D}Nanše dumu Eridu^{ki}⟨-ga⟩-ke$_4$ eš.bar.kíĝ.ĝá mí ba-ni-dug$_4$, /ba-ni-(n-)dug$_4$/ 'Nanše, the daughter of Eridu, cared for the oracle' (Gudea, cyl. A XX 16)

(682) eš.bar.kíĝ mí mi-ni-dug$_4$, /bi-ni-(n-)dug$_4$/ 'he cared for the oracle' (Gudea, cyl. B V 24)

Compare the verbs with inanimate reference but without the locative prefix:

(683) ĝiri$_3$ ní-te-(a-)na-ka^a igi lib-ba^b bí-in-du$_8$-ru (a: -ke$_4$; b: -a), /bi-n-du$_8$.r-e/ 'he looks with downcast eyes at his own feet' (Enmerkar and the Lord of Aratta 238)

(684) nam-bi (ha)-ba-an-tar-re-eš, /(ha-)ba-n-tar-eš/ 'they have (indeed) decided its fate (i.e., for the city)' (Lamentation over Sumer and Ur 55 = *UET* VI/2, 124: 54 = *STVC* 27 rev. 7)

§ 481. *2. person plural* forms are of course few, but at least in one case -ri- and the suffix /-enzen/ are used:

(685) lú-ulu₃ hé-me-en-zé-en nam ga-mu-ri-ib-tar(-en-zé-en), /ha-ī-me-enzen/, /ga-mu-ri-b-tar-enzen/ 'if you(pl.) are mortal, I will decree (your) fates for you(pl.)' (Inanna's Descent 270, the parallel line 243 has: nam-zu-ne hé-eb-tar-re, /ha-ī-b-tar-e/ 'may she decree your(pl.) fates')

§ 482. *3. Grammatical Function: Causative.* -ni- is often found in causative verbs and probably denotes the underlying agent. Strictly speaking only three-participant forms like 'he causes him to lift the head' are real causatives, but -ni- is also found with 'intransitive' verbs like ku₄.r 'to enter' and è 'to go out' in two-participant forms, cf. ex. 662-663 above, and see §§ 284-286 with examples 289-300.

The causative use of -ni- is clearly demonstrated in OBGT where Akkadian Š-forms are translated by Sumerian verbs with -ni- (cf. Th. Jacobsen, 1956 p. 28*ff.). In the Sumerian texts the use of -ni- in causative forms seems less consistent.

THE SUBORDINATION SUFFIX /-a/

§ 483. The suffix /-a/ can occur with a finite verb. Its rank is at the end of the verbal form after the pronominal suffixes. The finite verb with /-a/ can be followed by postpositions or possessive suffixes and the verb is in this case treated like a noun. Therefore, /-a/ has usually been called 'nominalization suffix' (for instance A. Falkenstein, 1959a p. 35), but /-a/ is a syntactic particle and not a morpheme used to derive nouns from other words. Its function can most properly be described as subordination.

Finite verbs with /-a/ occur in the following cases: 1. Dependent on another verb: Subjunctive (§§ 484-485). 2. Dependent on a noun: Relative and various subordinate clauses (§§ 486-490).

/-a/ occurs also in non-finite forms, for which see §§ 512-518; 522-523.

Subjunctive

§ 484. The subjunctive is directly dependent on another verb which is not necessarily a finite verb. A noun or a non-finite verb followed by the enclitic copula can also serve as main verb (ex. 688).

The subordinate verb precedes the main verb which is usually a verb of speaking, for instance: dug$_4$ 'to say', ge.n 'to confirm', mu lugal...pàd 'to swear by (lit.: call) the name of the king', nam.erim$_2$... TAR 'to swear'. The subjunctive indicates indirect speech which, however, is rarely used in Sumerian.

The finite subjunctive verb can be compared with the non-finite form R-ed-a, see §§ 522-523.

242

§ 485. *Examples:*

(686) la-ba-gi$_4$-gi$_4$-da igi di.kud-ne-šè Ur.^{D}Suen-ke$_4$ mu lugal-bi in-pàd, /nu-ba-gi$_4$.gi$_4$-ed-a/ 'Ur-Suen has sworn by the name of the king before the judges that he will not return (in this matter)' (*NG* nr. 103, 10-13)

(687) Ur.^{D}Lama ensi$_2$-ke$_4$ é Ha.la.^{D}Ba.ba$_6$-ka in-na-sum-ma-a Ur.íd.da di-ta ba-tag$_4$-a Uru.in.da.zal maškim-e nam.erim$_2$-bi in-TAR, /í-na-(n-)sum-a/, /ba-tag$_4$-a/ 'that Ur-Lama, the *ensi*, has given the house to Hala-Baba and that the claim of Ur-ida has been dismissed has Uru-indazal, the bailiff, confirmed by oath' (*NG* nr. 106, 5-9)

(688) mu-lugal Nin.dub.sar dumu Ka$_{10}$ dam-šè ha-tuku bí-in-dug$_4$-ga Nin.nam.ha.ni Ur.^{D}Lama nam.erim$_2$-àm, /bi-n-dug$_4$-a/ 'it is the oath of Ninnamhani and Ur-Lama that he has said: 'by the name of the king I shall marry Nin-dubsar, the daughter of Ka'' (*NG* nr. 15, 4-9)

Relative

§ 486. A finite verb or a whole sentence can be subordinate to a noun. The subordinate, or in other words, relative clause stands after the noun which it qualifies, and the subordination suffix /-a/ is added at the end of the finite verb. Between the noun and the relative clause an 'indefinite' noun can be inserted: for animate beings: lú 'someone' = 'who', for inanimate beings: níg 'thing' = 'which'. This 'relative pronoun' is not obligatory.

> lugal lú é in-dù-a ba-úš 'the king who has built the house has died'

The noun which is qualified by the relative clause can be subject, object or some other case in relation to the relative clause, but the relevant postposition is not applied (cf. lú and ki in ex. 689-692).

The case of the head noun (lugal in the example above) according to the main clause is added after the subordination suffix:

> lugal lú é in-dù-a-ra mu-na-an-sum-mu-uš 'they have given it to the king who has built the house'

Cf. also ex. 690 and 692. The ergative postposition /-e/ is assimilated with /-a/ (ex. 689; 691).

As a rule the verb of subordinate clauses cannot occur with modal prefixes other than the prospective /u-/ and the negative /nu-/. An exception is the form na-bé-a = /na-ī-b-e-e-a/ in the introductory passage of letters.

§ 487. *Relative Clauses: Grammatical Analysis*

(689) DNin.g̃iš.zid.da(-ra) Gù.dé.a   lú   É.ninnu in-dù–a(-e)   é   mu–na–dù

Relative Clause		Virtual Object	Verb			
		erg.				
Main Clause	Dative	Subject		Object	Verb	

'Gudea, who has built Eninnu, has built the temple for Ning̃išzida'
(Cf.: DNin.g̃iš.zid.da dig̃ir–ra–ni Gù.dé.a ensi₂ Lagaš^ki lú É.ninnu DNin.g̃ír.su–ka in–dù–a é G̃ír.su^ki–ka–ni mu–na-dù, Gudea, Brick D)

(690) alam Gù.dé.a ensi₂ Lagaš^ki   lú   É.ninnu   in–dù–a–ke₄   (...) sá.dug₄–ba   g̃ál–la–àm
/í–n–dù–a–ak–e/

Relative Clause			Virtual Object	Verb	
			erg.		
Main Clause	Regens	Genitive	Locative-Terminative	Subject Predicate	Verb

'for the statue of Gudea, the *ensi* of Lagaš, who has built the Eninnu, (these) are the offerings' (Gudea, St. B I 3-12)

(691)

Relative Clause:

lú	diĝir-ĝu$_{10}$-gin$_7$	^{D}Nin.ĝír.su-ke$_4$	diĝir-ra-ni	ùĝ-ĝá	gù	ù-ma-na-ni-dè-a(-e)	(...)	na-ab-ak-ke$_4$
Virtual dative	Equative	Subject		Locative Object		Verb		

Main Clause: Subject / Object / Verb

'the man whom Ninĝirsu, being his god like being my god, has called among the people shall not do ...' (Gudea, St. P III 12 - IV 2; parallel: St. I, III 11 - IV 1, with the var.: diĝir-ĝá-gin$_7$)

(692)

Relative Clause:

ki	^{D}Nin.ĝír.su-ke$_4$	kur-kur-ra	igi	mi-ni-ĝál-la-šè	(...) ensi$_2$-ke$_4$	(...) mi-ni-dab$_5$-dab$_5$
Virtual loc.	Subject	Locative Object		Verb		

Terminative / Subject Object / Verb

Main Clause: Subject Object / Verb

'to the place from where Ninĝirsu has looked at the mountains, the *ensi* has brought (numerous sheep and goats)' (Gudea, cyl. A VIII 7-9) The plural of the object, sheep and goats, is expressed by the reduplication of the verb dab$_5$

§ 488. The subject of the relative clause can be the 2. person, for instance:

(693) lú gùd-g̃á^a ne.en ba-e-(a-)ak-a^b (a: -g̃u$_{10}$; b: -e), /ba-e-ak-a/ 'you, who have done this to my nest' (Lugalbanda and Enmerkar 105)

Sometimes the head noun of the relative clause is absent:

(694) uru-bi-a ga-tuš bí-in-dug$_4$-ga ki-tuš na-an-dùg-ge, /bi-n-dug$_4$-a(-e)/, /na-ì-n-dùg-e/ '(the man who) has said: let me live in this city, shall not have a good place to dwell' (Curse of Akkade 272)

Subordinate Clauses

§ 489. The relative construction, NOUN ... VERB+a+CASE, forms various types of subordinate clauses: A. Temporal Clauses; B. Causal Clauses.

A. Temporal Clauses

/ud ... ... VERB-a-a(loc.)/ 'on the day when ...' (ex. 695-698)
/ud ... ... VERB-a-ta/ 'from the day when ...' = 'after' (ex. 699)
/eg̃er ... ... VERB-a-ta/ 'from the back of ...' = 'after' (ex. 700)
/... ... VERB-a-ta/ 'after' (ex. 701-702)
/en-na ... ... VERB-a- $\left\{ \begin{matrix} eše \\ a \end{matrix} \right\}$ / 'until' (ex. 703-704)

B. Causal Clauses

/bar ... ... VERB-a-ak-eše/ 'for the sake of, because'
/mu ... ... VERB-a-eše/ 'because'

§ 490. *Temporal Clauses: Examples*

ud ... ... VERB-a-a(loc.), lit.: 'on the day when': 'when, if'

(695) ud ^{D}Nin.g̃ír.su ur.sag̃ ^{D}En.líl-lá-ke$_4$ Uru.inim.gi.na-ra nam. lugal Lagaš^{ki} e-na-sum-ma-a šà lú šár-u-ta šu-ni e-ma-ta-dab$_5$-ba-a nam.tar-ra ud-bi-ta e-šè-g̃ar, /ì-na-(n-)sum-a-a/, /ì-ba-ta-(n-)dab$_5$-a-a/, /ì-ši-(n-)g̃ar/ 'When Ning̃irsu, the warrior of Enlil, gave the kingship of Lagaš to Uruinim-gina, and when he seized his hand from among 36.000 men,

(then) he restored the practice of former days' (Ukg. 4 VII 29 - VIII 9)

(696) ud ^{D}Aš.ím.babbar ǧizkim šag$_5$-ga-ni igi ma-ni–in-du$_8$-a igi nam.ti.la-ka-ni mu-ši–in-bar-a é-a-ni dù-ù-dè ki-bi gi$_4$-gi$_4$-dè ǧá-a-ar ma-an-dug$_4$-ga (...) É.temen.ní.guru$_3$ mu-na-dù, /mu-DAT.1.sg.-ni-n-du$_8$-a-a/, /mu-ši-n-bar-a-a/, /mu-DAT.1.sg.-n-dug$_4$-a-a/, /mu-na-dù/ 'when Ašimbabbar let me see his good sign, when he looked at me with his eye of life, and when he commanded me to build and restore his house (...), (then) I built for him the E-temen-niguru' (Waradsin 10, 25-39) (Note that R-ede is used here as subordinate to ma-an-dug$_4$-ga and not R-eda, see § 522)

(697) ud nu-šè-sa$_{10}$-sa$_{10}$-a-a ugula lipiš-bi na-na-tag-ge, /nu-ï-ši-sa$_{10}$.sa$_{10}$-e-a-a/, /na-ï-na-tag-e/ 'if he does not buy it, the ugula must not be angry with him' (Ukg. 4 XI 29-31), variant has: ud-da nu-šè-sa$_{10}$-sa$_{10}$.

(698) ud temen-ǧu$_{10}$ ma-si-ge$_4$-na é-ǧu$_{10}$ ud šu zid ma-ši-tùm-da (...) im si ma-ra-ab-sá-e, /mu-DAT.1.sg.-si.g-en-a-a/, /mu-DAT.1.sg.-ši-tùm-ed-a-a/, /mu-DAT.2.sg.-b-sá-en/ 'when you make my foundation, when (the building of) my house begins (lit.: 'the hand is brought to the house for me') (...), (then) I shall make favorable winds blow (lit.: 'put straight the winds')' (Gudea, cyl. A XI 18-23)

ud ... ... VERB-a-ta 'from the day when ...': 'after';
eǧer ... ... VERB-a-ta 'from the back of ...': 'after'

(699) ud é.gal-e ba-ab-túm-ma-ta igi nu-ni-du$_8$-a, /ba-b-túm-a-ta/, /nu-ï-ni-(n-)du$_8$-a/ '(he has sworn) that he has not seen him after the palace took him away' (*NG* nr. 190, 23-24)

In the Neo-Sumerian texts LUM is written instead of eǧer; LUM is probably to be read eǧer$_5$ or murgu$_2$ (cf. J.J. Finkelstein, 1969 p. 75):

(700) LUM in-tag$_4$-a-ta, /ï-n-tag$_4$-a-ta/ 'after he has left her' (*NG* nr. 23, 5)

ud and eǧer is often omitted:

(701) Ba.gara$_2$ é íd-dè lá-a-e im-ti-a-ta, ninda ǧiš bí-tag a šed$_7$

ì-dé, /ì-m-ti-a-ta/, /bi-(n-)tag/, /ì-(n-)dé/ 'after he has approached Bagara, the house which is ... at the river, he sacrificed bread, he poured out cold water' (Gudea, cyl. A II 7-8)

(702) ᴰŠul.gi-me-en ba-tu-(ud-)dè-en-(na-)ta nita kalag-ga-me-en, /ba-tu.d-en-a-ta/ 'I, Šulgi, am from birth on a strong man' (lit.: 'since I was born') (Šulgi Hymn A 2)

en-na ... ... VERB-a-a(loc.)/VERB-a-eše(term.) 'until'

(703) Ur.ᴰG̃á.tùm.dùg-ke₄ en-na íb-bé-a 0.1.0 še (gur-)lugal-ta ha-ba-ab-sum-mu, /ì-b-e-e-a/, /ha-ba-b-sum-e/ 'until Ur-G̃atumdug will speak, they shall give them 1 *nigida* barley each' (*TCS* nr. 141, 4-7)

(704) i.bí na.ám.ti.la en-na ba-ug₅-ge-a i.bí ba-ra-an-bar-re-en, /bara-ì-n-bar-en/ 'I will not look upon him with the eye of life as long as he lives' (lit.: 'until he dies') (Enki and Ninhursag̃ 219) The verbal form ba-ug₅-ge-a is difficult, we expect /ba-ug₅-ed-a/ = ba-ug₅-ge-da.

§ 491. *Causal Clauses: Examples*

bar ... ... VERB-a-ak-eš(e)(term.) 'for the sake of, because'

(705) lú Dub.ru.um-ma-ke₄ ᴰUtu.hé.g̃ál bar lugal ᴰEn.líl-le á sum-ma ì-me-a ì-zu-a-ke₄-éš, /ì-zu-a-ak-eš(e)/ 'because the people of Dubrum knew that Utu-heg̃al is a king to whom Enlil has given strength' (Utu-heg̃al IV 15-18)

Instead of the terminative also locative can be used:

(706) bar še-bi nu-da-sù-sù-da-ka Ur.lum.ma (...-e) e ki.sur-ra ᴰNin.g̃ír.su-ka (...) a-e ì-mi-è, /nu-ì-da-sù.sù-ed-a-ak-a/, /ì-bi-(n-)è/ 'because this barley ... Ur-lumma let the water go out of the boundary ditch of Ning̃irsu' (Ent. 28 II 27-35)

bar can be omitted:

(707) ur.sag̃ ug₅-ga ì-me-ša-ke₄-éš, /ì-me-eš-a-ak-eš(e)/ 'because they are dead heroes' (Gudea, cyl. A XXVI 15)

(708) á-nun-g̃ál zag.še-ni-šè húl-la ì-me-na-ke₄-eš, /ì-me-en-a-ak-eš(e)/ 'because I am a strong man rejoicing in his (own) strength' (Šulgi Hymn A 27)

mu ... ... VERB-a-eš(e)(term.) 'because'

(709) mu inim-bi nu-ù-zu bí-in-né-ša-šè ğeme$_2$ Lú.gú.gal dumu Lú.^{D}Ba.ba$_6$-ka ba-na-gi-in, /bi-n-e-eš-a-(e)še/, /ba-na-gi.n/ 'because they said that they did not know this case, the slave girl was given to Lu-gugal, the son of Lu-Baba' (*NG* nr. 89, 12-14)

(710) mu ^{D}Ašnan nu-ub-da^a-tu-da(-aš) nu-ub-da-(an-)sig$_7$-ga ⟨-aš⟩ kalam-ma^b gu ^{D}Uttu nu-ub-da-(an-)dím-ma-(a-)aš (a: -ta-; b: -e), /nu-ī-b.da-tu.d-a-eš(e)/, /nu-ī-b.da-sig$_7$-a-eš(e)/, /nu-ī-b.da-dím-a-eš(e)/ 'because Ašnan was not (yet) born and not (yet) created, because the thread of Uttu has not (yet) been made in the land' (Lahar and Ašnan 3-4 = *MBI* 8, 3-4 = *UET* VI/1, 33: 3-4) For the case prefix -da-, cf. Gragg, *SDI* p. 64: 'it is uncertain whether the comitative infix serves a conjunctive function, or whether, since the three verbs involved are all verbs of making, it implies 'putting together, assembling, etc.'.'

In the Isin-Larsa royal inscriptions the terminative is deleted:

(711) mu (...) erim$_2$.ğál-ğá šu-ğu$_{10}$-uš bí-in-si-a, /bi-n-si-a/ 'because he has filled my enemies into my hand' (Warad-Sin 15, 15-18) -ğá is not correct, we expect erim$_2$.ğál-ğu$_{10}$, absolutive.

§ 492. *VERB + a + ri*

This construction is found almost exclusively in Emesal laments. The meaning of -ri is disputed, especially because of the difficult context of the Emesal texts.

-ri seems to serve as a postposition, probably with the meaning 'to', 'concerning'. It is thus very similar to the terminative -šè, but -ri has also an isolating, emphasizing effect, comparative to that of the enclitic copula. Instead of -ri the suffix -ra is sometimes used in the same way (cf. Krecher, 1965 p. 23; 27).

For the function of -ri, see J. Krecher, 1965: (-ri ist) 'eine heraushebende Partikel, die soviel wie 'da(s) ist', 'ich meine (auch, damit)', 'was ... anbelangt' bedeutet und sich syntaktisch wie die enklitische Kopula -àm verhält' (p. 16). 'Als gesichert erscheint nach allem die Existenz eines Element -ri (oder -re), das primär als dimensionale Postposition 'für', 'hin zu', in temporaler Verwendung 'zum Zeitpunkt von', 'als' o.ä. meint, vor allem aber zur syntaktischen Isolierung ('was ... anbelangt') nominaler Glieder verwandt wird' (p. 27).

Examples:

(712) ud gig za-ra ma-ra-ni-ib-gi$_4$-a-ri an-úr hé-eb-gi$_4$, /mu-DAT.2.sg.-ni-b-gi$_4$-a-ri/, /ha-ī-b-gi$_4$/ 'concerning the evil storm which has turned against you — it has returned to heaven's base' (*TEP* 176)

(713) mu.lu(?) i.bí-g̃u$_{10}$ i.bí bí-in-du$_8$-a-ri mùš-àm na-ma-ab-bé, /bi-n-du$_8$-a-ri/, /na-mu-DAT.1.sg.-b-e-e/ 'the man who has seen my face, he says indeed: "it is enough" (*CT* XLII 7 iii 32 = 16 rev. 27)

§ 493. *VERB + a + POSS + CASE*

A possessive suffix can be added after the relative clause:

(714) g̃išguzza lú mu-na-gub-a-ni sahar-ra hé-em-ta-tuš, /mu-na-(n-)gub-a-ani/, /ha-ī-m-ta-tuš/ 'from his throne which he has erected for him, may he be seated in the dust' (Gudea, St. B. IX 10-11)

(715) níg maš.g̃i$_6$-ke$_4$ ma-ab-de$_6$-a-g̃á šà-bi nu-zu, /mu-DAT.1.sg.-b-de$_6$-a-g̃u-ak/ 'I do not know the sense of the things which my dream has brought to me' (Gudea, cyl. A I 27-28) The relative clause is an anticipatory genitive.

(716) DŠu.DSuen ba-šag$_5$-ge-na-g̃u$_{10}$, /ba-šag$_5$-en-a-g̃u/ 'my Šu-Suen, you who are pleasing' (*SRT* 23, 23)

The person of the possessive suffix can be identical with the subject of the subordinate verb. In these cases the suffix emphasize the subject:

(717) mu lugal ud ba-záh-dè-na-g̃á nir.da hé-a bí-in-dug$_4$, /ba-záh-ed-en-a-g̃u-a/ 'he has declared by the name of the king: when I shall run away (lit.: on the day of my running away) — let it be cursed' (*BE* III 1, 5-7)

(718) níg g̃á-e ì-zu-a-g̃u$_{10}$ ù za-e in-ga-e-zu, /ī-zu-a-g̃u/, /ī-ga-e-zu/ 'what I know (lit.: my thing that I know), you know it also' (*PBS* I/2, 127: II 6-7)

§ 494. *Bibliography*

G.B. Gragg, 1972b. 'Sumerian and Selected Afro-Asiatic Languages'. In *The Chicago Which Hunt*. Papers from the Relative Clause Festival, April 13, 1972. A Paravolume to Papers from the Eighth Regional Meeting. Edited by P.M. Peranteu, J.N. Levi, Gloria C. Phares. Chicago Linguistic Society, p. 153-168.

G.B. Gragg, 1973a. 'A Class of 'When' Clauses in Sumerian'. *JNES* 32: 124-134.

THE IMPERATIVE

§ 495. The imperative is formed by changing the order of the verbal root and the prefix chain of the finite form. The order of the elements of the prefix chain is, however, not changed, e.g.,

(719) sum–ma–ab = /sum + mu-DAT.1.sg.-b/ 'give it to me' (Schooldays 47)

§ 496. In the imperative 2.pl. the pronominal suffix /-enzen/ is added after the prefix chain, e.g.,

(720) sum–ma–ab–zé–en = /sum + mu-DAT.1.sg.-b + enzen/ 'give(pl.) it to me' (Schooldays 14)

When the prefix chain ends in a vowel the suffix is written –en-zé-en (ex. 735). If it ends in a consonant the suffix appears as /-zen/ (ex. 732-733). In forms like

(721) nin$_9$-ǧu$_{10}$ de$_6$-mu-un-zé-en 'bring my sister!' (Dumuzi's Dream 20),[100]

it is not clear whether the [n] should be interpreted as the pronominal prefix of 3.sg. animate, /de$_6$ + mu-n + (en)zen/, or as the [n] of the suffix, /de$_6$ + mu(-n?) + enzen/. However, the fact that no form like *sum–ma–ab–bé–en–zé–en occurs, may suggest that the pronominal suffix of the 2. person plural, at least in the imperatives, sounds /-zen/ (or /-nzen/) and not /-enzen/.

§ 497. The prefix chain in imperative forms is normally very short. /ĭ-/ most often appears as [a], e.g.,

(722) dub-ǧu$_{10}$ zi-ra-ab = /zi.r + ĭ-b/ 'destroy my tablet!' (NG nr. 208, 17), cf. also ex. 727-728. /ĭ-/ is here either changed to

---

100. According to § 498 the singular stem must be expected here, i.e. de$_6$, and not the plural stem which is lah$_4$ = $\dfrac{\text{DU}}{\text{DU}}$.

[a] because of the enclitic position, or the prefix is /ã-/, which, on the other hand, probably is a variant form of /ī-/, see §§ 316-321.

Between the verbal root and the prefix chain a vowel may be inserted, e.g.,

(723) húl-húl-la-mu-un-da = /húl.húl + a + mu-n-da/ 'rejoice over him!' (Inanna Hymn 17 and 19), and ex. 725

M. Yoshikawa, 1979c, considered /a/ an aspectual morpheme: 'The grammatical function of the /a/ morpheme (...) may be completive or perfective, while *marû* and *hamṭu* may denote the durative and punctive respectively. The primary distinction, however, in the Sumerian aspectual system must be *marû* and *hamṭu*. On the other hand, /a/ aspect may be secondary in that it is morphologically based on the *hamṭu*' (p. 175). Cf. also p. 167ff.: 'There exist two kinds of imperative': I. Imperative in *hamṭu* aspect, i. without postposed prefix, ii. with postposed prefix. II. Imperative in /a/ aspect, i. without postposed prefix (gub-ba, gi₄-a etc.), ii. with postposed prefix (ku₄-ra-ma-ni-ib, zi-ga-ab etc.).

§ 498. The *hamṭu* stem is always used in the imperative, in some cases the reduplicated *hamṭu* stem.[101] It must be noted that the singular *hamṭu* stem is used in the plural imperative too, even if the verb has a plural stem. So we have dug₄ (ex. 733) and ĝen (ex. 734), and not the plural verbs e and e.re₇.

§ 499. *Examples: Imperative, singular forms*

(724) lá-ma = /lá + mu-DAT.1.sg./ 'pay me!' (lit.: 'weigh it for me') (Ukg. 4 XI 27)

(725) ki.tuš dùg-ga-ma-ni-íb = /dùg + ī-ba-ni-b/ 'make (your) residence pleasant!' (Gudea, cyl. B III 1)

(726) ká é.gal-šè mu lugal pàd-mu-ni-ib = /pàd + mu-ni-b/ 'make him swear by the name of the king at the palace gate!' (*TCS* I nr. 39, 8-9)

(727) é-a-ni gul-a = /gul + ī/ 'destroy his house!' (*TCS* I nr. 142, 9)

(728) é-zu kalag-ga-ab = /kalag + ī-b/ 'strengthen your house!' (Codex Lipit-Ištar III 27)

(729) mušen ambar-ta è-ba-ra = /è + ba-ra(abl.)/ 'bird, go out of

---

101. This was pointed out by D.O. Edzard, 1971a p. 225.

the swamp!' (Bird and Fish 51, cf. *SDI* p. 94) Cf. the frequent phrase: ...-ta ba-ra-à 'he went out of ...'

(730) igi-zu ğar-ì, var.: ğar-ra-ni, = /ğar + ì(-ni)/ 'set your eye upon him', i.e. 'keep an eye on him' (Georgica 49 = *UET* VI/2, 172 ii 11 = *OECT* I pl. 33 ii 24)

(731) i.lu ğar-ù = /ğar + ì/ 'set up a lament' (Dumuzi's Dream 5)

Imperative, plural forms

(732) è-mu-na-ra-ab-zé-en = /è + mu-na-ra(abl.)-b + enzen/ 'bring it out for him!' (Nanna-Suen's Journey to Nippur 322, var.: è-mu-na-ni-ib-zé-en)

(733) dug₄-ga-na-ab-zé-en = /dug₄ + ì-na-b + enzen/ 'prepare it for him!' (Nanna-Suen's Journey to Nippur 325, var.: hé-dug₄-ga-na-ab-zé-en)

(734) ğe₂₆-nam-ma-an-zé-en (var. om. -an-), /ğen + ì-ba + enzen/ 'come!' (Dumuzi's Dream 140) The imperative of ğen is always written ĞA-na, etc.

(735) gù téš-a sè-ke-bí-ᵃen-zé-enᵃ suhuš ma.da ᵇge-né-bí-zé-enᵇ (a-a: var. omits; b-b: ge-né-eb-zé-en; ge-en-ge-bí), /sè.k + bí(-n?) + enzen/, /ge.n + bí + enzen/ 'make them obedient! make firm the foundation of the country!' (Letter A 2, 31-32)

NON-FINITE FORMS

Introduction

§ 500. The non-finite forms are verbs without prefix chain or pronominal elements or, more precisely, the verbal root and possibly some (syntactic) suffixes. The non-finite verb is either the *hamṭu* stem (R), the reduplicated *hamṭu* stem (R-R), or the *marû* stem with /ed/ (R(m)-ed). The *marû* stem without /ed/ does not occur as non-finite verb (cf. § 509).

Basically there are four syntactic constructions in which the non-finite verb may occur: I. the asyntactic constructions: the verb has no affixes; II. the subordinate constructions: the verb with the suffix /-a/ is subordinate to another verb; III. the verb with the suffix /-e/ is dependent on a verb and expresses a purpose: 'in order to do so and so'; IV. the verb occurs as predicate with the enclitic copula.

A case postposition can be added to the subordinate forms, except to the forms ending in /-da/.

§ 501.

	Hamṭu	Reduplicated *Hamṭu*	*Marû* + /ed/
I. Asyntactic (§§ 505-511)	R	R-R	R(m)-ed
II. Subordinate (§§ 512-523)	R-a		R(m)-ed-a
'Pronominal Conjugation' (§§ 519-521)	R-a- { ani / bi / anene }		R(m)-ed-a- { ani / bi / anene }
	R-a- { g̃u / zu } -da	R-R-g̃u-da	R(m)-ed-a- { g̃u / zu } -da
III. (§§ 524-525)			R(m)-ed-e
IV. Predicate (§ 526)	R-COP	R-R-COP	R(m)-ed-COP

255

For the writing of forms with /ed/, see § 253.
/-da/ in the 'pronominal conjugation', 1. and 2. person, is always written -dè.
For the identification of -dè with the comitative -da, see § 521.

§ 502. Negative Forms

The non-finite forms can be negated by the negative prefix /nu-/ (cf.
§§ 359-365). For examples, see to the various constructions below.
The negative non-finite forms cannot always be distinguished from
the finite forms without pronominal elements, e.g., /nu-ī-VERB/.

The Functions of the Non-Finite Forms

§ 503. Earlier Treatments

In the traditional Sumerian grammars the non-finite forms are classified rather according to their translation than to their grammatical
functions:

1. Active, transitive participle: R, R(m)-ed
2. Intransitive and passive participle: R-a
3. Transitive and intransitive infinitive: R-a, R-ed-a, R-ed-e

So for instance A. Falkenstein, 1959a p. 43; GSGL I p. 132-146. I.
Kärki, 1967 p. 97-108. A. Poebel used the terms: 1. Nomen agentis;
2. Nomen actionis in infinitivischer Bedeutung; 3. Das appositionell
gebrauchte Nomen actionis (GSG p. 279-301).

It is evident that the Sumerian forms do not function exactly as the
participles and infinitive of our languages. Sometimes the 'active,
transitive participle', R, seems to be passive/intransitive, in other cases
the 'intransitive/passive participle', R-a, must be translated as active
and transitive. Several Sumerologists have studied the Sumerian non-
finite forms, concentrating especially on the contrast between
R/R(m)-ed and R-a:
I.T. Kaneva, 1970 p. 541-565, considered the difference between
R and R-a chiefly aspectual. R she called 'transitive participle of the
imperfective aspect', R-a 'transitive participle of the perfective aspect and/or intransitive participle regardless of aspect'. However,
Kaneva did not recognize the morphological and aspectual distinctions of the hamṭu and marû stems.
In his study of the hamṭu and marû aspect D.O. Edzard, 1972,

stated that /-a/ can be combined with the *hamṭu* stem only. R–a, therefore, is originally perfective and neutral with regard to active and passive. Its function as passive participle is a secondary development, from the end of the Old Sumerian period on (1972 p. 33).

Several studies have especially concentrated on the function of the suffix /-a/ in the R–a form:

H. Limet, 1975 p. 5-19, regarded R–a as a perfective participle. /-a/, he considered, gives the verbal root 'une valeur de perfectif'.

B. Kienast, 1975 p. 1-27, on the other hand, assumed that the main function of /-a/ is to make nominal forms of the verb. Therefore, originally all non-finite forms had the ending -a and, according to Kienast, the non-finite form without suffix, R or R(*m*)-ed, is a secondary development. There is then no fundamental difference in meaning between the two forms, R–a and R.

J. Krecher, 1978c p. 376-403, investigated both non-finite verbs and adjectives, with and without /-a/, standing attributively to nouns. His main conclusion is that the attributive adjective or verb with /-a/ makes the noun definite. An adjective without /-a/ qualifies the noun, but ADJ + /-a/ qualifies *and* makes it definite. The verbal form R(*hamṭu*) indicates a quality of the noun, whereas R(*marû*)-ed denotes either an imminent action or an action which occurs frequently and a quality, but never a state. The verbal root without /-a/ can never make the noun definite, but R(*hamṭu*)-a indicates a state or the result of an action and makes the noun definite, just like ADJ + /-a/.

For references to the studies mentioned here, see Bibliography below § 527.

§ 504. The studies on non-finite forms quoted above (§ 503) almost all considered aspectual differences or differences between active and passive as the fundamental distinctions and some ascribed an aspectual function to the suffix /-a/. However, in my opinion, it must first of all be stated that the main distinction of the non-finite forms is between the verbal stem without suffix and the stem with /-a/. These forms are used in constructions which are substantially different as to syntax. Possible differences in aspect, like the frequently mentioned perfective: imperfective, are certainly due to the choice of either *hamṭu* or *marû* and not to the presence of /-a/. Forms with and without /-a/ occur both in *hamṭu* and *marû* stem, R(*h*) and R(*m*)-ed : R(*h*)-a and R(*m*)-ed-a. The suffix /-a/ is therefore not an aspectual suffix but it denotes subordination, in the non-finite forms as well as in the relative and subjunctive clauses (cf. §§ 484-488).

The non-finite verb without suffix occurs in asyntactic constructions, whereas the form with /-a/ is subordinate either to a noun: R(*h*)-a, or to a verb: R(*m*)-ed-a. The form R(*h*)-a makes the noun definite as J. Krecher, 1978, stated (cf. above § 503), and, depending on whether this noun is the agent or the patient of the action, we must translate either active or passive. The distinction active:passive is thus not expressed morphologically in Sumerian, but our various translations are due to changes in the syntax.

The distinction between the asyntactic and subordinate constructions may tentatively be described by the following rather theoretical examples:

Asyntactic	Subordinate
N_2 N_1 R(*h*) : (lú) dub sar 'man who writes tablet(s)' = 'scribe'	N_2 N_1 R(*h*)-a : lú dub sar-ra 'the man who has written this tablet'
N_2 N_1 R(*m*)-ed : lú dub sar-re 'the man (at this moment occupied by) writing a tablet'	
N_1 R(*h*) : níg ba 'something to give' = 'gift'	N_1 R(*h*)-a : dub sar-ra 'this tablet which has been written'

Asyntactic Constructions

§ 505. This type of non-finite construction consists of one or two nouns and the verbal root: (N_2) N_1 R. N_2 represents the ergative subject, N_1 the absolutive object of a corresponding finite clause, but the nouns in the non-finite construction occur without case postpositions. Therefore they are called an asyntactic sequence of nouns and verbs.

N_2 N_1 R corresponds to N_2-e(erg.) N_1(abs.) PREF-VERB(trans.)

e.g., (lú) á tuku 'man having strength (lit.: arm)', corresponding to

258

/lú-e á ī-n-tuku/ 'the man has strength'. N_2 is mostly animate and agentive, N_1 is inanimate and non-agentive.

A dimensional unit can be inserted between N_2 and N_1 or between N_1 and the verb (ex. 740, 744-746).

The verb occurs both in the *hamṭu* stem, the reduplicated *hamṭu* stem, and in the *marû* stem + /ed/.

§ 506. The asyntactic construction denotes in most cases a transitive action, so at least in our eyes. This is the case whether the verb is *hamṭu* or *marû*, or whether all three members of the construction, N_2 N_1 R, or only two, N_1 R, are mentioned: diğir sağ zìg 'god who lifts the head', dub sar 'scribe'.

But there are a few cases where N_1 R seems to denote a *nomen concretum* or the result of an action, e.g., níg ba 'gift', še ba 'barley ration'. In these forms the verb is always *hamṭu*.

The reason why dub.sar is understood as (lú) dub sar 'one who writes tablet(s)', but níg.ba and še.ba not as 'giver' and 'distributor', respectively, is not obvious. níg.ba, še.ba and a few similar expressions (see below § 508) could be 'frozen' forms, perhaps very old, and their meaning have been lexicalized, whereas the 'active' form of the asyntactic construction is the common and productive type. However, since the Sumerian verbal root is neutral as regards the categories intransitive(one-part.) and transitive(two-part.), it might be asked whether the 'active' meaning of the asyntactic form originally depended on the syntax. This means that N_2 N_1 R was the 'active' type, because N_2 represented the animate agent of the action, whereas N_1 R was the 'passive' forms, since no agent is mentioned. The 'active' dub.sar is then an abbreviated form from original lú dub sar, but the meaning 'scribe' is lexicalized for the short form, dub sar. The *nomen concretum*, N_1 R, seems to be replaced by constructions with nam or níg (see § 59).

§ 507. *Examples:*

Hamṭu Forms:

(736) nin-ğu$_{10}$ (...) diğir sağ zìg 'my queen, goddess who lifts the head' (Gudea, cyl. A II 29)
(737) lugal kur dúb 'king who smashes the foreign land' (Gudea, cyl. A XIV 18)

(738) ur.saĝ níg.ba-e(loc.-term.) ki áĝ-ra(dat.) 'to the hero who loves gifts' (Gudea, cyl. A VI 26)

(739) gud huš zìg-ga gaba.gi$_4$ nu-tuku 'the wild bull rising, having no opponent' (Gudea, cyl. A XIV 14) Note the intransitive /zìg-a/ as opposed to the transitive nu-tuku and gi$_4$.

(740) ĝiš.nu$_{11}$ íl-la-(a-)ni kur.šà-ga igi ĝál 'his rising light which looks straight into the heart of the mountain' (Enlil Hymn 4)

(741) ^{D}Nè.eri$_{11}$.gal en ní gur$_6$ 'Nergal, awe-inspiring lord (lit.: who wears fear)' (Nergal Hymn 6)

Reduplicated Hamṭu Forms:

(742) tukul-ĝu$_{10}$ Šár.ùr kur šu-šè ĝar-ĝar 'my weapon, Šarur, which makes all lands submit' (Gudea, cyl. A IX 24)

(743) ud kalam til-til-e(erg.) ki-a ur$_5$ im-ša$_4$ 'the storm, which totally annihilates the land, roars on the earth' (Ur Lament 183)

(744) nin (...) inim kug An-(na-)ta inim dug$_4$-dug$_4$ (...) kur gul-gul 'queen, making all decisions at the holy command of An, destroyer of all the lands' (Exaltation of Inanna 15-17)

Marû Forms: /R(*marû*)-ed/

(745) si.ĝar-bi-ta muš.šà.tur muš.huš am-šè eme è-dè, /è.d-ed/ 'from its bolt ...-snakes and dragons are stretching out their tongues against the bull' (Gudea, cyl. A XXVI 24-25)

(746) AN.IM.DUGUD^{mušen} an.šár-ra sig$_4$ gi$_4$-gi$_4$ 'the Anzu-bird, crying in heaven' (Gudea, cyl. A XI 3)

(747) ^{D}Nin.ĝír.su Abzu-a gal di 'Ningirsu, speaking great (things) in Abzu' (Gudea, cyl. A II 11)

(748) é ^{D}Nanše-ka bar-ra ku$_4$-ku$_4$ šà-ga nu-è^a (a: so three texts, two texts have nu-è-e, one text has nu-è-a), /ku$_4$.ku$_4$-ed/, /nu-è-ed/ or /nu-è-a/ 'what enters the house of Nanše from outside shall not go out from the inside' (Nanše Hymn 84)

(749) ^{D}En.ki (...) di pàd-dè Utu è-ta Utu šú-uš-šè ĝalga sum-mu, /pàd-ed/, /sum-ed/ 'Enki, finding the decision, giving advice from sunrise to sunset' (Ur-Ninurta Hymn B 4)

§ 508. *The Asyntactic Form as* nomen concretum

Examples are:

níg.ba 'gift' ǧiš hur 'drawing, plan'
še ba 'barley ration' níg kud (a tax)
sá dug$_4$ (regular delivery)

For these expressions, cf. D.O. Edzard, 1972 p. 8f.

§ 509. *The Asyntactic Marû Form*

It is here assumed that the asyntactic *marû* form always has the morpheme /ed/. This means that forms like, e.g., /ǧá.ǧá/ or /du/ do not occur, but exclusively /ǧá.ǧá-ed/(*marû*) and /ǧar/(*hamṭu*) or /du-ed/(*marû*) and /ǧen/(*hamṭu*), and also, of course, the reduplicated *hamṭu* forms. Theoretically ǧá-ǧá, gi$_4$-gi$_4$, ku$_4$-ku$_4$ etc. can be *marû* forms both with and without /ed/, since the [e] and [d] of /ed/ are not written after a vowel and when no suffix follows. However, since the *marû* stems of the other non-finite constructions are always followed by /ed/, e.g., ǧá-ǧá-dè, nu-gi$_4$-gi$_4$-dam etc., it seems logical to restore /ed/ in the asyntactic constructions too.[102] This assumption is also supported by asyntactic forms of regular verbs with the ending –e or –Ce (or –Cu). e.g.. pàd-dè and sum-mu (in ex. 749).[103]

The future meaning of /ed/ (cf. §§ 255-257) can apparently not be found with the non-finite forms in the asyntactic construction.

§ 510. *The Reduplicated Hamṭu Forms*

Sometimes the reduplicated *hamṭu* form occurs with the suffix –e. In most cases this –e can be interpreted as the ergative postposition (ex. 743), but in other cases it remains unexplained. The only possible explanation seems to be that it represents /ed/. This use of /ed/ with the reduplicated *hamṭu* stem is, however, unique.[104]

(750) nin ^{D}En.líl-gin$_7$ nam tar-tar-re ^{D}Nanše-ǧu$_{10}$ dug$_4$-ga-zu zid-dam 'lady who decides all fates like Enlil, my Nanše, your word is righteous' (Gudea, cyl. A IV 9-10)

(751) dub sar-sar-re-me-en 'you are (like) one who is writing tablets all the time' (Lugalbanda and Enmerkar 122)

---

102. For *marû* + /ed/ in these forms, cf. D.O. Edzard, 1972 p. 3f.
103. Cf. M. Yoshikawa's theory about the *marû* affix -e, above § 233, and M. Yoshikawa, 1968a.
104. Cf. D.O. Edzard, 1972 p. 4.

(752) šà lugal-la-na dùg-dùg-ge-ra 'to him who pleases the heart of the king again and again' (Letter B 16, 7)

§ 511. *Hamṭu Versus Marû Forms*

The difference in meaning between the *hamṭu* and the *marû* forms is difficult for us to grasp and to express in the translation. Generally it seems that the *hamṭu* forms denote some constant quality of the 'subject' (N_2), cf. (lú) á tuku 'a strong man', and the form is therefore also used as *nomen agentis*, e.g., dub sar 'scribe', kug dím 'silversmith', lit.: 'who forms silver'. The reduplicated *hamṭu* form is used in the same way, but stresses the plurality of the object (N_1).

The *marû* forms, on the other hand, seems to describe an action which actually takes place while telling the story, but it also denotes an action of some duration.

Subordinate Constructions

§ 512. The verbal root + /a/ occurs in various syntactically different constructions. There is also a grammatical difference between the constructions with *hamṭu* stem and those with *marû* + /ed/. The first is relative, subordinate to a noun (§§ 513-518), the latter subordinate to a verb and thus comparable to the subjunctive (cf. §§ 522-523).

The reduplicated *hamṭu* stem is very rare in subordinate constructions and seems to occur only as R-R-a-POSS-dè. *Marû* forms can also occur in this construction, cf. §§ 519-521.

In all constructions listed below, N_1 corresponds to the absolute subject/object of a one-part./two-part. verb, while N_2 denotes the ergative subject of a two-participant verb.

The Subordinate Hamṭu Forms

§ 513. The non-finite form R(*hamṭu*)-a is traditionally described as 'intransitive and passive participle'. This agrees with the type:

(a) N_1 R(*h*)-a, Utu è-a 'the rising sun',
inim dug₄-ga 'the spoken word'

The intransitive or passive translation depends on whether N_1 is agentive or not. In both cases the verbs, è-a and dug₄-ga, make the noun definite, just like the relative clauses: Utu ì-è-a 'the sun which rose', inim ba-dug₄-ga 'the word which was spoken'.

Cf. ex. 753-756 in § 517.

§ 514. The ergative agent of the verb can also be specified in the subordinate construction, either in the ergative or in the genitive:

(b) $N_1 N_2$-e R(h)-a, inim An-né dug$_4$-ga 'the word spoken by An'
(c) N_1 R(h)-a N_2-ak, inim dug$_4$-ga An-na 'the word spoken by An', lit.: 'An's spoken word'

Both constructions correspond to the finite relative clause: inim Anné in-dug$_4$-ga 'the word which An has spoken'. I cannot explain the possible semantic difference between (b) and (c).

For examples, see § 517.

§ 515. In one subordinate construction the verbal form cannot be translated as passive, but is rather active:

(d) $N_2 N_1$ R(h)-a, lú é dù-a 'the man who has built this house'

Here the agentive noun, N_2 = lú, is determined by the phrase é dù-a, and it seems therefore active. It corresponds to the finite relative clause: lú é in-dù-a, 'the man who has built the house'.

For examples, see § 517.

§ 516. The seeming active meaning of type (d) above has confused those who thought R-a to be a passive participle. But, like the asyntactic form R, the subordinate R(h)-a is neither active nor passive, neither transitive nor intransitive. The active and passive forms in our languages consider the action from different viewpoints: from the point of view of the agent(active) or of the patient(passive). Sumerian does not have morphologically distinct forms for this, but expresses almost the same by changing the syntax.

§ 517. *Examples:*

Type (a): N_1 R(h)-a

(753) igi-zu-šè dusu kug gub-ba 'the holy basket which stands before you' (Gudea, cyl. A VI 6)
(754) kur a-ta íl-la 'the mountain rising out of the water' (Gudea, cyl. A III 19)
(755) gal$_5$.lá ti-la 'the sitting demon' (Dumuzi's Dream 134)
(756) An-gin$_7$ dím-ma 'created like An' (Angim 1)

Type (b): N_1 N_2-e R(h)-a

This is the so-called Mes-anne-pada construction, after the personal name: mes An-né pàd-da 'the young man, called by An'.

(757) É.ninnu An-né ki ğar-ra 'Eninnu founded by An' (lit.: 'placed on the ground') (Gudea, cyl. A IX 11)

(758) a nun-né šà kug-ga ru-a 'the seed engendered by the prince in the holy womb' (Šulgi Hymn X 93)

(759) ú-a Uri$_2$^{ki}-ma ^{D}En.líl-le ğar-ra 'provider of Ur, installed by Enlil' (Warad-Sin 12, 7-8)

Type (c): N_1 R(h)-a N_2-ak

(760) Gù.dé.a unu$_6$ mah-a(loc.) tu-da ^{D}Ğá.tùm.dùg-ga-kam 'Gudea, born by Ğatumdug in the sanctuary' (Gudea, cyl. A XVII 13-14)

Type (d): N_2 N_1 R(h)-a

(761) lugal-ğu$_{10}$ ^{D}Nin.ğír.su en a huš gi$_4$-a 'my king, Ningirsu, the lord who returns the wild water' (Gudea, cyl. A VIII 15)

(762) Gù.dé.a lú é dù-a-ra mu-na-ab-ús-e 'he brings it to Gudea, the man who has built the house' (Gudea, cyl. A XV 13-14)

(763) A.kal.la lú sağ sa$_{10}$-a 'Akala, the man who has bought the slave' (NG nr. 37, 17)

(764) ama dumu-ni gù á-zi dé-a, dumu ama-a-ni-ir ka-dù-a dug$_4$-ğa 'a mother who shouts at her child, a child who speaks obstinately to his mother' (Nanše Hymn 168-169)

§ 518. The subordinate constructions (a)-(c) can, like the relative clause, qualify a noun which represents a dative or another dimensional case:

(e)　N_3 N_1 R(h)-a (N_2-ak)

N_3 is a virtual dative or another case, the two-part. subject N_2, is often added at the end of the construction, with genitive.

Example:

(765) En.te.me.na ensi$_2$ Lagaš^{ki} ğidru sum-ma ^{D}En.líl-lá(-k) 'Entemena, the *ensi* of Lagaš, to whom Enlil has given the sceptre' (Ent. 28 V 19-23)

The Pronominal Conjugation

§ 519. A possessive suffix can be added to the subordinate form, both in the *hamṭu* and the *marû* form: R(*h*)-a-POSS and R(*m*)-ed-a-POSS. The possessive suffix denotes the subject of the verb: as subject of a two-participant verb it corresponds to N_2-ak in type (c) above, but the suffix can also represent the absolute subject of a one-participant verb.

The pronominal conjugation serves almost as a temporal clause, denoting an action simultaneous with or immediately preceding the action of the main verb.

§ 520. The constructions of the 3. person forms on the one side and the 1. and 2. person forms on the other side are slightly different.

Examples, 3. person forms:

(766) ur.saĝ é-a-na ku₄-ku₄-da-ni ud mè-šè KA ĝá-ĝar-àm, /ku₄.ku₄-ed-a-ani/ 'when the hero enters his house he is (like) the storm calling for fight' (Gudea, cyl. B V 4-5)

(767) ᴰBa.ba₆ (...) á ná-da-ka-na ku₄-ra-ni ⁱᵈIdigna a.ù-ba ĝá-ĝar-àm, /ku₄.r-a-ani/ 'having stepped to her bed (lit.: the side of her bed), Baba is (like) the Tigris at high water' (Gudea, cyl. B V 10-13)

(768) BIR.HUR.TUR-raᵃ abul-la è-da-ni ká-abul-la-ka ᵇmu-ni-inᵇ-dab₅-bé-eš (a: -re; b-b: mu-un-) 'As B. goes out of the gate they catch him in the gateway' (Gilgameš and Aka 60-61) Since the *marû* stem of è is è.d (cf. the form è-dè-dam), we would expect è-dè-da-ni = /è.d-ed-a-ani/

§ 521. To the 1. and 2. person forms an element -dè is mostly added. This form does not occur before the Old Babylonian period. -dè is probably the comitative postposition /-da/, denoting 'with my/your (going, etc.)'. Another possibility is that -dè derives from the ablative-instrumental /-ta/: -ta > -da > -dè. This was suggested by G.B. Gragg, 1973a p. 128f., on the basis of the form ku₄-ku₄-da-ni-ta, /ku₄.ku₄-ed-a-ani-ta/ 'when she has entered' (Inanna's Descent 100). Cf. the temporal clauses with -ta (§§ 489-490). No postposition can follow after -dè.

Plural forms are not attested.

Cf. D.O. Edzard, 1972 p. 20-24, with many examples.

Examples:

(769) a.šà a dé-a-zu-dè 'when you water the field' (Georgica 4 = *UET* VI/2, 172: 4)

(770) ká é.gal–la–šè ĝen-a-ĝu₁₀-dè silim-ma lugal-ĝá-ke₄ èn li-bí-in-tar 'When I came to the gate of the palace, no one asked about the health of my king' (Letter A 1, 9-10)

(771) ku₄-ku₄-da-ĝu₁₀-dè ĝⁱˢgu.za gaba-ba KUG.GI ĝìr.ĝar.ra lú na-ma-an-de₆, /ku₄.ku₄-ed-a-ĝu-da/, /na-mu-DAT.1.sg.-n-de₆/ 'when I was entering, someone brought me a chair with golden ... (and) a footstool' (Letter A 1, 23-24)

The Subordinate Marû Form

§ 522. The subordinate *marû* form, (N₁) R(*m*)-ed-a, is mostly directly subordinate to a finite verb, e.g., 'to say', 'to declare', 'to order' etc. It is thus exactly parallel to the subjunctive clause (see §§ 484-485). Possibly due to the morpheme /ed/ the form denotes an action which has not yet taken place. The subject of the subordinate verb is, as a rule, not the same as the subject of the main verb.

The form R(*m*)-ed-a is often confused with the construction R(*m*)-ed-e (see §§ 524-525). In the Old Babylonian literary texts the writings -da and -dè often occur as variants in the duplicates. The distinction between R(*m*)-ed-a and R(*m*)-ed-e as described here and in § 524 is thus not consistently carried through in all texts, and we can perhaps say that the two, originally distinct forms, at some moment, in post-Sumerian times, have merged into one category.

The R(*m*)-ed-a and R(*m*)-ed-e forms have been discussed in detail by D.O. Edzard, 1967, especially p. 43 and 46.[105]

§ 523. *Examples:*

(772) é-a-ni dù-da ma-an-dug₄, /dù-ed-a/, /mu-DAT.1.sg.-n-dug₄/ 'he has ordered me to build his house' (Gudea, cyl. A IV 20)

(773) ùĝ-bi ug₅-ge-daᵃ á mu-un-áĝ-eš-a-ba (a: var. has -dè), /ug₅-ed-a/, /mu-n-áĝ-eš-a-bi-a/ 'after they have ordered that its people be put to death' (Ur Lament 142)

---

105. The form LAL-ad-a, discussed in Edzard, 1967 p. 47, and 1972 p. 25-29, is to be analysed: R(*h*)-a + -da(com.), as demonstrated by J. Krecher, 1978c p. 401f. n. 21.

Cf. the R(*m*)-ed-e forms, subordinate to the verb á...áĝ, in the next example:

(774) ùĝ-e ú nir.ĝál gu₇-(ù-)dè a dùg na₈.na₈-dè ᴰEn.líl-le á-bi mu-da-na-áĝ, /gu₇-ed-e/, /na₈.na₈-ed-e/, /mu-da-na-(n-)áĝ/ 'Enlil has ordered you to let the people eat fine grass and drink sweet water' (Iddin-Dagan Hymn B 10-11)

Note the change from R(*m*)-ed-a to R(*m*)-ed-e in the next example; the subordinate form is expected:

(775) Ì.si.inᵏⁱ nam.ĝá.nun ᴰEn.líl-la-šè ĝá-ĝá-da mu TUKU. TUKU-da nam.ra.ak-(ka-)ne-ne(-a) ak-dè uruᵏⁱ uruᵏⁱ-bi TUŠ.TUŠ-ù-dè, ᴰEn.líl-le ĝá-a-ra ma-an-dug₄ 'Enlil has ordered me to establish Isin as the ... of Enlil, to let it have a name (i.e. be famous), to gather their booty, to inhabit their cities' (Letter A 3, 12-14)

See also the examples in § 525.

§ 524. The Form R(*m*)-ed-e

The construction (N₁) R(*m*)-ed-e is indirectly dependent on a main verb. In contrast to the form R(*m*)-ed-a, the subject of the verb R(*m*)-ed-e and the subject of the main verb are, as a rule, identical. The form R(*m*)-ed-e denotes an intention or a purpose, something to take place in the future, as indicated by the morpheme /ed/. R(*m*)-ed-e and R(*m*)-ed-a are often confused, se above § 522.

The form R(*m*)-ed-e has been discussed in D.O. Edzard, 1967, especially p. 41-44.

§ 525. *Examples:*

(776) é dù-dè igi-zu ù dùg-ga nu-ši-ku₄-ku₄, /dù-ed-e/, /nu-í-ši-ku₄.ku₄-en/ 'in order to build the house you will not let sweet sleep enter your eyes' (Gudea, cyl. A VI 11)

(777) é ᴰNin.ĝír.su-ka dù-dè Gù.dé.a uru-ni Ĝír.suᵏⁱ-šè gú mu-na-si-si, /dù-ed-e/, /mu-na-si.si-e/ 'in order to build the house of Ninĝirsu they (Magan and Meluhha) assemble for Gudea in his city Ĝirsu' (Gudea, cyl. A XV 9-10)

(778) ud šu bal ak-dè ĝiš.hur ha.lam-e-dè, (...) me Ki.en.gi-ra šu bal ak-dè, bala šag₅-ga é-ba gi₄-gi₄-dè, uru gul-gul-lu-dè é gul-gul-lu-dè, tùr gul-gul-lu-dè amaš tab-tab-bé-dè, gud-bi

tùr-bi-a nu-gub-bu-dè, udu-bi amaš-bi-a nu-dağal-e^a-dè (...), An ^{D}En.líl ^{D}En.ki ^{D}Nin.hur.sağ.ğá-ke$_4$ nam-bi ba-an-tar-re-eš (a: -lu-) 'that the days shall be changed, the plans be ruined, that the *me*'s of Sumer shall be destroyed, that the rulership returns to its house, that cities shall be destroyed that houses shall be destroyed, that stalls shall be destroyed, sheep-folds destroyed, that its ox shall not stand in its stall, that its sheep shall not be numerous in its sheep-fold, (...) — An, Enlil, Enki and Ninhursağa have decided it as its (Ur's) fate' (Lamentation over Sumer and Ur 1-8 and 55 = *BE* XXXI, 3 = *UET* VI/2, 124; 125)

(779) É.kur ^{ğiš}má mah-gin$_7$, gul-gul-lu-dè, kur kug ba.al-gin$_7$ sahar du$_8$^{a}-ù-dè, hur.sağ ^{na_4}za.gìn-na-gin$_7$ kud-re-dè, uru ^{D}Iškur-e ba-an-de$_6$-a-gin$_7$ gú ki-šè ^{b}ğá-ğá-dè^b, é-e kur ^{ğiš}eren kud nu-me-a ^{urudu}ha-zi.in gal-gal ba-ši-in-dé-dé (a: dù-; b-b: ba-an-da-ab-lá) 'in order to destroy Ekur like a huge boat, to turn it into dust like a mountain where silver is dug, to cut it into pieces like a mountain of lapis lazuli, to bow its neck to the earth like a city that Iškur has carried away, (therefore) he cast big axes against the house, although it is no mountain where cedars are felled' (Curse of Akkade 110-115)

§ 526. Non-finite Forms with Enclitic Copula

The enclitic copula can be added after the non-finite forms, e.g.,

(780) lú é lugal-na dù-dam, /dù-ed + -a-m/ 'this is the man who builds the house of his king', or probably: 'who is going to build' (Gudea, cyl. A XVI 18)

(781) mu Lú.^{D}Ba.ba$_6$-šè Dug$_4$.ga.zid.da Ğeme$_2$.^{D}Lama-ra sum-mu-dam, /sum-ed + -a-m/ 'Instead of Lu-Baba it is Duga-zida who shall give this to Ğeme-Lama' (*NG* nr. 7, 11-14)

With the 1. and 2. person the enclitic copula probably replaces the personal pronoun (cf. § 545):

(782) nin ama Lagaš^{ki} ki ğar-ra-me, /ğar-a + -me-en/ 'you, the lady, the mother who has founded Lagaš' (Gudea, cyl. A III 3)

In the form N_1 R(m)-ed-a-m the morpheme /ed/ surely points to the future; R(m)-ed-a-m denotes something which has to be done, something inevitable (cf. D.O. Edzard, 1967 p. 39):

(783) èn-bi tar-re-dam, /tar-ed + -a-m/ 'it has to be examined' (*NG* nr. 212, 25)

(784) é-e gu$_7$-dam, /gu$_7$-ed + -a-m/ '(things) to eat for the palace' (*AWL* nr. 44 III 4)

§ 527. Bibliography

D.O. Edzard, 1967. 'Das sumerische Verbalmorphem /ed/ in den alt- und neu-sumerischen Texten'. *HSAO* I, p. 29-62.

D.O. Edzard, 1972. '*Hamṭu, marû* und freie Reduplikation beim sumerischen Verbum. II'. *ZA* 62: 1-34.

I.T. Kaneva, 1970. 'Participles in Sumerian'. *MIO* 16: 541-565.

B. Kienast, 1975. Zur Wortbildung des Sumerischen'. *ZA* 65: 1-27.

J. Krecher, 1978c. 'Die Form und der Gebrauch der nominalen Verbalformen und die Determination im Sumerischen'. *OrNS* 47: 3 76-403.

H. Limet 1975. 'Le morphème suffixe /-a/ en sumérien'. *RA* 69: 5-19.

COMPOUND VERBS

§ 528. A compound verb is a frequently occurring combination of a verb and a certain direct object making up a semantic unit, e.g., igi... bar 'to look at', lit.: 'to open the eye', ğeštug₂ ...gub 'to set the mind (lit.: ear) to'. The meaning of a compound verb cannot always be explained from the meaning of the individual members, for instance: sá...dug₄ 'to reach' = 'to say ..(?)', si...sá 'to make straight' = '...'.

An adjective or an adverbial expression can occur as an established part of the compound: igi zid...bar 'to look faithfully at', sağ an-šè... íl 'to lift the head towards heaven'.

Grammatically the compound verbs do not differ substantially from other verbs. The object of the compound verb usually stands immediately before the verb, or possibly separated by the adjective or adverb as mentioned above. This is of course the normal position of the object, but with other verbs the word order is more free. The criterion whether a verb must be considered as a compound verb is fairly vague, it is usually not based entirely on grammatical reasons, but rather on the meaning of the verb.

> For the definition of the category compound verb, see the comments by E. Sollberger, 1952 p. 41f. See also J.N. Postgate, 1974 p. 35f.

§ 529. Some examples of compund verbs are:

kig...áğ 'to love'	sá...dug₄ 'to reach'
šu...bal 'to change'	pa...è 'to make resplendent'
igi...bar 'to look at'	ad...gi₄ 'to take counsel'
ğá.la...dag 'to cease doing something'	ğeštug₂ ...gub 'to set the mind to'
gù...dé 'to call, to cry'	gú...ğar 'to submit'
igi...du₈ 'to look upon'	sağ an-šè...íl 'to lift the head
al-dug₄ 'to demand'	towards heaven'

ù...ku 'to sleep'   ğál...tag₄ 'to open'

sağ.e.eš...rig₇ 'to grant'   nam...tar 'to decree the fate'

si...sá 'to make straight, to pre-   šu...ti 'to receive'
pare'

A list of the compound verbs occurring in the Gudea texts can be found in A. Falkenstein, *GSGL* I p. 119-128. A similar list for the Isin-Larsa royal inscriptions is in I. Kärki, 1967 p. 88-94. See also Catalogue of Verbs below p. 295-323.

§ 530. Examples:

(785) ^{ğiš}gigir-bi kug.NE za.gìn-na šu ù-ma-ni-tag, /u-ī-ba-ni-e-tag/ 'when you have decorated this chariot with ...-metal and lapis lazuli' (Gudea, cyl. A VI 19)

(786) mu-bi kur šà-šè pa bí-è, /bi-(n-)è/ 'he made its name resplendent until the center of the mountains' (Gudea, cyl. A XXIV 11-12)

(787) nam ù-mu-tar a.ba(-a) šu ^{a}mi-ni-ib^{a}-bal-e (a-a: i-ni-ib-), /bi-ni-b-bal-e/ 'after you have decreed the fate – who will change it?' (Lugalbanda and Enmerkar 103)

(788) ^{D}Nanše(-er) sağ-e gu aš-a^{a} si mu-(un-)na-ab-sá-e (a: -àm for -a), /mu-na-b-sá-e/ 'for Nanše she makes straight the (row of) the servants as a single thread' (Nanše Hymn 101)

(789) ì.ne.šè ab.làl kur-ra^{a} ğál ^{b}ù-bí-in^{b}-tag₄ (a: -re; b-b: [um]-ma-an-), /u-bi-n-tag₄/ 'now, after you have opened a hole in the underworld' (Gilgameš, Enkidu and the Netherworld 240)

(790) níg.dùg-ge níg.dùg-ge al na-an-ga-àm-mi-in-dug₄, /na-ī-ga-bi-n-dug₄/[106] 'sweet things, sweet things he has indeed also wished' (Nanna-Suen Hymn E 6)

(791) ^{kuš}á.lá nu-ğál-la ki-bi-šè sá im-dug₄, /ī-m-dug₄/ 'where there is no *ala*-drum, he let it reach its place' (Enki's Journey to Nippur 94)

(792) níg.si.sá(-e) ki ha-ba-áğ-ğá(-àm) níg.erim₂-e ki la-ba-ra-áğ-ğá(-àm), /ha-ba-áğ-a-m/, /nu-ba-ra(abl.)-áğ-a-m/ 'I love the right, I do not love the evil' (Šulgi Hymn A 23-24)

---

106. For the analysis of the verbal form, see § 325.

(793) ^DUttu šà húl-la-ni-ta é-e ğál ba-an-tag₄, /ba-n-tag₄/ 'Uttu opened the house with a joyful heart' (Enki and Ninhursağ 173)

(794) ^DNin.líl nin-a-ni inim šag₅-šag₅-ge-da-ni šùd-da-a-ni ğiš in-ni-in-tuku-àm, /ĩ-ni-n-tuku-a-m/ 'Ninlil, his mistress, has heard his prayers (and) his appeals' (Rim-Sin 10, 35-37)

§ 531. Since the Sumerian verb cannot have two direct objects, the noun corresponding to the object in the translation (the second or indirect object) stands in a dimensional case, very often the locative-terminative, for instance: sağ-e (ex. 788), níg-dùg-ge (ex. 790), níg. si.sá-e (ex. 792), é-e (ex. 793). But a compound verb can also take other cases, cf. § 476.

In one-participant constructions the nominal member of the compound (ğiš in ex. 795, gù in ex. 796) is the absolutive subject of the verb, and the 'second object' still stands in the dimensional case, in ex. 795 and 796 in the locative-terminative.

(795) gù.dé-a-ni ğiš ba-tuku-àm, /ba-tuku-a-m/ 'his cry has been heard' (Gudea, cyl. B III 2) Cf. ex. 794

(796) im síg.ba-ke₄ gù ba-dé, /ba-dé/ 'the wool-ration tablet has been called for' (*TCS* I nr. 149, 3-4) Cf. Postgate, 1974 p. 36f.

§ 532. A construction which seems to be peculiar to the compound verb is that in some cases the noun and the verb occur as the direct object of an 'auxiliary' verb, ak or dug₄. There seems to be no semantic distinction between the ordinary compound verbs and such 'double compounds'.

(797) temen-bi ì ir.nun-ka šu tag ba-ni-dug₄, /ba-ni-(n-)dug₄/ 'he has decorated its foundation with fine oil' (Gudea, St. C III 8-10) Cf. ex. 785

(798) É.ninnu me-bi an ki-a pa è mu-ak-ke₄, /mu-ak-e/ 'he makes the *me* of Eninnu resplendent in heaven and earth' (Gudea, cyl. A I 11) Cf. ex. 786

(799) inim (...-a) šu bal bí-in-ak-éš, /bi-n-ak-eš/ 'they have changed (their) statement' (*NG* nr. 113, 23-24) Cf. ex. 787

§ 533. In post-Sumerian texts, especially after the Old Babylonian period, the compound is sometimes misunderstood and taken as the verbal stem. This is probably due to a misunderstanding of the lexical texts where the whole Sumerian compound is quoted with the Akkadian translation, e.g., si sá = *ešēru*. But sometimes only the verbal root (e.g., sá) is listed in the lexical texts with translations of various compounds (sá = *ešēru*, etc.).

(800) An.àm (...)-me-en (...) É.ği₆ .pàr en–na ki.tuš šà húl–la–na la. la–bi–šè túm–ma mu–un–ki–ğar 'I, Anam, have founded the Eğipar of the *en*-priestess, the residence of her joyous heart, worthy of their delight' (Anam 4, 4-19) The correct verbal form should be: /ki mu–ğar/

§ 534. Bibliography

J.N. Postgate, 1974. 'Two Points of Grammar in Gudea'. *JCS* 26: 16-54. P. 35ff. Postgate deals with the syntax of compounds verbs.

A. Salonen und P. Siro, 1958. *Studien zur neusumerischen Syntax. AASF*, Ser. B, Tom. 112, 2. Helsinki. (P. 34-39: Abschnitt III: Über die zusammengesetzten Verba.)

THE VERB ME 'TO BE' AND THE ENCLITIC COPULA

§ 535. The root of the Sumerian verb 'to be' is me. It has only this basic stem which cannot be differentiated according to tense or aspect.

The meaning of me both as finite verb and in enclitic position is simply 'to be', and it expresses the predicate. It has no semantic overtones like 'to exist'.

> Cf. for instance Th. Jacobsen in Gordon, 1958 p. 549: 'me always means 'to be (in some fashion)'/'Sosein', and not 'to be (somewhere)'/'Dasein', which is always gál or gá-gá.'
> G.B. Gragg, 1968 p. 102: 'In fact it is misleading even to speak of the meaning of the copula in Sumerian. The copula is not present in the deep structure generated by the P(hrase) S(tructure) rules. It is introduced into Sumerian sentences solely by a copula-insertion transformation, and has no other function than to mark certain types of predication and to act as a verb-like carrier of affixes.'

me is used both as a finite and a non-finite verb as well as in enclitic position. The enclitic form is perhaps the most common. Finite forms, on the other hand, are almost exclusively found with modal prefixes, or occasionally with case prefixes, which cannot be expressed with the enclitic copula.

The Finite Forms of me

§ 536. me occurs always as a one-participant verb with pronominal suffixes:

1.sg.	...–me–en	1.pl.	...–me–enden
2.sg.	...–me–en	2.pl.	...–me–enzen
3.sg.	...–me	3.pl.	...–me–eš

§ 537. *Examples:*

(801) pi.lu$_5$.da ud–bi–ta e–me–a (var.: e–me–am$_6$), /ī–me–a(–m)/ 'these were abuses of former days' (Ukg. 4 VII 26-28)

(802) ur.sağ ug$_5$–ga ì–me–ša–ke$_4$–éš ka–bi ki a nağ–šè mu–ğar, /ī–me–eš–a–ak–eš(e)/ 'because they are dead heroes he set their mouth to the water-drinking place' (Gudea, cyl. A XXVI 15-16)

(803) ^{m}Šeš.kal.la dumu Ur.^{D}Lama–ka–ke$_4$ ìr Ur.^{D}Sahar.^{D}Ba.ba$_6$– ka nu–ù–me–en bí–in–dug$_4$, /nu–ī–me–en/ 'Šeš-kala, the son of Ur-Lama, said: 'I am not the slave of Ur-Sahar-Baba' (*NG* nr. 32, 2-4) In other cases the same phrase is written nu–me, see *NG* III p. 140.

(804) mí.ús.sa–zu mí.ús.sa–ğu$_{10}$ ba–ra–me, /bara–ī–me/ 'your son-in-law shall not be my son-in-law' (*NG* nr. 18, 24)

(805) diğir hé–me–en–zé–en inim ga–mu–ra–an–dug$_4$, /ha–ī–me–enzen/ 'should you be gods, I will say you a word' (Inanna's Descent 242)

(806) É.kur–šè za.e lú–bi hé–me–en, /ha–ī–me–en/ 'for Ekur you are indeed its man' (Iddin-Dagan Hymn B 43)

(807) dumu–ni Ğír.ğír ⌈e⌉.ne–bi–da ^{D}Udug eden–na ^{D}Lama eden–na hé–em–ma–da–me–eš–àm, /ha–ī–ba–da–me–eš–a–m/ 'her son Ğirğir and she herself shall be the Udug of the plain and the Lama of the plain' (Inanna and Bilulu 111-112) Note both finite and enclitic form of me.

§ 538. **Emesal Forms**

In Emesal the verb apparently has the form [ğe], see J. Krecher, 1967a p. 100 and 104, e.g.,

(808) ze ši–in–ga–ğe$_9$ (NE)–na, /ša–ī–ga–me–en–a/ 'you are indeed' (Manch. Tam. VI 23, see Krecher, 1967a p. 100f.)

(809) é mu.tin ba–ra–ğen–na–ğu$_{10}$ a.še.er ba–da–ti, /ba–ra(abl.)– me–en–a–ğu(–a)/ 'in my house from where there was wine, is (now) lamentation' (Krecher, 1966 p. 57: IV 10)

§ 539. The form nu–me–a is probably a non-finite form. It is found in the expression ...–da nu–me–a 'without':

(810) kur gal ^DEn.líl-da nu-me-a uru nu-dù á.dam ki li-bí-ib-ǧar, /nu-ī-dù/, /nu-bi-b-ǧar/ 'without Enlil, the big mountain, no city is built, no village is founded' (Enlil Hymn 108-109)

§ 540. The verb me also occurs in some fixed expressions like: ga-nam-me-àm 'it is indeed', ur₅ hé-en-na-nam-me-àm 'let it be so'. These forms can hardly be analysed according to the normal rules for the presence of verbal prefixes.

(811) šeš-ǧu₁₀ ^DNin.ǧír.su ga-nam-me-àm 'it was certainly my brother Ninǧirsu' (Gudea, cyl. A V 17)

The form hé-àm 'let it be', which can also be used as a noun in the sense 'consent, approval', is probably an extremely short finite form: /ha-ī-m(e)/. See § 400.

The Enclitic Copula

§ 541. The enclitic form of the verb me is added immediately after nouns, adjectives, pronouns and non-finite verbs, sometimes even after postpositions (cf. § 45). The enclitic copula can also be added to finite verbs.

The enclitic copula terminates the form or the clause, and no other suffix normally follows. The suffix of direct speech, /-eše/, may come after a noun + COP, see ex. 829.

1.sg. –me-en	1.pl. –me-enden
2.sg. –me-en	2.pl. –me-enzen
3.sg. (-a)-m	3.pl. –me-eš

The 3.sg. form is written -am₆ (in OS texts) or -àm (later than OS) and -Cam after consonants. After words ending in a vowel other than [a] it is often written -Vm (see ex. 815, 829), but also -àm (ex. 824). Theoretically the 1. and 2. person forms as well as the 3.pl. can be analysed both /-me-SUFFIX/ and /-m-SUFFIX/. In the Old Sumerien and Gudea texts the pronominal suffixes are not written and –me stands for both /-me-en/ and /-me-eš/. 1. and 2. plural forms are not attested in the early texts.

The Emesal form of 1. and 2.sg. is often written DU = -ǧen, cf. § 538 above.

§ 542. The enclitic copula is the normal way to express the predicate. The enclitic copula can be regarded as a form of the verb me 'to be' of which the prefix chain has been deleted. A phrase ending with the enclitic copula is therefore a full sentence similar to those ending with a finite verb.

Examples

(812) diğir-ra-ni ^{D}Šul.utul-am$_6$ 'his god is Šulutul' (Ent. 2 III 2-3)

(813) pa.bìl.ga-ni Ur.^{D}Nanše ensi$_2$ Lagaš^{ki}-kam 'his grandfather, Ur-Nanše, was the *ensi* of Lagaš' (Ean. 2 VIII 4-7)

(814) An.ta.sur.ra ğá-kam, /ğa-ak-a-m/ 'Antasura is mine' (Ukg. 6 IV 7-9)

(815) zà.mí mu.ru-bi-im 'it is the middle of the hymn' (anticipatory genitive: /zà.mí(-ak) mu.ru.b-bi-m/) (Gudea, cyl. A XXX 16)

(816) ama nu-tuku-me ama-ğu$_{10}$ zé-me, /nu-tuku-ed-me-en/, /zé-me-en/ 'I am one having no mother, you are my mother' (Gudea, cyl. A III 6)

(817) min-kam ur.sağ-ğá-àm á mu-gur, /min-ak-a-m/, /ur.sağ-a-m/ 'secondly there was a hero, he has bent his arm' (Gudea, cyl. A V 2-3)

(818) (... ...) sağa-sağa-ne dusu-šè ì-íl-am$_6$ 'these were the things which the temple administrators brought as offferings' (Ukg. 4 V 19-21)

§ 543. The enclitic copula is regularly used with numerals, both with cardinal and ordinal numbers, see §§ 140-141.

(819) tu^{mušen} min-nam igi-ba šembi ba-ni-ğar 'the pigeons are two, he placed kohl on their eyes' (Ean. 1 XVIII 2-3)

§ 544. The enclitic copula may also be used in descriptions and comparisons, almost equivalent to -gin$_7$ 'like'. In post-Sumerian texts the copula and the equative are often used side by side. In other cases -gin$_7$ replaces the enclitic copula of earlier texts (ex. 822).

Post-Sumerian lexical texts translate the copula with Akkadian *kīma* 'like' (*NBGT* IX 270f. = *MSL* IV p. 175), cf. W. Heimpel, 1968 p. 33 ff.

(820) é-a dub.lá-bi šu$_4$.šu$_4$-ga-bi La.ha.ma Abzu-da šu$_4$-ga-àm

'the portals of the house (as) they stand (there) are the Lahama-gods standing by in Abzu' (Gudea, cyl. A XXIV 26-27)

(821) é kur gal-àm an-né im-ús 'the house is a big mountain, it reaches to heaven' (i.e. 'it reaches heaven like a big mountain') (Gudea, cyl. B I 6)

(822) ud-gin₇ an-⌐úr-ra⌐ dum.dam mu-ni-íb-za = ⌐ki⌐-ma u₄-me i-na i-⌐šid⌐ šamê ⌐ud-da⌐-az-za-am 'he howled like a storm at the horizon' (Angim 74) This is the Neo-Assyrian version of Angim, the OB texts have ud-dam.

§ 545. When an apposition or an epithet is present the enclitic copula is used instead of the personal pronoun: ğá-e é mu-dù 'I indeed have built the house', but

(823) sipa-me(-en) é mu-dù 'I, the shepherd have built the house' (Gudea, cyl. B II 5). In this case sipa-me(-en) means probably simply 'I, the shepherd', and not 'I am the shepherd'. The construction *ğá-e sipa etc. seems to be ungrammatical, or it is at least not very frequent (cf. § 95).

§ 546. When the enclitic copula occurs after a finite verb it possibly emphasizes the whole sentence:

(824) lugal-ni-ir ud-dè maš.ği₆-ka Gù.dé.a en ᴰNin.ğír.su-ra igi mu-ni-du₈-àm, /mu-ni-(n-)du₈-a-m/ 'Gudea saw his king, the lord Ningirsu, on this day in a dream' (or perhaps: 'it was his king he saw ...') (Gudea, cyl. A I 17-18)

(825) bur an-na mu-de₆ tin mu-ni-dé-dé ᴰA.nun ki Lagašᵏⁱ en ᴰNin.ğír.su-da ki-bi mu-da-rín-né-éš-àm é-a nam.išib-ba šu mi-ni-du₇ /mu-(n-)de₆/, /mu-ni-(n-)dé.dé/, /mu-da-rín-eš-a-m/, /bi-ni-(n-)du₇/ 'he brought the bowl of heaven, he poured wine into it, — it is the Anun of Lagaš who are shining there with Ningirsu — in the house he completed the rites of the purification priest' (Gudea, cyl. B V 21-23) If the translation is correct the phrase with -àm seems to be an interpolation in the passage.

(826) ᴰIš.me.ᴰDa.gan (...)-ra ud ᴰEn.líl-le ᴰNin.urta ur.sağ kalag-ga-ni maškim-šè mu-ni-in-tuku-a, šita mi.tum sağ ninnu

mu–na–dím, sig₄ al–ùr–ra ᵍⁱˢtukul ki–áĝ–a–ni mu–na–an–
gub–ba–àm, /mu–ni–n–tuku–a/, /mu–na–(n–)dím/, /mu–na–
n–gub–a–m/ 'when Enlil has made Ninurta, his mighty warrior, the bailiff of Išme-Dagan, he (Išme-Dagan) fashioned
for him (Ninurta) the šita and the mitum weapon with the
50 heads, and he placed his beloved weapons on a brick'
(Išme-Dagan 3, 1-12)

§ 547. Bibliography

G.B.Gragg, 1968. 'The Syntax of the Copula in Sumerian'. In J.W.M. Verhaar
(ed.), The Verb 'Be' and Its Synonyms. (3. Foundations of Language Supplementary Series, 8) Dordrecht, p. 86-109.

THE SUFFIXES /-EŠE/ AND /-ĜIŠEN/

/-eše/

§ 548. /-eše/ is a particle indicating direct quotation. It occurs immediately after the direct speech, in most cases after a finite verb, but it may also occur after an imperative or the enclitic copula.

/-eše/ does not occur before the Old Babylonian period. It is particularly frequent in proverbs, fables and Eduba compositions (for instance Schooldays, Father and Son).

For a possible occurrence of /-eše/ in a Neo-Sumerian letter, see W.W. Hallo, 1969 p. 173: kug in-da-tu ku-ši 'he owes him money, quoth he' (= *TCL* II 5557, 3).

The suffix is always written -e-še.

§ 549. *Examples*

(827) lú ĝiš.hur-ra-ke$_4$ a.na-aš-àm ĝá-da nu-me-a ì-zìg-[a]ge-en[a]-
e-še in-túd-dè-en (a-a: -gin$_7$-), /ì-zìg-en/, /ì-n-túd-en/
'who was in charge of drawing said: 'why did you stand up when I was not here?' — and he beat me' (Schooldays 37)

(828) [a]me.re-za[a] en.nu.un ak-ab-e-še (a-a: ĝiri$_3$-zu) "watch your feet!' he said' (Proverb 1.192)

(829) a.ab.ba TÙN-bi kàš-ĝu$_{10}$-um-e-še '(the fox having urinated into the sea:) 'the whole of the sea is my urine' he said' (Proverb 2.67)

§ 550. *Bibliography*

A. Falkenstein, 1952. 'Das Potentialis- und Irrealissuffix -e-še des Sumerischen'. *Indogermanische Forschungen* 60: 113-130. (Berlin).

/-g̃išen/

§ 551. /-g̃išen/ which occurs at the end of the clause, mostly but not exclusively after a finite verb, indicates irrealis: 'where it that'. It is not very frequently used, in the OB literary texts only a couple of instances can be found. In lexical and bilingual texts /-g̃išen/ corresponds to the Akkadian irrealis suffix -*man*.

The irrealis particle is written -g̃iš-en or -g̃iš-še-en.

§ 552. *Example:*

(830) á   mu–e–da–ág̃–g̃iš–še–en   á   ág̃–g̃á   ma–ab–sum–mu–un–e–še,
/mu–e.da–ág̃ + g̃išen/, /mu–DAT.1.sg.–b–sum–en + eše/ 'if I try to teach you something, you say, 'are you giving me instructions?' (Father and Son 43-44)

Other instances are: Father and Son 48 (var.); 119; 120; the translation of this text is, however, highly difficult.

§ 553. *Bibliography:* See above § 550. A. Falkenstein, 1952, deals also with the suffix /-g̃išen/.

UNUSUAL ORTHOGRAPHY

§ 554. A number of Sumerian literary texts are usually characterized as 'syllabic' because of their uncommon orthography. The most remarkable feature of these texts is the extensive use of monosyllabic signs, but other unusual writings are also found. J. Krecher has therefore suggested 'unorthographic' as the most appropriate term (1967b p. 17-19).[107]

Syllabic writings are for instance: ba-ra for bar-ra, bu-ru or bu-ur = $buru_5$, da-am = dam, en-gu-ra = engur-a. The syllabic writings may often differ phonetically from the standard orthography: ù-ki stands for ùz-gin_7 'like a goat', ki-bi-la-ba for ki gibil-la-bi 'its new place', etc.[108]

In the unorthographic texts, not only are polysyllables written with monosyllabic signs, but two syllables can be written with one sign, e.g., a-sa-gaba for a-sàg-ga-ba. Moreover, homophones often replace the usual word sign, for instance du, normally 'to go', for dù 'to build'.

A text can be unorthographic throughout, but mostly both unorthographic and standard writings are used side by side in the same text.

§ 555. Unusual writings can be found sporadically in almost every Sumerian text of all periods depending on the scribal tradition, the ability of the scribe, etc. For instance many syllabic and unorthographic writings occur in Neo-Sumerian juridical documents (see H. Sauren, 1969), and some can also be found in the Gudea inscriptions (listed in *GSGL* I p. 23-34).

Texts which exclusively or to a great extent are written in an extraordinary orthography occur only from the beginning of the second

---

107. For the writings quoted in the following, see the lists in J. Krecher, 1967b p. 43; A. Falkenstein, 1952-53 p. 63f. For other syllabic and unorthographic writings, see M. Civil, 1967 p. 210.

108. See J. Krecher, 1967b p. 48.

millennium B.C., or maybe already at the end of Ur III. In all there are about 200 such texts, most of them written in Babylonia during the Old Babylonian period. Later on unorthographic texts almost exclusively come from regions outside Babylonia, e.g., Boğazköy and Assyria. From the first millennium B.C. there are only few unorthographic texts.[109]

Most of the Babylonian texts are cultic songs and laments in Emesal, but a smaller number from the Old Babylonian period is written in the main dialect. Several of the texts are moreover bilingual.

§ 556. The unorthographic texts make up only a very small part of the Sumerian text material, and they do not represent any homogeneous scribal tradition. The purposes and reasons for the unusual orthography seem to be very different.

The Emesal orthography is anyhow largely syllabic and it is, therefore, very probable that other syllabic and unorthographic writings in these texts have come into being in consequence.[110] But the main reason, it seems, must be the simplification of the Sumerian writing, which of course is rather complicated for those who do not know the language very well like the scribes outside Babylonia. Writing syllabically the scribe uses the well-known syllabic signs common to the Akkadian writing instead of the many Sumerian word signs and ideograms. Another reason for the unusual orthography could be the intention of giving more exact information about the pronunciation of the text. This could for instance be the case of the Emesal songs and laments to be recited by the *kalû* priest.

In all cases, however, the unorthograhic texts belong to a scribal tradition inferior to that of the Old Babylonian literary texts in general, and they give the impression of a considerable neglect of the content and lack of understanding. These texts can therefore hardly be used for a reliable reconstruction of the original Sumerian phonetics, but the syllabic and unorthographic writings may, on the other hand, give some hints as to the scribal tradition in which these texts came into being.

---

109. J. Krecher, 1967b p. 21-30, gives an outline of the occurrence and age of the unorthographic texts.
110. Cf. J. Krecher, 1967b p. 20.

Cf. M. Civil, 1967 p. 209: 'To assume that the syllabic texts imply an inter-mediate step in which the transmission took place exclusively by oral means seems unavoidable in some cases, although definite proof is still lacking. Such a step did not exist in the cases where the syllabic version is written beside the text in standard orthography, as in the Nippur and Susa examples which, with their obvious didactic purposes and as products of schools of high stand-ing, represent the most reliable and useful type of syllabic texts. At the other extreme we have tablets like Nat.Mus. Copenhagen 10051 (Jacobsen, *JCS* 8, 82f.), a poor man's compact version of the great series am-e bara$_2$-na-ra.' (... The tablet) 'represents the work of some scribe unfamiliar with the rules of Sumerian orthography, who knew by heart, and not very well at that, the series am-e bara$_2$-na-ra.'

§ 557. Example:

The unorthographic texts are extremely difficult to read and trans-late, if we do not have exact parallels. As example may serve the be-ginning of a hymn to the moon-god, probably from Sippar dating to the late OB period and composed in the main dialect:

(831) úr-NE-ru an kug-ge si-a 'light(?) filling the pure heaven'
ku-zu-e mi-li gur-ù-a, 'the wise one(?), dressed in radiance'
(kug zu-e me.lám gùr-ru-àm)
^{D}Nanna me-en-zu ku-ku-gu 'Nanna, your crown is pure(?)'
(^{D}Nanna men-zu kug-kug-ga)
en di-il$_5$ en bar$_6$-bar$_6$ an-ne ši x 'lord, ..., shining lord, An
has ...'
(en dili(?) en bar$_6$-bar$_6$ an-né ...)
(Nanna-Suen Hymn J 6-9)
In parenthesis the probable equivalence of the main dialect is rendered. There is no text or duplicate in normal ortho-graphy.

For editions of unorthographic texts, see Bibiliography below § 558, especially the studies of E. Bergmann and J. Krecher.

§ 558. Bibliography

E. Bergmann, 1964. 'Untersuchungen zu syllabisch geschriebenen sumerischen Texten. I'. *ZA* 56: 1-43.
E. Bergmann, 1965. 'Untersuchungen zu syllabisch geschriebenen sumerischen Texten.II'. *ZA* 57: 31-42.

EMESAL

§ 559. eme-sal is the Sumerian term for the language used in certain texts such as hymns and laments. It thus seems to be a sort of literary dialect. Emesal may, however, also occur in shorter passages of other literary compositions and then especially in direct speech of women. In contrast to the main dialect of Sumerian which is called eme-gir$_{15}$, the Emesal dialect is characterized by certain phonetic differences and by the use of specific Emesal words, whereas there are no grammatical differences between Emesal and the main dialect.

eme-sal probably means 'thin tongue' or 'fine tongue', sal being equivalent to Akkadian *raqqu* 'thin' (cf. *AHW* II p. 958). Cf. also the Sumerian loan word in Akkadian *emesallu* 'fine taste, fine tongue, genteel speech' (*CAD* E p. 148). See further J. Krecher, 1967a p. 87 n. 1. I.M. Diakonoff, on the other hand, suggested as the translation of eme-sal 'twisted, slanted sideways' in the sense 'quaint' or 'corrupted language' (1976 p. 113).

eme-gir$_{15}$ probably means 'princely tongue', see J. Krecher, 1966 p. 108.

§ 560. The Emesal Text Genres

The oldest texts written in Emesal are cultic songs of the early Old Babylonian period and most Emesal texts are dated to the later part of this period. The cultic song is the only Sumerian genre which is continued after the Old Babylonian period, since we have Neo-Assyrian and Seleucid copies of Emesal compositions probably copied from older originals. Besides these texts there are Emesal passages of varying length in other Old Babylonian literary texts, primarily the laments and the love songs (the so-called sacred marriage texts).

Cultic Songs

The Emesal compositions belong to different genres, in OB they are called: ér.šèm.ma, balag̃ and šìr.nam.šub, after this period they are: šu.íl.la and ér.šà.hug̃.g̃á. These songs are hymns of praise to gods or laments over the destruction of temples or cities. Very often, but not always, the laments are spoken by a goddess and many songs are connected with the god Dumuzi. Characteristic of the Emesal compositions are moreover the many repetitions. In the Neo-Assyrian and Seleucid texts it is explicitly noted that they were recited by the *kalû*-priest, and it is very probable that this was also the case in the older periods, although we cannot say for certain since no ritual directions are preserved.

A detailed representation of the Emesal genres and their history is given by J. Krecher, 1966 p. 11-51, together with a list of the Old Babylonian texts, p. 16-17.

Literary Texts

Outside the cultic songs we find Emesal in the speech of the goddess Inanna in the love songs (cf. Krecher, 1966 p. 12f.); moreover Emesal occurs in the laments (for instance in the first ki.ru.gú of the Ur Lament, and in passages of the Eridu and Nippur Lament), and in myths etc. where goddesses are speaking (e.g., Inanna's Descent 29-67; Inanna and Enki II i 15-16, 21-26). But Emesal is not used in every case where a goddess or women is speaking, thus the speech of Inanna in Lugalbanda and Enmerkar 389-412 is in Emegir.

The Emesal Vocabulary

Another source for the study of the Emesal dialect is the Emesal Vocabulary, a lexical list consisting of three tablets. This 'lexicon' gives the Emesal and the Emegir forms of a word and its Akkadian translation, as well as the Emesal form of many divine names. The Emesal Vocabulary dates to the first half of the first mill. B.C., it is published in *MSL* IV p. 1-44.

§ 561. Phonetic Alterations

Characteristic for the Emesal dialect is that certain phonemes have been replaced by others: [d] > [z], [g] > [b], etc. These alterations are not always carried through, cf. [d] in dìm.me.er (= dig̃ir), and the first [g] in mu.gi$_4$.ib (= nu.gig). The phonetic alterations are dealt with by J. Krecher, 1967a p. 87-110 with many examples.

Cf. S. Parpola, 1975 p. 254: 'Most of the phonetic differences between Main Dialect and Emesal noted here can be explained as auton-
omous sound changes occasioned by a forward shift of the basis of
articulation (u > i = high back > high front; k > p, t = velar > labial/
dental stop; ŋ > m, n = velar > labial/dental nasal; š > s = post-al-
veolar > alveolar fricative; s > Θ = alveolar > dental fricative) which
seems to indicate that 'backward-flanged' phonemes (i.e. narrow
vowels, and labial or dental, including alveolar consonants) were considered 'finer' than their 'forward-flanged' counterparts.

Consonants:

Main Dialect		Emesal	Examples:
d	>	z	udu = e.zé 'sheep'
			dùg = zé.eb 'good, sweet'
			dugud = zé.bi-da 'heavy'
g	>	b	igi = i.bí 'eye'
			nu.gig = mu.gi$_4$.ib 'hierodule'
			sig$_4$ = še.eb 'brick'
			šà-g = šà-b 'heart'
g̃	>	m	diğir = dìm.me.er 'god'
			g̃á-e = ma-e 'I'
			g̃ál = ma.al 'to be'
			g̃ar = mar 'to place'
			g̃ír = me.er 'dagger'
			g̃iri$_3$ = me.ri 'foot'
			g̃iš = mu 'tree'
g̃	>	n	sag̃ = še.en 'head'
h	>	g	ha.lam = ge.le.èg̃ 'to destroy'
m	>	n	munus = nu.nus 'woman'
m	>	g̃	ha.lam = gel.le.èg̃ 'to destroy'
			nam = na.ág̃
			sum = zé.èg̃ 'to give'
			kalam = ka.na.ág̃ 'land'
n	>	l	niğir = li.bi.ir 'herald'
n	>	m	nu.gig = mu.gi$_4$.ib 'hierodule'
n	>	š	nin = šen 'lady'
			nir = še.er
			^{d}Nirah = ^{d}Še.ra.ah, the snake god
			nundum = šu.um.du.um 'lip'

Main Dialect		Emesal	Examples:
s	>	z	sum = zé.èg̃ 'to give'
s	>	š	sig₄ = še.eb 'brick'
			sag̃ = še.en 'head'

Vowels:

a	>	e	alim = e.lum 'deer'
i	>	e	inim = e.ne.èg̃ 'word'
i	>	u	ì = u₅ 'fat'
u	>	e	udu = e.zé 'sheep'

§ 562. The Emesal Lexicon

It is not intended here to give a complete list of Emesal words, but merely the most common words and forms are given below. Other lists of Emesal words can be found in:

MSL IV p. 1-44: 'The Emesal Vocabulary'. (= *ESV*)

R. Borger, 1978. *Assyrisch-babylonische Zeichenliste.* (*AOAT* 33) Neukirchen-Vluyn, p. 215-217. (= *ABZ*)

J. Krecher, 1967a. 'Zum Emesal-Dialekt des Sumerischen'. *HSAO* I p. 87-110. (= 1967a)

See also the bibliography in § 566.

Specific Emesal words are the following:

Emesal	Emegir	
aš.te/ti	gu.za	'throne' (*ABZ* p. 215)
ga	túm or de₆	'to bring'
gašan, ga.ša.an	nin	'lady', cf. Ga.ša.an.an.na = ᴰInanna
mu.ud.na	g̃itlam, nitadam etc.	'spouse' (*ESV* 73)
mu.lu	lú	'man'
ù.mu.un, umun	en	'lord', '*en*-priest'
ta(-àm)	a.na(-àm)	'what?'

Emesal forms of Emegir words:

Emesal	Emegir	
a.da.ar	a.gàr	'field' (*ESV* III 71)
á.mar	é.g̃ar₈	'figure' (*ESV* III 93-94)
ág̃	níg̃	'thing' (1967a p. 106)

Emesal	_Emegir_	
^{D}Am.an.ki	^{D}En.ki	Enki (_ESV_ I 38)
aš...tar	èn...tar	'to ask' (1967a p. 106)
a.še.er	a.nir	'lament' (_ESV_ III 73)
da-, dè-, du$_5$-	/ga-/, ha-/	the cohortative and precative/ affirmative prefixes (cf. §§ 385, 395)
da.ma.al	dağal	'wide'
di.ìm	gin$_7$	the equative postposition (_ABZ_ p. 217)
dìm.me.er	diğir	'god' (_ESV_ I 1)
di.ta, di.id	diš	'one' (_ESV_ III 131, _ABZ_ p. 217)
du$_5$.mu	dumu	'child, son'
e.lum	alim	'aurochs' (_ESV_ II 23)
é.mar	é.ğar$_8$	'figure' (_ABZ_ p. 216)
e.ne.èğ	inim	'word' (1967a p. 103f.)
e.ri	ìr, arad	'slave' (_ABZ_ p. 216)
e.zé	udu	'sheep' (_ESV_ II 89)
gel.le.èğ	ha.lam	'to destroy' (1967a p. 103f.)
gi$_4$.in	ğeme$_2$	'slave-girl' (_ABZ_ p. 216)
i.bí	igi	'eye' (_ESV_ II 185)
ka.na.áğ	kalam	'land, Sumer' (1967a p. 103f.)
li.bi.ir	niğir	'herald' (1967a p. 89)
ma(-e)	ğá-e	'I'
ma.al	ğál	'to be' (_ESV_ III 77)
ma–ma	ğá–ğá	'to place', _marû_ (_ESV_ III 76)
mar	ğar	'to place', _hamṭu_ (_ESV_ III 78)
mar.za	ğar.za	'rite' (_ESV_ III 81)
^{D}Ma.zé.eb.zib	^{D}Ğá.tùm.dùg	The goddess Ğatumdug (_ESV_ I 96)
me.er	mer	'anger' (_ESV_ III 87)
me.ri	ğiri$_3$	'foot' (_ESV_ II 197)
mu(.uš)	ğiš	'tree'
mu.du.ru	ğidru	'sceptre' (_ABZ_ p. 215)
mu.gi$_4$.ib	nu.gig	'hierodule' (1967a p. 89)
mu.nu$_{10}$/nu$_{12}$	unu$_3$, utul	'shepherd' (_ABZ_ p. 215)
mu.tin	ğeštin	'wine' (1967a p. 89)
^{D}Mu.ul.líl	^{D}En.líl	Enlil
mu.un.gàr/ğar	engar	'farmer' (_ABZ_ p. 215)

Emesal	Emegir	
mu.uš.túg$_{PI}$	ĝeštug$_2$	'ear' (*ABZ* p. 215)
na.áĝ	nam	(1967a p. 103f.)
na.ma	naĝa	'soap' (*ABZ* p. 215)
nu.nus	munus	'woman' (*ESV* II 68)
si.mar	si.ĝar	'bolt' (*ABZ* p. 215)
su$_8$.ba	sipa	'shepherd'
šà.ab	šà.g	'heart' (1967a p. 89)
še.eb	sig$_4$	'brick' (1967a p. 89)
še.en	saĝ	'head' (*ESV* II 181)
še.en.bún.na	níĝ.bún.na	'tortoise' (*ABZ* p. 216)
še.er.ma.al	nir.ĝál	'prince' (= *etellu*)
^{D}Še.ra.ah	^{D}Nirah	The snake-god (*ESV* I 19)
šu.um.du.um	nundum	'lip' (*ESV* II 187)
u$_5$	ì	'grease' (*ESV* II 175)
zé.eb	dùg	'sweet', 'knee'
zé.ed	túd	'to hit' (*ESV* III 117)
zé.bi.da	dugud	'heavy' (*ESV* II 22)
zé.èĝ	sum	'to give' (*ESV* III 118)

§ 563. Orthography

The specific Emesal words are necessarily written syllabically, e.g., zé-eb = /zeb/, 'sweet' (Emegir: dùg), but syllabic writings also turn up where they are not absolutely required, and in fact Emesal texts have to a large extent syllabic and unusual orthography (see §§ 554-558).

On the other hand the Emesal is often not consistently carried through in a text, but mixed with forms of the main dialect, even where a special Emesal form exists.

The question may be raised whether the more or less consistent occurrences of Emesal words and forms mixed with Emegir forms reflect the actual pronunciation of the text, or whether we have to restore or reconstruct the Emesal throughout in the text as for instance A. Falkenstein (1952-53) and S.N. Kramer (1940) do. Cf. S.J. Lieberman, 1977 p. 33 n. 89: 'Word graphemes usually employed for emegir words when found in emesal context are to be read in emesal. This is shown not only by the arrangement of the emesal lexicon, dimir = diĝir = *ilu* which presents the emesal orthographies as though they were pronunciations of the emegir spellings, but also by the variants in which one manuscript writes the emegir word and another manuscript writes the emesal form.' So also I.M. Diakonoff, 1976 p. 116, describing this as 'another feature of mnemonic techniques used in Sumerian writing'. J. Krecher, 1967a p. 95, on the contrary, argued against this practice and stated that Emegir forms cannot be excluded in Emesal context.

To me it seems most probable that the Emesal dialect was pronounced more consistently and not only in some words, and the reason why it is not always explicitly written is that the Emesal forms imply more syllabic signs, that means more space and they are therefore avoided if possible. In spite of this it seems preferable not to reconstruct the Emesal forms in order not to blur the original orthography of the text, and also since it is not always certain how the Emesal actually is to be read.

§ 564. What is Emesal?

There is no general agreement as regards the problem what Emesal actually denotes. It is thought to be either a local dialect or a women's language.

See for instance J. Krecher, 1967a p. 110: 'Trotz der unterschiedlichen Gestalten des Emesal in altbabylonischer Zeit postulieren wir wohl zu Recht einen in sich einheitlichen Dialekt des Sumerischen, der uns nur in seinem verschieden starken Anteil am altbabylonischen Emesal erhalten ist. Allerdings sind uns Zeit und Ort eines solchen ursprünglichen sumerischen Dialekts unbekannt, ja wir sind nicht einmal sicher, ob nicht verschiedene Dialekte dem altbabylonischen Emesal zugrunde liegen'.

I.M. Diakonoff, 1976 p. 113ff., took the opposite view: 'There are certainly no indications that it is a territorial or a tribal dialect, although elements of such dialects may be present in Emesal'. ... 'Both internal evidence and anthropological analogies seem to suggest that Emesal, whatever the exact meaning of the term might be, was actually a women's language. Tabooing of the use of 'men's' words and 'men's' pronunciation is known the world over, more especially among peoples speaking structurally archaic, 'ergative' languages'.[111]

---

111. For various earlier theories, see A. Falkenstein, 1959a p. 18.

The fact that Emesal occurs primarily in direct speech of women in the literary texts is of course a strong argument in favor of the theory of Emesal as a women's language. Moreover, as I.M. Diakonoff, 1976 p. 113f., pointed out, the differences between Emegir and Emesal are exactly those distinguishing men's language from women's language in other cultures, namely phonetic and lexical alterations, but not grammatical differences. The occurrence of Emesal in cultic songs is thus explained as due to the fact that the *kalû*-priests who recited these songs were eunuchs, and not being regarded as men, they had to use women's language.[112]

On the contrary, it must be noted that there are practically no Emesal occurrences outside the literary texts and we have thus no Emesal piece of actual speech at least pretending to be written down as it was spoken (there are for instance no Emesal words in the juridical documents quoting the statement of a woman). Moreover, the oldest Emesal texts are from the early Old Babylonian period, that means after Sumerian has died out as a spoken language. Emesal, therefore, appears most of all as a literary dialect, and we can say only little about its original character and extension.[113]

§ 565. Examples:

(832) šu ud-da an-ta ba-ma-al^a-la-ke$_4$-eš (a: -ǧál- for -ma-al-)
    (*šu ud-da an-ta ba-ǧál-la-ke$_4$-eš)
    KA hu-mu-dúb eden(!)-na ud gi$_4$-a me.e hé-em-ma(!)-na^b-di^c (b: om.; c: -dug$_4$)
    (*KA hu-mu-dúb eden-na ud gi$_4$-a ǧá.e hé-em-ma-na-dug$_4$)
    ud-da gaba-bi ^{d}ba-ra-mu-da-zi^d (d-d: ba-ra-ba-ra-zi; ba-ra-mu-da-ab-zi)
    (*ud-da gaba-bi ba-ra-mu-da-zi)

---

112. So I.M. Diakonoff, 1976 p. 115; Th. Jacobsen in E.I. Gordon, 1959 p. 483, and J. Renger, 1969 p. 192f. argued against this; see also J. Krecher, 1966 p. 36.

113. Note, however, that there are also other possible restrictions for a 'taboo language', cf. for instance in some Australian languages, where a certain dialect is used in communication with some relatives of the opposite sex (for instance betweeen a man and his mother-in-law); this 'taboo language' has the same grammar as the normal language, but an entirely different vocabulary (cf. R.M.W. Dixon, 1972. *The Dyirbal Language of North Queensland*. Cambridge, p. 32-34).

^{e}nu.nus–ǧen^e é.nun.kug^f é na.áǧ–ga.ša.an–na–ǧu$_{10}$ (e-e: munus–e; f: -ga)

(*munus–me–en É.nun.kug é nam–nin–na–ǧu$_{10}$)

bal–ba ud sù–rá na–ma(!)–ni–in–ǧar–re–eš–àm^g (g: -a for -àm)

(*bal–ba ud sù–rá na–ma–ni–ǧar–re–eš–àm)

ír a.še.er–ra ki ha–ma–ab^h–ús–e^i (h: -an- for -ab-; i: -àm for -e)

(*ír a.nir–ra ki ha–ma–ab–ús–e)

'Because the hand of the storm is from heaven (?)

I screamed and cried to it: Storm, return to the plain!

(But) the storm's breast did not rise.

To me, the woman, in Enunkug, my house of ladyship,

a rule of long days they have not granted.

Weeping and lamentation may follow me'

(Ur Lament 110-115)

(833) ga.ša.an–ǧen ša.ga.ba–ta ud zal–la–ǧu$_{10}$–dè

(*nin–me–en etc.)

Ga.ša.an.an.na–ǧen ša.ga.ba–ta ud zal–la–ǧu$_{10}$–dè

(*^{D}Inanna–me–en etc.)

ud zal–la–ǧu$_{10}$–dè e.ne di–da–ǧu$_{10}$–dè

(Emegir: the same)

ud zal ǧi$_6$–di–a–šè èn.du dug$_4$–ga–ǧu$_{10}$–dè

(Emegir: the same)

gaba mu–un–ri gaba mu–un–ri

(Emegir: the same)

ù.mu.un ku.li An–na gaba mu–un–ri

(*en ku.li An–na etc.)

ù.mu.un–e šu–ni–a šu im–ma–an–dù

(*en–e etc.)

^{D}Ušum.gal.an.na gú–ǧá–a gú–da ba–an–lá

(Emegir: the same)

me–a am šu ba–mu–u$_8$ é–me–šè da–ǧen

(*me–a am šu ba–mu–u$_8$ é–ǧu$_{10}$–šè ga–ǧen)

ku.li ^{D}Mu.ul.líl–lá šu ba–mu–u$_8$ é–me–šè da–ǧen

(*ku.li ^{D}En.líl–lá šu ba–mu–u$_8$ é–ǧu$_{10}$–šè ga–ǧen)

ama–[ǧu$_{10}$] lul–la–šè ta mu–na–ab–bé–en

(*ama–ǧu$_{10}$ lul–la–šè a.na mu–na–ab–bé–en)

ama–ǧu$_{10}$ ^{D}Ga.ša.an.gal–e lul–la–šè ta mu–na–ab–bé–en

(*ama–ǧu$_{10}$ ^{D}Nin.gal–e lul–la–šè a.na mu–na–ab–bé–en)

'I, the lady, having whiled away the time since yesterday,
I, Inanna, having whiled away the time since yesterday,
having whiled away the time, having danced,
having sung songs all day to evening,
he met me, he met me!
The lord, the friend of An, met me,
the lord took my hand in his,
Ušum-gal-ana embraced me,
where (are you taking me)? wild bull set me free! let me go
to my house!
Friend of Enlil, set me free! Let me go to my house!
What shall I say to my mother as a lie?
What shall I say to my mother, Ningal, as a lie?
(Love song, *PAPS* 107 nr. 4, 1-12; translation in Th. Jacobsen,
1976a p. 28f.)

§ 566. Bibliography

B. Alster, 1982. 'Emesal in Early Dynastic Sumerian? What is the UD.GAL.NUN-Orthography?' *ASJ* 4: 1-6.
A. Falkenstein, 1952-53. 'Zu einem syllabisch geschriebenen Emesal-Text'. *AfO* 16: 60-64.
J. Krecher, 1966. *Sumerische Kultlyrik*. Wiesbaden. (With an outline of the Emesal text genres)
J. Krecher, 1967a. 'Zum Emesal-Dialekt des Sumerischen'. *HSAO* I, p. 87-110.

CATALOGUE OF VERBS

Introduction

The list of verbs given below is not exhaustive. It contains the most frequently attested verbs and their compounds, especially those found in the examples in the grammar. Adjectives are also listed here if they occur in verbal forms.

The main purpose of the catalogue is to show the classification of the verbs as well as their meanings with various case elements. As regards the differentiation of meaning with case prefixes and postpositions, I rely mainly on G.B. Gragg's basic study *Sumerian Dimensional Infixes*, cited here as *SDI*.

A real dictionary of the Sumerian verbs would deserve detailed lexical studies and is of course beyond the scope of this grammar. I have therefore generally omitted references of the occurrences of the verb's various forms, and bibliographical references are only exceptionally given. Such references can be found through the lexical indices in the Sumerian text editions (cf. for instance Bibliography).

áĝ   Regular verb: áĝ-e-dè (*NRVN* I 56, 11).
'to measure,' ex. 345.
á . . . áĝ 'to command, to instruct (someone: -da-)'. Ex. 193, 308, 311, 576, 773, 774, 830.
ki . . . áĝ 'to love (someone: dative; something: loc./loc.-term.)'. Ex. 174, 175, 738.

ak   Regular verb, cf. ak-dè (ex. 775, 778). See Powell, 1982.
'to make, to do'. Ex. 73, 78, 107, 190, 233, 239, 557, 691, 693, 828.
ak is used with several compounds and as an 'auxiliary' verb in

double compounds:

a.da.mín...ak 'to compete (with someone: -da-)'.

á dúb...ak 'to beat the wings'; with -ši-, 'to fly towards' (*SDI* p. 24).

bar...ak 'to choose, to examine'.

du$_{14}$...ak 'to quarrel (with someone: -da-)'.

g̃eštug$_2$ ...ak 'to turn the mind (?)', with -ši-, cf. *SDI* p. 22.

gizzal...ak 'to listen', with -ši-. Also without -ši-, cf. § 458 and *SDI* p. 22.

kin...ak 'to work, to manufacture'.

sa gaz...ak 'to rob (someone: dat.)'.

sag̃ kéš...ak 'to pay attention to, to give heed to', with -ši-. Ex. 581, 632.

Double compounds are: pa è...ak (ex. 798) and šu bal...ak (ex. 460, 799); see pa...è and šu...bal.

ba   Regular verb.

'to give as a gift or a ration'. Ex. 118, 206, 228, 589, 615, 616.

ka...ba 'to converse'.

bad.r Regular verb, cf. bad-e-dè (ex. 358).

'to be remote, to remove'.

dùg...bad.r 'to run, to hurry' (lit.: 'to remove the knees from each other').

igi...bad.r 'to open the eye'.

ba.al Regular verb(?).

'to dig', ex. 234, 237, 560.

bal   Regular verb, cf. šu nu-bal-e-dam (ex. 358).

'to cross, to transfer (to someone: dat.)', with -ta-: 'to pour off, to libate' (cf. *SDI* p. 33). Ex. 248, 262, 336, 460, 496, 525, 654.

áš...bal 'to curse'.

dub-bi...bal 'to go over the account', with -da-. Ex. 613, 614.

g̃iš.gan...bal lit.: 'to hand over the pestle', i.e. 'to conclude a sale' (= *bukannam šūtuqu*).

KA...bal 'to converse, to discuss' (the reading of KA is not known, either inim 'words', or gù 'voice').

sag̃...bal 'to shake the head'.

šu...bal 'to change, to set aside', also šu.bal...ak. Ex. 33, 125, 358, 787.

bar   Regular verb, cf. ka.aš bar-re-da (ex. 606).
'to open, to split', with -ta-: 'to keep away' (*SDI* p. 33).
igi...bar 'to look at, to examine'; with -ši-: 'to gaze at some object in
a certain manner' (*SDI* p. 21), in this sense also with dative about
persons; with -ni-: 'to examine, to peer into' (*SDI* p. 21). Ex. 102,
160, 360, 380, 381, 574, 627, 630, 631, 634, 696, 704.
ka...bar 'to open the mouth'.
ka.aš...bar 'to make decision', ex. 606.
šu...bar 'to release', ex. 521.

bi₆ (=BA) Regular verb?
'to tear', with -ta- 'to tear off', cf. *SDI* p. 34.

bil   The verbal class is not known
'to burn'.

bir   The verbal class is not known.
'to scatter', ex. 424.

bi.z   The verbal class is not known. Reduplicated form: ...-bi-bi-zé.
'to drip.'

bu.úh Probably a shortened form of bu.luh, cf. Alster, 1972a p. 88f.
'to tremble'.

buluĝ₃   Regular verb, cf. nu-buluĝ₃ -ĝe₂₆ -e-dè (Lamentation over Sumer
and Ur 15 = *UET* VI/2, 124: 15).
'to grow, to make grow'.

bu.luh The verbal class is not known.
'to tremble' (cf. bu.úh).

bu.r or bù.r Regular verb.
'to tear out'. ex. 508.

búr   Reduplication class? The verb is most often reduplicated, also in
hamṭu forms, cf. ga-mu-ra-búr-búr (ex. 43).
The basic meaning of búr is perhaps 'to spread out (said of a garment)', then also 'to loosen, to dissolve', 'to reveal, to interpret
(a dream)' (see Wilcke, 1969a p. 143f.; Sjöberg, 1960, p. 105 f.).

gur₅ .(ru.)uš...búr (also du.ru.uš búr, Enmerkar and Ensukhešdana 47). The meaning of this compound verb is rather obscure, cf. Sjöberg, 1969 p. 133f. and 154, where he translates 'to rage against someone/something'; the compound is translated g/kaṣāṣu which means 'to bare the teeth' (*CAD* G p. 52). It is most often used about snakes.

bùr   Regular verb, cf. ì-bùr-dè (ex. 268).
'to pierce, to break into (a house)'.

dab₅   Regular verb, cf. dab₅ -bé-dè (Lamentation over Sumer and Ur 34); also written da-b, da₅ -b or dab.
'to seize, to catch'. Ex. 55, 224, 229, 259, 510, 511, 526, 536, 657, 692, 768.
šu.kin...dab₅ 'to prostrate' (see Civil, 1976c p. 184ff).

dadag (= UD.UD) is the reduplicated form of dág (= UD so far only attested in lexical texts). (For dadag, see Sjöberg, 1969 p. 137f.) 'to be/make clean'. Ex. 641.

dag   Regular verb.
'to run, to rove about' (cf. Berlin, 1979 p. 70).
ǵá.la...dag 'to cease (doing something)', often with -ta-. (See Wilcke, 1969a p. 130f.)
šu...dag 'to roam about, 'to run away'. (Cf. Wilcke, 1969a p. 207.)

daǵal Regular verb, cf. nu-daǵal-e-dè (Lamentation over Sumer and Ur 8 = *UET* VI/2, 124: 8).
'to be/make wide'. Ex. 260, 778.

dah   Regular verb, cf. dah-he-dam (Edzard, 1967 p. 39: *YOS* IV 18, 10).
'to add, to say further', 'to help' (cf. Römer, *SKIZ* p. 122). Ex. 84, 87, 585, 598.

dal   Regular verb.
'to fly', towards something: -ši-; out of: -ta- or -ra- (cf. *SDI* p. 24 and 94). Ex. 215, 216.

dar   Reduplication class, cf. dar-dar-re-dam (Uruk Lamentation
    = *UET* VI/2, 141: 2).
    'to split'.
    á...dar 'to confiscate' (cf. Falkenstein, *NG* III p. 90).
    ki...dar 'to split the earth' (said about plants).

dé   Regular verb.
    'to pour', often with -ni-. Ex. 779, 825.
    a...dé 'to pour out water'. Ex. 701.
    gù...dé 'to call, to cry, to speak to', lit.: 'to pour out the voice'.
    Ex. 19, 167, 168, 383, 583, 691, 796.
    ú.gu...dé 'to disappear, to lose'. Ex. 415, 416.

de$_6$ Singular verb, see § 265.
    Singular, *hamṭu*: de$_6$, singular, *marû*: túm, tùm
    Plural, *hamṭu*: lah$_4$, singular, *marû*: lah$_4$
    'to bring', wih -ši- or -ta- denoting the direction (cf. *SDI* p. 24: 'túm
    in itself simply means 'carry' (. . .) but with -ši- it becomes 'bring
    in''). Ex., de$_6$: 76, 89, 323, 363, 391, 414, 487, 597, 715, 771,
    779, 825; túm/tùm: 47, 66, 91, 257, 326, 355, 357, 699.
    ar/ár...de$_6$ 'to praise', ex. 400.
    ki...de$_6$ 'to bury'.
    mùš...de$_6$ 'to stop, to cease'.
    šu...de$_6$ 'to bring the hand to something', 'to set to work', ex. 698.

di,   see dug$_4$.

dib and díb Regular verb.
    'to pass (by)'.
    igi-šè...dib/díb 'to pass in front of/before'.

dím   Regular verb, cf. dím-me-dè (Lamentation over Sumer and Ur
    74 = *UET* VI/2, 124: 73).
    'to make, to fashion, to create'. Ex. 8, 71, 214, 354, 414, 478, 710,
    826.

dirig   Regular verb (?).
    'to float, to be extra, to be supreme over (dat./loc.)'. Ex. 93, 401.

du, see ḡen.

dù   Regular verb, cf. dù-ù-dè (ex. 696), dù-da (ex. 271).
'to erect something on the ground': 'to build'.
The initial consonant is probably the dr-phoneme, cf. § 23, and cf.
the Sumerian loanword in Akkadian *narû* 'stone monument',
from na dù-a 'erected stone'. Ex. 11,180, 197, 202, 324, 325, 332,
334, 370, 401, 422, 478, 531, 592, 689, 690, 696.
en.nu.ùg̃...dù 'to guard, to watch'.
ga.ba.al...dù 'to challenge'. (For ga.ba.al, see Gordon, 1958 p. 67:
'It is perhaps likely that ga-ba-al is acutally a Sumerian loanword
from the Akkadian *qablum*, 'controversy', rather than a derivative
of the Sumerian verbal root bala.') `
šu...dù 'to bind the hands'. (See Alster, 1972a p. 113.)

du$_7$ Reduplication class (?), cf. du$_7$-du$_7$-da/-dam (Iddin-Dagan
Hymn A 27; Keš Hymn 62), but du$_7$-dè (*RTC* 339, 5).
'to butt, to gore' (see Heimpel, 1968 p. 300-307).
šu...du$_7$ 'to be/make perfect, to complete' (with -ta- cf. *SDI* p. 36);
ex. 98, 319, 421, 825.

du$_8$ Regular verb, cf. du$_8$-ù-dè (Curse of Akkade 111).
The verb possibly ends in [h] or [r], see Falkenstein in *MSL* IV
p. 29 to line 25; cf. also igi bí-in-du$_8$-ru (Lugalbanda and Enmerkar
207-208 and Enmerkar and the Lord of Aratta 238).
'to open, to loosen, to release', ex. 133,559.
igi...du$_8$ 'to see, to look at', most often with -ni- or /bi-/. Ex. 65,
129, 666, 674, 675, 676, 677, 678, 683, 696, 699, 713, 824.
šu...du$_8$ 'to hold in the hand', with -ni- or /bi-/. Ex. 256, 335, 378,
379.
zar.re.eš...du$_8$ 'to pile up', see Cooper, 1978 p. 109.

du$_{12}$ The verbal class is not known.
'to play (an instrument)', 'to sing', ex 103.

dub   Reduplication class (?).
'to heap up', as objects often gur$_7$ 'grain', sahar 'sand', or zì 'flour'.
With -ta- in the sense 'to sprinkle off, to strew', see *SDI* p. 33.
múš...dub, cf. Reisman, 1973 p. 194: 'the verb has to do with
combing or setting of hair'.

dúb   Regular verb, cf. ní dúb-bu-dè (Iddin-Dagan Hymn B 9).

'to tremble, to make tremble'.

á...dúb, most often á.dúb...ak, 'to beat the wings', with -ši- and -šè indicating the direction: 'to fly towards' (*SDI* p. 24).

in(-šè)...dúb 'to insult, to taunt', with -ni- (see *SDI* p. 80).

sag̃...dúb 'to smash the head', mostly with -da- (for examples, see Sjöberg, 1969 p. 103, and 1973a p. 121).

dùg Adjective/Regular verb. Emesal: zé.b.
'to be/make good, pleasant', ex. 22, 422, 487, 694, 725.

dug₄ Complementary verb.
Singular, *hamṭu*: dug₄, singular, *marû*: e
Plural, *hamṭu*: e, plural, *marû*: e
The non-finite *marû* forms are: di, di-da, di-dam, di-dè; ex. 15, 152, 200, 443, 747.
'to say, to speak, to tell, to order', with -da- 'to speak with, to converse'. Ex., dug₄: 52, 56, 74, 87, 133, 134, 182, 250, 251, 267, 271, 276, 336, 337, 352, 382, 458, 459, 479, 480, 501, 506, 554, 582, 588, 717, 733; e: 14, 18, 44, 58, 97, 122, 254, 318, 423, 457, 471, 479, 480, 505, 519, 550, 555, 568, 703, 709, 713.
al...dug₄ 'to demand, to desire', very often with -ni-. Ex. 790.
di...dug₄ 'to carry on a lawsuit', against someone: -da-. Ex. 456, 609.
e.ne.sù.ud...dug₄ 'to rejoice, to copulate', with -da-. Cf. Sjöberg, 1969 p. 107. Ex. 509.
g̃iri₃ .sag₁₁ ...dug₄ 'to trample', see Cooper, 1972 p. 81-83.
mí...dug₄ 'to care for, to flatter, to praise', often with -ni-. Ex. 502, 562, 563, 564, 681, 682.
sá...dug₄ 'to reach, to overwhelm', often with -ni-. Ex. 88, 791.
ság...dug₄ 'to scatter', with -da- or -ta-, cf. *SDI* p. 65. Ex. 152.
še.er.ka.an...dug₄ 'to cover with, to adorn', with -ni-.
šu (dag̃al)...dug₄ 'to supply, to provide (generously) with', with -ni-. Cf. Jacobsen, 1943 p. 120 n. 13. Ex. 664.
šu.tag...dug₄ 'to decorate', with -ni-. Ex. 334, 797. See tag.

dugud Adjective/Regular verb.
'to be/make heavy or important'.

duh, see du₈ .

dul   Regular verb or reduplication class? Cf. dul-lu (Šu-ilišu Hymn A 6), but du$_6$.ul-du$_6$.ul-e (Nusku Hymn IV 7).
'to cover', the object which is covered is mostly in the locative, cf. ex. 309.

dun   The verbal class is not known.
'to dig (with a hoe)'.

dúr.ru.un, see tuš.

e,   see dug$_4$.

è   Complementary verb: è, *hamṭu*: è.d, *marû*. Cf. è-a: è-dè-dam (Gudea, cyl. A XXI 27). è sometimes alternates with e$_{11}$. è is also written i, especially in the reduplicated form i-i, see for instance Sjöberg, 1969 p. 104.
'to go out, to bring out'. Ex. 40, 251, 297, 298, 333, 358, 427, 466, 570, 571, 575, 639, 640, 646, 647, 648, 650, 651, 706, 729, 732, 745, 768.
á...è 'to bring up'.
dalla...è 'to appear, to shine, to make resplendent'.
pa...è 'to make resplendent, to manifest', also pa.è...ak; often with -ni- or /bi-/. Ex. 358, 786.

e$_{11}$.d   Regular verb.
'to go down (or up), to bring down (or up)'. Ex. 419, 495, 649.

e.re, er, see ǧen.

ga, Emesal, see de$_6$.

gal   Adjective/Regular verb.
'to be/make big'.

galam   Adjective/Regular verb.
'to be/make artfully'. According to A. Falkenstein, 1959c p. 75, the basic meaning of galam is 'stufenweise emporsteigen'; cf. Römer, *SKIZ* p. 120, who translates 'erhöhen'.

gam   Regular verb. It is also possible to read gúr.

'to bow down, to kneel' for someone: dative.
The terminative -ši- stresses the directionality of the action, cf.
SDI p. 26. Ex. 104, 269, 362, 554.

gaz Regular verb? Cf. ha-ni-gaz-e (ex. 532); Yoshikawa, 1968b
p. 406, classified gaz in the Reduplication Group.
'to slaughter, to kill', 'to strike, to break, to crush'. Ex. 105, 532,
536.

ge.n Regular verb, cf. ge-né-dè (Iddin-Dagan Hymn B 7).
'to be/make firm, to strengthen'. In juridical documents ge.n is
used in the sense 'to establish something as the property of someone (dat.)' (cf. ex. 709). Ex. 203, 209, 491, 673, 735.

gi₄ Reduplication class, cf. gi₄-gi₄-dè (ex. 696, 778).
'to return , to come back'. Ex. 48, 90, 185, 333, 361, 462, 559,
686, 712.
'to send (back)', with -ši-; ex. 230, 301, 312. Cf. *SDI* p. 25.
'to answer', with dative prefix (the person to whom the answer is
given) and -ni-, ex. 317.
ad...gi₄ 'to take counsel (with someone: -da-)', without -da- the
verb is reflective, cf. ex. 404 and *SDI* p. 62. Ex. 335, 403, 405.
Ka/inim/gù...gi₄ 'to answer', with dative prefix and -ni-, ex. 338;
with /bi-/ 'to call back the word', ex. 535.
ki-bi(-šè)...gi₄ 'to restore', lit.: 'to return to its place'; mostly with
/bi-/, or with dative prefix. Ex. 429, 543.
sa...gi₄ 'to prepare'. See Römer, 1980 p. 64f.
saĝ...gi₄ 'to topple', see Falkenstein, 1964 p. 54; Cooper, 1978 p.
117.
sig₄/še₂₅/še₂₆...gi₄ 'to cry, to shout' (cf. Sjöberg, 1969 p. 77 and
152). Ex. 117, 244, 418.
šu(-a)...gi₄ 'to repay, to repeat'; ex. 569, 522.

gib or gil Regular verb?
'to be crossed, twisted', 'to block, to cause difficulty' (cf. Sjöberg,
1969 p. 128f.).

gibil Adjective/Regular verb.
'to renew, to renovate'.

gíd   Regular verb.
'to be/make long', 'to measure out' (ex. 413), 'to draw' (cf. Falken-stein, *NG* III p. 113).
ğišmá...gíd 'to sail', lit.: 'to draw a boat', with -da-. Ex. 368.
saĝ(.ki)...gíd 'to be angry (with someone: -da-)', 'to be enraged'.
šà-šè...gíd 'to bear in mind', ex. 158.
šu...gíd 'to accept', lit.: 'to stretch out the hand'. šu...gíd is also used in the specific sense 'to observe the offering animal', cf. ex. 392.

gig   Regular verb?
'to be/make sick', 'to be painful to (= dative)'.
hul...gig 'to hate'.

gu₇   Regular verb, cf. gu₇-(ù-)dè (ex. 774), gu₇-dam (ex. 784).
'to eat'; with -ni-: 'to feed'. Ex. 296, 498, 607.
For the reading gu₇ instead of kú, see Borger, 1967.

gub   Singular verb; regular verb; see § 267.
Singular, *hamṭu*: gub, singular, *marû*: gub
Plural, *hamṭu*: su₈.g, plural, *marû*: su₈.g
'to stand, to erect'; with -da-: 'to stand by, to serve' (ex. 602); with -ta-: 'to stand aside'. Ex. 15, 119, 255, 270, 273, 274, 275, 277, 278, 285, 328, 384, 420, 431, 474, 593, 602, 611, 670, 714, 826.
ĝeštug₂ ...gub 'to set the mind to', with -ši-; ex. 129, 386, 494.
ù.ma/ù.na...gub 'to attain victory, triumph'.

gu₄.ud   Reduplication class? Written gu₄-ud and gu₄-gu₄-ud.
'to jump'.

gu.ul   Regular verb, cf. gu.ul-lu-dè (Warad-Sin 18 I 14).
'to enlarge, to increase, to make numerous'; the verb is often re-duplicated.
gu-ul can also stand for gul 'to destroy'.

gul   Reduplication class, cf. gul-gul-lu-dè (ex. 778).
'to destroy'. With -ši-: 'to fall upon' (*SDI* p. 24); with -ta-: 'to wreck to pieces, to destroy utterly' (*SDI* p. 37). Ex. 135, 159, 261, 320 (gu.ul), 350, 353, 467, 472, 538, 727, 744.

gùn   The verbal class is not known; the verb is often reduplicated. 'to be/make multicoloured'. Ex. 334.

gur   Regular verb, cf. nu-gur-re-dè (Lamentation over Sumer and Ur 37 = *UET* VI/2, 126 III 7).
'to come back, to return', in juridical documents in the sense 'to return in a legal case, to reject (evidence)'.
With ablative: 'to turn away from', see *SDI* p. 49. Ex. 272.
á...gur 'to bend the arm'. Ex. 256.
gú...gur 'to gather, to collect', often with -da- and often reduplicated.
šu...gur 'to roll, to wrap'.

gúr, see gam.

gur₄   Adjective/Reduplication class (?).
'to be/make thick', 'to feel wonderful'.

ǧál   Regular verb.
'to be (somewhere)', 'to be available'.
'to place' (with -ni- or /bi-/); with -ši-: 'to place into' (cf. *SDI* p. 25).
'to be with someone', with -da- also 'to have on one's person, to carry', ǧál with -da- is also used in the sense 'to be possible', see *SDI* p. 55. Ex. 191, 200, 253, 335, 394, 530, 566, 567, 572, 660, 791.
gú ǧiš...ǧál 'to submit' (to someone: dative), ex. 232.
igi...ǧál 'to look upon', often with -ši-.
kiri₄ šu...ǧál 'to pay homage to (dative)', lit.: 'to place the hand on the nose'.
nir...ǧál lit.: 'authority or confidence is with someone (-da-)', 'to have authority', 'to be reliable, to trust in'. Ex. 158, 599.
zi šà...ǧál 'to provide (someone: -ši-) with life'.

ǧar   Reduplication class, *marû* stem: ǧá.ǧá, cf. ǧá-ǧá-dè (ex. 210).
'to place', occasionally with -ni-; ex. 24, 34, 35, 46, 74, 115, 252, 256, 658, 659.
'to restore', with -ši-, ex. 224.
'to remove', with -ta-, ex. 558, 642. (Cf. *SDI* p. 33: 'With the verb gar 'set, place', on the other hand the semantic specification added by -ta- seems to be that of setting at some other level'.)

á...ĝar 'to resist, to rebel (?)'. See Berlin, 1979 p. 77 with examples; Berlin translates: 'to behave arrogantly'.

du₁₄...ĝar 'to start a fight'.

dùg...ĝar 'to bend the knees, to kneel down', for someone: dative.

dúr...ĝar 'to seat, to take seat'.

gú...ĝar 'to submit', to someone: dative; lit.: 'to place the neck'. Ex. 49, 126, 226, 327, 520, 554.

gú-a...ĝar 'to place on the neck'. Ex. 613, 614.

ĝeštug₂...ĝar 'to listen to', usually with -ši-. For the use of -ši- with this and similar verbs, see § 458. Ex. 331.

ĝiri₃...ĝar 'to move forward, to make one's way', with -ni-.

ĝiri₃-šè...ĝar 'to place something under the authority of someone', the terminative is not repeated in the prefix chain.

igi...ĝar 'to look at', for the use of -ši- with this verb, cf. § 458. Ex. 61, 730.

inim...ĝar 'to bring an action against someone (before the court)', 'to claim', ex. 92, 364.

i.si.iš...ĝar 'to wail', to someone: dative, cf. *SDI* p. 89.

ki...ĝar 'to found', lit.: 'to place on the ground', ki is virtually locative; often with -ni- or /bi-/. Ex. 6, 197.

ki-šè...ĝar 'to fall/throw upon the ground', ex. 265.

me...ĝar 'to make silent', cf. Sjöberg, 1969 p. 143.

saĝ...ĝar 'to oppose someone/something (-da-)'.

saĝ sig...ĝar 'to bend the head', before someone/something: -ši-, ex. 385.

šu...ĝar 'to perform a task, to carry out', ex. 307, 512. With -ta-: 'to cease doing something'.

šu-a/šè...ĝar 'to be/place in the hand'.

ù.gul...ĝar 'to pray to, to entreat', with dative. Ex. 39.

ĝen   Singular verb, complementary verb. See § 268.
Singular, *hamṭu*: ĝen, singular, *marû*: du
Plural, *hamṭu*: (e.)re₇. er, plural, *marû*: su₈ .b
'to go, to come', with dative or -ši-. Ex., ĝen: 44, 99, 198, 249, 255, 366, 375, 395, 398, 514, 601, 734, 770; du: 80, 127, 330, 643; re₇, e.re, er: 31, 281, 282, 283, 365, 517, 580, 608, 628; su₈ b: 280, 284.

ĝír   Regular verb (?), cf. ĝír-re-da (Šulgi Hymn B 108).
'to lighten, to flash', often nim-gin₇...ĝír 'to flash like lightning'. Ex. 417.

hal   Reduplication class (?), cf. hal-ha-dam (*DP* 222 XII 2).
'to deal out, to distribute'.

ha.lam   Regular verb, cf. ha.lam-e-dè (ex. 778).
'to ruin, to destroy', often with -ta-, cf. *SDI* p. 37 and 48. Ex. 778.

ha.luh, see hu.luh.

har   Regular verb (?). It is also possible to read hur.
'to chew', ex. 235.

ha.za   Regular verb (?).
'to hold, to grasp'.

he or hi   Reduplication class (?).
'to mix', ex. 31.

hug̃   Regular verb.
'to hire, to rent', ex. 437.
šà...hug̃ 'to calm down the heart, to pacify'.

hul   Regular verb?
'to destroy', ex. 231, 267, 393.

húl   Regular verb, cf. nu-húl-le-dè (ex. 443).
'to rejoice over', usually with -da-, but also -ši-; -da- is perhaps more
original, cf. mu-da-húl in Ean. 1 IV 17 and V 5. Ex. 194, 195, 255,
341, 518, 529, 541, 555, 605, 659, 708, 723.

hu.luh   Regular verb. Also ha.luh.
'to become frightened', ex. 468.

hur   Probably regular verb.
'to scratch, to grind'.
g̃iš...hur 'to draw'.
ki...hur 'to scratch the earth'.

i and i-i = è, è-è.

íl   Regular verb or reduplication class? Cf. íl-dam (Gudea, cyl. A
XXVIII 22) and íl-íl-dam (cyl. A XX 6).

308

'to lift, to carry', ex. 246, 302, 391, 398, 401, 552, 754, 818.
igi...íl 'to lift the eyes', both with and without -ši-, cf. *SDI* p. 21:
'With -ši-, igi-íl means to look at some specific object, usually
an individual thing, without it however it means rather to look
over (perhaps usually a multitude).' Ex. 199, 240.
saĝ (an-šè)...íl 'to lift the head (towards heaven)', usually without
-ši-.

ir   The verbal class is not known. ir seems to occur only as a compound verb together with zi:
zi...ir 'to be worried', see Römer, *SKIZ* p. 113 f.

kal   Adjective/Regular verb.
'to be/make precious'.

kalag   Adjective/Regular verb.
'to be/make strong, to strengthen', ex. 51, 728.

kàm   Regular verb. kàm seems to occur exclusively in the form
nu-kàm-me(-da/dam) 'which cannot be changed'.

kar   Regular verb, cf. kar-re-dè (Rim-Sin 18, 31).
'to flee away (from), to take away, to remove', with -da-, see § 449.
Ex. 129, 426, 557, 621.

kár   Reduplication class, cf. igi kár-kár-dè (or better ka_x-ka_x-dè ?)
(Iddin-Dagan Hymn A 172).
'to shine, to illuminate'.
igi...kár 'to look upon, to examine, to select', often with -ši-, cf.
§ 458. See P. Steinkeller, 1982. 'On the Reading and Meaning of
igi-kár and gúrum (IGI.GAR).' *ASJ* 4: 149-151. Ex. 132.

KÉŠ   Probably regular verb. KÉŠ can be read kéš or kešda, it probably ends in [dr]: /kešdr/, cf. KÉŠ-re_6-dè (*BIN* IX 332, 3)
'to bind'.
KA...KÉŠ 'to bind the word/mouth', 'to make an agreement', ex.
252. According to *SDI* p. 36: 'to be bound, to have a structure',
but with -ta-: 'to become undone, to be disorganized'.
zag...KÉŠ 'to seize, to grasp', with -ni-.

kíd or kid_7 The verbal class is not known.
'to pinch off (clay), to break off'.

kin, or perhaps better kíǧ (= KIN). Reduplication class, cf. nu-KIN-
-KIN-dè (nu-ki$_x$-ki$_x$-dè?) (Lamentation over Sumer and Ur 12 =
UET VI/2, 124: 12).
'to seek' (cf. Krecher, 1978d p. 51: 'Die Grundbedeutung ist be-
kanntlich nicht 'etwas Verlorenes hier und da suchen', sondern
'eine Sache angehen, eine Person (mit Rücksicht auf eine Sache,
Lok.-Term.) in Anspruch nehmen''). Ex. 376, 636.
ki...kin 'to seek', with -ši-. Cf. *SDI* p. 26: 'With (ki+)kin-kin 'seek'
(perhaps 'scour the ground for'), -ši- designates the object of the
search'. Ex. 635; cf. § 459.
umbin...kin 'to shear'.

kìr Reduplication class? Cf. ex. 561.
'to nip off (clay)'.

ku Reduplication class, cf. ù nu-ku-ku-dè (Ur Lament 81). The verb
is always reduplicated; it is found in the following compound only:
ù...ku-ku 'to sleep', with -ši-. In Gudea texts: ù...ku$_4$-ku$_4$. Ex. 435,
436.

kú, see gu$_7$.

kud.r Regular verb, cf. kud-re-dè (ex. 779).
'to cut off', with -ta-. Ex. 622, 623.
nam...kud.r 'to curse', often with -ta-. Ex. 540.
nam.erim$_2$ (-bi)...kud.r 'to swear', ex. 316.

ku$_{10}$.g Adjective, as verb always (?) reduplicated: ku$_{10}$-ku$_{10}$ (-g).
'to be black or dark'.

kug Adjective/Regular verb, cf. kug-ge-da (Gudea, cyl. B IX 6).
'to cleanse'.

ku$_4$.r Reduplication class, cf. nu-ku$_4$-ku$_4$-da (ex. 442). It has been
suggested that the verb has a plural stem sun$_5$, see § 263.
'to enter, to let enter, to bring in', with -ni- (loc.) or dative prefix
('to enter before someone'); -ni- is also used in the causative
sense 'to let enter'. With other case prefixes, cf. *SDI* p. 24: 'With
-ši- (...ku$_4$.r) seems to have the sense 'enter into the presence of'';
p. 60: -da- 'can occur with ku$_4$ also in the sense of 'to turn into; to

become'.' Ex. 9, 10, 59, 74, 106, 181, 240, 286, 299, 300, 342, 343, 348, 374, 533, 534, 555, 748, 766, 767, 771.

kúr Regular verb, cf. kúr-ru-dè (Lamentation over Sumer and Ur 17 = *UET* VI/2, 124: 17).
'to change', often with -da- (com. or abl. ?). Ex. 536, 558.

kúš.ù Regular verb, cf. kúš.ù-dè (Ur Lament 80).
'to be troubled, to care about, to become tired'.
šà...kúš.ù 'to rest the heart', 'to make love to', 'to take counsel with' with -da-.

lá Regular verb, cf. lá-e-dè (Lamentation over Sumer and Ur 18 = *UET* VI/2, 124: 18 = *BE* XXI 3, 18); lá-dè (ex. 437).
a) 'to carry', 'to hang (from)', with -ta-. Ex. 23, 96, 241.
b) 'to weigh out, to pay', ex. 724.
c) 'to bind, to harness', with -ši-.
d) 'to be few, to diminish', ex. 535.
e) 'to stretch', ex. 129.
gú...lá lit.: 'to let the neck hang down', 'to bow down', also 'to embrace', with -ta-. Ex. 161.
ğiš...lá 'to be silent' (cf. Heimpel, 1968 p. 157).
sa...lá 'to stretch the net'.
šu-šè...lá 'to bind at the hand, to hold in the hand', cf. Wilcke, 1969a p. 156-157.

lah$_4$ /$_5$, see de$_6$.

lu (Reduplication class ?)
'to be/make numerous, abundant'.

lu.g Probably regular verb.
'to swarm (said of fish and birds)', see Wilcke, 1969a p. 158.

luh The verbal class is not known.
'to be clean, to cleanse, to wash'.

ma$_5$ Reduplication class ? The verb seems to occur exclusively in the reduplicated form.
'to burn', 'to grind', see Cooper, 1978 p. 131.

mah   Adjective/Regular verb.
'to be/make great, magnificent'.

me   The verb occurs in the basic form, me, only.
'to be'. See §§ 535-547. Ex. 54, 60, 197, 201, 250, 278, 356, 430,
461, 482, 486, 504, 546, 588, 705, 707, 708.

mú   Reduplication class, cf. mú-mú-dè (Lamentation over Sumer and
Ur 10 = *UET* VI/2, 124: 10).
'to grow', ex. 245.
áš...mú 'to curse'.
du$_{14}$ ...mú 'to start a quarrel', ex. 464.
šu...mú a) 'to enlarge, to expand', ex. 113, 672; with -ni-. b) 'to
pray', with dative. Ex. 372.

mu$_4$.r Reduplication class (?), cf. mu$_4$-mu$_4$-da-zu-dè (Samsuiluna
Hymn 50).
'to dress, to clothe, to put on clothing'.

mul   The verbal class is not known.
'to shine, to radiate (said about branches, pa)'.

ná   Probably regular verb. NÁ should perhaps rather be read nú, cf.
ba-e-dè-NÁ-un/ù-nam (Ur Lament 319); NÁ-ù-dè (Samsuiluna A II
27-28).
'to lie', with -da-: 'to lie together'; with -ni-: 'to lay down'. Ex. 367,
534, 671.

naŋ   Reduplication class, cf. na$_8$-na$_8$-dè (ex. 774).
'to drink, to let drink'; with -ta-: 'to drink out of' (*SDI* p. 36). Ex.
81, 125, 248, 265, 296.

niŋin   For the *marû* form, see Krecher, 1978d p. 71 n. 80: '/niŋin/,
geschrieben LAGAB = niŋín, ist offenbar die *hamṭu*-Basis; in *marû*-
Belegen wird (immer) LAGAB.LAGAB (= NIGIN$_1$), auch LAGAB.
LAGAB.E/NÉ (= 'NIGIN-e/né') geschrieben, was wahrscheinlich
(immer?) /nini/ zu lesen ist (nini/ninnì, nín-né)'. Cf. the non-finite
form nu-LAGAB.LAGAB-NE = nu-nini-dè (?) (Lamentation over
Sumer and Ur 45 = *UET* VI/2, 124: 44).
'to wander around, to surround', ex. 493.

šu...niĝin 'to proceed, to hurry'.

pad.r Regular verb. That the verb ends in the phoneme [dr] can be
seen from the form ba-ra-pad-re₆ (ex. 460).
'to break'.

pàd Regular verb, cf. pàd-dè-da (Gudea, cyl. B VI 20).
'to call', 'to see, to show, to reveal, to find'; *SDI* p. 95: with abl.
prefix 'to choose out of'. Ex. 344, 369, 415, 416, 473, 539, 558,
661.
ér...pàd 'to weep'.
mu lugal...pàd 'to swear by the king's name', ex. 272, 293, 294,
295, 686.

peš Probably regular verb, cf. šu mu-da-peš-e (ex. 3).
'to be/become thick'.
šu...peš 'to expand', ex. 3, 4.

pil, píl, pi.il or pe.el The verbal class is not known.
'to be/make obscure, dirty, defiled'.

ra Reduplication class.
'to beat, to press'; with -ta-: 'to throw away' (*SDI* p. 34). Ex. 266.
gù...ra 'to shout'.
ĝiš...ra 'to beat with a wooden stick, to thresh'.
kišib...ra 'to seal'.
šu...ra 'to knead clay and form it into a tablet' (cf. *SDI* p. 54, and
Enmerkar and Ensuhkešdana 77).
ti...ra 'to shoot an arrow', cf. Wilcke, 1969a p. 175.

ra.g Regular verb (?), cf. šu bí-íb-ra-ge-a (ex. 187).
šu...ra.g 'to erase'.

re₇ , see ĝen.

ri Alternating class, *hamṭu*: ri, *marû*: ri.g. As plural stem probably
ri.ri.g.
a) 'to pour, to inject into'.
b) 'to place upon, to impose, to lean against', with -ši-. Cf. *SDI*
p. 25: 'ri does not take -ši- in its frequent meaning 'pour, inject

into' even when the adverbial complement is in -šè. It does however take -ši- in those contexts where it could be translated by
Akk. *emēdu*.'
c) 'to throw away', with -ta- (*SDI* p. 34).
na...ri 'to give instructions', ex. 1, 2, 510, 511.
ní...ri 'to be afraid of something, to inspire fear', with -da-.
šu...ri 'to wring the hands over', with -ši-, see *SDI* p. 25.

rig₇   The verbal class is not known; perhaps regular verb.
saĝ.e.eš/saĝ-šè...rig₇ 'to bestow, to grant', with -ni- and -ri-. Ex. 497,
665, 667, 673, 679.

rín   Reduplication class, cf. rín-rín-dam (or better ri_x-ri_x-dam?)
(Gudea, cyl. A XIX 18).
'to be/make bright', ex. 825.

ru   The verbal class is not known.
a...ru 'to dedicate, to give as a votive gift', with dative.

ru.gú   Regular verb? Cf. nu-ru-gú-dè (Lamentation over Sumer and Ur
42 = *BE* XXI 3 rev. 13).
'to withstand, to oppose'.

rú, see dù.

sá   Regular verb.
'to be equal to, to compare with, to compete', with -da-. Ex. 51, 79,
612.
si...sá 'to make straight, to put in order, to prepare', often with -ni-
or /bi-/. Ex. 5, 21, 153, 169, 170, 233, 247, 264, 410, 411, 560,
698, 788.

sa₄   The verbal class is not known.
'to name, to call by name', ex. 205.

sa₁₀   Reduplication class, cf. sa₁₀-sa₁₀-dè (see Edzard, 1967 p. 41:
Nik. 293 I 3).
'to buy', with -ši-, ex. 490, 513.
'to sell', with -ra-, abl.; ex. 95, 114.

sal   Adjective/Regular verb.
'to be thin', 'to spread'.
zar.re.eš...sal 'to spread', 'to heap up'.

sar   Regular verb.
'to write', ex. 13, 121, 751.
'to drive', with -ni-; 'to chase away', with -ta-, cf. *SDI* p. 34.

sè.g/k Regular verb, cf. sè-ge-dam (*NG* nr. 12, 18), sè-ke-dè (Iddin-
-Dagan Hymn B 8).
'to place', ex. 249, 439.
gù...sè.g/k 'to make obedient', ex. 735.
sá...sè.g/k 'to plot, to plan', see Sjöberg, 1969 p. 103f.
sãg̃...sè.g/k 'to take care of', see Römer, 1980 p. 58.

si   Probably reduplication class.
'to be full, to fill'; with -da-: 'to fill with'. Ex. 551.
gú...si 'to assemble', ex. 171, 399, 777.
šu-šè...si 'to fill into the hand', 'to hand over, to deliver'. Ex. 711.

si.g, si.ig Probably regular verb.
The meaning of this verb is not very clear; it is sometimes used
about things which are placed on or into the ground, for instance
foundation (cf. ex. 698) or standards, but it also seems to be confused with si 'to fill'. (Cf. for instance Sjöberg, 1969 p. 139f.)
Ex. 100, 101, 425.

sig The verbal class is not known; sig is only rarely used as finite verb.
'to be weak', ex. 108.

sìg Regular verb.
'to beat (rhythmically, for instance a drum) to tremble, to smite',
ex. 476.
sãg̃...sìg 'to move the head from side to side', 'to tremble', with -da-
(*SDI* p. 63).
šà...sìg 'to be oppressed'.

sig$_7$, see ti.

sig$_7$ or sa$_7$.g The verbal class is not known.

'to be/make pleasant, beautiful, to create' (see Gragg, 1969 p. 177). Ex. 710.

sikil Adjective/Regular verb, cf. sikil-e-da (Gudea, cyl. B VI 24). 'to be/make pure, clean', ex. 641.

si.il Regular verb or reduplication class? Cf. si.il-le-dè (Lamentation over Sumer and Ur 30 = *UET* VI/2, 124: 29), si.il.si-le-dè (Nungal 23).
'to split, to tear apart', also 'to go away, to absent.oneself'.
ka.tar...si.il 'to praise'.

silig Regular verb, cf. nu-silig-ge-dam (Gudea, cyl. A XXIX 6). 'to cease, to lay aside one's work'. The verb occurs almost exclusively in non-finite forms. See Sjöberg, 1969 p. 64.

silim Adjective/Regular verb. 'to be/make good, healthy'.

su Reduplication class. 'to replace', ex. 121, 225.

su and sù Probably reduplication class.
'to drown, to go down (said about ships), to set under water'.
kuš₇...su(sù) 'to level, to devastate', see Cooper, 1978 p. 113.
It is not certain that the compound belongs here.

sù The verbal class is not known.
'to sprinkle'.
ù...sù 'to dine, to eat', see Sjöberg, 1969 p. 54.

su.ub The verbal class is not known.
The basic meaning of su.ub is probably 'to rub'; it occurs mostly as a compound verb. See Deller and Watanabe, 1980.
ki-a...su.ub 'to kiss the ground, to prostrate oneself'.
naǧa...su.ub 'to rub with soap'.
ne...su.ub 'to kiss'.
šu...su.ub 'to gather up, to collect, to scrape together'.

su₈.b, see ǧen.

sud.r Reduplication class, cf. sù-sù-ud-dè (Lamentation over Sumer and Ur 28 = *UET* VI/2, 124; 27).
'to be/make remote, lasting'.
šu...sud.r 'to stretch the hand out after something' (lit.: 'to make the hand remote').
á...sud.r 'to make the arms wide (?)', see Wilcke, 1969 p. 180.

sù.g The verbal class is not known.
'to be/make naked, empty, waste'.

su$_8$.g, see gub.

suh The verbal class is not known.
igi...suh 'to stare with wide-open eyes'. (See Römer, 1980 p. 68.)

sùh The verbal class is not known.
'to be/make confused'.

sukud The verbal class is not known.
'to be/make high' (cf. ex. 552).

sum Regular verb, cf. sum-mu-dè (Lamentation over Sumer and Ur 32 = *UET* VI/2, 124, 31), sum-mu-dam (ex. 781). Emesal: zé.èm.
'to give', with dative. Ex. 38, 57,77, 85, 120, 211,212,213, 225, 232, 258, 287, 288, 303, 304, 322, 329, 346, 347, 387, 388, 389, 397, 527, 528, 542, 586, 590, 687, 695, 703, 719, 720, 749, 830.
gù...sum 'to talk to', with dative. Ex. 402.
g̃eštug$_2$ ...sum 'to give ear to, to listen to', with dative.
sag̃...sum 'to rush towards', ex. 93, 358.

sur Reduplication class (?), cf. sur-sur-ru-dè (Nungal 15).
'to perform an action from which a liquid product results', so Civil, 1964 p. 81.
kàš...sur 'to urinate'.
ki...sur 'to fix the boundary', cf. Römer, *SKIZ* p. 219. Ex. 189.
šà...sur 'to have diarrhea', cf. Sjöberg, 1960 p. 160.

ša$_4$ The verbal class is not known.
ad...ša$_4$ 'to wail', 'to resound', see Sjöberg, 1969 p. 148. Ex. 412.
še...ša$_4$ 'to moan'.

ur₅ ...ša₄ 'to roar', ex. 743.

šag₅   Reduplication class, *marû*: ša₆ .ša₆ (.g).
'to be/make good, favourable', 'to be/make pleasing to', with dat.
or -da-. Ex. 223, 339, 392, 716.

šám,   see sa₁₀ .

šár   The verbal class is not known.
a) 'to mix', with -da- (cf. § 204). See Römer, 1980 p. 82f. Ex. 220,
221, 222, 223, 561.
b) 'to slaughter', cf. Farber-Flügge, 1973 p. 89.
ul...šár 'to gladden', see Sjöberg, 1969 p. 67.

še.ba   Probably regular verb.
'to be careless, neglient', see Falkenstein, *NG* III p. 132; Ali, 1964
p. 75 n. 12.

šed₇ , šed₁₁   Probably regular verb.
'to be/make cool'.
šà...šed₇ 'to cool/soothe the heart'.

še.g   Regular verb.
'to be obedient, to obey, to agree'; with -ši-: 'to comply with someone's prayer'. Ex. 203, 438.

šèg̃   The verbal class is not known.
'to rain'.

šeg̃₆   The verbal class is not known.
'to boil'.

šéš, šeš₄   Reduplication class, *marû*: še₈-še₈ .
'to anoint', ex. 493.
ér...šéš 'to weep'.

šid   Probably regular verb.
'to count, to recite, to read aloud', ex. 516.

šú   Reduplication class, cf. šú-šú-(ù-)dè (Lamentation over Sumer

and Ur 51 = *UET* VI/2, 124: 50 = *BE* XXXI, 3, rev. 22).
'to cover, to overwhelm', with -da- (see *SDI* p. 44 and 53).
ud...šú 'to become dark, dusky', said about the sun, day(light), see
Sjöberg, 1969 p. 136; Berlin, 1979 p. 84.

šub   Regular verb.
'to fall (upon), to throw'; with -ta-: 'to throw away, to remove';
with -da-: 'to drop, to let fall', cf. *SDI* p. 44. Ex. 16, 108, 305,
545, 549.
gú...šub 'to be lax with respect, to scorn', with -ši-, see *SDI* p. 27.

šum   Regular verb.
'to slaughter'.

šúr   Regular verb.
'to be enraged (against someone: -da-)', cf. *SDI* p. 63.

tab   The verb tab seems in some instances to be a regular verb, but
cf. tab-tab-bé-dè (ex. 778).
'to be/make double, to clutch, to clasp to'; with -da-: 'to join' (see
SDI p. 59).
gaba(-a, loc.)...tab 'to hold to the breast'.

tag   Regular verb, cf. nu-tag-(ge-)dè (Lamentation over Sumer and
Ur = *UET* VI/2, 124: 41 and 47), or reduplication class (so Yoshikawa, 1968a p. 253) tag-tag-ge-dè (Curse of Akkade 22).
'to touch'.
g̃iš...tag 'to sacrifice', often with dative. Ex. 377, 406.
ki...tag 'to lay something on the ground', especially used in the
meaning 'to lay the foundation', cf. Römer, *SKIZ* p. 62 n. 151.
kušu/kušum(= U+PIRIG̃) (ki)...tag 'to crawl, to run (?), see Civil,
1976a p. 135f.; Berlin, 1979 p. 70.
šu...tag 'to cover, to decorate', often with -ni-. Ex. 188.
zag...tag 'to push, to put off'. Cf. Gragg, 1973c p. 70: 'In most of
the clear instances zag-tag seems to mean 'overthrow, reject' —
frequently with negative implications.'

tag₄   Reduplication class.
tag₄ is the traditional reading of the verb KÍD. On the basis of lexical texts Powell, 1978 p. 181ff., suggested a reading taka₄ for the

hamṭu stem, and da$_x$.da$_x$ (= TAG$_4$-TAG$_4$) for the *marû* stem.
'to leave, to divorce, to neglect, to disregard', ex. 62, 687, 700.
g̃ál...tag$_4$ 'to open', ex. 789, 793.
šu...tag$_4$ 'to send', with dative.

tál   The verbal class is not known.
'to be/make wide, broad, to spread wide', perhaps rather: 'to be/
make unfold'; said about wings, arms. See Berlin, 1979 p. 74;
Gragg, 1969 p. 183.

tam   The verbal class is not known.
bar...tam, bar.tam...ak 'to choose', see Hallo, 1973.

tar   Regular verb, cf. tar-re-dè (ex. 673), tar-re-dam (ex. 783).
'to cut'.
èn...tar 'to question, to ask (someone: dat.)', 'to examine'. Ex. 770,
783.
nam...tar 'to decide the fate', most often with -ni- (or -ri-, 2. sg.).
The verb occurs also with -da-, cf. *SDI* p. 57: 'The comitative infix
is also used to signify engagement in some activity along with
someone else (. . .). Under this heading it is fairly frequent with
nam-tar 'to decide the fates' in situations where a number of gods
do this together.' Ex. 45, 60, 594, 668, 669, 673, 680, 684, 685,
750, 778, 787.
nam.erim$_2$-bi...TAR 'to swear, confirm by oath', ex. 687. The
readings tar and kud are both possible in this compound verb.

te or ti   Alternating class, *hamṭu*: te, ti, *marû*: te.g̃, ti.g̃, cf. te-g̃e$_{26}$-e-
-da-g̃u$_{10}$-dè (Letter A 1, 12). See Edzard, 1976a p. 52f.
'to approach (someone: dat.)', ex. 300, 595, 701.
šu...ti 'to receive', lit.: 'to approach the hand to something', with
terminative and -ši-, cf. § 459. Ex. 237, 558, 626, 637.
ní...te/ti 'to be afraid of', with -da- (cf. § 447).

te.en   Probably reduplication class.
ní...te.en 'to relax, to cool off', with -ši- (cf. § 459). Ex. 321.

ti.1   Singular verb, see § 269.
Singular, *hamṭu*: ti.1, singular, *marû*: ti.1
Plural, *hamṭu*: sig$_7$, plural, *marû*: sig$_7$

'to be alive, to live, to dwell, to let live'. Ex. 1, 2, 75, 313, 755.

til   Regular verb, cf. til-le/e-dè (Lamentation over Sumer and Ur = *UET* VI/2, 124: 46 and 49).
'to be completed, to finish, to cease, to perish'. Ex. 491.

tu_5 Probably reduplication class (so Yoshikawa, 1974 p. 25).
a...tu_5 'to bathe, to wash'.

tu_{10}.b, tu_{11}.b   Regular verb. tu_{10} = HUB, tu_{11} = HÚB. The readings hub and húb for this verb are not totally excluded, but cf. Cooper, 1978 p. 119 for arguments in favour of /tub/.
'to strike, to smite', 'to pile up'.

tu.d, ù.tu.d   The verbal class is not known.
'to bear, to fashion'. Ex. 30, 37, 111, 204, 357, 702, 710, 760.

túd   Probably regular verb.
'to hit', ex. 827.

tuk_4 Probably reduplication class.
'to tremble'; see Wilcke, 1969a p. 150.

tuku   Reduplication class? (See Powell, 1978 p. 181 n. 28.) The reading of the reduplicated form, TUKU-TUKU, is not clear.
'to have'. In juridical documents tuku is used in the sense 'to marry'. Ex. 2, 12, 94, 207, 238, 252, 289, 290, 291, 292, 420, 432, 441, 503, 688, 739, 775, 826.
ǵiš...tuku 'to hear', ex. 230, 794, 795.

tu.lu   Probably regular verb.
'to be/make loose, limp', ex. 340.

tur   Adjective/Regular verb, cf. tur-re-dè (Lamentation over Sumer and Ur 47 = *UET* VI/2, 124: 46).
'to be/make small, to reduce', ex. 424.

tuš   Singular verb, see § 270.
Singular, *hamṭu*: tuš, singular, *marû*: tuš
Plural, *hamṭu*: durun, plural, *marû*: durun

'to sit, to live somewhere, to seat'. Ex. 41, 119, 242, 285, 296, 477, 694, 714, 775.

u₅ The verbal class is not known.
'to ride, to mount'.
má(-a)...u₅ 'to go on board, to embark', ex. 499.

ug₅, ug₇, see úš.

ul₄ Probably regular verb (so Yoshikawa, 1974 p. 34).
'to hurry, to hasten'.

u₁₈.lu The verbal class is not known.
See Sjöberg, 1969 p. 102-103; and cf. *CAD* A /1 p. 376: u₁₈.lu
'seems to have denoted a supernatural awe-inspiring phenomenon
and is also used to describe winds abnormal in intensity'.
ǧeštug₂ ...u₁₈.lu 'to forget'.

ùr Reduplication class, cf. ùr-ùr-ru-dam (Nungal 24).
'to drag (over the ground)', often with -ni-.
ǧiš...ùr 'to harrow', often with -ni-.
šu...ùr 'to erase', with -ni- and /bi-/; also with -ta-, cf. *SDI* p. 95.
Ex. 640.

ur₄ Probably reduplication class.
'to reap, to collect, to harvest'.

uru₄, ur₁₁(.ru) Probably regular verb (so Yoshikawa, 1968 p. 410).
'to plow.'

ús Regular verb.
'to follow, to join, to reach, to let reach'. Ex. 53, 165, 172, 173,
407, 587, 679, 762, 821.
gú...ús 'to raise the neck'.
gùd...ús 'to build a nest', ex. 162.
ki...ús 'to set on the ground, to establish', often with -ni-. Ex. 263,
558.
šu...ús 'to lay the hand on something'. In the sense 'to send, to dis-
patch', see Sollberger, *TCS* I p. 187; 'to push on (the door)', see
Sladek, 1974 p. 191.

zag...ús 'to border on, to stand by, to set aside'.

úš   Singular verb, see § 271.
Singular, *hamṭu*: úš, singular, *marû*: ug₅ , ug₇
Plural, *hamṭu*: ug₅, ug₇, ug₇-ug₇ , plural, *marû*: ug₅, ug₇
'to die, to kill'. Ex. 118, 161, 704, 707, 773.

ù.tu, see tu.d.

za   The verbal class is not known.
This verb occurs always in compounds with onomatopoetic words
like for instance dum dam...za 'to howl' (see ex. 822), others are:
bu.ud-ba.ad, bùl-bal, dub-dab, du.bu.ul-da.ba.al, gúm-ga.àm,
gun_x(KUN)-ga.an, hu.um-ha.am, mul-ma.al, pu.ud-pa.ad, pu.ug-
-pa.ag, sùh-sah₄, zur-za.ar, wu-wa. See Civil, 1966 p. 119: 'All
these forms mean 'to make noise', usually a repeated, monotonous
kind of noise'.

záh, zàh Probably regular verb, cf. ì-zàh-dè-na (ex. 267).
'to run away, to flee', ex. 259, 717.

zal   Regular verb.
'to pass (said about time), to spend the day', often with -ni-; with
-ta- in a temporal sense, cf. *SDI* p. 36. Ex. 74, 229, 465, 618, 619,
620, 644.

zalag The verbal class is not known.
'to be/make bright'. zalag is often reduplicated, for this form, see
Sjöberg, 1969 p. 137f. Ex. 341.

zé.eb (Emesal), see dùg.

zé.èm (Emesal), see sum.

zé.er, zi.r Regular verb, cf. zi-re-dam (ex. 415).
'to tear out, to remove, to break', often with -ta-. Ex. 351.

zìg   Reduplication class, *marû*: zi-zi.
'to rise, to stand up'; with -ta- or -ra-: 'to rise up from'. Ex. 50, 151,
396, 409, 624, 736, 739, 827.

su...zìg 'to be afraid of', with -da-. Lit.: 'to stand (said about) the body hair', 'to have gooseflesh', see Sjöberg, 1969 p. 58.

zil   The verbal class is not known.
'to peel off, to strip off'. Cf. Sladek, 1974 p. 199.

zíl   The verbal class is not known. The verb is mostly reduplicated.
'to make pleasing', see Sjöberg, 1974 p. 169.

zu   Possibly reduplication class.
'to know'; with -da-: 'to learn from someone'. Ex. 72, 86, 257, 417, 433, 440, 444, 463, 470, 554, 600, 604, 705, 715, 718.

zuh   The verbal class is not known.
'to steal'.

Some Comments on the Transliteration

It is not recommendable to aim at a transliteration phonetically more exact than the original text. Therefore, the transliteration lugal-ni = /lugal-ani/ is preferred to lugala$_x$-ni etc. (cf. Civil, 1973b p. 32-34). In order to facilitate the understanding forms like dug$_4$, pàd, zid or zìg, etc. are preferred rather than du$_{11}$, pà, and zi (cf. Diakonoff, 1977 p. 110-112). Although it is probable that reduplicated stems are phonetically reduced they are written in full, e.g., zalag-zalag, tuku-tuku, since the pronunciation of such forms as a rule is not known.

Dots are used in a succession of signs forming a semantic unit and in proper names, for instance ur.sàĝ 'hero', ki.sikil 'girl' (but ki sikil 'pure earth'), ^{D}En.líl, the god Enlil, Ur.^{D}Nammu, the king Ur-Nammu, etc. Hyphens are used between roots and grammatical elements: è-a 'in the house', ki-bi-šè 'to its place', mu-na-an-dug$_4$ 'he said it to him'.

Sign values are according to R. Borger, 1978. *Assyrisch-babylonische Zeichenliste. (AOAT* 33) Neukirchen-Vluyn. Words of two syllables, however, are written with numbers: ensi$_2$ instead of énsi, ĝiri$_3$, instead of ĝìri, etc.

Words with the phoneme [ĝ] have the same index numbers as the sign values with [g], thus ĝá = gá, ĝu$_{10}$ = gu$_{10}$ = MU.

Abbreviations and Symbols

abl.	ablative
abs.	absolutive
acc.	accusative
ADJ	adjective
affirm.	affirmative
Akkad.	Akkadian
an.	animate
C	consonant
CAS	case postposition or prefix
com.	comitative
COP	the enclitic copula
dat.	dative
DAT	the dative element of the prefix chain
ED III	Early Dynastic III
erg.	ergative
gen.	genitive
GEN	the genitive postposition /-ak/
IL	Isin-Larsa period
inan.	inanimate
instr.	instrumental
intrans.	intransitive
lit.	literary
loc.	locative
loc.-term.	locative-terminative
MOD	modal prefix
N	noun
NA	Neo-Assyrian
nom.	nominative
NS	Neo-Sumerian
OAkk	Old Akkadian
OB	Old Babylonian
OBJ	object
om.	omit(s)
one-part.	one-participant
OS	Old Sumerian
pl.	plural
PLUR	the plural suffix /-ene/

PN	personal name
POSS	possessive suffix
pron.	pronominal
PRON	pronominal prefix or suffix
PREF	element of the prefix chain of the finite verb
R	verbal root: non-finite forms
R(*h*)	the *hamṭu* stem
R(*m*)	the *marû* stem
R-R	the reduplicated *hamṭu* stem
sg., sing.	singular
SUBJ	subject
Sum.	Sumerian
term.	terminative
three-part.	three-participant
trans.	transitive
two-part.	two-participant
Ur III	The Third Dynasty of Ur
V	vowel
var.	variant
VERB	the verbal root, regardless of stem
{ }	morphemes in this parenthesis have the same rank and cannot occur together
{ }	this parenthesis in the transliteration indicates that the sign should be deleted
< >	indicates that the sign does not occur in the text but is restored in the transliteration
[ ]	indicates phonemes
/ /	indicates morphemes

BIBLIOGRAPHY

Abbreviations

References are to the general bibliography below.

AASF	*Annales Academiae Scientiarum Fennicae.* Helsinki.
Acta Antiqua	*Acta Antiqua Academiae Scientiarum Hungaricae.* Budapest.
AfO	*Archiv für Orientforschung.* Berlin, Graz.
AJA	*American Journal of Archaeology.* Boston, Concord, Princeton.
AHw	*Akkadisches Handwörterbuch.* Unter Benutzung des lexikalischen Nachlasses von Bruno Meissner bearbeitet von Wolfram von Soden. Wiesbaden 1965-81.
AnOr	*Analecta Orientalia.* Rome.
AOAT	*Alter Orient und Altes Testament. Veröffentlichungen zur Kultur und Geschichte des Alten Orients und des Alten Testaments.* Neukirchen-Vluyn.
AOAT 1	*Lišān mithurti. Festschrift Wolfram Freiherr von Soden zum 19. VI.1968 gewidmet von Schülern und Mitarbeitern.* Unter Mitwirkung von M. Dietrich herausgegeben von W. Röllig. Neukirchen-Vluyn 1969.
AOAT 25	*Kramer Anniversary Volume. Cuneiform Studies in Honor of Samuel Noah Kramer.* Edited by Barry Eichler. Neukirchen-Vluyn 1976.
AOATS	*Alter Orient und Altes Testament, Sonderreihe.* Neukirchen-Vluyn.
AS	*Assyriological Studies* (University of Chicago).
AS 16	*Studies in Honor of Benno Landsberger on his Seventy-Fifth Birthday April 21, 1965.* Chicago 1965.
AS 20	*Sumerological Studies in Honor of Thorkild Jacobsen on His Seventieth Birthday June 7, 1974.* Edited by S.J. Lieberman. Chicago and London 1976.
ASJ	*Acta Sumerologica.* Hiroshima.
ASK	Paul Haupt, 1882. *Akkadische und sumerische Keilschrifttexte nach den Originalen copirt und mit einleitenden Zusammenstellungen sowie erklärenden Anmerkungen herausgegeben. (Assyriologische Bibliothek,* 1) Leipzig.
AWL	See Josef Bauer, *AWL.*
BE	*The Babylonian Expedition of the University of Pennsylvania,* Series A: Cuneiform Texts.

328

BE I	Hermann V. Hilprecht, 1893-96. *Old Babylonian Inscriptions Chiefly from Nippur.* 1-2. Philadelphia.
BE III	David W. Myhrman, 1910. *Sumerian Administrative Documents Dated in the Reigns of the Second Dynasty of Ur from the Temple Archives of Nippur.* Philadelphia.
BE XXXI	Stephen H. Langdon, 1914. *Historical and Religious Texts from the Temple Library of Nippur.* München.
BIN	*Babylonian Inscriptions in the Collection of J.B. Nies.* New Haven.
BIN VIII	George G. Hackman, 1958. *Sumerian and Akkadian Administrative Texts from Predynastic Times to the End of the Akkad Dynasty.*
BIN IX	Vaughn E. Crawford, 1954. *Sumerian Economic Texts from the First Dynasty of Isin.*
BiOr	*Bibliotheca Orientalis.* Leiden.
BL	Stephen H. Langdon, 1913. *Babylonian Liturgies. Sumerian Texts from the Early Period and from the Library of Ashurbanipal.* Paris.
BSOAS	*Bulletin of the School of Oriental and African Studies.* London.
CAD	*The Assyrian Dictionary of the Oriental Institute of the University of Chicago.* Chicago 1956-.
CT	*Cuneiform Texts from Babylonian Tablets in the British Museum.* London.
CT XV	Leonard W. King, 1902.
CT XXXVI	Cyril John Gadd, 1921.
CT XLII	Hugo Heinrich Figulla, 1959.
CT XLIV	Theophilus G. Pinches, 1963. *Miscellaneous Texts.*
DP	François-Maurice Allotte de la Fuÿe, 1908-13. *Documents présargoniques.* Fasc. I-II. Paris.
ECTJ	See Aage Westenholz, *ECTJ.*
ESV	*Emesal Vocabulary,* in: *MSL* IV, p. 1-44.
Genava	*Bulletin du Musée d'Art et d'Histoire de Genève.* Genève.
GSG	See Arno Poebel, *GSG.*
GSGL I, II	See Adam Falkenstein, *GSGL* I and II.
HSAO I	*Heidelberg Studien zum Alten Orient, Adam Falkenstein zum 17. September 1966.* Wiesbaden 1967.
ISET I	*Istanbul Arkeoloji Müzelerinde Bulunan. Sumer Edebî Tablet ve Parçalari (Sumerian Literary Tablets and Fragments in the Archaeological Museum of Istanbul),* I. By Muazzez Çiğ and Hatice Kızılyay. Introduction and Catalogue by Samuel Noah Kramer. *(Türk Tarih Kurumu Yayınlarından,* VI/13) Ankara 1969.
ISET II	*Istanbul Arkeoloji Müzelerinde Bulunan. Sumer Edebî Tablet ve Parçalari (Sumerian Literary Tablets and Fragments in the Archaeological Museum of Istanbul),* II. By Samuel Noah Kramer. *(Türk*

	Tarih Kurumu Yayınlarından, VI/13 Ankara 1976.
JANES	The Journal of the Ancient Near Eastern Society of Columbia University.
JAOS	Journal of the American Oriental Society. New Haven.
JCS	Journal of Cuneiform Studies. New Haven, Cambridge Mass.
JNES	Journal of Near Eastern Studies. Chicago.
LIH	Leonard W. King, 1898-1900. The Letters and Inscriptions of Hammurabi, King of Babylon, about B.C. 2200, to which are added a Series of Letters of Other Kings of the First Dynasty of Babylon, I-III. London.
MBI	George Aaron Barton, 1918. Miscellaneous Babylonian Inscriptions. Part I Sumerian Religious Texts. New Haven.
MDOG	Mitteilungen der Deutschen Orient-Gesellschaft. Berlin.
MIO	Mitteilungen des Instituts für Orientforschung. Berlin.
MSL	Materialien zum sumerischen Lexikon. Rome.
MSL I	Benno Landsberger, 1937. Die Serie ana ittišu.
MSL II	Benno Landsberger, 1951. Die Serie Ur-e-a = nâqu.
MSL IV	Benno Landsberger, R. Hallock, Thorkild Jacobsen and Adam Falkenstein, 1956. Introduction. Part I: Emesal-Vocabulary (Series dimir-dingir-ilum), Part II: Old Babylonian Grammatical Texts. Part III: Neobabylonian Grammatical Texts.
MSL XII	Miguel Civil, 1969. The Series lú = ša and Related Texts.
MSL XIII	Izi = išátu, Ká-gal = abullu and Níg-ga = makkūru. Edited by Miguel Civil with the collaboration of Hans G. Güterbock, William W. Hallo, Harry A. Hoffner, Erica Reiner. Rome 1971.
NG	See Adam Falkenstein, NG.
NRVN I	Muazzez Çığ and Hatice Kızılyay, 1965. Neusumerische Rechts- und Verwaltungsurkunden aus Nippur. I. (Türk Tarih Kurumu Yayınlarından, VI/7) Ankara.
OECT I	Stephen Langdon, 1923. The H. Weld-Blundel Collection in the Ashmolean Museum, Sumerian and Semitic Religious and Historical Texts. (Oxford Editions of Cuneiform Texts, I) Oxford.
OIP	Oriental Institute Publications. Chicago.
OIP 99	See Robert D. Biggs, 1974.
OLZ	Orientalistische Literaturzeitung. Berlin und Leipzig.
Or	Orientalia. Rome.
OrNS	Orientalia Nova Series. Rome.
PAPS	Proceedings of the American Philosophical Society. Philadelphia.
PAPS 107	See Samuel Noah Kramer, 1963.
PBS I/2	Henry F. Lutz, 1919. Selected Sumerian and Babylonian Texts. (University of Pennsylvania, The Museum, Publications of the Babylonian Section, I/2) Philadelphia.

PBS VII	Arthur Ungnad, 1915. *Babylonian Letters of the Hammurapi Period. (University of Pennsylvania, The Museum, Publications of the Babylonian Section,* VII) Philadelphia.
RA	*Revue d'Assyriologie et d'Archéologie Orientale.* Paris.
RTC	François Thureau-Dangin, 1903. *Recueil de tablettes chaldéennes.* Paris.
SAK	See François Thureau-Dangin, *SAK.*
SBH	George Andrew Reisner, 1896. *Sumerisch-babylonische Hymnen nach Thontafeln griechischer Zeit. (Mitheilungen aus den orientalischen Sammlungen,* 10) Berlin.
SDI	See Gene B. Gragg, *SDI.*
SEM	Edward Chiera, 1934. *Sumerian Epics and Myths. (OIP* 15) Chicago.
SKIZ	See Willem H. Ph. Römer, *SKIZ.*
SLTNi	Samuel Noah Kramer, 1944. *Sumerian Literary Texts from Nippur in the Museum of the Ancient Orient at Istanbul. (Annual of the American Schools of Oriental Research,* 23) New Haven.
SR	See Dietz Otto Edzard, *SR.*
SRT	Edward, Chiera, 1924. *Sumerian Religious Texts.* Upland (Pa.)
StOr	*Studia Orientalia edidit Societas Orientalis Fennica.* Helsinki.
STVC	Edward Chiera, 1934. *Sumerian Texts of Varied Contents. (OIP* 16) Chicago.
TCL	*Musée du Louvre. Département des Antiquités Orientales, Textes Cunéiformes.* Paris.
TCL II	Henri de Genouillac, 1911. *Tablettes de Dréhem publiées avec inventaire et tables.*
TCL XV, XVI	Henri de Genouillac, 1930. *Textes religieux sumériens du Louvre.*
TCS	*Texts from Cuneiform Sources.* Locust Valley, New York.
TCS I	See Edmond Sollberger, *TCS* I.
TDr	Henri de Genouillac, 1911. *La trouvaille de Dréhem. Etude avec un choix de textes de Constantinople et Bruxelles.* Paris.
TMH(NF)	*Texte und Materialien der Frau Professor Hilprecht Sammlung im Eigentum der Universität Jena. (Neue Folge).*
TMH V	Alfred Pohl, 1935. *Vorsargonische und sargonische Wirtschaftstexte.* Leipzig.
TMHNF I-II	Alfred Pohl, 1937. *Rechts- und Verwaltungsurkunden der III. Dynastie von Ur.* Leipzig.
TMHNF III	Samuel Noah Kramer and Inez Bernhard, 1961. *Sumerische literarische Texte aus Nippur. Bd. I. Mythen, Epen, Weisheitsliteratur und andere Literaturgattungen.* Berlin.
TMHNF IV	Samuel Noah Kramer and Inez Bernhardt, 1967. *Sumerische literarische Texte aus Nippur. Bd. II, Hymnen, Klagelieder, Weisheitstexte und andere Literaturgattungen.* Berlin.

TSŠ	Raymond R. Jestin, 1937. *Tablettes sumériennes de Šuruppak conservées au Musée de Stamboul. (Mémoires de l'Institut français d'archéologie de Stamboul,* 3) Paris.
UET	*Ur Excavations, Texts.* London.
UET II	Eric Burrows, 1935. *Archaic Texts.*
UET III	Léon Legrain, 1947. *Business Documents of the Third Dynasty of Ur.*
UET VI/1-2	Cyril John Gadd and Samuel Noah Kramer, 1963 and 1966. *Literary and Religious Texts.*
VS II	Heinrich Zimmern, 1912. *Sumerische Kultlieder aus altbabylonischer Zeit.* Erste Reihe. *(Vorderasiatische Schriftdenkmäler der Königlichen Museen zu Berlin,* II) Leipzig.
VS X	Heinrich Zimmern, 1913. *Sumerische Kultlieder aus altbabylonischer Zeit.* Zweite Reihe. *(Vorderasiatische Schriftdenkmäler der Königlichen Museen zu Berlin,* X) Leipzig.
WO	*Welt des Orients.* Wuppertal, Stuttgart, Göttingen.
WZKM	*Wiener Zeitschrift für die Kunde des Morgenlandes.* Wien.
YNER	*Yale Near Eastern Researches.* New Haven and London.
YOS IV	Clarence Elwood Keiser, 1919. *Selected Temple Documents of the Ur Dynasty. (Yale Oriental Series, Babylonian Texts,* IV) New Haven.
ZA	*Zeitschrift für Assyriologie und Vorderasiatische Archaeologie.* Berlin.
ZDMG	*Zeitschrift der Deutschen Morgenländischen Gesellschaft.* Wiesbaden.

General Bibliography

V. Afanasjeva, 1974. 'Mündlich überlieferte Dichtung ('Oral Poetry') und schriftliche Literatur in Mesopotamien.' *Acta Antiqua* 22: 121-135.

Fadhil Abdulwahid Ali, 1964. *Sumerian Letters: Two Collections from the Old Babylonian Schools.* Dissertation Philadelphia. University Microfilms Ann Arbor 64-10, 343.

Bendt Alster, 1972a. *Dumuzi's Dream. Aspects of Oral Poetry in a Sumerian Myth. (Mesopotamia* 1) Copenhagen.

— 1972b. 'A Sumerian Incantation against Gall.' *OrNS* 41: 349-358.

— 1972c. "Ninurta and the Turtle', *UET* 6/1, 2.' *JCS* 24: 120-125.

— 1974. *The Instructions of Suruppak. A Sumerian Proverb Collection. (Mesopotamia* 2) Copenhagen.

— 1982. 'Emesal in Early Dynastic Sumerian? What is the UD.GAL.NUN-Orthography? ASJ 4: 1-6.

Josef Bauer, *AWL. Altsumerische Wirtschaftstexte aus Lagasch.* Würzburg 1967 (Dissertation).

— 1970. 'Ein Nachtrag zu Edmond Sollberger, Le syllabaire présargonique de Lagaš, *ZA* 54 (1961) 1-50.' *RA* 64: 188-189.

— 1975. 'Zum /dr/-Phonem des Sumerischen.' *WO* 8: 1-9.

— 1982. 'Das sumerische Pronomen des 2. Ps. Pl.' *Altorientalistische Notizen* 18-20. Höchberg, im Selbstverlag des Verfassers, p. 2-4.

Adele Berlin, 1979. *Enmerkar and Ensuḫkešdanna. A Sumerian Narrative Poem. (Occasional Publications of the Babylonian Fund,* 2) Philadelphia.

Eugen Bergmann, 1964. 'Untersuchungen zu syllabisch geschriebenen sumerischen Texten. I.' *ZA* 56: 1-43.

— 1965. 'Untersuchungen zu syllabisch geschriebenen sumerischen Texten. II. *ZA* 57: 31-42.

Robert D. Biggs, 1967. 'Semitic Names in the Fara Period.' *OrNS* 36: 55-66.

— 1974. *Inscriptions from Tell Abū Ṣalābīkh. (OIP* 99) Chicago.

Rykle Borger, 1967. 'SU-GU₇ = *sugû* 'Hungersnot' und GU₇ 'essen'.' *OrNS* 36: 429-431.

— 1978. *Assyrisch-babylonische Zeichenliste (AOAT* 33) Neukirchen-Vluyn.

Antoine Cavigneaux, 1976. *Die sumerisch-akkadischen Zeichenlisten. Überlieferungsprobleme.* München (Dissertation).

Miguel Civil, 1964. 'A Hymn to the Beer Goddess and a Drinking Song.' In: *Studies presented to A. Leo Oppenheim.* Chicago, p. 67-89.

— 1966. 'Notes on Sumerian Lexicography, I.' *JCS 20*: 119-124.

— 1967: Erica Reiner and Miguel Civil, 'Another Volume of Sultantepe Tablets.' *JNES* 26: 177-211.

— 1968. 'Išme-Dagan and Enlil's Chariot.' *JAOS* 88: 3-14.
— 1973a. 'From Enki's Headaches to Phonology.' *JNES* 32: 57-61.
— 1973b. 'The Sumerian Writing System: Some Problems.' *OrNS* 42: 21-34.
— 1973c. 'Notes on Sumerian Lexicography, II.' *JCS* 25: 171-177.
— 1976a. 'Lexicography.' *AS* 20: 123-157.
— 1976b. 'Enlil, the Merchant: Notes to *CT* 15, 10.' *JCS* 28: 72-81.
— 1976c. 'Notes on Sumerian Lexicography, III.' *JCS* 28: 183-187.
Miguel Civil and Robert D. Biggs, 1966. 'Notes sur des textes sumériens archaïques.' *RA* 60: 1-16.
Bernard Comrie, 1976. *Aspect.* Cambridge.
Jerrold S. Cooper, 1972. 'gìr-KIN 'to stamp out, trample'.' *RA* 66: 81-83.
— 1973. 'Sumerian and Akkadian in Sumer and Akkad.' *OrNS* 42: 239-246.
— 1978. *The Return of Ninurta to Nippur: an-gim dím-ma. (AnOr* 52) Rome.
Scott DeLancey, 1981. 'An Interpretation of Split Ergativity and Related Patterns.' *Language* 57: 626-657.
Karlheinz Deller and Kazuko Watanabe, 1980. '*šukkulu(m), šakkulu* 'abwischen, auswischen'.' *ZA* 70: 198-226.
Igor M. Diakonoff, 1965. *Semito-Hamitic Languages.* Moscow.
— 1976. 'Ancient Writing and Ancient Written Language: Pitfalls and Pecularities in the Study of Sumerian.' *AS* 20: 99-121.
J.J.A. van Dijk, 1960. *Sumerische Götterlieder. II.* Heidelberg. *(Abhandlungen der Heidelberger Akademie der Wissenschaften. Philosophisch-historische Klasse,* Jahrg. 1960, 1. Abhandlung) Heidelberg.
— 1964-65. 'Le motif cosmique dans la pensée sumérienne.' *Acta Orientalia* 28: 1-59.
— 1967. 'VAT 8382: ein zweisprachiges Königsritual.' *HSAO* I: 233-268.
— 1970. 'La 'confusion des langues'. Note sur le lexique et sur la morphologie d'Enmerkar, 147-155.' *OrNS* 39: 302-310.
Robert M.W. Dixon, 1972. *The Dyirbal Language of North Queensland.* Cambridge.
— 1979. 'Ergativity.' *Language* 55: 59-138.
Dietz Otto Edzard. *SR. Sumerische Rechtsurkunden des III. Jahrtausends, aus der Zeit vor der III. Dynastie von Ur.* (Bayerische Akademie der Wissenschaften. Philosophisch-Historische Klasse, Abhandlungen, Neue Folge, Heft 67. Veröffentlichungen der Kommission zur Erschliessung von Keilschrifttexten. Serie A, 4. Stück) München 1968.
Dietz Otto Edzard, 1959. 'Fragen der sumerischen Syntax.' *ZDMG* 109: 235-252. (Review article of Salonen and Siro, 1958.)
— 1960. 'Sumerer und Semiten in der frühen Geschichte Mesopotamiens.' *Genava* 8: 241-258.
— 1963. 'Sumerische Komposita mit dem 'Nominalpräfix' nu-.' *ZA* 55: 91-112.

334

- 1964. (Review of *BIN* VIII) *ZA* 56: 275-278.
- 1965. 'Die frühdynastische Zeit.' In: *Fischer Weltgeschichte*, Bd. II: *Die altorientalische Reiche*, 1. Frankfurt am Main, p. 57-90.
- 1967. 'Das sumerische Verbalmorphem /ed/ in den alt- und neusumerischen Texten.' *HSAO* I, p. 29-62.
- 1971a. '*Ḫamṭu, marû* und freie Reduplikation beim sumerischen Verbum. I.' *ZA* 61: 208-232.
- 1971b. 'Grammatik.' In: *Reallexikon der Assyriologie und vorderasiatischen Archäologie*, III. Berlin, p. 610-616.
- 1972. '*Ḫamṭu, marû* und freie Reduplikation beim sumerischen Verbum. II.' *ZA* 62: 1-34.
- 1975. 'Zur 'Wortbildung im Sumerischen'.' *ZA* 65: 254-257. (Cf. Kienast, 1975.)
- 1976a. '*Ḫamṭu, marû* und freie Reduplikation beim sumerischen Verbum. III.' *ZA* 66: 45-61.
- 1976b. 'Du hast mir gegeben', 'ich habe dir gegeben'. Über das sumerische Verbum sum.' *WO* 8: 159-177.
- 1980. 'Sumerisch 1 bis 10 in Ebla.' *Studi Eblaiti* III: 121-127.
- Dietz Otto Edzard, Walter Farber und W.R. Mayer, 1978. *Ergänzungsheft zu A. Falkenstein, Grammatik der Sprache Gudeas von Lagaš (AnOr* 29A) Rome.
- Adam Falkenstein, *GSGL* I. *Grammatik der Sprache Gudeas von Lagaš. I. Schrift- und Formenlehre. (AnOr* 28) Rome 1949.
- *GSGL* II. *Grammatik der Sprache Gudeas von Lagaš. II. Syntax. (AnOr* 29) Rome 1950.
- *NG. Die neusumerischen Gerichtsurkunden.* I-III. (Bayerische Akademie der Wissenschaften. Philosophisch-Historische Klasse. Abhandlungen, Neue Folge, Heft 39, 40, 44. Veröffentlichungen der Kommission zur Erschliessung von Keilschrifttexten, Serie A, 2. Stück, 1-3.). München 1956-1957.
- 1931. 'Zum sumerischen Tempussystem.' *OLZ* 34: 791-794.
- 1933. (Review of *TCL* XV and XVI) *OLZ* 36: 299-306.
- 1936. *Archaische Texte aus Uruk. (Ausgrabungen der Deutschen Forschungsgemeinschaft in Uruk-Warka*, 2.) Berlin-Leipzig.
- 1939. 'Untersuchungen zur sumerischen Grammatik: 1. Der Plural des Kohortativs. 2. Das richtungsanzeigende Infix -ra-.' *ZA* 45: 169-194.
- 1942. 'Untersuchungen zur sumerischen Grammatik. 3. Das affirmative Präformativ na-.' *ZA* 47: 181-223.
- 1944. 'Untersuchungen zur sumerischen Grammatik. 4. Das affirmative Präformativ ši-/ša-.' *ZA* 48: 69-118.
- 1949. 'Ein sumerisches Kultlied auf Samsuiluna.' *ArOr* 17/1: 212-226.
- 1950. 'Ibb Isîn - Išbi'erra.' *ZA* 49: 59-79.
- 1951. 'Zur Chronologie der sumerischen Literatur' In: *Compte rendu de la seconde Rencontre Assyriologique Internationale*. Paris: p. 12-27.
- 1952. 'Das Potentialis- und Irrealissuffix -e-še des Sumerischen.' *Indogermanische Forschungen* 60: 113-130.
- 1952-53. 'Zu einem syllabisch geschriebenen Emesal-Text.' *AfO* 16: 60-64.

335

- 1953. 'Zur Chronologie der sumerischen Literatur. Die nachaltbabylonische Stufe.' *MDOG* 85: 1-13.
- 1957-58. 'Zur Grammatik der altsumerischen Sprache.' *AfO* 18: 89-96. (Review of Sollberger, 1952.)
- 1959a. *Das Sumerische. (Handbuch der Orientalistik*, 1. Abt./ Bd. 2, 1-2/Lfg. 1) Leiden.
- 1959b. 'Untersuchungen zur sumerischen Grammatik. 5. Zum Akzent des Sumerischen.' *ZA* 53: 97-105.
- 1959c. *Sumerische Götterlieder.* I. *(Abhandlungen der Heidelberger Akademie der Wissenschaften.* Philosophisch-historische Klasse, Jahrg. 1959, 1. Abhandlung) Heidelberg.
- 1960. 'Kontakte zwischen Sumerern und Akkadern auf sprachlichem Gebiet.' *Genava* 8: 301-314.
- 1964. 'Sumerische religiöse Texte. 5. Enki und die Weltordnung. 6. Ein sumerischer Liebeszauber.' *ZA* 56: 44-129.

Adam Falkenstein and Wolfram von Soden, 1953. *Sumerische und akkadische Hymnen und Gebete.* Zürich-Stuttgart.

Gertrud Farber-Flügge, 1973. *Der Mythos 'Inanna und Enki' unter besonderer Berücksichtigung der Liste der me. (Studia Pohl, 10)* Rome.

Jacob J. Finkelstein, 1969. 'The Laws of Ur-Nammu.' *JCS* 22: 66-82.

Benjamin R. Foster, 1982. 'Ethnicity and Onomastics in Sargonic Mesopotamia.' *OrNS* 51: 297-354.

Daniel A. Foxvog, 1975. 'The Sumerian Ergative Construction.' *OrNS* 44: 395-425.

Ignace J. Gelb, 1960. 'Sumerians and Akkadians in their Ethno-Linguistic Relationship.' *Genava* 8: 258-271.
- 1961. *Old Akkadian Writing and Grammar.* Second Edition, Revised and Enlarged. *(Materials for the Assyrian Dictionary*, 2) Chicago.

Edmund I. Gordon, 1958. 'Sumerian Animal Proverbs and Fables: 'Collection Five'. *JCS* 12: 1-21 and 43-75.
- 1959. *Sumerian Proverbs: Glimpses of Everyday Life in Ancient Mesopotamia.* Philadelphia 1959.

Gene B. Gragg, *SDI. Sumerian Dimensional Infixes. (AOATS* 5) Neukirchen-Vluyn 1973.
- 1968. 'The Syntax of the Copula in Sumerian.' In: J.W.M. Verhaar (ed.). *The Verb 'Be' and its Synonyms, 3. (Foundations of Language Supplementary Series*, 8) Dordrecht, p. 86-109.
- 1969. *The Keš Temple Hymn.* In: Å. W. Sjöberg and E. Bergmann, 1969. *The Collection of the Sumerian Temple Hymns. (TCS* III) Locust Valley, p. 155-188.
- 1972a. 'Observations on Grammatical Variation in Sumerian Literary Texts.' *JAOS* 92: 204-213.

— 1972b. 'Sumerian and Selected Afro-Asiatic Languages.' In: *The Chicago Which Hunt.* Papers from the Relative Clause Festival, April 13, 1972. A Para-volume to Papers from the Eighth Regional Meeting. Edited by P.M. Peranteu, J.N. Levi and Gloria C. Phares. Chicago, p. 153-168.

— 1973a. 'A Class of 'When' Clauses in Sumerian.' *JNES* 32: 124-134.

— 1973b. 'Linguistics, Method and Extinct Languages: The Case of Sumerian.' *OrNS* 42: 78-96.

— 1973c. 'The Fable of the Heron and the Turtle.' *AfO* 24: 51-72.

William W. Hallo, 1963. 'On the Antiquity of Sumerian Literature.' *JAOS* 83: 167-176.

— 1966. 'New Hymns to the Kings of Isin.' *BiOr* 23: 239-247.

— 1969. 'The Neo-Sumerian Letter Orders.' *BiOr* 26: 171-176.

— 1973. 'Choice in Sumerian.' *JANES* 5: 165-172.

— 1976. 'Toward a History of Sumerian Literature.' *AS* 20, p. 181-203.

William W. Hallo and J.J.A. van Dijk, 1968. *The Exaltation of Inanna. (YNER* 3) New Haven and London.

Wolfgang Heimpel, 1968. *Tierbilder in der sumerischen Literatur. (Studia Pohl,* 2) Rome.

— 1974-77. 'Sumerische und akkadische Personennamen in Sumer und Akkad.' *AfO* 25: 171-174.

Malcolm J.A. Horsnell, 1977. 'The Grammar and Syntax of the Year-Names of the First Dynasty of Babylon.' *JNES* 36: 277-285.

Thorkild Jacobsen, 1943. 'Parerga Sumerologica.' *JNES* 2: 117-121.

— 1954. 'Texts and Fragments 17-23.' *JCS* 8: 82-86.

— 1956. 'Introduction to the Chicago Grammatical Texts.' In: *MSL* IV, p. 1*-50*.

— 1957. 'Early Political Development in Mesopotamia.' *ZA* 52: 91-140.

— 1965. 'About the Sumerian Verb.' *AS* 16: 71-102.

— 1973. 'Notes on the Sumerian Genitive.' *JNES* 32: 161-166.

— 1974. 'Very Ancient Texts: Babylonian Grammatical Texts.' In: Dell Hymes (ed.), *Studies in the History of Linguistics. Traditions and Paradigms.* Bloom-ington-London, p. 41-62.

— 1976a. *The Treasures of Darkness. A History of Mesopotamian Religion.* New Haven and London.

— 1976b. 'The Stele of the Vultures Col. I-X.' *AOAT* 25: 247-259.

— 1982. 'Oral to Written.' In: (J.N.Postgate (ed.),) *Societies and Languages of the Ancient Near East.* Studies in Honour of I.M. Diakonoff. Warminster, p. 129-137.

Raymond R. Jestin, 1943. *Le verbe sumérien. Déterminations verbales et infixes. (Etudes Orientales* VII) Paris.

— 1946. *Le verbe sumérien. Préfixes, particules verbales et noms verbaux. (Études Orientales* IX) Paris.

— 1949. 'Le Phonème g̃ en sumérien.' *RA* 43: 41-53.

— 1950. 'Le phonème g̃ en sumérien. Notes additionnelles.' *RA* 44: 72.

— 1951. *Abrégé de grammaire sumérienne.* Paris.

337

— 1954. *Le verbe sumérien. Complément. (Études Orientales* XIII) Paris.
— 1965. *Notes de graphie et de phonétique sumériennes. (Bibliothèque de l'École des Hautes Études,* IVe section. Sciences historiques et philologiques, 317) Paris.
— 1967. 'Sur les particules verbales sumériennes.' *RA* 61: 45-50.
— 1973. 'Les noms de profession en nu-.' In: M.A. Beek, A.A. Kampman, C. Nijland, J. Ryckmans (eds.), *Symbolae biblicae et mesopotamicae Francisco Mario Theodoro de Liagre Böhl dedicatae.* Leiden, p. 211-213.
— 1976. 'Quelques notes complémentaires sur le système préfixal sumérien.' *AOAT* 25, p. 261-263.
Ilmari Kärki, 1967. *Die Sprache der sumerischen Königsinschriften der frühaltbabylonischen Zeit. (StOr* 35) Helsinki.
— 1968. *Die sumerischen Königsinschriften der frühaltbabylonischen Zeit in Umschrift und Übersetzung.* (Textband zu *'Die Sprache der sumerischen Königsinschriften der frühaltbabylonischen Zeit'* desselben Verfassers, *Studia Orientalia* 35.) Helsinki.
— 1980. *Die sumerischen und akkadischen Königsinschriften der altbabylonischen Zeit. (StOr* 49) Helsinki. (Revised edition of Kärki, 1968.)
Irina T. Kaneva, 1970. 'Participles in Sumerian.' *MIO* 16: 541-565.
— 1982. 'Notes on Sumerian Grammar.' In: (J.N. Postgate (ed.),) *Societies and Languages of the Ancient Near East. Studies in Honour of I.M. Diakonoff.* Warminster, p. 160-164.
Burkhart Kienast, 1975. 'Zur Wortbildung des Sumerischen.' *ZA* 65: 1-27.
— 1980a. 'Probleme der sumerischen Grammatik. 2. Zu den Personalpronomina. 3. Die Personalelemente in der Verbalbildung.' *ASJ* 2: 52-66.
— 1980b. 'Probleme der sumerischen Grammatik. 4. Bemerkungen zu *hamṭu* und *marû* im Sumerischen.' *ZA* 70: 1-35.
Samuel Noah Kramer, 1936. *The Sumerian Prefix Forms be- and bi- in the Time of the Earlier Princes of Lagaš. (AS* 8) Chicago.
— 1940. *Lamentation over the Destruction of Ur. (AS* 12) Chicago.
— 1956. *From the Tablets of Sumer.* Indian Hills.
— 1963. 'Cuneiform Studies and the History of Literature: The Sumerian Sacred Marriage Texts.' *PAPS* 107: 485-527.
Fritz Rudolf Kraus, 1970. *Sumerer und Akkader. Ein Problem der altmesopotamischen Geschichte. (Mededelingen der Koninklijke Nederlandse Akademie van Wetenschappen. Afd. Letterkunde. Nieuwe Reeks - Deel 33 - No. 8.)* Amsterdam-London.
Joachim Krecher, 1965. 'Zur sumerischen Grammatik. 1. Isolierende Postpositionen. 2. -(e)n nach Verbalwurzeln.' *ZA* 57: 12-30.
— 1966. *Sumerische Kultlyrik.* Wiesbaden.
— 1967a. 'Zum Emesal-Dialekt des Sumerischen.' *HSAO* I, p. 87-110.
— 1967b. 'Die sumerischen Texte in 'syllabischer' Orthographie. I.' *ZA* 58: 16-65.
— 1968a. 'Die pluralischen Verba für 'gehen' und 'stehen' im Sumerischen.' *WO* 4: 1-11.

338

- 1968b. 'Die sumerischen Texte in 'syllabischer' Orthographie. II.' *WO* 4: 252-277.
- 1969. 'Verschlusslaute und Betonung im Sumerischen.' *AOAT* 1, p. 157-197.
- 1978a. 'Sumerische Literatur.' In: Wolfgang Röllig (ed.), *Neues Handbuch der Literaturwissenschaft.* Bd. I. Wiesbaden, p. 101-150.
- 1978b. 'Sumerische Literatur der Fara-Zeit: Die UD.GAL.NUN-Texte (I).' *BiOr* 35: 155-160.
- 1978c. 'Die Form und der Gebrauch der nominalen Verbalformen und die Determination im Sumerischen.' *OrNS* 47: 376-403.
- 1978d. 'Das sumerische Phonem /ǧ/.' In: B. Hruška und G. Komoróczy (eds.), *Festschrift Lubor Matouš.* Bd. II. (*Assyriologia* V) Budapest, p. 7-73.

Raphael Kutscher, 1975. *Oh Angry Sea (a-ab-ba hu-luh-ha). The History of a Sumerian Congregational Lament. (YNER* 6) New Haven.

Maurice Lambert, 1961. 'Le préfixe sumérien HÉ-, indice de l'inéluctable.' *RA* 55: 35-40.

Wilfred George Lambert, 1960. *Babylonian Wisdom Literature.* Oxford.
- 1976. (Review of R.D. Biggs, 1974). *BSOAS* 39: 428-432.
- 1981. 'Studies in UD.GAL.NUN.' *OA* 20: 81-97.

Emmanuel Laroche, 1965. 'Le pluriel en sumérien.' *Bulletin de la Faculté des Lettres.* Strasbourg, p. 589-592.

Stephen J. Lieberman, 1977. *The Sumerian Loanwords in Old Babylonian Akkadian.* Vol. I: *Prolegomena and Evidence. (Harvard Semitic Series,* 22) Missoula.
- 1979. 'The Phoneme /o/ in Sumerian.' In: Marvin A. Powell jr. and Ronald H. Sack (eds.), *Studies in Honor of Tom B. Jones. (AOAT* 203) Neukirchen-Vluyn, p. 21-28.

Henri Limet, 1975. 'Le morphème suffixe /-a/ en sumérien.' *RA* 69: 5-18.

John Lyons, 1968. *Introduction to Theoretical Linguistics.* Cambridge.

Isaac Mendelsohn, 1949. *Slavery in the Ancient Near East. A Comparative Study of Slavery in Babylonia, Assyria, Syria and Palestine from the Middle of the Third Millennium to the End of the First Millennium.* New York.

Piotr Michalowski, 1980. 'Sumerian as an Ergative Language, I.' *JCS* 32: 86-103.

Karl Oberhuber, 1953/55. 'Zur sumerischen Postposition -e.' *WZKM* 52: 81-89.
- 1954. 'Zur Struktur des Sumerischen.' *OLZ* 49: 5-20. (Review article of Sollberger, 1952.).
- 1979. (Review of G. Farber-Flügge, 1973). *OLZ* 74: 447-451.

Simo Parpola, 1975. 'Transliteration of Sumerian: Problems and Prospects.' *StOr* 46, p. 239-257.

Arno Poebel, *GSG. Grundzüge der sumerischen Grammatik.* Rostock 1923.
- 1925. 'Sumerische Untersuchungen. II: Die Präfixverbindung eri- in der Inschrift der Geierstele.' *ZA* 36: 5-7.
- 1931. *The Sumerian Prefix Forms e- and i- in the Time of the Earlier Princes of Lagaš. (AS* 2) Chicago.
- 1938. 'Another Case of the Predicative Use of the Genitive in Sumerian.' *JAOS* 58: 148-150.

– 1934. 'The Tenses of the Intransitive Verb in Sumerian.' *American Journal of Semitic Languages and Literatures* 50: 143-170.

J.N. Postgate, 1974. 'Two Points of Grammar in Gudea.' *JCS* 26: 16-54.

Marvin A. Powell, Jr., 1978. 'Ukubi to Mother . . . The Situation is Desperate. A Plaidoyer for Methodological Rigor in Editing and Interpreting Sumerian Texts with an Excursus on the Verb taka: da$_x$-da$_x$ (TAG$_4$).' *ZA* 68: 163-195.

– 1982. 'On the Verb AK in Sumerian.' In: (J.N. Postgate (ed.),) *Societies and Languages of the Ancient Near East. Studies in Honour of I.M. Diakonoff.* Warminster, p. 314-319.

Daniel Reisman, 1973. 'Iddin-Dagan's Sacred Marriage Hymn.' *JCS* 25: 184-202.

Johannes Renger, 1969. 'Untersuchungen zum Priestertum der altbabylonischen Zeit. 2. Teil.' *ZA* 59: 104-230.

– 1971. 'Überlegungen zum akkadischen Syllabar.' *ZA* 61: 23-43.

Willem H. Ph. Römer, *SKIZ. Sumerische 'Königshymnen' der Isin-Zeit.* Leiden 1965.

– 1970. 'Einige Bemerkungen zu einer Grammatik der frühaltbabylonisch-sumerischen Königsinschriften.' *BiOr* 27: 160-167. (Review article of Kärki, 1967.)

– 1974. 'Fünf und zwanzig Jahre der Erforschung sumerischer literarischer Texte.' *BiOr* 31: 207-222.

– 1975. 'Kleine Beiträge zur Grammatik des Sumerischen. 2. Das präfigierende Element iri-.' *BiOr* 32: 3-5.

– 1976. 'Kleine Beiträge zur Grammatik des Sumerischen. 1. Das modale grammatische Element nu-uš-.' *AOAT* 25, p. 371-378.

– 1980. *Das sumerische Kurzepos 'Bilgameš und Akka'. (AOAT* 209/1), Neukirchen-Vluyn.

– 1982. *Einführung in die Sumerologie.* Nijmegen.

Armas Salonen und Paavo Siro, 1958. *Studien zur neusumerischen Syntax. (AASF* Ser B, Tom. 112, 1) Helsinki.

Herbert Sauren, 1969. 'Untersuchungen zur Schrift- und Lautlehre der neusumerischen Urkunden aus Nippur.' *ZA* 59: 11-64.

Nikolaus Schneider, 1936. *Die Zeitbestimmungen der Wirtschaftsurkunden von Ur III. (AnOr* 13) Rome.

– 1946. 'Die Wunschpartikel ha-, hé- und hu- in der Ur III-Texten.' *OrNS* 15: 89-94.

Wolfgang Schramm, 1983. 'Die Pluralbildung der Nomina im Sumerischen.' In: *Althistorische Studien.* Hermann Bengtson zum 70. Geburtstag dargebracht von Kollegen und Schülern. Herausgegeben von Heinz Heinen in Verbindung mit Karl Stroheker und Gerold Walser. *(Historia*, Zeitschrift für alte Geschichte. Einzelschriften. Heft 40.) Wiesbaden, p. 1-7.

Aaron Shaffer, 1963. *Sumerian Sources of Tablet XII of the Epic of Gilgameš.* Dissertation Philadelphia. University Microfilms Ann Arbor 63-7085.

– 1969. '*TA ša kīma ītenerrubu:* A Study in Native Babylonian Philology.'

340

OrNS 38: 433-446.

Bernard J. Siegel, 1947. *Slavery During the Third Dynasty of Ur. (Memoir Series of the American Anthropological Association,* 66) Menasha. (Reprint, New York 1969)

Åke W. Sjöberg, 1960. *Der Mondgott Nanna-Suen in der sumerischen Überlieferung.* Stockholm.

— 1969: Åke W. Sjöberg and Eugen Bergmann, *The Collection of the Sumerian Temple Hymns and the Keš Temple Hymn by Gene B. Gragg.* (TCS III) Locust Valley and New York.

— 1970. 'Beiträge zum sumerischen Wörterbuch.' *OrNS* 39: 75-98.

— 1973a. 'Der Vater und sein missratener Sohn.' *JCS* 25: 105-169.

— 1973b. 'Nungal in the Ekur.' *AfO* 24: 19-46.

— 1974. 'A Hymn to ^{d}Lama-sa$_6$-ga.' *JCS* 16: 158-177.

— 1975. 'In-nin šà-gur$_4$ -ra. A Hymn to the Goddess Inanna by the en-Priestess Enheduanna.' *ZA* 65: 161-253.

— 1976. 'The Old Babylonian Eduba.' *AS* 20, p. 159-179.

William R. Sladek, 1974. *Inanna's Descent to the Netherworld.* Dissertation John Hopkins University. University Microfilms Ann Arbor 74-27, 928.

Wolfram von Soden, 1952. *Grundriss der akkadischen Grammatik. (AnOr* 33) Rome.

— 1965. 'Das akkadische *t*-Perfekt in Haupt- und Nebensätze und sumerische Verbalformen mit den Präfixen ba-, imma- und u-.' *AS* 16, p. 103-110.

Edmond Sollberger, *TCS* I. *The Business and Administrative Correspondence under the Kings of Ur. (Texts from Cuneiform Sources,* I) Locust Valley and New York 1966.

— 1950. 'Etudes de linguistique sumérienne.' *Cahiers Ferdinand de Saussure* 9: 51-88.

— 1952. *Le système verbal dans les inscriptions 'royales' présargoniques de Lagaš.* Genève. (Reprint: Niederwalluf bei Wiesbaden 1971)

— 1959. (Review of *BIN* VIII) *BiOr* 16: 113-119.

— 1969a. 'Genre et nombre en Sumérien.' *Cahiers Ferdinand de Saussure* 26: 151-160.

— 1969b. 'Samsu-ilūna's Bilingual Inscriptions C and D.' *RA* 63: 29-43.

— 1976. 'Some Legal Documents of the Third Dynasty of Ur.' *AOAT* 25, p. 435-450.

Edmond Sollberger and Jean-Robert Kupper, 1971. *Inscriptions royales sumériennes et akkadiennes.* Paris.

Horst Steible, 1975. *Rīmsîn, mein König. Drei kultische Texte aus Ur mit der Schlussdoxologie* ^{d}*ri-im-*^{d}*sîn lugal-mu. (Freiburger altorientalische Studien,* 1) Wiesbaden.

— 1982. *Die altsumerischen Bau- und Weihinschriften.* I-II. Bearbeitet von H. Steible, unter Mitarbeit von Hermann Behrens. (*Freiburger altorientalische Studien,* 5/I-II) Wiesbaden.

Gerd Steiner, 1976. 'Intransitiv-passivische und aktivische Verbalauffassung.' *ZDMG* 126: 229-280.

— 1981a. 'The Vocalization of the Sumerian Verbal Morpheme /= ED/ and its Significance.' *JNES* 40: 21-41.

— 1981b. *'Hamṭu* und *Marû* als verbale Kategorien im Sumerischen und im Akkadischen.' *RA* 75: 1-14.

Piotr Steinkeller, 1979. 'Notes on Sumerian Plural Verbs.' *OrNS* 48: 54-67.

— 1982. 'On the Reading and Meaning of igi-kár and gúrum(IGI.GAR).' *ASJ* 4: 149-151.

A.J. Taylor, 1970. 'Reduplication in Motu.' In: S.A. Wurm and D.C. Laycock (eds.), *Pacific Studies in Honour of Arthur Capell. (Pacific Linguistic Series C,* Book 13, 1-2) Canberra, p. 1235-1245.

François Thureau-Dangin, *SAK. Die sumerischen und akkadischen Königsinschriften. (Vorderasiatische Bibliothek,* 1) Leipzig 1907. (Reprint: Leipzig 1972)

A.A. Vaiman, 1974. 'Über die protosumerische Schrift.' *Acta Antiqua* 22: 15-27.

H.L.J. Vanstiphout, 1979. 'How Did They Learn Sumerian? *JCS* 31: 118-126.

Aage Westenholz, *ECTJ. Early Cuneiform Texts in Jena. Pre-Sargonic and Sargonic Documents from Nippur and Fara in the Hilprecht-Sammlung vorderasiatischer Altertümer, Institut für Altertumswissenschaften der Friedrich-Schiller-Universität, Jena. (Det Kongelige Danske Videnskabernes Selskab. Historisk-Filosofiske Skrifter 7,3.)* Copenhagen 1975.

Claus Wilcke, 1968. 'Das modale Adverb i-gi₄-in-zu im Sumerischen.' *JNES* 27: 229-242.

— 1969a. *Das Lugalbandaepos.* Wiesbaden.

— 1969b. 'ku-li.' *ZA* 59: 65-99.

Mamoru Yoshikawa, 1968a. 'On the Grammatical Function of -e- of the Sumerian Verbal Suffix -e-dè/-e-da(m).' *JNES* 27: 251-261.

— 1968b. 'The *Marû* and *Hamṭu* Aspects in the Sumerian Verbal System.' *OrNS* 37: 401-416.

— 1974. 'The *Marû-* Conjugation in the Sumerian Verbal System.' *OrNS* 43: 17-39.

— 1977a. 'Some Remarks on the Sumerian Verbal Infixes -n-/-b- in the Preradical Position.' *JCS* 29: 78-96.

— 1977b. 'On the Sumerian Verbal Prefix Chains ì-in-, ì-íb- and ì-im-.' *JCS* 29: 223-236.

— 1977c. 'On the Sumerian Verbal Infix -a-.' *OrNS* 46: 447-461.

— 1978. 'Sumerian Ventive and Ientive.' *OrNS* 47: 461-482.

— 1979a. 'The Sumerian Verbal Prefixes mu-, ì- and Topicality.' *OrNS* 48: 185-206.

— 1979b. 'Verbal Reduplication in Sumerian.' *ASJ* 1: 99-119.

— 1979c. 'Aspectual Morpheme /a/ in Sumerian.' *ZA* 69: 161-175.

— 1981. 'Plural Expressions in Sumerian Verbs.' *ASJ* 3: 111-124.

— 1982. 'The Sumerian Verbal Infix Chains -e-ni- and -e-a-.' *ASJ* 4: 153-169.

342

Textual Material: Bibliographical References

For abbreviations, see above p. 327. Other references are to the general bibliography p. 332. Bibliographical references to the textual material can moreover be found in Rykle Borger, 1967 and 1975, *Handbuch der Keilschriftliteratur*. I-II. Berlin.

Amar-Sin, king of the Third Dynasty of Ur, 2045-2037 B.C. Brick E: Inscription. F. Thureau-Dangin, *SAK* p. 198.

Ana ittišu: Lexical text from the first millennium B.C. *MSL* I.

Anam, king of Uruk, ca. 1821-1817 B.C. Anam 4: Inscription. I. Kärki, 1968 p. 99-100.

Angim: OB lit. text. Jerrold S. Cooper, 1978.

ASK: 7: Hymn to the Sun god. Neo-Assyrian.

AWL: Old Sumerian administrative texts from Lagaš. See J. Bauer, *AWL*.

BE III 1: Neo-Sumerian document. H. Sauren, 1970. 'Zum Bürgschaftsrecht in neusumerischer Zeit.' *ZA* 60: p. 77f.

BIN IX 332: Economic text from the First Dynasty of Isin. No text edition.

Bird and Fish: Disputation between Bird and Fish: OB lit. text. No text edition.

Codex Lipit-Ištar: Law code from the reign of Lipit-Ištar of Isin (1934-1924 B.C.), OB copy. Francis Rue Steele, 1948. 'The Code of Lipit-Ishtar.' *AJA* 52/3: 425-450.

CT XV 14: Cultic song.

CT XLII 7 = CT XLII 16: Cultic song.

CT XLII 13: Cultic song.

Curse of Akkade: OB lit. text. Adam Falkenstein, 1965. 'Fluch über Akkade.' *ZA* 57: 43-124.

Dialogue 1 = Dialogue between Two School Graduates: OB lit. text. No text edition.

Dialogue 2 = Dialogue between Enkita and Enki-hegal: OB lit. text. No text edition.

Dialogue 3 = Dialogue between Enki-mansum and Girine-išag: OB lit. text. No text edition.

DP 222: Old Sumerian document. Anton Deimel, 1920. 'Die Listen über den Ahnenkult aus der Zeit Lugalandas und Urukaginas.' *Or* 2: 34f.

DP 278: Old Sumerian document. Anton Deimel, 1926. 'Fisch-Texte der Zeit Urukaginas.' *Or* 21: 48.

Dumuzi and Enkimdu: OB lit. text. J.J.A. van Dijk, 1953. *La sagesse suméro-accadienne. Recherches sur les genres littéraires des textes sapientiaux.*

Leiden: p. 65-73.
Dumuzi's Dream: OB lit. text. B. Alster, 1972a.
Ean. = Eanatum, ruler of the First Dynasty of Lagaš, ca. 2470 B.C.
Ean. 1 = Stele of the Vultures. H. Steible, 1982 I p. 120-145. Th. Jacobsen, 1976b.
Ean. 2: Boundary stone. H. Steible, 1982 I p. 145-151.
Ean. 62: Inscription on a mortar. H. Steible, 1982 I p. 172-175.
En. I = Enanatum the First, ruler of the First Dynasty of Lagaš, ca. 2440 B.C.
En. I, *AOAT* 25 = En. I 29: Inscription on a clay tablet. Robert D. Biggs, 1976. 'Enannatum I of Lagash and Ur-Lumma of Umma: A New Text.' *AOAT* 25 p. 33-40. H. Steible, 1982 I p. 198-202.
Enki and Ninhursaḡ: OB lit. text. Samuel Noah Kramer, 1945. *Enki and Ninhursag: A Sumerian 'Paradise' Myth. (Bulletin of the American Schools of Oriental Research, Supplementary Studies,* 1) New Haven.
Enki and Ninmah: OB lit. text. Carlos A. Benito, 1969. *Enki and Ninmah and Enki and the World Order.* Dissertation Philadelphia. University Microfilms Ann Arbor 70-16,124.
Enki and the World Order: OB lit. text. Carlos A. Benito, 1969. (See to Enki and Ninmah above).
Enki's Journey to Nippur: OB lit. text. Abdul-Hadi A. Al-Fouadi, 1969. *Enki's Journey to Nippur: The Journeys of the Gods.* Dissertation Philadelphia. University Microfilms Ann Arbor 70-7772.
Enlil and Namzitara: OB lit. text. Miguel Civil, 1974/1977. 'Enlil and Namzitarra.' *AfO* 25: 65-71.
Enlil and Ninlil: OB lit. text. Hermann Behrens, 1978.*Enlil und Ninlil. Ein sumerischer Mythos aus Nippur. (Studia Pohl, Series Maior,* 8) Rome.
Enlil Hymn: OB lit. text. A. Falkenstein, 1959c, Nr. 1, p. 11-25.
Enlil Hymn, *CT* XV pl. 11-12.: Both OB and NA duplicates. Translation: A. Falkenstein and W. von Soden, 1953 p. 77-79.
Enmerkar and Ensukhešdana: OB lit. text. A. Berlin, 1979.
Enmerkar and the Lord of Aratta: OB lit. text. Sol Cohen, 1973. *Enmerkar and the Lord of Aratta.* Dissertation Philadelphia. University Microfilms Ann Arbor 72-24, 127.
Ent. = Entemena, ruler of the First Dynasy of Lagaš ca. 2430 B.C.
Ent. 2: H. Steible, 1982 I p. 214-215.
Ent. 28 (and 29): Clay cones. H. Steible, 1982 I p. 230-245.
Ent. 36: Brick. H. Steible, 1982 I p. 254-255.
Ent. 41: Brick. H. Steible, 1982 I p. 256-257.
Enz. = Enentarzid, ruler of the First Dynasty of Lagaš, ca. 2380 B.C.
Enz. 1: Letter. Translation: E. Sollberger and J.R. Kupper, 1971 p. 75-76.
Eridu Lamentation: OB lit. text. M.W. Green, 1978. 'The Eridu Lament.' *JCS* 30: 127-167.
Exaltation of Inanna: OB lit. text. W.W. Hallo and J.J.A. van Dijk, 1968.
Father and Son: OB lit. text. Å.W. Sjöberg, 1973a.

Georgica: OB lit. text. No text edition. Transliteration (by J. Aro) and translation (by S.N. Kramer) can be found in Armas Salonen, 1968. *Agricultura Mesopotamica nach sumerisch-akkadischen Quellen. (AASF,* Ser. B 149) Helsinki, p. 202-212.

Gilgameš and Aka: OB lit. text. W.H.Ph. Römer, 1980.

Gilgameš and Huwawa: OB lit. text. Samuel Noah Kramer, 1947. 'Gilgamesh and the Land of the Living.' *JCS* 1: 3-46.

Gilgameš, Enkidu and the Netherworld: OB lit. text. A. Shaffer, 1963.

Gudea, ruler of the Second Dynasty of Lagaš ca. 2144-2124 B.C.

Gudea, Brick D: F. Thureau-Dangin, *SAK* p. 140-141.

Gudea, cyl. A and B: Two cylinders inscribed with a hymn concerning the building of the Ningirsu temple in Lagaš, F. Thureau-Dangin, *SAK* p. 88-141. Translation: A. Falkenstein and W. von Soden, 1953 p. 137-182.

Gudea, St.: Inscriptions on statues.

Gudea, St. A: F. Thureau-Dangin, *SAK* p. 66-67.

Gudea, St. B: F. Thureau-Dangin, *SAK* p. 66-75.

Gudea, St. C: F. Thureau-Dangin, *SAK* p. 74-77.

Gudea, St. D: F. Thureau-Dangin, *SAK* p. 76-79.

Gudea, St. E: F. Thureau-Dangin, *SAK* p. 78-83.

Gudea, St. I: F. Thureau-Dangin, *SAK* p. 86-87.

Gudea, St. P: See St. I.

Hammurapi, king of the First Dynasty of Babylon 1792-1750 B.C. *OECT* I 18 and duplicates: Bilingual inscription. Translation: E. Sollberger and J.R. Kupper, 1971 p. 214-215.

Hendursaĝa Hymn : OB lit. text. Dietz Otto Edzard and Claus Wilcke, 1976. 'Die Hendursanga Hymne.' *AOAT* 25 p. 139-176.

Home of the Fish: OB lit. text. Miguel Civil, 1961. 'The Home of the Fish. A New Sumerian Literary Composition.' *Iraq* 23: 154-175.

HSM 1384: Document dated in the reign of Enlil-bani of Isin (1860-1837 B.C.). D.O. Edzard, 1976b p. 160-161.

Hymn to the Hoe: OB lit. text. No text edition.

Iddin-Dagan, king of Isin 1974-1954 B.C.

Iddin-Dagan Hymn A: OB lit. text. W.H.Ph. Römer, *SKIZ* p. 128-143. D. Reis--man, 1973. (Translation and commentary.)

Iddin-Dagan Hymn B: OB lit. text. W.H.Ph. Römer, *SKIZ* p. 209-214.

Inanna and Bilulu: OB lit. text. Thorkild Jacobsen, 1953. 'The Myth of Inanna and Bilulu.' *JNES* 12: 160-187.

Inanna and Ebih: OB lit. text. No text edition.

Inanna and Enki: OB lit. text. G. Farber-Flügge, 1973.

Inanna Hymn (*CT* XXXVI p. 33-34): OB lit. text. A. Falkenstein, 1944 p. 105-113.

Inanna's Descent: OB lit. text. W.R. Sladek, 1974.

Innin: OB lit. text. Å.W. Sjöberg, 1975.

Instructions of Šuruppak: OB lit. text. B. Alster, 1974.

Iškur Hymn (*CT* XV pl. 15-16): OB lit. text. Translation: Adam Falkenstein and W. von Soden, 1953 p. 81-83.

Išme-Dagan, king of Isin, 1953-1935 B.C.

Išme-Dagan 3: Inscription. I. Kärki, 1968 p. 4f.

Išme-Dagan Hymn A: OB lit. text. W.H.Ph. Römer, *SKIZ* p. 236-240.

Išme-Dagan Hymn D: OB lit. text. W.H.Ph. Römer, *SKIZ* p. 39-55.

Išme-Dagan Hymn K: OB lit. text. W.H. Ph. Römer, *SKIZ* p. 21-22.

Keš Hymn: OB lit. text. G.B. Gragg, 1969.

Lahar and Ašnan = Disputation between Sheep and Grain: OB lit. text. No text edition.

Lamentation over Sumer and Ur: OB lit. text. Lines 1-59: Adam Falkenstein, 1950. 'Die Ibbīsîn-klage.' *WO* 1: 377-384.

Letter A and B: OB lit. texts. F.A. Ali, 1964.

Letter to Nanna: OB lit. text. Å·W. Sjöberg, 1960 p. 104-105.

Letter of Sin-iddinam to Utu: OB lit. text. William W. Hallo, 1982. 'The Royal Correspondence of Larsa: II. The Appeal to Utu.' In: *Zikir šumim. Assyriological Studies Presented to F.R. Kraus on the Occasion of his Seventieth Birthday.* Leiden, p. 95-109.

LIH 98 and 99, see Samsuiluna A.

Lugalbanda and Enmerkar: OB lit. text. C. Wilcke, 1969a.

Lugalbanda in Hurrumkura: OB lit. text. Partial edition i C. Wilcke, 1969a:

Lines 19-37	p. 196f.	Lines 73-82	p. 189	Lines 169-195	p. 67-69
− 43-57	p. 35f.	− 83-136	p. 54-60	− 196-222	p. 75-77
− 58-69	p. 49f.	− 137-168	p.78-81	− 223-256	p. 81-84

Lugal-e = Lugal-e ud me.lám-bi nir ǵál, Ninurta Myth: OB lit. text. No text edition. See now: J. van Dijk, 1983. *Lugal ud me-lám-bi nir-ǵál. Le récit épique et didactique des Travaux de Ninurta, du Déluge et de la Nouvelle Création.* I. Leiden.

Lugalzagesi, king of Uruk ca. 2350 B.C.

Lugalzagesi, *BE* I 87: Inscription on a stone vessel. H. Steible, 1982 II p. 310-325.

Manch. Tam. = Manchester Tammuz, Sumerian cultic song concerning Dumuzi. Theophilus G. Pinches, 1903/04. *Manchester Memoirs (Memoirs and Proceedings of the Manchester Literary and Philosophical Society)* 48. N. 25.

Martu Hymn: OB lit. text. Adam Falkenstein, 1959c Nr. 4 p. 121-125.

Nanna-Suen Hymn A: OB lit. text. Å. W. Sjöberg, 1960. Nr. 1 p. 13-17.

Nanna-Suen Hymn E: OB lit. text. Å.W. Sjöberg, 1960. Nr. 5 p. 65.

Nanna-Suen Hymn J: OB lit. text. Å.W. Sjöberg, 1960. Nr. 9 p. 97f.

Nanna-Suen's Journey to Nippur: OB lit. text. A.J. Ferrara, 1973. *Nanna-Suen's Journey to Nippur. (Studia Pohl, Series Maior, 2)* Rome.

Nanše Hymn: OB lit. text. W. Heimpel, 1981. 'The Nanshe Hymn.' *JCS* 33: 65-139.

NBGT: Neo-Babylonian Grammatical Texts. *MSL* IV p. 129-178.

Nergal Hymn: OB lit. text. J.J.A. van Dijk, 1960. Nr. 1 p. 7-11.

346

NG: Neo-Sumerian documents. A. Falkenstein, *NG.*
Ni 2461 (*ISET* I pl. 90): OB lit. text: Emesal love song. No text edition.
Ninurta and the Turtle: OB lit. text. B. Alster, 1972c.
Ninurta Hymn: OB lit. text. Åke W. Sjöberg, 1976. 'Hymns to Ninurta with Prayers for Šūsîn of Ur and Būrsîn of Isin.' *AOAT* 25: 411-426.
Nisaba Hymn: OB lit. text. Daniel Reisman, 1976. 'A Royal' Hymn of Išbi-Erra to the Goddess Nisaba.' *AOAT* 25: 357-365.
NRVN I: Neo-Sumerian juridical documents. No text edition.
Nungal: OB lit. text. Å.W. Sjöberg, 1973b.
Nusku Hymn: OB lit. text. J.J.A. van Dijk, 1960, p, 108-113.
OBGT = Old Babylonian Grammatical texts. *MSL* IV p. 45-128.
Or 47-49 nr. 411: Neo-Sumerian document. Nikolaus Schneider, 1930. *Die Geschäftsurkunden aus Drehem und Djoha in den Staatlichen Museen (VAT) zu Berlin in Autographie und mit systematischen Wörterindices herausgegeben. (Or* 47-49) Rome.
PAPS 107 nr. 1 and nr. 4: OB lit. texts: love songs. S.N. Kramer, 1963, p. 485-495; 499-500.
PBS I/2, 127: OB lit. text: incantation. Adam Falkenstein, 1931. *Die Haupttypen der sumerischen Beschwörung, literarisch untersucht. (Leipziger Semitistische Studien,* Neue Folge, 1) Leipzig, p. 89-93. (Reprint: Leipzig 1968)
Proto-Ea: OB lexical text. *MSL* II.
Proverb 1 and 2: OB lit. text: proverb collections. E.I. Gordon, 1959.
Proverb 5: OB lit. text: proverb collection. E.I. Gordon, 1958.
Rim-Sin, king of Larsa 1822-1763 B.C.
Rim-Sin 4: Inscription. I. Kärki. 1968 p. 72-73.
Rim-Sin 8: Inscription. I. Kärki, 1968 p. 76-78.
Rim-Sin 10: Inscription. I. Kärki, 1968 p. 79-80.
Rim-Sin 11: Inscription. I. Kärki, 1968 p. 81-82.
Rim-Sin 15: Inscription. I. Kärki, 1968 p. 86-87.
Rim-Sin 18: Inscription. I. Kärki, 1968 p. 89-91.
RTC 339: Old Sumerian document. No text edition.
Samsuiluna, king of the First Dynasty of Babylon 1749-1712 B.C.
Samsuiluna A: Inscription. Translation: E. Sollberger and J.R. Kupper, 1971 p. 220-221.
Samsuiluna C: Inscription. E. Sollberger, 1969b.
Samsuiluna Hymn: OB lit. text. Adam Falkenstein, 1949.
SBH: Sumerian cultic songs from the first millenium B.C., mostly Emesal.
Schooldays: OB lit. text. Samuel Noah Kramer, 1949. *Schooldays: A Sumerian Composition Relating to the Education of a Scribe.* Philadelphia.
Sin-iddinam, king of Larsa 1849-1843 B.C.
Sin-iddinam 2: Inscription. Ilmari Kärki, 1968 p. 31-32.
Sin-iddinam 3: Inscription. Ilmari Kärki, 1968 p. 32-33.
Sin-iddinam 6: Inscription. Ilmari Kärki, 1968 p. 33-35.

Sin-kašid, king of Uruk ca. 1865-1833 B.C.

Sin-kašid 10: Inscription. Ilmari Kärki, 1968 p. 97.

SR: Old Sumerian documents. D.O. Edzard, SR.

SRT 23: OB lit. text: hymn to Šu-Sin of Ur. Translation: A. Falkenstein and W. von Soden, 1953 p. 119-120.

STVC 83: OB lit. text. No text edition.

Šu-ilišu, king of Isin 1984-1975 B.C.

Šu-ilišu Hymn A: OB lit. text. W.H.Ph. Römer, SKIZ p. 91-95.

Šulgi, king of the Third Dynasty of Ur 2093-2046 B.C.

Šulgi Hymn A: OB lit. text. Adam Falkenstein, 1952. 'Sumerische religiöse Texte. 2.: Ein Šulgi-Lied.' ZA 50: 61-91. Also: Jacob Klein, 1981.. Three Šulgi Hymns. Sumerian Royal Hymns Glorifying King Šulgi of Ur. Ramat Gan, p. 167-217.

Šulgi Hymn B: OB lit. text, royal hymn. Giorgio R. Castellino, 1972. Two Šulgi Hymns (BC). (Studi Semitici, 42) Rome, p. 9-242.

Šulgi Hymn C: OB lit. text, royal hymn, Giorgio R. Castellino, 1972. Two Šulgi Hymns (BC). (Studi Semitici, 42) Rome, p. 243-294.

Šulgi Hymn D: OB lit. text. J. Klein, 1981 (See to Šulgi Hymn A) p. 50-123.

Šulgi Hymn X: OB lit. text. J. Klein, 1981 (see to Šulgi Hymn A) p. 124-166.

TCL XV nr. 1: OB lit. text, cultic song. No text edition.

TCL XVI nr. 89: OB lit. text: incantation. Raymond R. Jestin, 1947. 'Textes religieux sumériens.' RA 41: 58ff. Erich Ebeling, 1949. 'Beschwörungen gegen den Feind und den bösen Blick aus dem Zweistromlande.' ArOr 17/1: 206-207.

TCS I: Neo-Sumerian letter-orders. E. Sollberger, TCS I.

TDr nr. 26: Neo-Sumerian document. No text edition.

TDr nr. 85: Neo-Sumerian document. No text edition.

Temple Hymns: OB lit. text. Å.W. Sjöberg, 1969.

TEP: OB lit. texts. Samuel Noah Kramer, 1960. Two Elegies on a Pushkin Museum Tablet. A New Sumerian Literary Genre. (Oriental Literature Publishing House) Moscow.

TMH V nr. 129: Sumerian document from the Old Akkadian period. A. Westenholz, ECTJ p. 68.

TMH V nr. 159: Sumerian document from the Old Akkadian period. A. Westenholz, ECTJ p. 79-81.

TMHNF I-II nr. 47: Neo-Sumerian document. No text edition.

TMHNF I-II nr. 53: Neo-Sumerian document. I. Mendelsohn, 1949 p. 14-15.

TSŠ 79: Literary text from Fara(= Šuruppak), ca. 2500 B.C. Cf. J.J.A. van Dijk, 1964-65 p. 34.

UET II Suppl. nr. 15: Archaic text. No text edition.

UET III nr. 14: Neo-Sumerian document. No text edition.

UET III nr. 26: Neo-Sumerian document. No text edition.

UET III nr. 51: Neo-Sumerian document. No text edition.

UET VI/I, 103: OB lit. text. No text edition.

Ukg. = Uru-inim-gina, ruler of the First Dynasty of Lagaš ca. 2355 B.C.

348

Ukg. 1: Inscription on clay cones. H. Steible, 1982 I p. 278-287.
Ukg. 4 (and 5)' Inscription on clay cones, the so-called 'Reform Texts'. H. Steible, 1982 I p. 288-312.
Ukg. 6: Inscription on a stone plate. H. Steible, 1982 I p. 312-324.
Ukg. 14: Inscription. H. Steible, 1982 I p. 332-333.
Ukg. 15: OS lit. text. J. van Dijk, 1964-65 p. 39ff.
Ukg. 16: Inscription. H. Steible, 1982 I p. 333-337.
Ur Lament: OB lit. text. S.N. Kramer, 1940.
Urn. = Ur-Nanše, ruler of the First Dynasty of Lagaš ca. 2520 B.C.
Urn. 49: Incantation on a diorite plate. H. Steible, 1982 I p. 110-111.
Ur-Nammu's Death: OB lit. text. Samuel Noah Kramer, 1967. 'The Death of Ur-Nammu and His Descent to the Netherworld.' *JCS* 21: 104-122.
Ur-Ninurta, king of Isin 1923-1896 B.C.
Ur-Ninurta Hymn B: OB lit. text. A. Falkenstein, 1950. 'Sumerische religiöse Texte. 1. Drei Hymnen auf Urninurta von Isin.' *ZA* 49: 112-117.
Uruk Lament: OB lit. text. No text edition.
Utu-heǧal, king of Uruk 2116-2110 B.C.
Utu-heǧal: Inscription, OB copy of a monumental inscription. François Thureau-Dangin, 1912. 'La fin de la domination gutienne.' *RA* 9: 111-120. Translation: E. Sollberger and J.R. Kupper, 1971 p. 130-132.
VS X 199 iii 42 - iv 23: OB lit. text: hymn to Nanše. No text edition.
Warad-Sin, king of Larsa 1834-1823 B.C.
Warad-Sin 1: Inscription. I. Kärki, 1968 p. 39.
Warad-Sin 5: Inscription. I. Kärki, 1968 p. 41.
Warad-Sin 6: Inscription. I. Kärki, 1968 p. 41-42.
Warad-Sin 7: Inscription. I. Kärki, 1968 p. 42-44.
Warad-Sin 8: Inscription. I. Kärki, 1968 p. 44-45.
Warad-Sin 10: Inscription. I. Kärki, 1968 p. 46-48.
Warad-Sin 11: Inscription. I. Kärki, 1968 p. 48-49.
Warad-Sin 12: Inscription. I. Kärki, 1968 p. 49-50.
Warad-Sin 15: Inscription. I. Kärki, 1968 p. 52-53.
Warad-Sin 17: Inscription. I. Kärki, 1968 p. 53-54.
Warad-Sin 18: Inscription. I. Kärki, 1968 p. 54-55.
Warad-Sin 27: Inscription. I. Kärki, 1968 p. 66-67.
Warad-Sin 28: Inscription. I. Kärki, 1968 p. 67-71.
YOS IV nr 2: Neo-Sumerian document. No text edition.
YOS IV nr. 18: Neo-Sumerian document. No text edition.

INDEX: TEXTS CITED

352

356

358

PAUL D. SANSONE, O.F.M.

921001   35.00